SAP PRESS e-books

Print or e-book, Kindle or iPad, workplace or airplane: Choose where and how to read your SAP PRESS books! You can now get all our titles as e-books, too:

▸ By download and online access
▸ For all popular devices
▸ And, of course, DRM-free

Convinced? Then go to **www.sap-press.com** and get your e-book today.

SAP® Integrated Business Planning

 PRESS

SAP PRESS is a joint initiative of SAP and Rheinwerk Publishing. The know-how offered by SAP specialists combined with the expertise of Rheinwerk Publishing offers the reader expert books in the field. SAP PRESS features first-hand information and expert advice, and provides useful skills for professional decision-making.

SAP PRESS offers a variety of books on technical and business-related topics for the SAP user. For further information, please visit our website: *www.sap-press.com*.

Baumgartl, Chaadaev, Choi, Dudgeon, Lahiri, Meijerink, Worsley-Tonks
SAP S/4HANA: An Introduction
2016, 449 pages, hardcover and e-book
www.sap-press.com/4153

Sandeep Pradhan
Demand and Supply Planning with SAP APO (2nd Edition)
2016, 831 pages, hardcover and e-book
www.sap-press.com/4011

Jochen Balla, Frank Layer
Production Planning with SAP APO (3rd Edition)
2016, 431 pages, hardcover and e-book
www.sap-press.com/3927

Elke Roettig
Inventory Management and Optimization in SAP ERP
2016, 523 pages, hardcover and e-book
www.sap-press.com/3977

Sandy Markin, Amit Sinha

SAP® Integrated Business Planning

Functionality and Implementation

Rheinwerk®
Publishing

Bonn • Boston

Editor Meagan White
Acquisitions Editor Emily Nicholls
Copyeditor Julie McNamee
Cover Design Graham Geary
Photo Credit Shutterstock.com/387960121/© Bubbers BB
Layout Design Vera Brauner
Production Graham Geary
Typesetting III-satz, Husby (Germany)
Printed and bound in the United States of America, on paper from sustainable sources

ISBN 978-1-4932-1427-3

© 2017 by Rheinwerk Publishing, Inc., Boston (MA)
1st edition 2017

Library of Congress Cataloging-in-Publication Control Number: 2017002799

Contents at a Glance

Dear Reader,

In today's fast-paced market, your supply chain needs to be faster, more responsive, and more flexible than ever. Enter SAP Integrated Business Planning!

As the buzz around SAP IBP has grown, SAP PRESS authors and editors have been working to provide information and insight into this much-anticipated cloud solution. Like you, we've been watching the solution come into focus for the SAP community, and have heard the queries transition from "What is it? What can it do? And how will it help *my* business?" to the more practical questions of implementation, like "How do I get it? And how do I use it?"

To this we say: Your next SAP PRESS resource has arrived. Between these pages, expert authors Amit Sinha and Sandy Markin have given you the lowdown on everything you need to know to set up and use SAP IBP. With step-by-step instructions, countless screenshots, and some intimidating equations (Chapter 8 strikes math-related fear into this editor's heart), this book has it all!

As always, your comments and suggestions are the most useful tools to help us make our books the best they can be. Let us know what you thought about *SAP Integrated Business Planning: Functionality and Implementation*! Please feel free to contact me and share any praise or criticism you may have.

Thank you for purchasing a book from SAP PRESS!

Meagan White
Editor, SAP PRESS

Rheinwerk Publishing
Boston, MA

meaganw@rheinwerk-publishing.com
www.sap-press.com

Contents

8   Demand Planning and Forecasting with SAP IBP 197

9   Implementing SAP IBP for Demand 225

10   Response and Supply Planning with SAP IBP 251

11 Implementing SAP IBP for Response and Supply 269

12 Inventory Management with SAP IBP 293

Preface

Welcome to the first ever book on SAP Integrated Business Planning (SAP IBP), SAP's strategic supply chain planning solution. Over the past five years, SAP IBP has matured into a best-in-class solution for managing and transforming supply chain planning processes. It contains advanced algorithms to help manage your planning processes, real-time analytics for end-to-end visibility and control, and enterprise social networking for seamless collaboration.

This book will provide you with an overview of SAP IBP, along with detailed instructions for configuring and using the SAP IBP system to manage your organization's supply chain network. Data elements and analytics receive a special focus, as do model configuration and planning process automation. You do not require extensive prior knowledge of the supply chain or SAP software to understand this text; planning processes are discussed in a logical sequence that will help you build knowledge as you progress through the chapters. Our hope is that this book will provide you with a broad understanding of supply chain planning processes, data management, modeling, and analytics—all through the lens of SAP IBP.

Target Audience

Business users, technical users, and consultants associated with supply chain planning and related business functions will find tremendous value in the ensuing pages. Furthermore, because this manual does not require any previous SAP training or business process expertise, it will be beneficial to other professionals working at various levels in a wide range of organizations.

An SAP IBP business user will gain insight into integrated supply chain planning and optimization within the SAP landscape. This book details solutions for individual planning processes and their integration to manage the supply chain network from end-to-end. The chapters focusing on data, analytics, and the agile project management approach will be highly useful for our business user readers.

A consultant will also find valuable system configuration information, along with the conceptual and process knowledge of supply chain planning. Both functional and technical consultant will gain an understanding of the optimization of supply chain planning processes, data, and integration architecture.

Finally, considering the widespread demand for supply chain skills in the market and the impact of supply chain management on an organization's success, we encourage students and anybody with interest in supply chain management to read this book.

How to Read This Book

We recommend that you read through the chapters in sequence, as concepts that are introduced in early chapters will be subsequently revisited. For example, data elements that are introduced in Chapter 3 will be applied to build a planning model in Chapter 4. Similarly, demand planning concepts that are discussed in Chapter 1 will later be explored as they relate to SAP IBP for demand or SAP IBP for sales and operations.

If a specific topic or chapter is of particular interest, we strongly recommend that you first read the introduction before proceeding to that section. For each of the planning processes (SAP IBP for sales and operations, SAP IBP for demand, SAP IBP for response and supply, SAP IBP for inventory, and the SAP Supply Chain Control Tower), two chapters are allocated. The first is focused on discussing the concepts related to that solution and the second on implementation of the process in SAP IBP. We recommend you read through both chapters in sequence. Topics like project management approach, planning data, user interface, etc., can be read independently, although we suggest reading Chapter 3 on planning data before delving into any planning process chapters.

How This Book Is Organized

This book is structured to serve the various individuals who work on supply chain planning processes in the SAP IBP environment. Each chapter illustrates a specific knowledge area and builds on the skills obtained in previous sections. The chapters are as follows:

▶ **Chapter 1: Introduction**
This chapter introduces the application and scope of SAP IBP for managing supply chain planning processes. It discusses supply chain challenges and opportunities for modern global organizations using SAP IBP to achieve maximum value. The individual planning applications of SAP IBP are discussed in this chapter, as is the system architecture of SAP IBP.

▶ **Chapter 2: Navigation**
This chapter introduces the SAP IBP user interfaces and navigation capabilities. The SAP IBP Excel planning view, the SAP Fiori view, and mobile views are discussed in detail.

▶ **Chapter 3: Planning Data**
Key to any organization's supply chain is its data, which is loaded into SAP IBP and used for various planning and execution activities. This chapter covers the master and transactional data used in SAP IBP processes. It explains how data is loaded into SAP IBP, through manual and automated processes, and how business users can analyze and review the data using visualization methods.

▶ **Chapter 4: Building Blocks of a Planning Model**
The planning model is the foundation of SAP IBP; therefore it is critical even for business users to understand how these pieces fit together, although they will typically not be configuring the system. This chapter covers the concepts of planning model building blocks and their applications.

▶ **Chapter 5: Configuring an SAP IBP System**
This chapter introduces the steps needed to create the planning model and associated elements in SAP IBP.

▶ **Chapter 6: Sales and Operations Planning with SAP IBP**
This chapter outlines the concepts of sales and operations planning (S&OP) and shows how related business sub-processes are accomplished with SAP IBP for sales and operations. This chapter is illustrated with screenshots and examples of how the functionality can be used in a variety of industries.

▶ **Chapter 7: Implementing SAP IBP for Sales and Operations**
Building on the conceptual knowledge of S&OP process and usage of SAP IBP for sales and operations, this chapter details the steps involved in configuring, building, and using SAP IBP for managing S&OP.

▶ **Chapter 8: Demand Planning and Forecasting with SAP IBP**
This chapter explores statistical demand forecasting and demand finalization and explains how SAP IBP for demand addresses these processes. Different statistical models, pre- and post-processing for generating the forecast are discussed, as is the collaboration process in SAP IBP to finalize the demand plan. This chapter illustrates the sophisticated method of demand sensing in SAP IBP for planning the demand in the short-term.

▶ **Chapter 9: Implementing SAP IBP for Demand**
This chapter provides instruction for configuring demand planning and demand sensing in SAP IBP.

▶ **Chapter 10: Response and Supply Planning with SAP IBP**
This chapter discusses the concepts of supply planning in the short, medium, and long-term with different supply methodologies. Forecast consumption and demand-supply matching is illustrated, as is using SAP IBP to manage response planning, demand prioritization, product allocation, and order confirmation processes.

▶ **Chapter 11: Implementing SAP IBP for Response and Supply**
This chapter walks through the configuration steps needed to build the supply and response planning solution in SAP IBP. SAP IBP for response and supply is also discussed using examples and screenshots.

▶ **Chapter 12: Inventory Management with SAP IBP**
This chapter introduces the concepts of inventory management, outlining the motivation for maintaining optimal inventory levels in a supply chain network. Different types of inventories along with the factors that impact inventory levels are discussed in this chapter. It also discusses inventory optimization calculations in a supply chain network.

▶ **Chapter 13: Implementing SAP IBP for Inventory**
SAP IBP for inventory and system configuration is discussed in this chapter. Network visualization chart building and inventory optimization algorithms SAP IBP are illustrated in the text, along with the planning model for inventory optimization.

▶ **Chapter 14: SAP Supply Chain Control Tower**
Supply chain analytics concepts and end-to-end integration with total visibility and control are discussed in this chapter. Process control, analytics, dashboards and custom alerts are also introduced.

▶ **Chapter 15: Implementing SAP Supply Chain Control Tower with SAP IBP**
This chapter demonstrates the SAP Supply Chain Control Tower. Analytics and dashboard applications are user-friendly and easily configured by planners. Custom alert and KPI (key performance indicator) configurations are also discussed in this chapter.

▶ **Chapter 16: Unified Planning and User Roles**
The SAP IBP unified planning area allows for end-to-end planning as part of one integrated system. An integrated planning approach through a common planning data set is discussed in this chapter. User roles and access management are covered with steps for managing the system user roles in SAP IBP.

▶ **Chapter 17: Implementation Methodology**
With newer planning applications, value delivery is materialized through an agile project management approach, as opposed to the traditional waterfall approach. This chapter delves into the details of agile implementation methodology and the recommendations for successful SAP IBP project implementation.

▶ **Chapter 18: Customer Use Cases**
Supply chain challenges present opportunities for SAP IBP, and this chapter uses real-world examples to show how SAP delivers value across different organizations in multiple sectors.

Conclusion

Reading this book will provide you with comprehensive knowledge of SAP IBP applications in managing supply chain planning processes. This book is a key reference in understanding supply chain planning processes and their value to an organization, and the use of SAP IBP to maximize the benefits from these processes. The depth and breadth covered in the text will help you develop both the business knowledge and system configuration skills for a successful SAP IBP implementation.

Acknowledgments

I would first like to thank my coauthor Amit Sinha whose boundless energy and deep knowledge of supply chain management and solutions have made this book possible. In addition, I would like to thank Amit's colleagues at Deloitte Consulting, particularly Deb Bhattacharjee and Jeroen Kusters, whose partnership has greatly contributed to the success of SAP Integrated Business Planning. Special thanks to our very patient editor Meagan White for her continuous support and guidance throughout the process. Emily Nicholls and Sarah Frazier from Rheinwerk Publishing were instrumental in the early development of this book. I thank both of them along with all of Rheinwerk Publishing for providing us with this opportunity.

There are many SAP colleagues who should be recognized for the remarkable success of SAP Integrated Business Planning. First, our top-notch development team, led by Franz Hero and Thomas Klemm, who have turned this product from a concept into a reality in record time. Next, my solution management team who, under the direction of Hans Thalbauer, Martin Barkman, and Patrick Crampton-Thomas, have set a new standard for market adoption of a new SAP solution. Our Cloud Operations team, led by Sunil Mampatta, helped us navigate through the challenges of delivering best-in-class customer service on a new cloud platform. Finally to our SAP Integrated Business Planning customers for whose trust, investment, and effort on behalf of SAP we offer our highest level of gratitude.

Last but not least, I'm truly grateful to my family, especially my son and SAP colleague Zach for his assistance with this book, and my wife Karen for her continuous encouragement, love, and support.

Sandy Markin
February 2017

I would first like to thank my co-author Sandy Markin for sharing this long, exciting journey of book authoring involving numerous late nights and vacation days spent on our work desks. Gratitude is due to our wonderful editor Megan White for her continuous support and guidance throughout the process. Emily Nicholls and Sarah Frazier from Rheinwerk Publishing have been instrumental in the concept of this book. I highly thank both of them along with other team members from Rheinwerk Publishing.

We thank SAP IBP product development team for building the best supply chain planning tool, SAP IBP, around which this book has been developed. In addition of development team, we thank the many system configurators and SAP IBP solution enthusiasts who have directly or indirectly helped the development of this text.

I would like to thank Brian Scott, Deb Bhattacharjee, Chris Verheuvel, Vadhi Narasimhamurti, Will Chadrow, Mike King, and Eric Monti for their support and opportunities, which helped me in building my skills and developing this text. I am grateful to my friends Jeroen Kusters, Akshay Oak, Sanchit Chandana, and Amber Mathur for our long discussions on varied topics on supply chain management and SAP IBP; it has helped in developing different sections of this book.

In the end, I am highly thankful to my family and friends, especially to my wife Surabhi and kids Ivan and Anaya for their encouragement, love, and support.

Amit Sinha
February 2017

This chapter describes the SAP view of how the digital economy is driving a new paradigm in supply chain planning, and the innovations that enable companies to meet the resulting challenges.

1 Introduction

In this introduction to SAP Integrated Business Planning (SAP IBP), the newest advanced supply chain planning suite from SAP, we'll explain the five applications (sales and operations planning [S&OP], demand planning, response and supply planning, inventory management, and SAP Supply Chain Control Tower), walk through the technical architecture that supports them, and identify the role of and advancements from SAP HANA, on which SAP IBP is built.

1.1 Supply Chain Complexity in the Digital World

Since integrated supply chain management became a business imperative several decades ago, companies have struggled to keep pace with the ever-increasing level of complexity in their networks. In the 1980s, it was all about operational efficiency and cost effectiveness. The mantra of the 1990s was flexibility and agility. Becoming a demand-driven organization was the major focus of the first decade of the new millennium. Most recently, a new phenomenon has evolved known as *supply chain digitization*, which incorporates many of the principles of previous approaches and is driven by major innovations in technology as well as market dynamics. Let's continue the discussion by exploring these dynamics in greater depth, how they give rise to strategic imperatives, and how disruptive technologies influence them.

1.1.1 Customer Centricity

Digital technology has dramatically changed how consumers research and purchase products of virtually every category, from staples to luxury items and everything in between. With mobile capabilities, they can connect on any device, anytime, anywhere.

These consumers expect products to be priced competitively, delivered quickly, and, in many cases, tailored to their unique needs. This new customer experience is changing the way businesses sense demand, produce products, and deliver them, and it is driving the need for more streamlined, flexible methods of engagement through an *omnichannel network*. Although there are complex interrelationships between the nodes in the network, the customer is squarely in the center. The following describes some of these customer-driven digital processes and enabling technologies:

▸ **Omnichannel sales**
The ability of consumers to shop online across channels requires retailers to bring the online experience to the store and the store experience to online sales. They need to enable customers to easily compare price and features as well as availability and delivery options, regardless of location.

▸ **Demand sensing**
With the digital economy comes digital demand signals, both structured and unstructured, from customers placing orders and making comments via social media on mobile devices. The ability to capture and analyze this new, unstructured sentiment data is key to getting closer to the customer and obtaining a clear picture of what is driving demand. The structured demand data provides the opportunity to improve both short-term and mid-term forecast accuracy through pattern recognition and predictive analytics. The challenge is to effectively capture, harmonize, and convert these huge volumes of raw data into something actionable.

▸ **Omnichannel fulfillment**
When customers have the ability to place orders through any channel in real time, they also expect the order to be fulfilled in near real time. This has created opportunities for companies: Amazon offers same-day delivery, many brick-and-mortar retailers enable consumers to buy online and pick up at the nearest store, and Google and UberRUSH offer businesses door-to-door delivery services for their products in urban areas such as New York, San Francisco, and Chicago.

▸ **Customer-centric business processes**
Customer-centric processes are created by harnessing order, forecast, point-of-sale, channel, and social data to sense both short-term and long-term demand. Companies are driving actual demand signals through the extended supply chain and connecting this data to R&D, manufacturing, and supply chain

processes. Solutions like the following enable them to design, produce, and deliver the most desirable products and services to the customer:

- Integrated business planning solutions that sense real-time demand signals and enable responsive planning to adjust to market dynamics

- Warehousing and transportation solutions that allow flexible logistics processes

1.1.2 Individualized Products

The digital economy is driven by the need and ability to personalize solutions for individual customer demands. This will transform the way that companies design, produce, and deliver goods and services.

Personalized solutions and products are everywhere. Consumers can design their shoes, customize their drinks in vending machines, configure cars and motorcycles, and print personalized chocolates.

Companies are beginning to understand the full potential of the close relationships between physical and digital assets and the Internet of Things (IoT). We're witnessing new use cases across industries with measurable results. This puts increasing pressure on manufacturers to introduce more flexibility into their platforms and processes, as follows:

- **Platform for personalization**
  The common feature of most companies' personalization strategy is a strong platform that is used as a base for customization. This practice has been common in the automotive industry for several years, where customers can build their vehicle by selecting options on top of a base model, or platform.

- **Smart products driving new business models**
  IoT and Industry 4.0, the digitally enabled "smart" factory, are changing traditional business models by connecting people, products, and assets. This explosion of big data is driving the growth of individualized products and *segment-of-one marketing* (marketing that is targeted to individual consumer via social media). As companies embed sensors in their assets and products, they are themselves becoming technology companies and rethinking the value delivered by their products.

- **Redesigning products for unique segments**
  In today's dynamic landscape, customers demand better, individualized products

faster. To satisfy the changing demand, people, processes, and technology must be connected across the organization to create the following types of solutions:

▶ Product lifecycle management solutions that enable the design of configurable and customizable products

▶ Manufacturing and supply chain solutions designed for responsiveness to deliver the lot size of one

▶ Asset management solutions that leverage the IoT to improve performance, reliability, and uptime

1.1.3   The Sharing Economy

The sharing economy is a social ecosystem built around the sharing of human and physical resources and collaborative processes. Examples of this include Airbnb, Uber, and Netflix. Each of these organizations is among the largest in its market but own virtually none of the physical assets that are used or consumed by its customers. In addition, the people who provide the services are in large part independent operators. The main driver behind the success of these organizations is the digital platform on which they operate. This platform provides both customers and providers an efficient, seamless experience by which they conduct business.

When we translate this sharing economy into the business world, we see an increasing emphasis on collaboration across the network with suppliers, contract manufacturers, logistic service providers, and other partners. There is also a need to collaborate not only with people and companies but also across assets. The IoT is a fundamental element in the digital platform that allows businesses to connect across assets. Figure 1.1 is an illustration of this concept.

Following are some of the key characteristics of such a network:

▶ **Transparency at the core of a strong business network**
Business networks help manufacturers gain the necessary insights into customers' needs, suppliers' actions, and contract manufacturers' performance. This ensures not only high quality and standards but also that increasing demands for sustainability are met. This process transparency improves collaboration and decision-making, as well as the flexibility to respond to changing customer and economic demands.

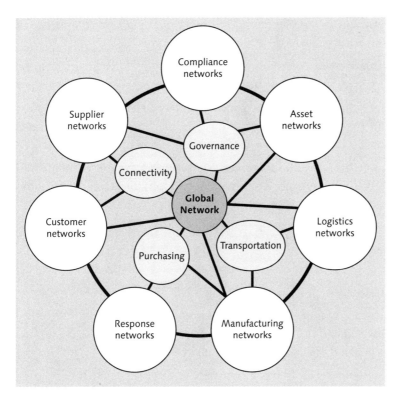

Figure 1.1 The Sharing Economy

- **Network of networks**
  As businesses expand globally, the ability to successfully operate within business networks will mean the difference between winning and losing. These networks (and networks of networks) will be the platforms on which successful businesses innovate, collaborate, grow, and continually evolve—at both speed and scale.

- **Connecting the business to the world and the world to the business**
  The extended supply chain is at the center of these business networks as we collaborate with customers, suppliers, outsourced (or contract) manufacturers, logistics service providers, and many other partners on a daily basis. Following are some examples of these collaborative business networks.

  - Project networks drive collaboration during the design process to share drawings, models, and 3D designs across departments and companies and to manage the change management processes.

▷ Supplier networks streamline the selection, onboarding, and compliance of suppliers and their materials.

▷ Manufacturing networks enable internal and contract manufacturers to be treated as a single, virtual plant floor.

▷ Asset networks optimize usage by collaborating on technical data, real-time insights, and predictive maintenance through machine-to-machine (M2M) connectivity.

▷ Customer networks enable a market-driven world where visibility and response to fluctuating demand and sentiment about the products and company are critical.

▷ Logistics networks track and trace materials, products, and assets throughout their complete lifecycle.

1.1.4 Sustainability

Efficient management of limited resources has become a major factor for economies around the world and the businesses that drive them. This isn't only limited to natural resources that are harvested for human consumption but also to the human resources themselves whose talent and creativity is required to solve some of the toughest problems we face. The modern-day digital supply chain can be seen as a microcosm of this global concern, which manifests itself in the following ways:

▸ **Talent shortage**
The skills required to run a digitized supply chain have evolved with the emergence of big data, both structured and unstructured, now available from informed customers, connected assets, social media, and the IoT. This drives the need for data scientists who can analyze and make sense of this wealth of information in real time. The ability to do so effectively can have a significant positive upstream effect on the supply chain by better aligning supply with demand and by eliminating process waste and excess consumption of scarce materials.

▸ **Environmental responsibility**
The need for raw materials such as water, minerals, oil, and gas is a key component to many supply chains, but these resources are becoming increasingly limited as global demand for finished goods continues to ramp up, particularly

in emerging markets. This trend has been building over the past several years and will continue to gain momentum. As a result, manufacturers will need to continue to find ways to utilize these scarce resources better to avert global shortages.

▶ **Risk minimization**
A key principle of sustainable operations is to encourage people and processes to embrace risk management. Risks fall into several major categories: operational, compliance, environmental, and geopolitical. Any of these can have a significant impact on supply chain operations. Companies that manage them effectively are able to make use of the availability of big data to perform simulation and scenario analysis and understand the probability and impact of different risks.

▶ **Sustainability in business processes**
Sustainability will play a particularly important role in how businesses run moving forward. Corporate social responsibility used to be a luxury, but not anymore. Sustainability is becoming the lens through which a business is judged by its consumers, workforce, society, and even its investors. Following are some of the approaches companies have adopted to foster sustainability in their organizations:

  ▷ Innovation and design processes that deliver sustainable products to the market

  ▷ Product stewardship networks that manage global product safety and compliance throughout the product lifecycle

  ▷ Supply chains that utilize assets and move products through the network in a manner that satisfies demand while minimizing environmental impact

  ▷ Track-and-trace solutions to ensure visibility from raw materials to finished products and contain the effects of product recalls

1.2　The Evolution of Supply Chain Planning at SAP

In 1998, SAP released the first version of its advanced supply chain planning solution, SAP Advanced Planning and Optimization (SAP APO) amid a mixture of anticipation and skepticism from the market. Today, SAP APO is the most widely used advanced planning solution in the industry, with more than 2,000 customers across all regions, industries, and market segments. The key design criteria for SAP APO included in-memory computing for performance and scalability, an enhanced user experience, and near real-time integration with the execution environment. In addition, SAP APO offered a complete set of advanced supply chain planning applications on a single integrated platform. Although SAP APO is considered to be a mature product in today's market, these design criteria remain valid as the SAP supply chain portfolio continues to evolve.

In 2011, SAP began development of a completely new supply chain planning solution, which was released in 2012 under the name SAP Sales and Operations Planning powered by SAP HANA (hereafter, SAP S&OP on SAP HANA). This product marked a number of firsts for SAP. It was the first supply chain application built natively on the SAP HANA platform, deployed in the cloud, and purpose-built to support a company's end-to-end S&OP process. Another very important key attribute was the underlying comprehensive demand, supply, and financial model, which meant that plans could be developed that weren't only operationally feasible but financially sound as well. For the first time, the information needs of all the stakeholders in the S&OP process could be addressed in a single tool.

A number of other significant innovations were built into SAP S&OP on SAP HANA. One was the ability for the end user to create analytics and dashboards based on the information in the SAP HANA-based data model in real time. That's correct—no batch updates required—just select the data elements, layout, and format, and the very latest available information would be displayed in a web-based view. Another was embedded, context-aware collaboration, powered by SAP Jam, which provided the ability to orchestrate both the formal and informal processes that are part of any organization's S&OP practice. Now not only did the S&OP stakeholders have the information they needed, they were also connected to all the other stakeholders in real time. This combination of capabilities promised to deliver unprecedented speed and precision in decision-making.

Probably the most notable characteristic of SAP S&OP on SAP HANA wasn't really an innovation, but a recognition that most planners are quite comfortable working in Microsoft Excel to perform their daily tasks. In every organization, one can find a multitude of basic to complex spreadsheets into which users download data from the main planning system so they can work with it in their way. Early on, the decision was made to not only support this practice but enhance it by making

Excel the primary user interface (UI) for SAP S&OP. There are several major advantages to this approach, as follows:

▸ The learning curve and acceptance by the user are highly accelerated because they aren't forced to learn a new interface.

▸ Users have tremendous flexibility to create customized "planning views" using their own Excel format and the data that reside in the system.

▸ These planning views can be used to create scenarios by using the standard features of Excel combined with the planning capabilities provided by the tool.

When a planner creates a scenario with which they are satisfied, they simply save it, and the system is updated in real time. All other users then have access to the information from within their own planning views, or dashboards. The importance of this can't be overemphasized. The single biggest complaint that companies express regarding their S&OP process is the burden of having to manage and reconcile multiple spreadsheets that aren't based on a consistent view of data. SAP has solved this problem with this product by connecting the planners and their spreadsheets to a single, unified data model.

This unified data model has been mentioned several times in different contexts. This may be the most important aspect of this product and bears discussing in greater detail. It's not an exaggeration to say that the data model is the heart and soul of the product because it defines the set of business objects (customers, products, resources, locations, etc.) that comprise a supply chain and the relationships between these objects (product structures, planning hierarchies, sourcing rules, etc.). The objects are defined by master data and key figures, and the relationships are defined by attributes and operators. As an example, *product* would be a master data element, *sales forecast* would be a key figure, and *region* would be an attribute. This type of structure makes it very simple to construct a planning view that shows product forecast by region across multiple time periods. These planning views can be built using virtually any combination of master data, key figures, and attributes to facilitate how the planners operate.

What makes this even more powerful is the fact that the data model is completely flexible. It's really a meta model that defines the actual data stored in the underlying SAP HANA tables. SAP provides a reference model with commonly used key figures, attributes, etc., but customers generally modify or add to them based on their business requirements. They can also create user-defined calculations that can be used to perform certain functions on the data. All of this is stored as customer-specific configuration and doesn't impact the base code. What this means is that SAP can continue to deliver frequent product updates with new capabilities without creating conflicts within the customer's environment.

The early versions of SAP S&OP on SAP HANA provided some basic planning functions that could be used in conjunction with the data model. These included basic statistical forecasting and single-level rough-cut capacity planning. This enabled the S&OP team to balance supply and demand at a finished goods level and use some of the financial key figures (product costs, pricing) to determine if the plan was profitable. One very powerful capability was simulation and scenario analysis, which was done by creating additional versions of the plan that could be modified using different conditions and assumptions performed by different planners on different segments of the plan. The team would work on one or more of these versions collaboratively until they achieved a particular result. For example, there could be baseline (active), upside, and downside versions showing the impact of different levels of demand on supply and revenue. If certain key figures from a particular version had a desirable outcome, they could be promoted to the baseline plan. This is where the advantage of having built the product on SAP HANA becomes apparent. Other solutions in the market can perform simulation and scenario analysis, but none can do so with the volume of data and speed of SAP S&OP on SAP HANA.

In later versions of the product, more advanced planning capabilities were added, including additional forecasting models, multilevel supply planning heuristics, and supply/profit optimization. These advanced capabilities were geared toward a different type of user and really began to leverage the performance and scalability of the SAP HANA platform. SAP S&OP on SAP HANA began to push the boundaries of traditional S&OP into a more operational realm and created the impetus for the next phase of development.

1.3 SAP IBP at a Glance

In mid-2014, after a successful launch of SAP S&OP on SAP HANA, SAP released the first version of SAP Integrated Business Planning (SAP IBP), which combined tactical and operational planning, analytics, and control in a single environment.

These planning processes were packaged into five individual applications, which will be described in the following sections of this chapter. From a technical perspective, these individual applications comprise a single product, sharing a common platform, data model, and UI, as shown in Figure 1.2 and discussed further in Section 1.4 and Section 1.5.

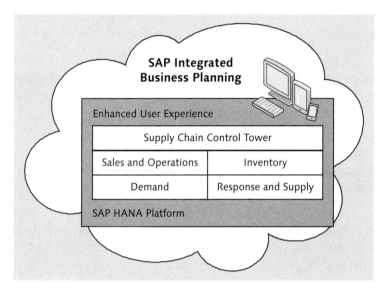

Figure 1.2 SAP IBP Planning Applications

Table 1.1 provides the important usage capabilities of SAP IBP.

Complete Scalable Model	Real-Time What-If Scenario Planning	Collaboration	Intuitive User Interfaces
Demand, supply chain, and financial model at aggregate and detailed levels	Real-time scenarios and simulation on entire model	Transparent communication, recorded decisions	Access anytime via web, Excel, and mobile UI

Table 1.1 Key Usage Capabilities of SAP IBP

In the following sections, we'll take a look at each of the five functionalities that make up SAP IBP: S&OP, demand planning, response and supply planning, inventory management, and SAP Supply Chain Control Tower.

1.3.1 SAP IBP for Sales and Operations

Much has already been said about SAP S&OP on SAP HANA and all of the key capabilities and innovations that were part of this solution, which was subsequently rebranded and became the flagship application for SAP IBP. The enhanced user experience, robust, flexible data model, and native SAP HANA performance and scalability provided a solid foundation on which to build the complete SAP IBP suite. The development teams working on the new applications were able to leverage this foundation by reusing and extending the data model and UI.

The end result was a fully integrated, high-performance suite of tactical and operational supply chain planning applications with a common, consistent UI. The importance of this can't be overstated in light of the supply chain planning architecture that has evolved in many companies over the past few decades, which are rife with data redundancy, non-integrated processes, and multiple UI's. Many customers have implemented SAP IBP for sales and operations to advance their S&OP process maturity, which had been severely hampered by their incumbent system landscapes. This solution has enabled them to orchestrate a cross-functional S&OP process, profitably balance supply and demand, and anticipate and respond to changing business conditions through simulation and scenario analysis. Their success has encouraged many of them to begin the next phase of the journey, which includes implementation of multiple SAP IBP applications.

1.3.2 SAP IBP for Inventory

SAP has been providing inventory planning solutions to its customers for many years, either natively as part of SAP Supply Chain Management (SAP SCM) or through third-party providers that were focused in the field of inventory optimization. While these solutions were helpful in managing inventory levels at a product or location level, the results were typically less than optimal. This was due to the fact that they ran in separate environments on different data models or didn't take into account the full supply chain network and all of its associated variability factors. Several years ago, SAP decided to expand its capabilities by acquiring SmartOps, which was recognized as the industry-leading provider of multistage inventory- and service-level optimization solutions.

The SmartOps solutions were subsequently integrated with SAP APO and SAP ERP, and then they were rebranded as SAP Enterprise Inventory and Service-Level

Optimization. The branding accurately describes the power of this solution, which is able to model the complete network, from the original raw material supplier to the end customer, and all nodes in between, as well as all the complex relationships between these nodes. The highly sophisticated algorithm uses a stochastic approach to determine the appropriate balance between inventory investment and service level at every node based on demand and supply variability characteristics specific to each product/location combination.

For example, with multi-sourcing, where a single product can be supplied to different distribution centers from different plants, each of these combinations would have a unique set of lead times on the supply side and forecast accuracy on the demand side. The SAP Enterprise Inventory and Service-Level Optimization algorithm would understand all of these unique characteristics and plan inventory and service levels individually, as opposed to in aggregate. This may result in higher inventory in some locations and lower inventory in others, with the final result being the inventory/service balance referred to earlier. Many SAP customers in the consumer, discrete, and process manufacturing industries have leveraged SAP Enterprise Inventory and Service-Level Optimization to achieve this balance and dramatically improve supply chain performance with regard to key metrics such as fill rate, customer service, inventory turns, and cycle times.

These capabilities became an integral part of SAP IBP 4.0 with the added benefit of the common platform, data model, and UI that provide seamless integration between the previously disconnected processes of S&OP and inventory optimization. Inventory investment can now be part of the S&OP plan along with investment in capacity and other key decision factors. Likewise, the S&OP constrained demand plan drives forecast accuracy, which is a factor in the inventory optimization process. Planners on both the S&OP and inventory side can look at multiple scenarios to arrive at a result that best meets customer service, revenue, and profitability objectives. This integrated process is commonly referred to as sales, inventory, and operations planning (SIOP) and is one of the key pillars of the SAP extended supply chain portfolio. Figure 1.3 shows an example of an SAP IBP dashboard that an inventory planner may use; it contains a summary of the inventory planning process, a heat map with safety stock information, and several bar charts which compare different financial and operational key figures.

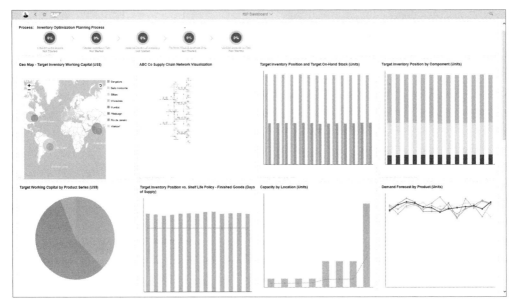

Figure 1.3 SAP IBP for Inventory Dashboard

1.3.3 SAP Supply Chain Control Tower

One of the biggest challenges with advanced supply chain planning systems has been the inability to easily extract and analyze the rich set of information that underlies the core functions. We know, for example, that a tremendous amount of data is required to support processes such as forecasting, supply planning, and inventory optimization. What we see when we run these processes is only the final result, which is the tip of the iceberg. If we have a high forecast error, repeated material shortages, or excess inventory, what is the underlying root cause? What is the impact of these issues on supply chain performance, and how can they most effectively be resolved. To answer these questions requires analytical tools that operate in real time and produce actionable information. Companies using classic SAP SCM solutions such as SAP APO had the SAP Business Warehouse (SAP BW) and SAP Supply Chain Info Center tools with which they could extract supply chain data to produce a variety of reports.

However, these tools were either very IT driven, requiring a lot of effort to maintain, or weren't flexible or broad enough in scope to produce actionable information. With SAP IBP 4.0, SAP delivered the SAP Supply Chain Control Tower, which was designed to overcome these shortcomings by providing real-time, end-to-end supply chain visibility. With SAP Supply Chain Control Tower, end users can configure their own dashboards to represent any combination of data that is resident within SAP IBP. They can create custom alerts that highlight exceptions and drill down on these exceptions to perform root-cause analysis. Using the advanced planning capabilities of SAP IBP, they can simulate different methods of resolving exceptions, such as changing inventory targets to resolve shortages or expediting orders to improve delivery performance. Finally, using the built-in case management capability, they can create a workflow that will track the issue through the resolution process.

SAP Supply Chain Control Tower also comes with a number of predefined key performance indicators (KPIs) based on standard metrics from the Supply Chain Operations Reference (SCOR) model, or companies can use the same framework to create their own KPIs that can be included in their dashboards. Finally, SAP Supply Chain Control Tower is equipped with the ability to connect to other rich sources of supply chain data, including SAP SCM, SAP ERP, SAP S/4HANA, SAP Transportation Management (SAP TM), SAP Extended Warehouse Management (SAP EWM), and even non-SAP data sources. The end result is a highly configurable self-service environment that provides supply chain managers unparalleled visibility and control across their network. Figure 1.4 shows an example of an SAP Supply Chain Control Tower dashboard that combines information from various sources such as manufacturing, inventory, and demand and supply planning into a single view.

Figure 1.4 SAP Supply Chain Control Tower Dashboard

1.3.4 SAP IBP for Demand

Getting demand planning right is essential for good supply chain performance, perhaps more so than any other planning process. This is reflected by the fact that there are many mature demand planning solutions in the supply chain applications market. SAP Demand Planning (formerly SAP APO Demand Planning) is arguably the most widely used tool in the industry and certainly one of the most mature. With SAP IBP 5.0, SAP introduced demand planning in the cloud. This included a number of core capabilities found in its SAP APO-based predecessor such as outlier detection, forecast alerts, powerful statistical algorithms, and multiple forecast error measures. This set of tools provides the demand planner with the ability to develop an accurate mid-to-long term forecast.

Forecast accuracy is perhaps the single most important metric in supply chain planning as it impacts every upstream process, including inventory, supply, and production planning. That is why so much of the professional demand planner's effort goes into determining the right statistical method used to generate a forecast given the nature of the historical data and level of variability. However, even the most advanced statistical method has its limitations with regard to accuracy, so other non-mathematical approaches are often deployed. The most common are collaborative and consensus forecasting, which incorporate the collective judgment of the demand planners and can further enhance the results of statistical methods. The ability to drive collaborative demand planning is one of the unique attributes of SAP IBP for demand and is powered by the embedded social collaboration capabilities of SAP Jam.

Another method of improving forecast accuracy is demand sensing, which looks at actual demand signals such as orders, shipments, and point-of-sale data and then uses a pattern recognition algorithm to forecast demand in the short term. Take the example of a weekly statistical forecast for 100 units. The typical approach would be to distribute this equally, that is, 20 units per day. However, the real pattern of demand signals may actually predict different amounts each day (15, 20, 25, 25, 15), which could drive how the product is produced and deployed to the distribution centers. The combination of more accurate short-term forecasts (as calculated by demand sensing) and sophisticated mid- to long-term forecasting methods increases the overall level of forecast accuracy. This, of course, translates into benefits across the supply chain such as improved service, reduced inventory, and higher revenue. Finally, for the demand analysts, there are customizable dashboards as shown in Figure 1.5 that allow them to monitor these processes in real time to enable a best-in-class demand management practice. Figure 1.5 shows is an example of an SAP IBP for demand dashboard illustrating the demand planning process and some key metrics such as forecast, sales, and revenue plans.

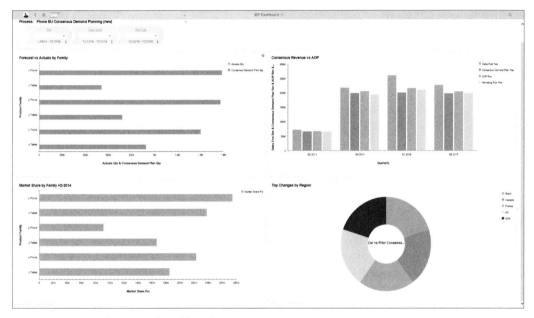

Figure 1.5 SAP IBP for Demand Dashboard

1.3.5   SAP IBP for Response and Supply

Despite all the noble efforts of demand planners and analysts to improve forecast accuracy, even the best in class are somewhere in the 70–80% range. There is simply a certain amount of demand variability that can't be planned for, which means that upstream processes such as supply and production planning need to have the flexibility to respond effectively. This flexibility is at the core of what is known as demand-driven planning and is fundamental to the design of a new category of solutions known as response management. With SAP IBP 6.0, SAP introduced this capability as part of a broader supply planning solution. SAP IBP for response and supply covers the full range of processes, including multilevel heuristics, constraint-based supply optimization, and priority-driven response planning. This addresses all levels of tactical and operational supply planning, similar to what is available with its predecessor, SAP Supply Network Planning (SAP SNP). Also similar to SAP APO, it incorporates a full representation of the SAP ERP order-level data model and offers real-time integration to SAP ERP via a utility called SAP HANA smart data integration (SAP HANA SDI). The advantage of SAP IBP for response and supply as compared to other solutions, both SAP and otherwise, is that it shares the platform, data model, and consumer-grade user experience with the other SAP IBP applications, which creates an unobstructed view of demand and supply conditions across the entire supply network. Following are a few examples to illustrate the benefit of this architecture:

- **Rough-cut capacity planning**
  One of the primary objectives of a mature S&OP process is to determine if sufficient capacity is available in the future to support the consensus demand plan or, in reverse, if there is insufficient demand resulting in excess capacity. This is typically done at an aggregated demand and capacity level to simplify the analysis and decision-making process and is effective in making long-term recommendations to adjust demand, supply, or capacity while maintaining profitability. However, this aggregation can sometimes mask underlying issues, such as the demand for a particular product or utilization of an individual resource that is the root cause of the problem. The SAP IBP data model combined with the multilevel heuristic provides the environment and tools necessary to address both of the scenarios in a single planning view. The planner can begin with the aggregate rough-cut plan and easily drill down to the underlying details to further investigate any problems and recommend adjustments. These recommendations can be done in simulation mode so that multiple alternatives can be evaluated before a final decision is made. The result is an S&OP process that is sensitive to demand and supply variability and can be executed across the complete planning horizon.

- **Supply optimization**
  Companies that have developed a more advanced S&OP practice have employed optimization as a way of maximizing delivery, profitability, or asset efficiency. SAP IBP for response and supply is equipped with an optimizer that can effectively cover these scenarios or objective functions. This tool is capable of considering several different operating constraints, including production,

storage, lot sizes, and lead times, as well as financial constraints such as transportation, production, procurement, and inventory costs. Most often, it's used in a tactical planning context as a means of constraining the S&OP consensus demand plan. Some customers have also found it useful as a method of developing an initial constrained supply plan that can be fed directly to manufacturing for more granular production planning and scheduling. As with the multi-level heuristic, the optimizer operates on the common SAP IBP data model in either live mode or simulation mode, which enables rapidly iterative scenario analysis and delivers more timely and accurate decision-making.

► **Response planning**
While the processes described previously provides the foundation for an efficient, profitable response to demand, modern supply chains are faced with daily challenges that threaten to disrupt even the most carefully laid out plans. These disruptions can come in the form of demand spikes caused by unanticipated orders, supply shortages caused by production issues, or emergency situations resulting from natural or human disasters (floods, fire, etc.). Supply planners are the "first responders" in such situations but often lack the tools to effectively handle them. The basic problem is how to prioritize demand and allocate supply in a way that minimizes the potential negative impact on customer service. These decisions often have to be made in a very short time frame and with a high degree of accuracy, so there isn't much time for traditional analysis and planning. SAP IBP for response and supply addresses this problem with a rules-based, priority-driven approach that can very quickly identify constraints, perform root-cause analysis, and propose a solution that meets business objectives at the highest feasible level. The solution can be a recommended change to the production schedule, reallocation of available supply, or reprioritization of delivery dates for customer orders. Because response planning is enabled by real-time integration with SAP ERP, these recommendations are based on the very latest information available and can be executed seamlessly.

Figure 1.6 shows an example of an SAP IBP dashboard that a supply planner would use as part of the S&OP process for an overview of the current supply situation.

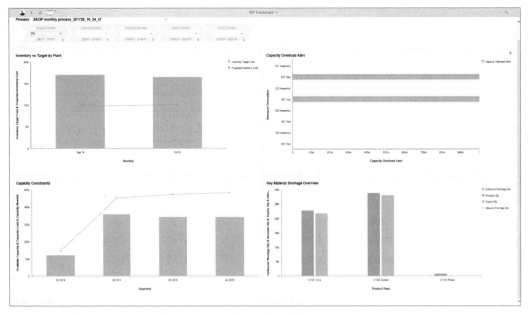

Figure 1.6 SAP IBP for Response and Supply Dashboard

1.4 SAP IBP Architecture

In Section 1.2, the SAP IBP unified planning model was discussed. This model is the core component of the SAP IBP planning architecture and is based on the individual building blocks, which are used together to define the unique planning model of an organization. Following is a list of the building blocks that are included with SAP IBP:

- Attribute
- Master data type
- Time profile
- Planning area
- Planning level
- Key figure
- Key figure calculation logic
- Planning operator

- ▸ Reason code
- ▸ Version
- ▸ Scenario
- ▸ Global configuration parameters
- ▸ Snapshot configuration

Chapter 4 will describe these building blocks in more detail, including how the model can be configured to execute the planning processes described in this and other chapters.

1.5 SAP HANA and SAP IBP

The reason SAP IBP is able to perform quick calculations with a high data volume is due to the inherent nature of SAP HANA's in-memory computation. This new generation of solutions leverages the disruptive technologies of in-memory, cloud, and mobile computing that will enable business to truly operate in real time, not just within functional silos but from end-to-end. Nowhere is the opportunity for these solutions greater than in the area of supply chain management. The supply chain professional of the very near future will have the ability to capture, organize, analyze, and execute massive amounts of information with unprecedented speed and accuracy.

At the heart of these solutions is the digital core, SAP S/4HANA. This is the new system of record, where all mission-critical data and processes are connected and operate as a single unified organism. SAP S/4HANA supports major shared business functions such as sales, finance, procurement, manufacturing, and human capital management.

Connected to the digital core are extensions that share a common architecture and data model with the digital core. In addition, they share a number of key attributes, as follows:

- ▸ **Real-time capabilities**
  Real-time optimization of business processes will have massive implications for how companies design, plan, make, and deliver products; how they respond to increasing supply and demand volatility; and how they operate and utilize assets.

▶ **Power of prediction and simulation**
Every employee can leverage real business insights, and planners can simulate scenarios and perform "what if" analyses. They can leverage predictive tools to drive more precise decisions, improve productivity, and increase profitability.

▶ **Agility**
Companies can rapidly bring new products to market, onboard new suppliers, or reflect changes in business dynamics and fluctuations in supply and demand.

▶ **Deployment choice and lower total cost of ownership (TCO)**
The consuming solution to run the core has to be simple. Companies now have the choice to deploy in house or in the cloud. In-memory computing will also have a significant impact on TCO and will free up more budget space for innovation.

▶ **Consumer-grade user experience**
User experience is key to success; it drives adoption, user engagement, and, ultimately, productivity.

SAP IBP is an excellent example of one of these extensions, as it is SAP's newest and most advanced supply chain planning solution.

1.6   Summary

With the recent advent of technology transformation, digitization, and changing customer behavior, supply chain planning is at the top of the minds of many business professionals. SAP IBP, with its unified model, advanced planning capabilities, and intuitive UI, is well equipped to optimize the supply chain planning processes of many organizations. SAP IBP seamlessly integrates S&OP, demand planning, supply planning, response planning, and inventory optimization. In addition, real-time embedded analytical capabilities further enhance the ability of leading organizations to become more responsive to the ever-changing and hyper-connected business environment.

Equipped with a good understanding of the basics of SAP IBP, we will now move into a more detailed review of the architecture and capabilities, beginning with the all-important user interface and navigation.

This chapter demonstrates basic navigation that provides you with personalized access to all of the powerful capabilities of SAP Integrated Business Planning.

2 Navigation

SAP has put a tremendous amount of effort into making SAP Integrated Business Planning (SAP IBP) a very efficient and intuitive solution from an end-user perspective. To this end, SAP has leveraged three user interface (UI) technologies—SAP Fiori, the web, and Microsoft Excel—to manage a specific type of user interaction. This chapter will explore some examples of these UIs and how planners work with them to more effectively manage their supply chains.

2.1 SAP Fiori

When you log in to SAP IBP via the web, you'll land on your home page, which is built on the SAP Fiori platform, as shown in Figure 2.1. The tiles on the home page each provide access to a specific function within SAP IBP, and they are organized by role. In the following sections, we'll look at the MY HOME page, and the GENERAL MAINTENANCE, DEMAND PLANNER, and RESPONSE PLANNER areas.

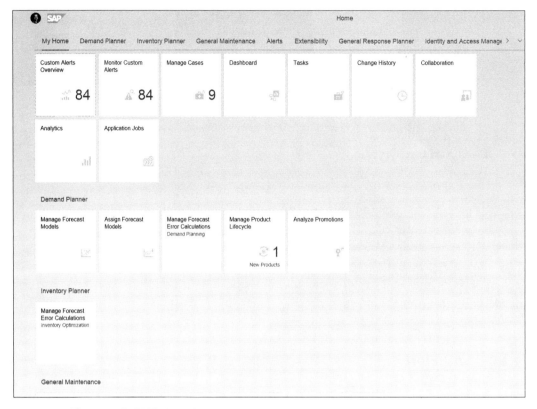

Figure 2.1 SAP IBP Home Page

2.1.1 My Home

The first home page is called MY HOME, which you can customize to include your most commonly used functions. The number on the first tile indicates that there are custom alerts, or exceptions, to review. Alerts will be covered in more depth in Chapter 14 and Chapter 15. Selecting this tile opens the SAP IBP alert window where you can investigate the situation.

The left panel in Figure 2.2 displays the alerts in both text and numeric format. By selecting one of these, a graphical display opens up in the main portion of the screen to provide a more visual representation of the data. From this view, you can drill down and see more details about what is causing the exception. This capability enables you to proactively manage issues in the supply chain.

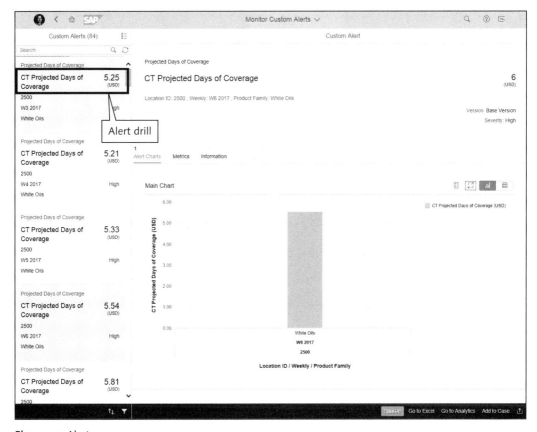

Figure 2.2 Alerts

Selecting the DASHBOARD tile in Figure 2.3 opens up one of the many web-based views that are available in SAP IBP.

Figure 2.4 provides an overview of the sales and operations planning (S&OP) process and some of the relevant analytics. These analytics are based on real-time data, which can be investigated further using the EXPLORE button that is found on all web-based views. In addition, from this screen, you can switch to another dashboard by selecting from a dropdown list in the upper-left corner.

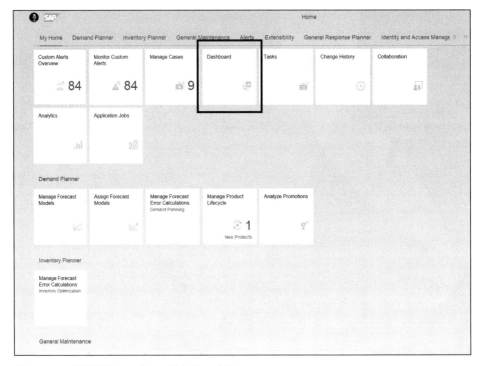

Figure 2.3 SAP IBP Home Page: Web-Based View

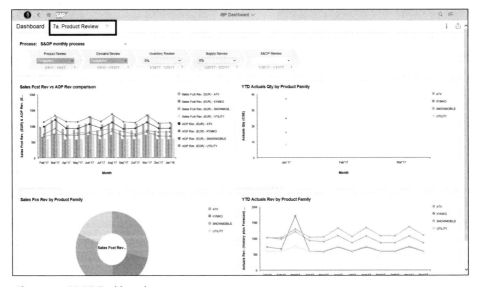

Figure 2.4 S&OP Dashboard

Moving further to the right on the HOME PAGE, you'll see the COLLABORATION tile (see Figure 2.5). Selecting it opens up an SAP Jam session (for more details, see Chapter 4), which is used to orchestrate the various steps and tasks in the S&OP or other planning processes.

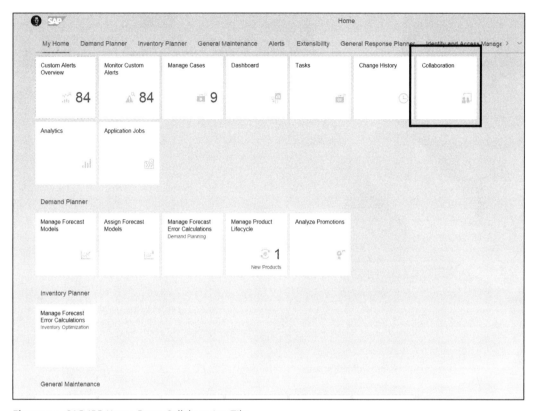

Figure 2.5 SAP IBP Home Page: Collaboration Tile

Figure 2.6 shows the DEMAND REVIEW page in SAP Jam, which is displaying a series of updates that have been made to the plan. From here, you can review these updates, share content with other stakeholders, conduct virtual meetings, create new tasks, and perform a number of other collaborative functions.

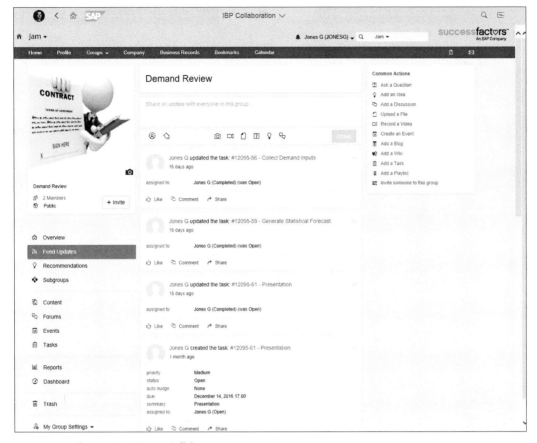

Figure 2.6 SAP Jam Collaboration

Finally, selecting the Analytics tile in Figure 2.7 opens a list of available SAP IBP analytics functions.

Figure 2.8 shows the customized list that provides a type, title, description, and relevant dates regarding each analysis. From this list, you can go directly to the chart you want to view.

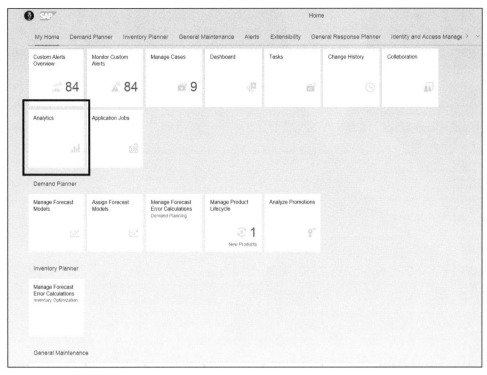

Figure 2.7 SAP IBP Home Page: Analytics Tile

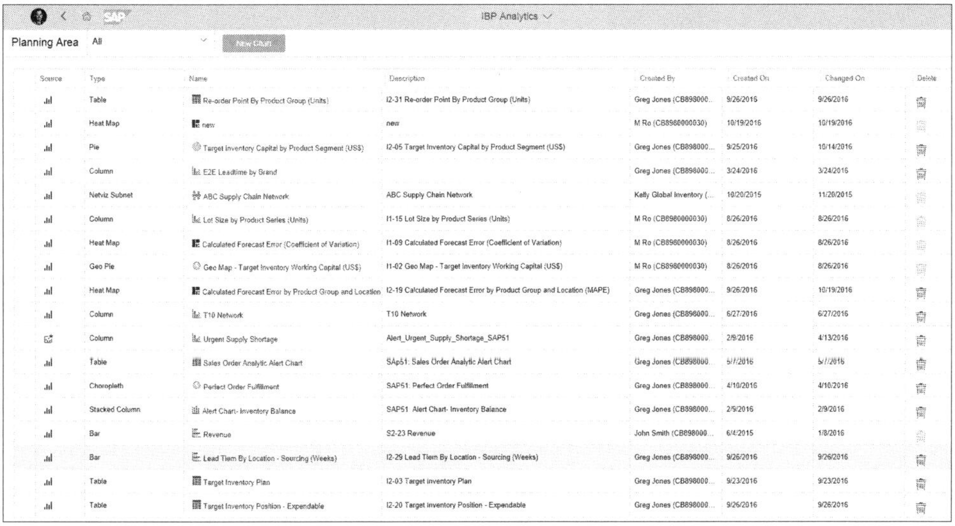

Figure 2.8 SAP IBP Analytics Selection Screen

Figure 2.9 is a good example of an SAP IBP analysis, which in this case, is showing inventory investment by period, type, and product group. As with all SAP IBP analytics, this data is from the very latest planning run or user update. You can dynamically change the view by simply selecting different key figures, attributes, or time buckets. You can also easily switch from a graphical to a tabular representation of the data, or change the chart type, all from within the view itself. This type of flexibility and real-time analysis enables you to make faster, more accurate decisions.

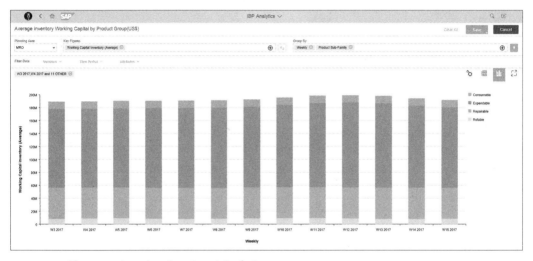

Figure 2.9 Inventory Investment Analysis

2.1.2   General Maintenance

The next area we'll take a look at is General Maintenance, where various cross-application functions such as alerts, process models, and visibility filters are maintained. In Figure 2.10, select the Configuration tile, which opens up the configuration menu.

Figure 2.11 shows the main configuration menu. Here is where the building blocks of the SAP IBP planning model, described in Chapter 3, are maintained under Set Up and Manage Your Master Data Library. Another important area is the Planning Area, which is where the planning model is instantiated for a given company or business unit based on their configuration.

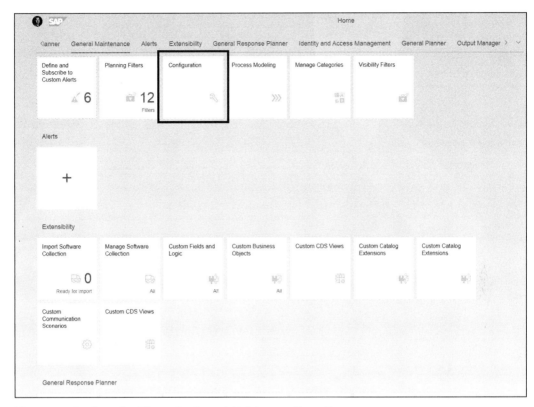

Figure 2.10 Configuration Tile on the General Maintenance Home Page

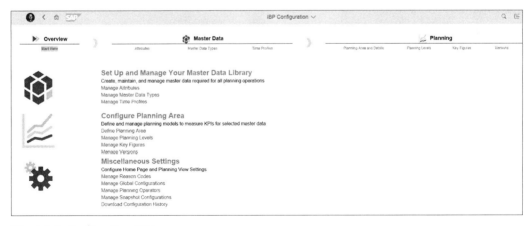

Figure 2.11 Configuration Menu

Figure 2.12 shows an example of a PLANNING AREA configuration screen, which is accessed by selecting PLANNING AREA AND DETAILS from the menu bar. This particular screen is where some of the basic parameters are maintained, such as TIME PROFILE and CHANGE HISTORY, and other functions are enabled such as supply planning or planning operators. It is also where master data and attributes are assigned to the planning area and parameters are maintained.

Figure 2.12 Planning Area Configuration

2.1.3 Demand Planner

The next area—DEMAND PLANNER—is a functional one. From the home page, you can execute many of the key maintenance and planning functions for this particular process. These include maintaining forecast models and error calculations, as well as analyzing promotions and managing the product lifecycle, which is the task of the MANAGE PRODUCT LIFECYCLE tile selected in Figure 2.13.

This selection opens another maintenance screen, which in this case is used to set up a new product in a particular planning area (Figure 2.14). Notice that there is a field for a REFERENCE PRODUCT from which the new product will inherit some of its characteristics. This greatly simplifies the task of creating a new product in the system as opposed to defining it from scratch.

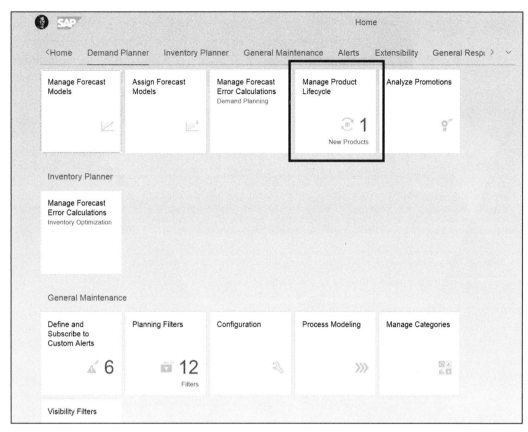

Figure 2.13 Demand Planner Home Page

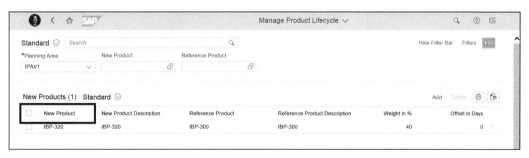

Figure 2.14 Manage Product Lifecycle

2.1.4 Response Planner

The last area we'll cover is the GENERAL RESPONSE PLANNER, which provides access to critical information about the supply network, including materials, locations, transportation lanes, and projected stock. On the far right is the MANAGE VERSIONS AND SCENARIOS, which has been selected in Figure 2.15 for further exploration.

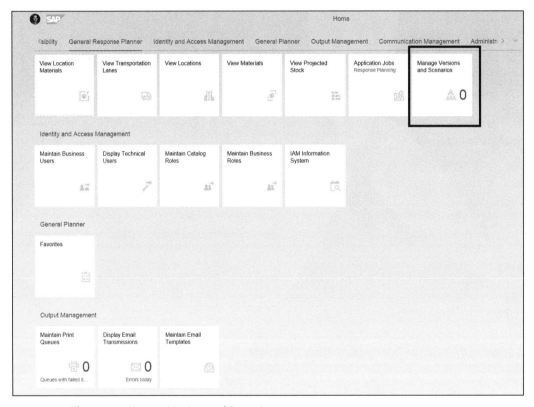

Figure 2.15 Manage Versions and Scenarios

Figure 2.16 is a good example of the results of a response management scenario, the objective of which is to evaluate the impact of an unexpected demand on the supply network. The main part of the screen shows the exploded ORDER NETWORK, which contains all the planned receipts and dependent requirements generated by the new demand. It also displays the requested and confirmed date for each, highlighting those that aren't in compliance, as well as the gating factors, or constraints, that are preventing the demand from being fulfilled as requested. With this complete picture, you can begin to investigate how to resolve the issue.

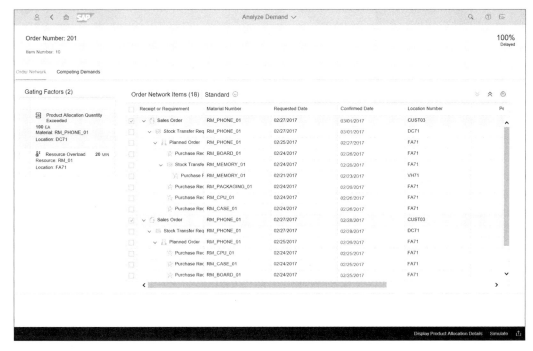

Figure 2.16 Response Planning Scenario

2.2 SAP IBP Excel Planning View

Many of the planning functions in SAP IBP are performed in the Excel planning view, which combines advanced capabilities with the familiarity and flexibility of Microsoft Excel. The Excel planning view in SAP IBP is functionally comparable to the planning book capability of SAP Advanced Planning and Optimization (SAP APO). In addition to planning, reviewing, and updating key figures, there are multiple planning-related options performed in the SAP IBP Excel planning view. In the following sections, we'll discuss some of the most widely used functions such as the planning view add-in, favorites, editing a planning view, simulations, and alerts.

2.2.1 Excel Add-In for SAP IBP Planning View

The very first requirement to be able to use the Excel planning view of SAP IBP is to download the SAP IBP Excel add-in on the user's computer. This add-in is available for download from within SAP IBP or through the SAP Service Marketplace. From the SAP Fiori ADMINISTRATOR home page, click the DOWNLOAD EXCEL ADD-IN tile, which opens a page with an option to download the Excel add-in software.

The SAP IBP ribbon appears in the Excel document, as displayed in Figure 2.17, after the add-in is successfully downloaded. Through the LOG ON screen of this page, access is created by providing the connection name, SAP IBP system web address, and the planning area. Login through the Excel interface activates all the buttons in the SAP IBP ribbon, as shown in Figure 2.17. An active logon screen connects the SAP IBP database with the Excel document for planning data viewing and editing. Clicking the LOG OFF button disconnects the document from the SAP IBP database, and the options displayed in Figure 2.17 are grayed out.

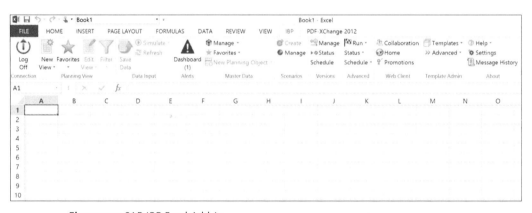

Figure 2.17 SAP IBP Excel Add-In

The SAP IBP Excel planning view has multiple options to perform different planning functions, which will be described in subsequent sections.

2.2.2 Planning View Options

A planning view is a specific combination of planning attributes, key figures, and master data to be displayed in the Excel planning document. Options available in the PLANNING VIEW group are NEW VIEW, FAVORITES, EDIT VIEW, and FILTER. Refer to the associated buttons in Figure 2.17.

A new planning view is created by clicking the NEW VIEW button in the PLANNING VIEW group. For a new planning view scenario, VERSIONS and PLANNING SCOPE are selected at the top of the page. Through the TIME SETTINGS option, the TIME PERIOD is selected, along with start and end times. Attributes are selected from the PLANNING LEVEL group, and the KEY FIGURES group is used to select the key figures whose values will be displayed in the planning view. Figure 2.23 shows an example of the planning view selection screen. After the planning view data is loaded, the view can be changed by using the EDIT VIEW button in the PLANNING VIEW group. Note the flexibility and ease in creating different views by simply selecting and deselecting per the planner requirement.

The FAVORITES option is used to select a predefined planning view. A planning view can be added as a favorite by using the FAVORITES option and clicking the ADD option as shown in Figure 2.18. The assigned name will appear in the FAVORITES name group in the dropdown list. This saves time, as after the next login, the data in the planning view can be accessed by just a click of a button, and you don't have to select the time profile, planning level, and key figures again.

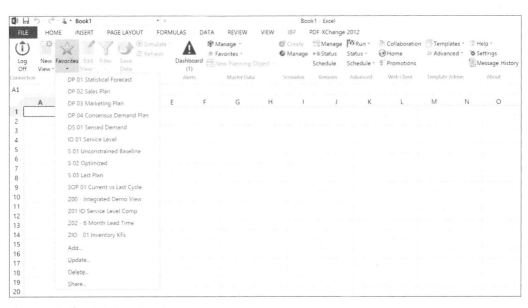

Figure 2.18 Planning View Favorites

The FAVORITES option is also used for collaboration. After saving your view as a favorite, you can click SHARE in the FAVORITES dropdown to provide the name of the system users with whom you want to share the planning view. Selected users will see a favorite in their SAP IBP Excel planning view screen with the name of the person who shared the favorite. The FILTER option provides a filtering criteria for the data selected in the SAP IBP Excel planning view, as shown in Figure 2.19.

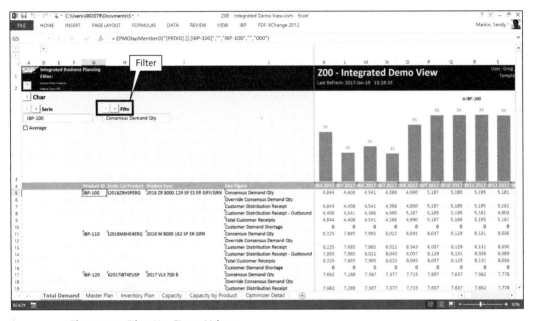

Figure 2.19 Filter Key Figure Values

A planning view can have multiple tabs in the same Excel document for different sets of planning data. Figure 2.20 shows an example of a planning view with different groups of information in different tabs of the planning view document. The capacity planning view is currently selected for review in the example, where row 4 displays the planning level attributes of LOCATION TYPE, LOCATION ID, and RESOURCE ID. There are five capacity-related key figures selected in this view, as shown in column J of the Excel document. Shifting to a different planning data set defined as a planning view can be done by toggling to another tab of the Excel document. Hence, by selecting the TOTAL DEMAND tab, the data associated with the new planning view will appear.

The Excel planning view also has integrated, context-sensitive system help capabilities, which are available when you click the HELP button as shown in Figure 2.21.

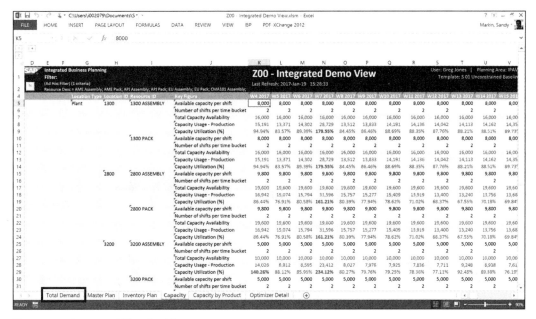

Figure 2.20 Integrated Planning View

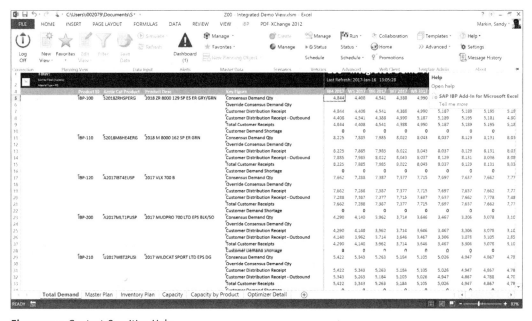

Figure 2.21 Context-Sensitive Help

To edit the scope of the planning data in the Excel planning view, the EDIT VIEW option is selected as shown in Figure 2.22. This opens the EDIT PLANNING VIEW option screen shown in Figure 2.23. Time setting, planning level, key figure selection, filtering, and planning scopes are examples of the options that planners can select to see a customized view of the data.

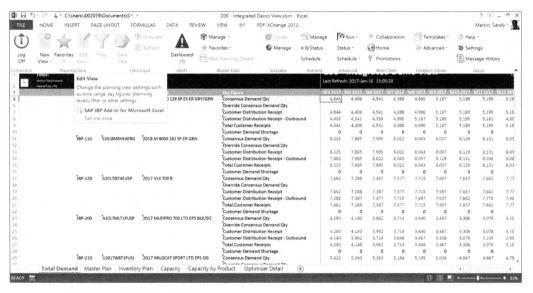

Figure 2.22 Edit View Option

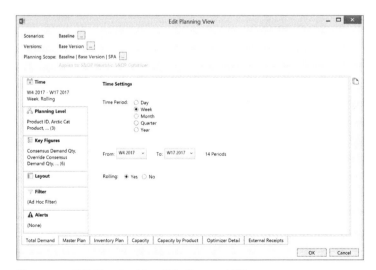

Figure 2.23 Edit Planning View Selections and Filters

2.2.3 Data Input Options

The DATA INPUT area in the Excel planning view contains the SAVE DATA, SIMU-LATE, and REFRESH options as shown in Figure 2.24. A planner can make a key fig-ure editable or non-editable (i.e. only for review) based on its definition in the planning model. An editable key figure generally appears with a white back-ground in the Excel planning view, whereas a non-editable key figure will have a gray background. If you edit key figure data in the planning view (e.g., the fore-cast of a product for a customer in a week is updated from 100 to 125 units), selecting the SAVE DATA button will save this change in the SAP IBP database.

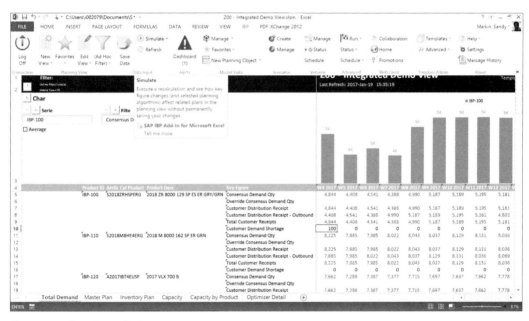

Figure 2.24 Data Input Options

The SIMULATE option is used for simulating the planning data without saving to the database. Planning algorithms in simulation mode can be executed with the SIMULATE option as displayed in Figure 2.24. If the forecast is changed, a simu-lated supply planning run (e.g., the S&OP heuristic) can be executed to analyze the impact of this change on capacity. The new capacity situation can then be reviewed without changing the live data. Figure 2.25 shows a list of other plan-ning functions that can be used to create a simulation, such as inventory or supply optimization.

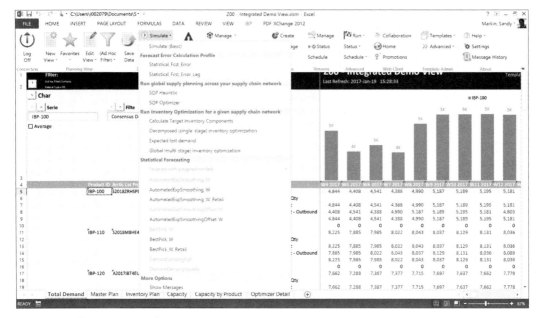

Figure 2.25 Simulation Options

The REFRESH button is used to bring the data in the Excel planning view back to its original state; any unsaved changes will be removed.

The SIMULATION, SAVE, and REFRESH functions are very useful in performing what-if scenario analyses and for improved decision-making. If the simulation exercise results in an optimum or preferred option, the SAVE DATA option will move the simulation to the active database. If the simulation data needs to be kept for further analysis, the SCENARIO option can be exercised (discussed in Section 2.2.6).

2.2.4   Alerts in the SAP IBP Excel Planning View

Alerts can also be generated in the Excel planning view, as shown in Figure 2.26. The DASHBOARD option indicates that there is an alert, which upon selection by the planner, opens up an alert window that provides additional information.

The ALERT DASHBOARD pop-up in Figure 2.27 indicates that there are several capacity issues along with the actual number of exceptions associated with each. The FAVORITE VIEW column also lists links that can be selected to bring up a planning view that will display the source of the exceptions. From here, you can use the planning and simulation capabilities previously discussed to resolve the situation. Note that all of this activity is occurring in real time, as of the latest update to the customer's SAP IBP database.

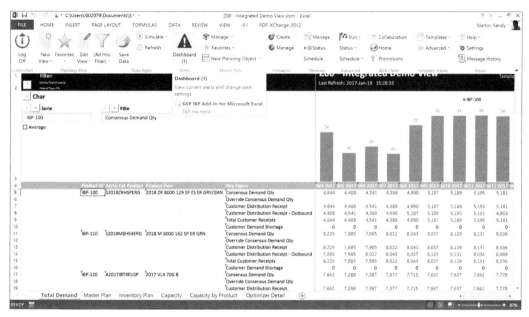

Figure 2.26 Alerts

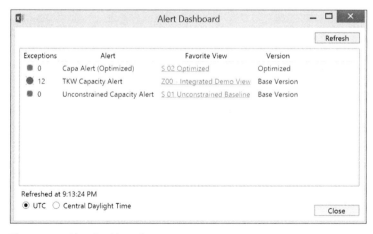

Figure 2.27 Alert Dashboard

2.2.5 Master Data Option in SAP IBP Excel Planning View

While the system of record for master data is normally the company's enterprise resource planning system, it's necessary to have the ability to maintain this data from within the planning system to add attributes or types to existing materials, new materials for planning purposes, and other master data functions. Access to this function is shown in Figure 2.28. As indicated, master data maintenance can be done for single or multiple records.

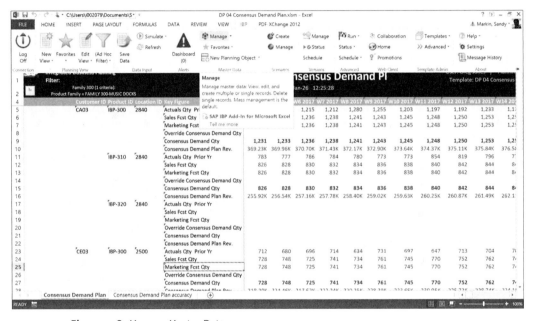

Figure 2.28 Manage Master Data

Figure 2.29 shows the CREATE MASTER DATA WORKBOOK pop-up where master data types are created and attributes are assigned to them.

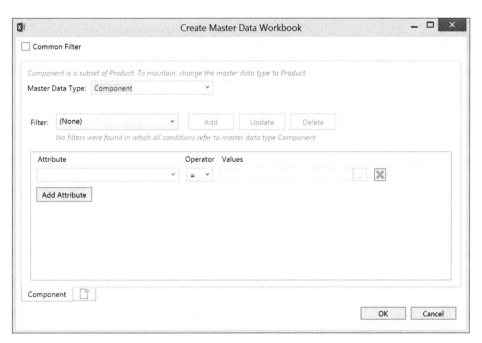

Figure 2.29 Create Master Data Workbook

2.2.6 Scenario and Version Options in the Excel Planning View

A key capability of SAP IBP is scenario planning where multiple versions of a plan can exist to test different conditions or assumptions. A version is a full copy of all planning and master data associated with a particular plan, unlike simulations that were covered earlier in this chapter, which only include local data. A common practice is to establish several versions of a plan to cover the baseline, upside, and downside scenarios. Figure 2.30 shows where the version management capability is accessed from the SAP IBP ribbon.

One of the powerful features of SAP IBP is the capability to copy data between versions based on specific key figures or attributes via the version management function shown in Figure 2.31. To commit certain data from a scenario version to the live plan, simply promote the appropriate key figures, and the data will be copied over.

DP 04 Consensus Demand Plan.xlsm - Excel

C:\Users\i002079\Documents\S...

FILE · HOME · INSERT · PAGE LAYOUT · FORMULAS · DATA · REVIEW · VIEW · IBP · PDF-XChange 2012 · Markin, Sandy

Log Off · New View · Favorites · Edit View · (Ad Hoc Filter) · Save Data · | Simulate · Refresh · Dashboard (0) · New Planning Object · | Manage · Favorites · Manage · | Create · Manage · | Manage · Status · Schedule · | Run · Status · Home · Promotions · | Collaboration · | Templates · Advanced · | Help · Settings · Message History

Filter:
Family 300 (1 criteria):
Product Family = FAMILY 300-MUSIC DOCKS

DP 04 Cons... Last Refresh: 2017-Jan...

Manage: Initialize, reinitialize, promote or copy version data from and to the base version or other version

SAP IBP Add-In for Microsoft Excel — Tell me more

Template: DP 04 Consensus

Customer ID	Product ID	Location ID	Key Figure	W4 2017	W5 2017	W6 2017	W7 2017	W8 2017	W9 2017	W10 2017	W11 2017	W12 2017	W13 2017	W14 20
CA03	IBP-300	2840	Actuals Qty Prior Yr	1,187	1,195					1,203	1,197	1,192	1,233	1,1
			Sales Fcst Qty	1,231	1,233					1,245	1,248	1,250	1,253	1,25
			Marketing Fcst Qty	1,231	1,233	1,236	1,238	1,241	1,243	1,245	1,248	1,250	1,253	1,25
			Override Consensus Demand Qty											
			Consensus Demand Qty	1,231	1,233	1,236	1,238	1,241	1,243	1,245	1,248	1,250	1,253	1,25
			Consensus Demand Plan Rev.	369.23K	369.96K	370.70K	371.43K	372.17K	372.90K	373.64K	374.37K	375.11K	375.84K	376.5
	IBP-310	2840	Actuals Qty Prior Yr	783	777	786	784	780	773	773	854	819	796	7
			Sales Fcst Qty	826	828	830	832	834	836	838	840	842	844	8
			Marketing Fcst Qty	826	828	830	832	834	836	838	840	842	844	8
			Override Consensus Demand Qty											
			Consensus Demand Qty	826	828	830	832	834	836	838	840	842	844	8
			Consensus Demand Plan Rev.	255.92K	256.54K	257.16K	257.78K	258.40K	259.02K	259.63K	260.25K	260.87K	261.49K	262.1
	IBP-320	2840	Actuals Qty Prior Yr											
			Sales Fcst Qty											
			Marketing Fcst Qty											
			Override Consensus Demand Qty											
			Consensus Demand Qty											
			Consensus Demand Plan Rev.											
CE03	IBP-300	2500	Actuals Qty Prior Yr	712	680	696	714	634	731	697	647	713	704	7
			Sales Fcst Qty	728	748	725	741	734	761	745	770	752	762	7
			Marketing Fcst Qty	728	748	725	741	734	761	745	770	752	762	7
			Override Consensus Demand Qty											
			Consensus Demand Qty	728	748	725	741	734	761	745	770	752	762	7
			Consensus Demand Plan Rev	318.30K	324.46K	317.62K	322.24K	320.32K	328.30K	322.66K	329.05K	325.73K	328.74K	324.1

Consensus Demand Plan · Consensus Demand Plan accuracy

READY · 100%

Figure 2.30 Version Management on SAP IBP Ribbon

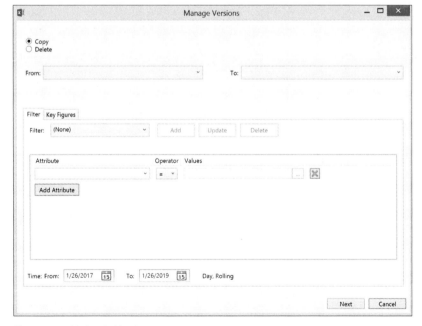

Figure 2.31 Maintain Versions

2.2.7 Advanced Planning Options in SAP IBP Excel Planning View

SAP IBP offers a robust set of advance planning capabilities and operators such as statistical forecasting, inventory optimization, and supply planning. These and other functions can be initiated directly from the SAP IBP ribbon as shown in Figure 2.32.

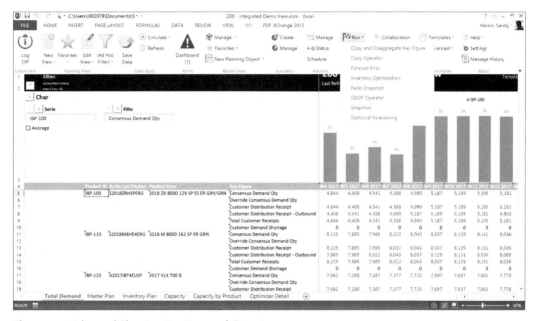

Figure 2.32 Advanced Planning Functions and Operators

Figure 2.33 shows the attribute selection screen for the statistical forecasting run. These selections will determine which data will be included in the forecast. There are also options for FORECAST MODEL ASSIGNMENT, PLANNING LEVEL, and TIME BUCKET. These types of selection criteria are available for other planning functions and help to customize the process based on your objectives.

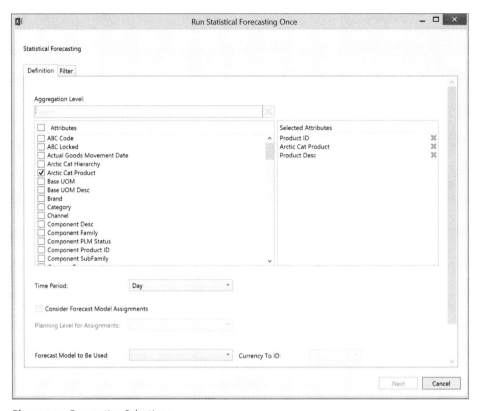

Figure 2.33 Forecasting Selections

2.2.8 Integration of the Planning View with Planning Collaboration

The final step in any planning process is to update the plan with fresh data. This is done by selecting SAVE DATA from the ribbon as shown in Figure 2.34. A best practice is to document and share the reasons why a change was made so that the history of the plan is visible and understood by all stakeholders.

Figure 2.35 shows the REASON CODE selections in the SAVE KEY FIGURE CHANGES window that pops up when SAVE is clicked. This is where the plan changes are documented with both codes and text that describe the reason for the change. This information is stored in the process record and displayed in the SAP Jam feed for other users to view. After you click the SAVE button, the planning process loop has been closed.

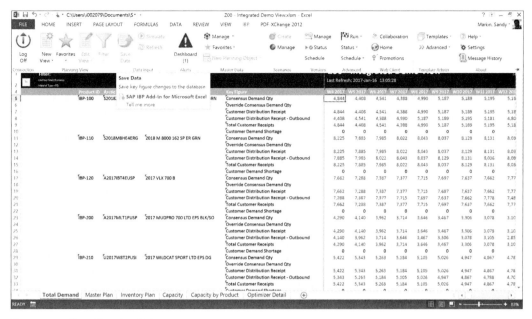

Figure 2.34 Save Planning Data

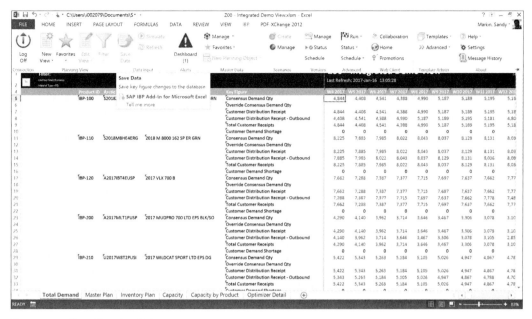

Figure 2.35 Reason Codes

2.3 Summary

Navigation in SAP IBP is enabled by a customizable set of UIs that allows you to have a highly productive and personalized experience. Examples of these are the role-based SAP Fiori home page, the intuitive web-based analytics, and the configurable Excel planning views. The primary benefit is an accelerated learning curve for users, which translates into rapid time to value for the company. The following chapters will provide many detailed examples of how this occurs.

The key to any organization's supply chain is its data, which are loaded into SAP IBP and used for various planning and execution activities. This chapter describes the use of master and transactional data throughout SAP IBP processes, including how data is loaded into SAP IBP through manual and automated modes, as well as how business users can analyze and review the data via visualization methods.

3 Planning Data

An organization's supply chain is an organized set of data elements. The fundamental unit of any supply chain is its data, which is the structural background of the supply chain network that facilitates the planning of products and resources. Data items in the supply chain can be categorized as master data or transactional data. Master data include products, locations, and resources, among others, and they are the building blocks of the supply chain network. Transactional data include sales orders, purchase orders, production orders, etc., and is used for planning and execution operations in the supply chain network. Transactional data in the planning system are also known as key figures. Data in SAP IBP can be integrated manually or on demand through SAP Cloud Platform or via data replication through SAP HANA smart data integration (SAP HANA SDI), which provides near real-time integration.

In this chapter, we'll cover both master data and transactional data in your supply chain network, before moving on to the standard data models in SAP IBP. We'll then cover each of the previously mentioned data integration options and end with a brief look at data visualization in SAP IBP.

3.1 Master Data in a Supply Chain Network

Master data represent physical entities of an organization's supply chain. For example, a manufacturer's location, products, resources, and other entities are created as master data elements in the supply chain.

The master data elements discussed in the first section are relevant for time bucket planning used in SAP IBP for sales and operations, SAP IBP for demand, SAP IBP for response and supply, and SAP IBP for inventory. Order series planning, used in response and supply, requires some extra sets of master data; we'll discuss those in Section 3.2. The data elements discussed here are a representative set of master data types for standard SAP IBP models. Special business scenarios may require an additional set of master data types.

3.1.1 Time Bucket Planning

The master data elements used in time bucket planning are as follows:

▶ **Location**
A physical place at which supply chain operations are performed is mapped as the location master data in SAP IBP. Operations such as production, inventory storage, and order processing are conducted at these locations. Table 3.1 shows an example of the data elements for location master data from SAP standard time series planning areas.

Location Data Element	Usage Example
Location ID	Unique number to represent a location
Location description	Name of a plant, distribution center, or other location
Location type	Plant, distribution center, other location type
Location region	Region in a network, for example, NA and EU
Latitude and longitude	Latitude and longitude as geographic coordinate information

Table 3.1 Location Master Data Elements in SAP IBP

▶ **Customer**
Customer master data groups the data elements for the customer. Most of the attributes for customer master data are similar to those of location master data. Table 3.2 is just a representative example of this data; actual data elements of the customer table are based on the information elements used for the forecast and sales order execution process for the customers.

Customer Data Element	Usage Example
Customer ID	Unique ID to represent a customer
Customer name	Name of the customer or customer organization

Table 3.2 Customer Master Data Elements in SAP IBP

Customer Data Element	Usage Example
Region	Sales region
Channel	Sales channel
Type	Type assignment for customers, for example, original equipment manufacturer (OEM), and trade
Sales representative	Office or name of the sales rep or sales manager
Latitude and longitude	Latitude and longitude as geographic coordinate information

Table 3.2 Customer Master Data Elements in SAP IBP (Cont.)

- ▶ **Product**

  Materials for the organization and partners such as suppliers and customers are represented using product master data. These data represent all the materials relevant to planning in SAP IBP, whether it's a finished product, components, direct materials, or indirect materials used by the organization. Component master data can also be used to represent the input material of the bill of materials (BOM). Every product is represented by a unique product ID, and operations related to production, purchasing, inventory management, and other processes are performed by referring to the product identification number. Table 3.3 shows the representative set of the standard product attributes and related information.

Product Data Element	Usage Example
Product ID	Unique number to represent a product
Product description	Product name/description
Family	Product family
Group	Group assigned to the product
Lifecycle status	States whether the product is live or obsolete
Unit price	Unit price for the product
UOM	Unit of measure

Table 3.3 Product Master Data Elements in SAP IBP

- ▶ **Location/product**

  A product created at a particular location is represented through location/product master data, which are actually compound master data, that is, a collection of two or more simple master data types. Location/product master data is made of the attributes from the simple master data types of location and product. For location/product master data, you must use the attributes for identification numbers (product ID and location ID) for both product and location. Other attributes or data elements can be considered a part of the location/product master data based on information requirements for performing planning and execution transactions. Table 3.4 contains the information elements for location/product data from SAP standard planning areas.

Location/Product Data Elements	Usage Example
Location ID	Location identification number
Product ID	Product identification number
Lot size	Lot size policy
Minimum order quantity	Minimum order quantity for purchase or production
Unit price	Unit price to procure/produce at this location
Service level	Service level for sales order fulfillment
Frozen horizon	Frozen horizon for planning
Subnetwork	Subnetwork within the supply chain network

Table 3.4 Location/Product Master Data Elements in SAP IBP

▶ **Customer/product**
Similar to location/product master data, customer/product is a compound master data for product and customer and represents a product extended to a customer location. Table 3.5 shows the data elements of the customer/product master data.

Customer/Product Data Elements	Usage Example
Customer ID	Customer number
Product ID	Product number
Market segment	Market segment information

Table 3.5 Customer/Product Master Data Elements in SAP IBP

▶ **Source customer**
Source customer represents an arc in the supply chain network connecting a customer location to an organization's internal location, such as a distribution center, a production plant, or an order processing location.

A node represents a fixed location in a supply chain network. It's a unit or independent entity; for example, a location master data with location type as a manufacturing plant, distribution center, customer, and so on are the nodes of the supply chain network. An arc is a connection between two nodes that allows material movement between the locations. A source customer, for example, is an arc that connects a customer location to a fulfillment location, such as a distribution center.

Source customer master data, then, allows you to place a sales order at a fulfillment location for a particular customer and also transfer material from the fulfillment location to the customer using the source customer master data. Table 3.6 shows an example of the source customer data element used in SAP IBP.

Source Customer Data Element	Usage Example
Customer ID	Customer number
Location ID	Location number to supply the customer
Lead time	Time required for supply from location to customer
Product ID	Product number for supplying from location to customer
Customer ratio	Ratio of supply percentage from location to customer
Time series ratio check	Identifies whether the customer ratio can change with time
Target service level	Target service level to fulfill the requirements of the selected product against the customer's order from this location

Table 3.6 Source Customer Master Data Elements in SAP IBP

▶ **Source location**

Source location is another example of an arc used in the supply chain to connect different internal or external locations to allow product movement. An example of a source location can be from or to a location, usually a production plant and distribution center, respectively. Source location and source customer together join all the locations (internal, customer, and supplier) to generate the supply chain network. Table 3.7 shows an example of a source location used in the SAP standard planning areas in SAP IBP.

Source Location Data Element	Usage Example
Location ID	Receiving location ID
Location from ID	Supplying location ID
Product ID	Product ID that can move from the supply to the receive location
Lead time	Transportation lead time
Transport ratio	Percentage of product supply at receiving location from supply location
Time series ratio check	Identifies whether the transport ratio can change with time
Maximum lot size	Maximum lot size for transport
Minimum lot size	Minimum lot size for transport
Rounding value	Rounding value for transport orders

Table 3.7 Source Location Master Data Elements in SAP IBP

▶ **Resource, resource/location, resource/location/product**

Assets used for manufacturing, storage, handling, etc. are created as resource master data in SAP IBP with the assigned category type. Every resource is expected to get created at one and only one location. Resource/location/product master data is another example of compound master data consisting of three separate types of master data: resource, location, and product. A production type resource is used to model a production or assembly process; the capacity consumption is calculated by SAP IBP through the number of the produced or assembled quantity and the consumption rate maintained in the master data. Table 3.8 shows the attributes used for resource and associated master data of resource/location and resource location/product.

Resource, Resource/Location, Resource/Location/Product Data Elements	Usage Example
Resource ID	Resource identifier name or number
Resource description	Resource name or description
Location ID	Location at which the resource is available
Product ID	Output product from this resource

Table 3.8 Resource Master Data Elements in SAP IBP

Resource, Resource/Location, Resource/Location/Product Data Elements	Usage Example
Resource type	Capacity type (production, storage, etc.)
Capacity supply	Available supply of resource in relevant unit based on the resource type
Time series relevance for capacity supply	Indicator for time variability of available capacity
Capacity consumption	Capacity consumption by the product ID
Time series relevance for capacity consumption	Indicator for time variability of capacity consumption

Table 3.8 Resource Master Data Elements in SAP IBP (Cont.)

▶ **Location-from and location-to**

Location-from and location-to master data types are used to represent the flow direction of materials in the supply chain through the arc of the chain. This master data type must have the information of the base location and the ship-from or ship-to location. Table 3.9 shows the ship-from master data example from the standard SAP planning area.

Location-From and Location-To Data Elements	Usage Example
Location from ID	Ship-from location ID
Location from description	Ship-from location name
Location to ID	Ship-to location ID
Location to description	Ship-to location name

Table 3.9 Location-From and Location-To Master Data Elements in SAP IBP

▶ **Source production**

Source production master data is created for the fulfillment of a product at a location. The source type defines whether a product will be fulfilled through in-house manufacturing or external procurements. The major source types are as follows:

▸ P is used for the materials produced in-house at the location ID mentioned in the master data.

▸ T is used for the transport rule for the product that will be supplied at the location from another place in the supply chain network. With a material with source type T at a location, location source data must exist in SAP IBP mentioning the supply location.

▶ U is used for an undefined supply location and represents the end of the chain for the supply network in SAP IBP for this product.

The component of the BOM isn't captured in the production source master data. Table 3.10 shows the data elements for the production source master data.

Source Production Master Data Element	Usage Example
Location ID	Location ID
Product ID	Product ID
Source ID	Source ID, normally maintained as `location-id_product-id`
Output coefficient	Quantity or volume of the product ID for the source ID
Time series ratio check	Identifies whether the output coefficient can change with time
Lead time	Lead time for manufacturing if in-house
Maximum production lot size	Maximum production lot size
Minimum production lot size	Minimum production lot size
Production lot size coverage	Coverage of period of demand
Source type	P, T, or U for production, transport, or undefined source

Table 3.10 Source Production Master Data Elements in SAP IBP

▶ **Production source item**
Production source item master data is maintained to represent the component information for producing a finished or semifinished material. In addition to the component materials, production source item contains the information about the quantity or volume used for producing a unit quantity or volume of the output product. Table 3.11 shows the example attributes for the production source item.

Production Source Item Master Data Element	Usage Example
Source ID	Source ID (note the relationship with source production master data)

Table 3.11 Production Source Item Master Data Elements in SAP IBP

Production Source Item Master Data Element	Usage Example
Source item ID	Component material ID, generally the BOM component ID maintained as 10, 20, 30, and so on for multiple components of a BOM
Product ID	BOM component ID for a particular source item ID
Component coefficient	Amount of the component product required for the output coefficient for the BOM header product maintained in the source ID

Table 3.11 Production Source Item Master Data Elements in SAP IBP (Cont.)

▸ **Product substitution relation (substitutable product)**
Product substitution relationship for planning in SAP IBP is controlled through the master data types related to product substitution. It represents the customer or the location at which a product can be substituted by another product. Table 3.12 shows the data elements for the product substitution master data element.

Product Substitution Master Data Element	Usage Example
Product ID	Product ID
Substitution product ID	Product ID that can substitute for the product ID in supply chain

Table 3.12 Product Substitution Master Data Elements in SAP IBP

3.1.2 Order Series Planning

The supply and response solution requires further master data elements in addition to these master data types. Master data used for the supply and response in order series planning can be represented as follows:

▸ Location

▸ Material

▸ Location material

▸ Transportation lane

▸ Supplier

- Resource

- Production data structure (PDS)

- Customer

Most of the master data elements used in order planning are similar to those in time series planning, although it can have a couple of different data elements. For example, material location data has the extra data elements of allocation procedure and requirement strategy, which are relevant only for response and supply planning in order series data. New master data elements introduced through supply and response planning are transportation lane and production data structure. These two data elements are similar to the time series data elements of source location and source production. Further information on these two data elements is as follows:

- **Transportation lane**
  Transportation lane contains the information for allowed product movement in the supply chain network. The transportation lane data element is similar to the source location master data element as discussed for time series planning. Transportation lane contains the ship-from location, ship-to location, product ID, and any relevant lot size data. Table 3.13 shows the data elements and usage example of transportation lane in SAP IBP.

Transportation Lane Data Elements	Usage Example
Location from	Supply location
Location to	Receiving location
Material	Material for supply through this transportation lane
Planned delivery time	Lead time for supply
Procurement priority	Priority
Info record	Info record number from the execution system
Purchase organization	Purchase organization for the info record
Base unit	Base UOM for the material
Maximum lot size	Maximum lot size for transfer
Available from	Validity start date for the transportation lane
Available to	Validity end date for the transportation lane

Table 3.13 Transportation Lane Master Data Elements in SAP IBP

▶ **Production data structure (PDS)**

Production data structure is master data for items produced in-house that require response and supply planning. It has the data elements of the output produced item, components needed to produce, output and input quantities, and the related resource consumption for the production. Table 3.14 shows the data elements for production data structure.

Production Data Structure Data Elements	Usage Example
Material	Output material
Plant	Plant location
Production version	Production version in execution system
Minimum lot size	Minimum lot size for production through PDS
Maximum lot size	Maximum lot size for production through PDS
Quantity	Amount of header material
Base unit	Base UOM for material
Procurement priority	Priority of PDS
Item number	Component item number
Material	Component product ID
Material description	Component product description
Component quantity	Component quantity in BOM
Base unit of measure	Component base UOM
Work center	Resource ID required for output product
Resource description	Resource name
Capacity category	Resource category (production, handling, etc.)
Valid from/to	Validity of resource
Bucket consumption	Resource consumption for output quantity in BOM
Bucket UOM	Consumption UOM

Table 3.14 Production Data Structure Master Data Elements in SAP IBP

3.2 Transactional Data in a Supply Chain Network

Transactions performed on the master data elements in a supply chain network generate transactional data. Transactional data is represented through key figures in SAP IBP.

Different business transactions are performed through different sets of transaction data. For example, to procure a product at a manufacturing location from a supplier, a purchase order transactional data element can be used to perform the transaction. A material is supplied to a customer by creating a sales order transaction data element and performing further activities such as inventory issue, invoice creation, and delivery document—all of which are examples of transaction data.

In addition to business transactions, transactional data is also used for information and planning for a supply chain network. Available inventory of a product with the further visibility of on-hand, quality control, and blocked inventory are also examples of transaction data. Planning elements such as projected inventory of a product at a location and safety stock requirements are further examples of information-specific transaction data.

Transactional data is much more dynamic in a supply chain network than master data. The transactional data set and key figures used for the design and build of a SAP IBP solution are based on the planning requirements of the organization. A representative set of general transaction data elements are as follows:

- Sales order
- Inventory
- Purchase order
- Purchase requisition
- Production order
- Planned production
- Stock transfer order
- Net inventory
- Safety stock

Some transactional data elements are relevant for order response and supply planning only. These data elements or key figures are as follows:

- ► Projected stock
- ► Demand by priority
- ► Sales order simulation
- ► Confirmations

3.3 Standard Data Models in SAP IBP

SAP's standard master data for representative planning models are available in the SAP IBP system. Different planning solutions are mapped through various planning areas and contain different master data models. Table 3.15 shows the demo planning area models available in the SAP IBP environment, along with their planning solution and data alignment.

Planning Area	Solution Alignment	Representative Master Data Type and Transaction Data (Key Figure)
SAP2	S&OP and supply (including demand forecasting)	To support S&OP, demand forecasting, and multilevel supply planning
SAP3	Inventory optimization	Inventory optimization and limited supply planning
SAP4	S&OP and supply (no demand forecasting)	S&OP and supply planning
SAP5	SAP Supply Chain Control Tower	SAP Supply Chain Control Tower functionalities
SAP6	Demand	Demand forecasting and demand sensitivity
SAP7	Response and supply	Supply planning and response management
SAP74	S&OP, supply and response	S&OP, response and supply solution
SAPIBP1	S&OP, demand, supply, and inventory	S&OP, demand forecasting, supply planning, and inventory optimization

Table 3.15 Production Data Structure Master Data Elements in SAP IBP

Sample planning models can be copied to create customer-specific planning models. Organization-specific changes to master data, related data elements, and key figures can be performed in the planning area, and data models can be set up for the customer's solution.

3.4 Data Integration

Data can be integrated with the SAP IBP system in three different approaches:

- Manual data integration
- SAP Cloud Platform Integration, formerly known as SAP HANA Cloud Platform Integration Services (SAP HCP-IS)
- SAP HANA Smart Data Integration (SAP HANA SDI)

The integration approach is the same for both master data and key figures. In the following sections, we'll look at each approach in turn.

3.4.1 Manual Data Integration

Both master data and key figures can be integrated with SAP IBP using the Data Integration app. The app allows loading a file (CSV format) into the SAP IBP system. Manual outbound data integration for key figures is much easier, as the planning data in SAP IBP exists in a normal Microsoft Excel spreadsheet.

To get data into the SAP IBP system, select the DATA INTEGRATION tile in the ADMINISTRATOR area of the app. The system will create a blank file with the right format for the data upload. You can then fill in the file and upload the data.

Figure 3.1 shows the relevant tiles and related information to upload the master data and key figures into SAP IBP system. The Data Integration app shows the success or failure of the data load through a notification on the same page. Any failure is reported with a rejection file, which can be analyzed to take action to resolve the root cause. A successful data load can also be taken as a report from the DATA INTEGRATION page. Uploaded data is available in the SAP IBP system for further use.

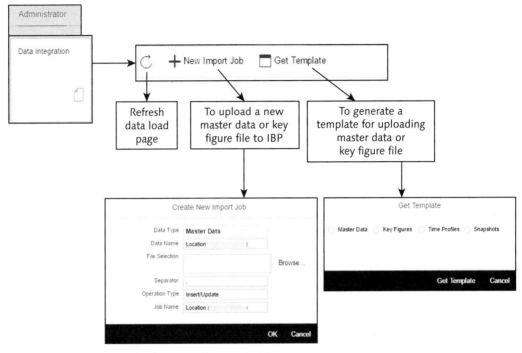

Figure 3.1 Manual Data Upload Functionality in SAP IBP

3.4.2 SAP Cloud Platform

SAP Cloud Platform is an in-memory comprehensive application tool for integration, enterprise mobility, collaboration, and analytics. In this chapter, we'll focus our discussion on its integration capabilities. SAP Cloud Platform is required for automated data integration to SAP IBP from an SAP environment or other legacy application. Integration through SAP Cloud Platform is executed through batch jobs. The frequency of the data transfer depends on the frequency adopted for the batch job execution.

The necessary steps for data integration are as follows:

1. **Install and configure SAP Cloud Platform.**
   SAP Cloud Platform agent installation enables the data transfer between the on-premise data source and the cloud-based SAP IBP system. Agent installation and configuration can be performed by following the steps provided in

the *SAP Data Service Agent Guide*. After the installation and configuration are performed successfully, the conduit for the data movement has been developed for usage of data flow.

2. **Create the data store.**
   Data stores are created to connect SAP Cloud Platform with the customer's application and database. Through the data store connection, SAP Cloud Platform can read the data from the data store and write it to the SAP IBP system as well as take the data from SAP IBP and write it back to the on-premise data system. Data stores are created in the SAP Cloud Platform web user interface. Objects or data elements of the data stores are available for usage by importing the objects from the data stores in SAP Cloud Platform. For detailed steps, refer to the technical configuration guide on this topic.

3. **Create the project, task, data flow, and process.**
   A project in SAP Cloud Platform is created as a container to hold similar processes and tasks. Figure 3.2 shows the conceptual functionalities of the project, process, task, and data flow. A task is created under a project. Data flow maps the fields with the extraction, transformation, and loading (ETL) logic.

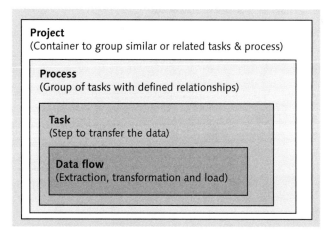

Figure 3.2 Project, Process, Task, and Data Flow Objectives in SAP Cloud Platform

Figure 3.3 shows an example of a project, process, and task. The EDIT, VIEW, SCHEDULE, RUN NOW, VIEW HISTORY, and MORE ACTIONS buttons are used for multiple operations with tasks and processes such as editing a task, executing a process chain, viewing the history of previous runs, or promoting the objects to the production environment. The data flow for the task allows the mapping of source and target fields through an easy drag-and-drop functionality.

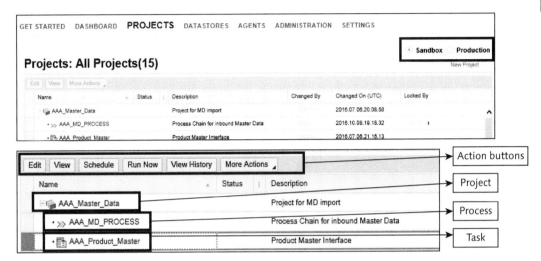

Figure 3.3 Project, Process, and Task Example in SAP Cloud Platform

Figure 3.4 shows a typical data flow for the location master data task. A process is created by taking multiple tasks with an assigned start and end relationship. The process provides the option to execute multiple tasks in a required sequence.

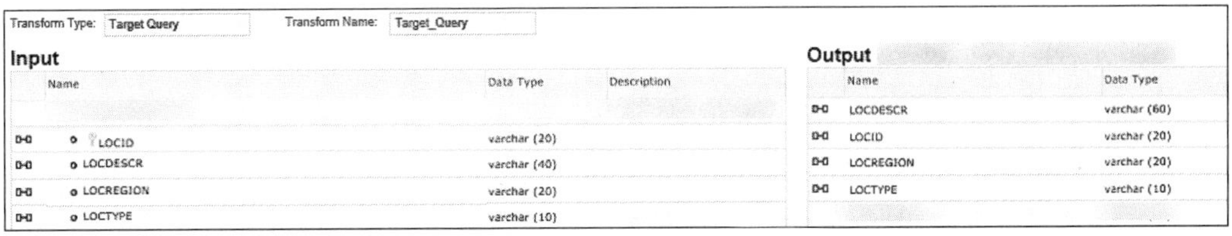

Figure 3.4 Data Flow Example for the SAP Cloud Platform Task

Figure 3.5 shows a process with multiple master data tasks assigned with a start-to-end relationship in a linear fashion. In this example, the task for location/product master data transfer represented by DF_LOCPRD is executed after execution of the location, customer, and product tasks.

Figure 3.5 SAP Cloud Platform Process to Execute Multiple Tasks with Assigned Relationships

4. **Execute the process/task.**

Execution of a task performs the data transfer for the data element selected for the task. A global variable is part of the execution property of a task and controls the logic for task execution for the planning area, update nature, etc. Update nature controls whether the data transfer follows an insert/update, replace, or delete methodology. The INSERT/UPDATE option adds the data in the target table from the source table without impacting the existing data in the target system. The REPLACE option removes the existing data in the target system while loading the data from the source system. The DELETE option will only remove the data in the target system while using the data from the source system. Process and task can be executed manually on demand or can be scheduled through a batch job. The batch job can be scheduled for single execution or created for periodic execution. Success or failure of the task is displayed in the SAP Cloud Platform through symbol and color (green for success and red for failure). SAP Cloud Platform's dashboard functionality also shows the analytics of the previously completed tasks and the information about scheduled tasks for execution.

3.4.3 SAP HANA Smart Data Integration

Based on the nature of the response planning, dynamic or real-time data integration is required from the execution system within the SAP IBP system. Real-time integration is achieved through SAP HANA SDI. Integration through SAP HANA SDI is performed for both master data and transactional data. SAP HANA SDI provides both replication and transformation capabilities. Replication connects the data from another system to the SAP HANA data environment in SAP IBP, and transformation helps in using logic for data editing through transformation.

Figure 3.6 shows an example of server architecture with SAP HANA SDI. If the driver can run inside the data provisioning server, the adapter is used inside the

SAP HANA database. If the driver can't run inside the data provisioning server, then the data provisioning agent is kept outside of the SAP HANA database. Performing the data integration through SAP HANA SDI, requires multiple steps of enablement, configuration, and integration. These are tasks for the technical developer and therefore not in the scope of this text. (If interested, you can follow the SAP HANA SDI configuration and administration documents for details.)

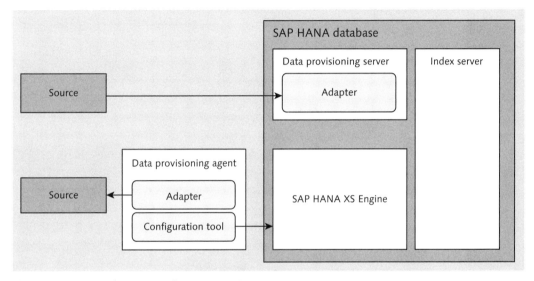

Figure 3.6 Server Architecture with SAP HANA SDI

3.5 Data Visualization in SAP IBP

Data in SAP IBP can be viewed, analyzed, and edited through an Excel planning view and through an SAP Fiori view. All the time series master data can be assessed through the Excel planning view. Time series planning key figures and some of the order series planning key figures are reviewed through the Excel planning view. Therefore, the data review for planning applications of S&OP, demand, inventory and analytics in SAP Supply Chain Control Tower are performed solely through the Excel planning view. Data review of planning applications for response and supply occurs through both the Excel view and the SAP Fiori view.

In the following sections, we'll look at the Excel planning view and the SAP Fiori view in SAP IBP.

3.5.1 Excel Planning View

In the SAP IBP Excel planning view, there is a separate section for master data in the header section of the IBP page. Figure 3.7 shows the master data toolbox for the time series master data. Mass display or single display of a master data item is controlled through the MANAGE dropdown. Under NEW PLANNING OBJECT, you can either choose NEW PLANNING OBJECT to create a new object or DELETE PLANNING OBJECT to delete an existing planning object.

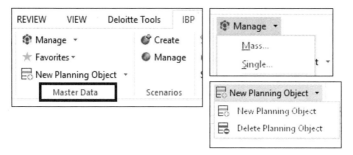

Figure 3.7 Master Data Toolbox in the SAP IBP Excel Planning View

Figure 3.8 and Figure 3.9 represent the mass and single master data display, respectively, through the MANAGE option of the Excel panning view.

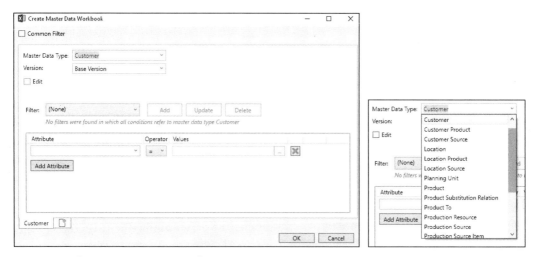

Figure 3.8 Mass Manage of Master Data

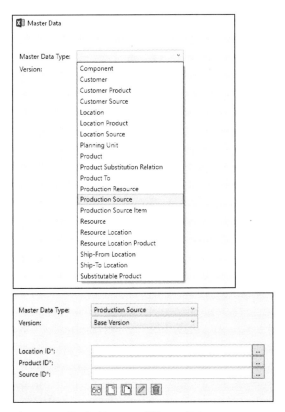

Figure 3.9 Single Manage of Master Data

Mass selection provides another screen to select master data element through the MASTER DATA TYPE dropdown. The FILTER option can also be used to select a group of master data elements en masse. For example, a production source data with filter for a particular production plan will generate a list of all the production source data maintained for this location. Without a filter, every valid data element for the identified master data type will be displayed by the system for review.

Single selection of master data requires entry of the key attribute of the master data. For example, for the PRODUCTION SOURCE item, LOCATION ID, PRODUCT ID, and SOURCE ID are the key attributes and need the input from the planner to display the data.

Mass selection of master data displays the data in an Excel planning view report. Figure 3.10 shows an example of a mass display of source production master data. A single selection of master data shows the data on the same page. Single selection also provides an opportunity to edit, delete, or create a master data element. Deletion or creation of master data is based on the logical relationship. For example, a product/location master data combination should only be created if both the product and location for this combination have already been created in the system. Similarly, master data should only get deleted if there are no dependent data in the system.

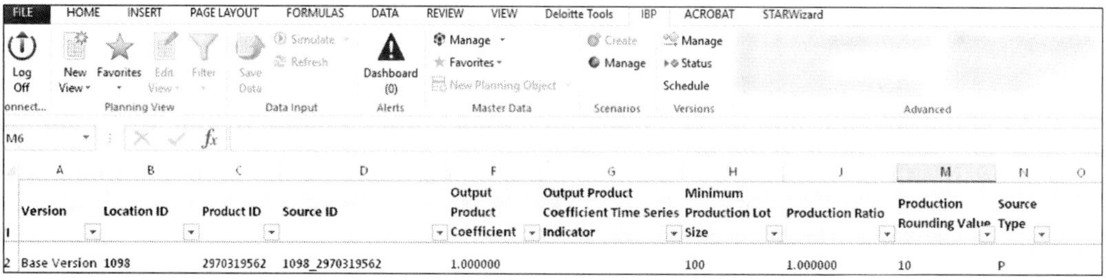

Figure 3.10 Mass Master Data Display for Source Production Data

Key figures in the SAP IBP environment can be displayed through the Excel planning view. Figure 3.11 illustrates the planning view tab in the Excel header view to create and display a planning view. It also shows an example of key figure display in the planning view. Key figures with their respective planning levels can be displayed in the planning view as shown. A key figure value can be edited in the planning view if the property of the key figure allows the same. For the different planning applications of S&OP, demand planning, response and supply planning, and inventory management, SAP has developed multiple ready-to-use planning views with selected planning levels and key figures. These views are available through different SAP Notes. Refer to those views in addition to creating your own views for reviewing key figure data in SAP IBP.

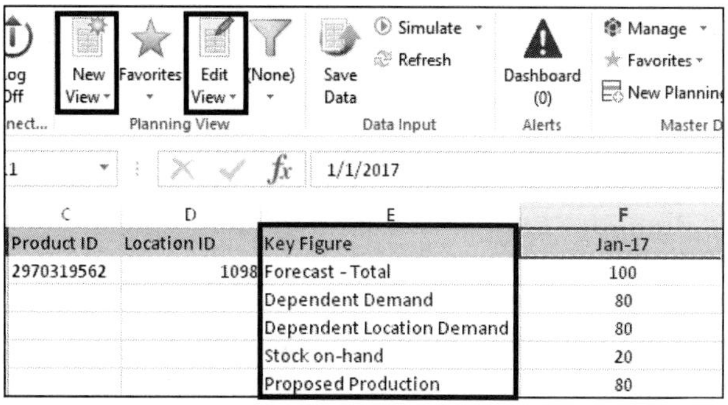

Figure 3.11 Key Display in the SAP IBP Environment

3.5.2 SAP Fiori View

Master data and some of the key figures for the response and supply planning solution can be displayed and reviewed through the SAP Fiori app of SAP IBP in the following groupings:

- General Response Planner
  - View Locations
  - View Materials
  - View Location Materials
  - View Transportation Lanes
  - View Projected Stocks
- Supply Planner
  - View Suppliers
  - View Resources
  - View Production Data Structure
- Account Planner
  - View Customers
  - View Demand by Priority
  - Simulate Sales Order
  - View Confirmations

Figure 3.12 shows the tiles of the SAP Fiori app for SAP IBP for review of master data and associated response and supply key figures. Most of the master data only have the view option in SAP IBP and aren't supposed to have their values changed in the planning system. The source system of this data is the execution system, which is the data owner. Any planning-relevant changes need to be performed in the source system. The dynamic integration through SAP HANA SDI makes this change available in the SAP IBP system. View Projected Stock, View Demands by Priority, Simulate Sales Order, and View Confirmation are examples of key figure usage in the SAP Fiori planning view for response and supply; all other tiles represent the master data elements for the response and supply solution.

Figure 3.12 Master Data and Key Access for Supply and Response Planning through SAP Fiori

3.6   Summary

Data is the building blocks of the planning system. In SAP IBP, data is grouped as master data and transaction data for use in the planning applications. These data sets can be sourced from both SAP and non-SAP backend systems, such as SAP ERP, using tools that SAP provides. SAP Cloud Integration is an ETL tool that is used for integrating master data and time series data which are represented as key figures in SAP IBP. SAP HANA SDI is used to integrate transactional data into the SAP IBP order data model. Both master and time series data can be managed in the system via the SAP Fiori user interface and the Excel planning views.

Now that you have a broad understanding of the data in the SAP IBP system for building the supply chain network and for planning the activities in the network, you're ready to explore the SAP IBP planning model.

To understand and use the SAP IBP planning solution, it's essential to know the basic concepts and building blocks of the SAP IBP system. This chapter will guide you through the concepts of a planning model for SAP IBP.

4   Building Blocks of a Planning Model

Supply chain planning in SAP Integrated Business Planning (SAP IBP) is performed through planning models. A planning model is a well-defined structure of master data, transaction data, and associated calculations to manage and optimize a supply chain network. As the foundation of SAP IBP, the planning model consists of entities that together define the structure of an organization's supply chain network and the flows in that network.

Because every organization is different in terms of its product and supply chain, every organization requires a unique planning model to plan, execute, and analyze the processes relevant to procurement, manufacturing, and delivery. However, the basic building blocks covered in this chapter are the same for most organizations. Along with understanding the organization's nature, products, material flow, customers, and planning requirements, the planning model entities can be used to develop the model in SAP IBP.

The entities of the planning model that will be discussed in this chapter are as follows:

- Attribute
- Time profile
- Planning level
- Key figure calculation logic
- Version
- Reason code
- Snapshot configuration

- Master data type
- Planning area
- Key figure
- Planning operators
- Scenario
- Global configuration parameters

4.1 Attribute

Attributes are basic information elements of a supply chain entity. In a logical group, combinations of attributes can define master data or a physical element of a supply chain network. A product in a company is normally associated with information such as product identification number (product ID), product name, and market segment. Hence, to model a supply chain network, the first required activity in the design phase is the identification of all the attributes relevant for the planning model.

Based on the property of the attribute, it can be created and used as a character, an integer, a decimal, or a time stamp, as follows:

- **Character**
  Characters are the most widely used attribute type in designing and building the supply chain solution in SAP IBP. Product description, market type, customer name, and resource name are examples of attributes used as character elements.

- **Integer**
  Integer values may be required for information elements such as lead time, period of coverage for safety stock, or system setting values of lot size policy indicator. Those information elements are created as integer attribute types in SAP IBP.

- **Decimal**
  Decimal attributes are used for numerical value maintenance across the time horizon and for using the attributes as key figure data. If the numeric value of an information element remains the same across the time period, mapping this as a decimal attribute can be considered. Information elements that are generally considered for the decimal attributes are cost, capacity supply, consumption rate, currency conversion exchange rate, and production rate.

- **Time stamp**
  Multiple information elements require the data maintenance in terms of date or time, and those information elements are created as time stamp attributes. Product introduction or discontinuation date, promotion start date, and material availability date are examples of the data elements that can be captured via the time stamp attribute.

After completing the attribute configuration, every attribute for the planning model design is created and is available to use in SAP IBP per the solution design.

4.2   Master Data Type

Multiple attributes together define a master data type. Master data represents a physical product, locations, flow directions, resources, components, or a combination of them. Master data elements together build the supply chain network and can be used to work with planning data. For example, a sales forecast is a number for the projected sales of a product from a selling location against a customer's requirement; here, the product, location, and customer are examples of master data elements whose combination is used for forecast planning data. A recommended set of master data types must exist for planning in SAP IBP. However, the information attached to a master data type can be specific to an organization and needs to be defined as an attribute for selection in the master data type.

For example, the product master data type, which is an essential master data type for SAP IBP, can be built of product ID, description, introduction date, product type, and multiple other attributes that are relevant for an organization to perform planning, execution, and analytics activities. For solution implementation, we recommend a top-down approach to master data and attribute types. The master data type relevant for the planning solution should be identified first, and then the required attributes can be created.

While adding the attributes for master data, an attribute can be further identified as a key or required attribute. A key attribute defines the basic building block of an independent dimension data element and becomes a required attribute by default. On the other hand, an attribute whose null value isn't an accepted criteria in the master data type can be assigned as a required attribute without marking it a root. For example, in product master data, product ID (represented by PRDID) is a root attribute that must have a value for the product to even exist in the system. Other attributes such as product group, product family, etc. are extensions of the product information identified by the product ID.

Table 4.1 shows an example of a product master data type and its associated attributes. Product ID is the key attribute, which defines the existence of product master data in the system. Without a valid value for this attribute, any combination of data for other attributes can't define product master data. Due to this restriction, product ID is a required attribute. Product geography isn't a key attribute but is a required attribute; hence, a blank value won't be accepted. The value example columns in Table 4.1 that highlight the importance and management of attribute characteristic while maintaining the master data in the system. Master data types source production and production source item have multiple keys.

Attribute	Technical Name	Value Example 1	Value Example 2	Key	Required
Product ID	PRDID	2345489210	2679012780	X	X
Product description	PRDDESCR	ABC1 product	ABC2 product		X
Market segment	MKTSGMNT	Retail			
Product family	PRDFAMILY		FRGCA		
Product geography	PRDGEOG	USA	EU		X

Table 4.1 Key and Required Attributes in the Master Data Type

Based on configuration and basic nature, master data types in SAP IBP are categorized as follows:

▸ **Simple master data type**
A simple master data type represents one independent master data element in the supply chain. Product, location, customer, resource, and so on are examples of simple master data types. To create a simple master data type, you select the name and ID of the master data and assign the relevant attributes, which together defines the property of the master data element.

▸ **Compound master data type**
Compound master data represent a combination of two or more simple master data types, which helps integrate the entities of the supply chain. A product and location individually represent the characteristics of a material and a location through simple master data; however, location/product as compound master data represents a product that has been extended to a particular location. On a similar note, product/location/customer is a compound master data type showing a product that has been extended to a location from which it can be supplied to a customer. Compound master data is created by selecting associated simple master data and relevant attributes of simple master data types.

In general, a simple master data type has a single key attribute, and a compound master data type is a combination of two or more simple master data types and can have multiple key attributes.

Figure 4.1 shows examples of simple and compound master data types. Simple master data type examples are represented with location and product master data. The compound master data type example consists of simple master data types of location and product to create the location/product master data type.

Figure 4.1 Examples of Simple and Compound Master Data Types

▶ **Reference master data type**
A reference master data type refers to another master data element and doesn't require a separate data load. A reference master data type is used when the primary data elements of a data set are the same as or a subset of another set of data. For example, every component is also a product, so the component can be created as a reference master data type while referring to the product master data. While creating a reference master data type, you need to refer to an attribute of the parent master data. Hence, if the component is created as reference master data while referring to product master data, the component ID will refer to the product ID, the component description will refer to the product description, and so on.

▶ **Virtual master data type**
A virtual master data type doesn't store any data; instead, it's used to join two or more master data types so that the attribute of one master data type is available for other. A virtual master data type can be built by joining two or more simple or compound master data types through a join condition, which can be a common attribute of different master data, so that other attributes are also available.

▶ **External master data type**
An external master data type is used to integrate the master data content from an external SAP ERP or SAP S/4HANA system. It allows a near real-time integration of the master data element from the source system to SAP IBP. For an external master data type, an external data source table is used, and the characteristics of the master data are mapped with the reference attribute of the source table from the external master data system.

4.3 Time Profile

Time periods and data storage parameters relevant for planning in SAP IBP are defined through time profile maintenance. Start and end times for planning relevant duration are maintained in the time profile. A time profile can have multiple buckets of planning time such as day, week, month, quarter, and so on. A base level value in a time profile is used to create parent-child relationships for aggregation and disaggregation. The smallest time bucket is assigned level 1, and so on up. For example, if a time bucket is relevant for day, week, and month, then the levels assigned will be 1, 2, and 3, respectively; the week planning level will get day as the base planning level. The relationship hierarchy of the planning level and base planning level allows seamless aggregation and disaggregation of data from daily to weekly, monthly, quarterly, yearly, and the other way round. The time profile also controls the default display of time periods for every planning time bucket in SAP IBP Excel planning view.

In SAP IBP, every time period of the time profile is represented by a unique identification number called PERIODID; for example, Week 24 (W24) of year 2018 will be assigned a period ID number of say 56234, W25 can be assigned a number as 56235, and so on. These unique identifiers in background tables help make data processing and retrieval more efficient for different buckets of the time horizon.

Every level of time profile is identified by a number assigned to another attribute: PERIODIDn. The lowest level of the time period is assigned the value of 0, value 1 is assigned to the highest level of the time level, and then it follows a sequence. Table 4.2 shows the PERIODIDn value for a time profile consisting of day, technical week, week, month, quarter, and year. Note that the technical week in a year starts from the first Monday (or any other day as desired) and considers subsequent weeks without considering the month's impact. The PERIODIDn value helps with data calculation, analysis, and processing by providing a lever to select a data element based on past, present, or future time periods.

PERIODIDn	Time Bucket (Consisting of D, TW, W, Q, M, Y)
PERIODID0	Day (D)
PERIODID1	Year (Y)
PERIODID2	Quarter (Q)
PERIODID3	Month (M)
PERIODID4	Week (W)
PERIODID5	Technical Week (TW)

Table 4.2 Period ID Values for Different Time Buckets

4.4 Planning Area

A planning area is a unified structure in which planning and analytics processes are performed in SAP IBP. It holds the entire set of master data, time periods, associated attributes, planning levels, and key figures to perform the planning in SAP IBP and to fetch the data in a unified set for analytics usage. The SAP IBP Excel planning view is connected to one planning area and can be set as a default planning area for a user. For project implementation and infrastructure management purposes, an organization can create multiple planning areas for configuration, test, and active environments. Data from one planning area to another can't be transferred automatically. To perform different planning methodologies (say demand planning, supply planning, and inventory optimization) in a singular planning area, SAP IBP supports the configuration of a unified planning area.

In the planning area, planning-relevant parameters are defined and used. Both the time profile and storage planning level of the time period are assigned in a planning area. The exact planning period, which can be a subset of the time profile horizon, is also defined in a planning area. The planning horizon works on a rolling basis, so a selection of –12 to 24 months in the planning horizon of the planning area makes the planning relevant for the preceding one year to the next two years on a rolling basis.

Master data types are selected for a planning area, which makes all the attributes of the master data type planning relevant. If the business requires you to move the current period to a period in the past (say a week or a month) for planning purposes, then it can be achieved by using the current period offset functionality in the planning area. Through settings in the planning area, you can be define whether a particular planning area is relevant for supply planning, external data integration, and change history enablement. Relevant planning calculation logic through planning operators is assigned in the planning area and can be used through interactive or batch modes to perform those operations for the data elements in the planning area.

4.5 Planning Level

Planning level is a combination of attributes from master data type and time period: it defines the label for the transaction data in the planning area. Every transaction data point exists at a planning level. Aggregation and disaggregation of the key figure is based on the hierarchical structure created by the planning levels. For example, forecast data can be defined for a time bucket (say, a month), a product, a replenishment location, and a customer; hence, a planning level period/product/location/customer can be created and assigned in the planning area for usage in the customer forecast key figure. Another planning level period/product/location can be used for calculating the aggregated forecast for all the customers in a particular time period for the selected product at a selected replenishment location.

In a planning level, the attributes selected can be further defined as a *root*. A root attribute defines an independent dimension that denotes the mandatory information for having a set of data selected at the relevant planning level. For reading data at a particular level, the root attribute must have a non-null value. Generally, a required attribute of master data is selected as the root attribute for the planning level, although any other attribute can also be made a root attribute of a planning level if relevant for aggregation or disaggregation. Figure 4.2 shows examples of the SAP sample planning level, Period|Product|Location, which is the combination of period, product, and location master data types with the root attributes selected as the required attributes of product and location, as well as the monthly attribute of the time period.

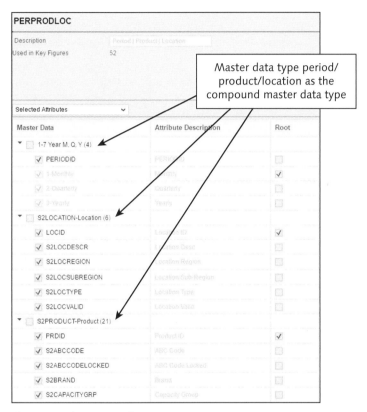

Figure 4.2 Planning Level

4.6 Key Figure

Key figures in SAP IBP represent supply chain planning and execution-relevant numerical values in periodic time buckets. Numbers such as sales orders, forecasts, and projected inventories are identified as key figure elements. Every key figure has a base planning level at which its value is stored, calculated, or manually edited. Values at other planning levels can be read through the defined aggregation and disaggregation in the key figure definition. A sales forecast number is generally calculated in SAP IBP at the period/product/location/customer planning level, and the period can be day, week, month, and so on. Forecast information at higher or lower planning levels is obtained through the respective aggregation and disaggregation logic maintained in the key figure. Aggregation logic in SAP IBP can be sum, minimum, maximum, average, or custom. An aggregation logic is selected during the system configuration per the nature of the key figure. For example, the projected inventory key figure will have a different aggregation logic than a sales order key figure. The disaggregation mode of a key figure can be copy, equal distribution, or proportional. Disaggregation in the SAP planning system distributes the data to lower planning levels. For example, if a forecast is updated in a monthly bucket, the update in the weekly bucket will be based on the disaggregation mode.

Key figures in SAP IBP can be categorized as key figures, helper key figures, or attribute transformations. Most of the standard key figures are created as key figures for which the values can be stored, calculated, or edited, and any specific calculation logic can be provided. These key figures can be accessed through the Excel planning view. Helper key figures are used to hold the intermediate values for complex calculations, and it's a standard practice to prefix helper key figures with "H". Helper key figures aren't applicable for the Excel planning view and aren't visible to the end user accessing the planning views. Because these are only used to perform intermediate calculations, helper key figures aren't relevant for storage, editing, aggregation, or disaggregation.

An attribute transformation key figure is used for changing the value of an attribute that can be used for further calculation or data editing. For example, time period is an attribute, and a specific time, for example, a week, is represented by an attribute, say PERIODID0. Through attribute transformation, we can copy the base planning level of PERIODID0 and change the value of this attribute by providing calculation logic (an example may be putting an offset for a few time periods), and this calculation can impact a key figure value as input. In this case, the attribute transformation may allow the values of the key figure to shift by the periods mentioned in the calculation. Usage of the functionalities of key figure, helper key figure, and attribute transformation key figure depend on the business requirements and are used to perform the required calculations in the most efficient fashion.

If a real-time integration with an execution system (e.g., SAP ERP or SAP S/4HANA) is required for the key figure, then the key figure must be assigned as an external key figure. The precondition of using the external integration in the key figure is that the planning area has been identified as relevant for external integration through the configuration checkbox in the planning area. Hence, key figures such as inventory, sales order, purchase order, etc. can be dynamically integrated in SAP IBP through external data integration to have the most recent value in the planning system as the execution system.

A standard key figure can be marked as an alert key figure by selecting the ALERT KEY FIGURE value. An alert key figure works in binary format in SAP IBP with the allowed value as 1 or 0, which represent "yes" and "no," respectively. An alert key figure must be calculated and can't be stored or edited. Alert key figures require defined calculation logic that results in either positive or negative (assigning the value as 1 or 0) and hence provide the information in the SAP IBP database to generate the alert based on this key figure.

Through system configuration settings, it's possible to control the logic of editing a key figure as well as its usage for supply planning. For an editable key figure, editing the key figure can be controlled for the time periods by setting whether the edit can be performed only in the past, current, or future bucket, or if it can be performed in all the past, present, and future time buckets. A key figure can also be marked as system editable, which is applicable for the values of the key figure as calculated by the SAP IBP planning algorithm. Usage in supply planning is marked if a key figure is either input, output, indirect input, or both input and output for supply planning. It may be possible that a particular key figure isn't relevant as I/O (input or output) for supply planning.

Figure 4.3 shows examples of standard, alert, and helper key figures from an SAP IBP system. DEPENDENTLOCATIONDEMAND is a stored key figure as an output of the planning algorithm and is available for planner's review in the planning view. CAPACITYOVERLOADALERT here can get the value of 0 or 1 and hence will either generate an alert or not. A helper key figure is used here for an intermediate calculation and isn't available for review in the planning view by planners.

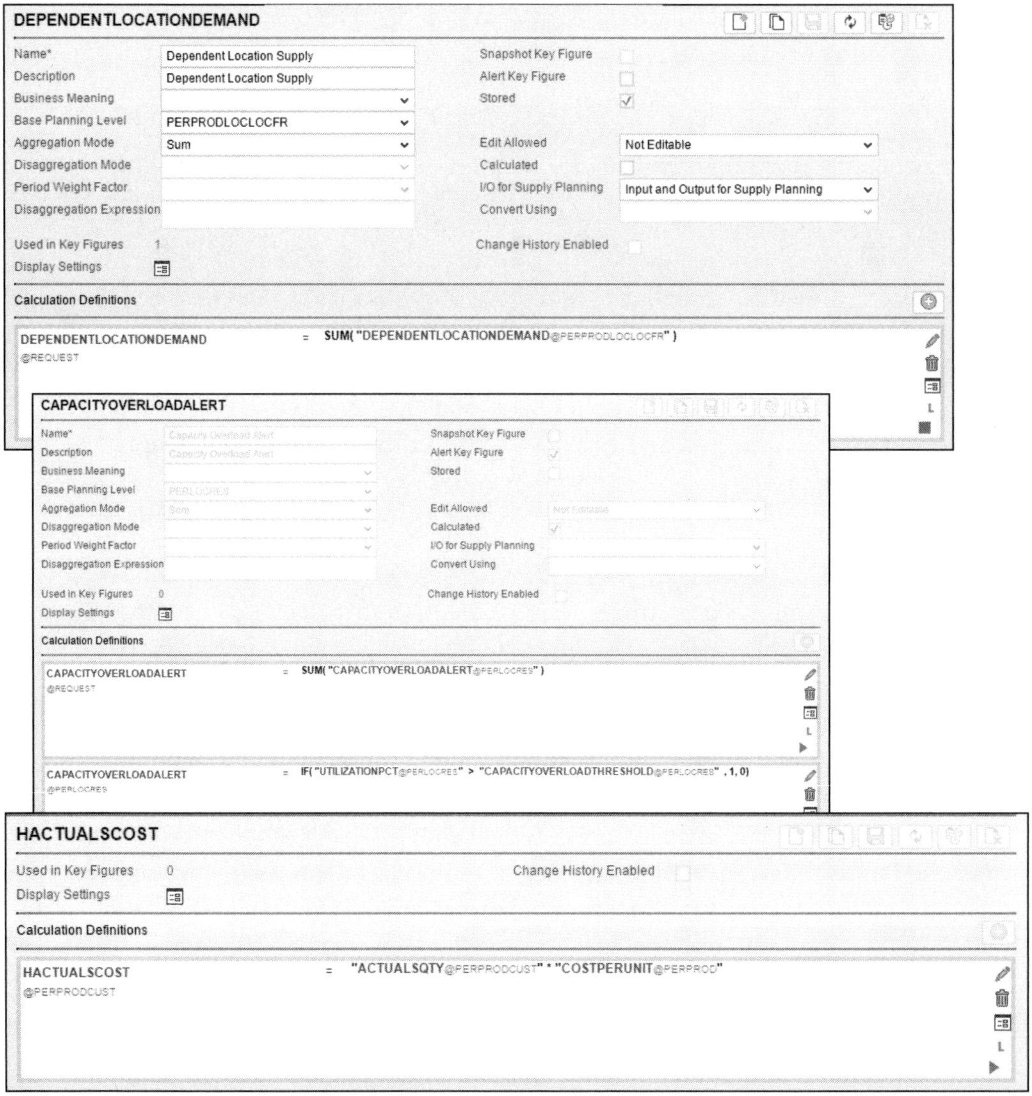

Figure 4.3 Standard, Alert, and Helper Keys

4.7 Key Figure Calculation Logic

As discussed in the previous section, calculation logic can be provided in the key figure to calculate the values as required in SAP IBP. A key figure stored, maintained, or edited at the base planning level may need to get the value from another planning level through a request-level calculation logic. Request level calculation defines the logic through which the key figure data can be fetched from other relevant planning levels in the key figure. Request level calculation happens through the aggregation logic (sum, minimum, maximum, average, or custom). Sum is the most popular request level aggregation logic used in SAP IBP as generally the roll-up of the planning level works with the sum logic. However, key figures such as projected inventory, capacity threshold value, and forecast error may require different logic, including custom, maximum, average, etc. For request level calculation, every key figure needs to be analyzed for the aggregation function usage.

When writing the key figure calculation, the key figure calculation functions are also important. The following examples are provided for referencing the key figure configuration calculation:

▸ **Aggregation logic**
Aggregation logic calculations are used to calculate the key figure value from the base planning level to the higher planning level. This is achieved by writing the request level calculation while referring to the base planning level number.

```
SALESORDER@Request = SUM("SALESORDER@PerProdLocCust)
```

This represents the calculation of key figures at the request level with the logic of summation from the base planning level of period/product/location/customer. For the planning calculation if the sales order key figure is displayed at period/product/location level, the value is calculated from the summation of all the sales orders for all the customers in the time period for a location/product combination.

▸ **Disaggregation logic**
Disaggregation logic calculations are based on using the disaggregation operators such as copy, equal, proportional, or custom, as discussed in the previous section.

▸ **Mathematical operation**
Mathematical operators are simplified tools used to perform key figure calculations based on the specific business requirement. Standard operators are used to perform the required calculation. Figure 4.4 shows one SAP standard example of the usage of mathematical operators. In this example, a helper key figure is used to hold the total cost value, multiplication of cost per unit, and

constrained demand, and the gross profit is calculated by subtracting the total cost from the revenue.

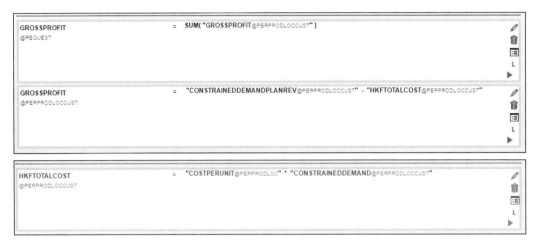

Figure 4.4 Mathematical Operator Usage for Key Calculation

▸ **Usage of IF criteria**

Conditional argument IF is used widely in SAP IBP key figure calculation to perform the calculations based on the required logic. The simple logic of the IF condition argument can follow the format Keyfigure@planning level = IF.

Usage of this format can be further illustrated by a key figure example in the SAP2 planning area of SAP IBP as represented in Figure 4.5. ACTUALSPRICE key figure at request level calculation is happening through an IF condition. If the ACTUALSQTY key figure in a time period is 0, then the ACTUALSPRICE gets the value assigned for the time period; if the ACTUALSQTY key figure's value isn't equal to 0, then the value of the ACTUALSPRICE key figure is calculated by dividing the ACTUALSQTY key figure's value from the ACTUALSREV key figure's value in the time period.

In Figure 4.5, the COMPONENTCOEFFICIENT key figure demonstrates the conditional argument IF along with another conditional argument ISNULL. The ISNULL argument is used to identify the values that aren't marked as 0 but have a blank or null value.

Figure 4.5 Usage of the IF Conditional Argument for Key Calculation

- **Nested IF criteria**

  Conditional arguments for key figure calculations can also work on the nested IF argument for performing complex calculations based on multiple conditions. The format to write and read the nested IF condition follows similar logic to an IF condition. Figure 4.6 shows an example of using a complex argument designed through a nested IF argument. Note that the ELSE value (when the IF condition isn't correct) has its own IF argument to calculate the value required for the consensus accuracy key figure percentage. The same key figure also uses another functional argument ABS (absolute value).

Figure 4.6 Nested IF Conditional Argument for Key Calculation

- **Usage of attributes in key figure calculation**

  Attributes created in SAP IBP can also be used for key figure calculations if required. The most widely used period-related attributes use the time buckets to identify past, present, or future time periods for the key figure calculations. The attribute in the key figure calculation is selected by using double quotation marks (e.g., "attribute"). The availability of the attribute for a key figure calculation is restricted by selection of the attribute at the planning level for which the key figure is being calculated through the key figure calculation expression.

For a planning configuration in which week represents the lowest time bucket and hence the `PERIODID0` value represents the weekly bucket, if a calculation is required for the future bucket only, the following can be used to perform the calculation only for the future:

```
IF("PERIODID0" > "$$PERIODID0CU$$
```

Using this, `PERIODID0` checks whether the relevant week for the calculation is greater than the current week as represented by standard attribute `$$PERIO-DID0CU$$` for the current time period.

Another example is performing a calculation only for the product of a particular product type. If the product type attribute is represented as `PRDTYPE`, and the check needs to happen for `ABCTYPE` to put a value of 1 if true and 0 otherwise, then the argument can be written as follows:

```
IF("PRDTYPE" = "ABCTYPE", 1, 0)
```

Figure 4.7 shows the calculations for a demand planning quantity using period ID. For the past period, the value is copied from the actuals quantity (ACTUALSQTY) key figure, and for the future, it's calculated through marketing promotion forecast (MKTGPROMOTIONFCSTQTY) and demand planning quantity (DEMANDPLANNINGQTY).

Figure 4.7 Attribute Value Condition Argument Usage Application for Key Calculation

4.8 Planning Operators

Planning operators are the algorithms that compute key figure data through a defined logic. They provide readily available references to perform supply chain planning and analytics operations. Examples of using the planning operators can be as simple as copying one key figure to another key figure or as complex as calculations such as statistical forecasting, supply heuristics, or inventory optimization.

Planning operators can be defined for their execution in interactive, filter, or batch mode. Some of the operators can be executed only in batch mode. Interactive mode allows you to work in the planning simulation without saving the data in the table; filter mode allows you to execute a selected set of master data while the batch mode executes in the background and saves the result in the table through the same execution. After interactive mode is used, you can save the data in the table.

Every action is controlled by a set of standard parameters. Parameters provide the option to customize SAP's provided planning operators. For example, the copy operator needs to be assigned the value of the source key figure and destination key figure along with the duration for which the copy should happen.

Table 4.3 lists the set of standard planning operators provided in SAP IBP.

Technical Name	Name	Usage
ABC	ABC classification/categorization	Attribute categorization based on time series values defined on attributes. Helps in analytics and to identify critical material groups.
ADVSIM	Advanced simulation	Perform copy and disaggregation on a predefined logic when the identified key figure value is simulated or a change in value is saved. The change in the disaggregation key figure can perform the copy of a key figure to another and can disaggregate the changed key figure by referring the copied key figure. It can also be used in changes in key figures such as sales forecast. However, it has a performance impact, and functionality can be considered through a copy and disaggregation operator.
COPY	Copy	Copy one key figure to another, and source and target key figures can be at different planning levels. The operator calculates the value of the source key figure at the base planning level of the target key figure before performing the copy. It's one of the most widely used planning operators. The functionality is limited by a single version in a single planning area. A period offset as well as a duration can be provided as parameters to control an offset or duration of performing the copy function.

Table 4.3 Standard Planning Operators

Technical Name	Name	Usage
DELABNDCOMBOS	Delete abandoned combinations	If some of the root master data types have been deleted from the system, clean the system and makes it consistent by deleting any abandoned planning combinations.
DISAGG	Disaggregate	Perform the copy and disaggregation of source key figures to target key figures while having the flexibility to select the duration and any period offset. The disaggregation operator can be used even if the source and target key figures are stored at different planning levels. Through parameters, the attribute is provided for the source key figure, which may be at the base planning level or higher than the base planning level for the target key figure. Consider a case where the source is at period/product/customer, and the target key figure is at period/product/location level. The planning operator can be executed at the product level, and the disaggregation at target happens for the location/product level.
GROUP	Group multiple operators	Define a group of planning operators to be executed as a single batch job. The execution can be triggered by the user or can be automated by assigning a key figure whose value import in the SAP IBP system triggers the group operator. A parameter can be assigned to control the execution of the remaining operators if any of the operators in the group results in an error.
IBPFORECAST	Statistical forecasting	Run the statistical forecast for the defined model in simulation or batch mode.
IO	IO (inventory optimization)	Perform single-stage or multistage inventory optimization through selection of relevant parameter such as SINGLE STAGE IO or MULTI STAGE IO. Other planning functions through this operator are expected demand loss, forecast error, and component inventory. We'll discuss these in detail in Chapter 13, which is devoted to inventory optimization in SAP IBP.

Table 4.3 Standard Planning Operators (Cont.)

Technical Name	Name	Usage
PCH	Purge change history data	Delete the record of any saved change history that is older than the specified time.
PURGE	Purge key figure data	Delete the key figure data for the records older than a specified time.
SCM	Supply planning across the global supply chain network	Execute supply planning algorithms such as heuristic, optimizer, and network consistency check. Each planning type has a separate algorithm and a set of recommended parameters to control the supply planning models. For example, through parameter selection, supply planning policies such as carry over shortages and lot size usage can be selected. Input to the supply planning operators are the master data and multiple key figures relevant to the planning, and output is saved in the supply planning-relevant key figures. Supply planning algorithms can be executed in batch mode for the global network or for a specified set by using the filter mode and by providing the values for the filter.
SNAPSHOT	Snapshot for a predefined set of key figures	Copy and store the value of a key figure at a particular point in time. For example, demand forecast snapshot can be used to analyze demand sensing. The SAP IBP system can save up to nine snapshots for a key figure, and the snapshot copy can be performed through a user's execution of the planning operator or through execution in the background.
SNAPSHOTREDO	Redo Snapshot	Generate a new snapshot by overwriting the most recent snapshot for the predefined set of key figures.

Table 4.3 Standard Planning Operators (Cont.)

For a planning operator to be relevant and available for a planning area, the operator must be assigned in the planning area during configuration.

4.9 Version

Version in SAP IBP provides the functionality to create and use alternative plans and what-if scenario planning. The base version is the inherent active version of the SAP IBP system that is used for active planning and data integration. Other simulation versions can be configured in the system to support the alternative plans. Alternative plans through versions can share the master data with the base version or can have their own set of master data.

Versions are highly efficient and useful tools for the planners to perform simulation planning to identify and finalize the best demand-supply plan as well as for easy collaboration with team members. Master data and key figure values can be copied from one version to another and can be analyzed and compared in a planning view. Planning operators can be executed for a specific version; for example, a planner can copy the master data and key figures from the active version to a simulation version; change the capacity, forecast, cost parameters; execute a supply or inventory optimization; and then compare the results in the simulated version with the base version. Planning data in the version is available to every other member in the planning team with the required authorization to work in the version, and it doesn't require an essential sharing of the version from one planner to another. The simulation version's key figures can be copied back to the base version's data if simulation decisions result in a better plan output.

Organizations also use the version capability to copy the data before the planning cycle ends (e.g., daily or weekly cycle) into a different version for analysis and comparison purposes. Version-specific simulation planning can be performed for the entire data set of the base or simulation version or by selecting a smaller set through the filter capability of using the versions in planning interfaces. Copying master data and key figures between versions can be performed interactively by users or can be scheduled in the background.

4.10 Scenario

Scenarios are used by planners to perform simulation planning on the fly. Planning data in a scenario are available only to the planner who has created the scenario and for the team members with whom the scenario has been shared by the scenario creator. The baseline scenario is provided in the system, which contains the data in the active database. Multiple simulation scenarios can be created by the planners for planning review and change impact analysis by adjusting a planning variable and using the planning operators to analyze its impact. Scenario planning data can be promoted to the baseline scenario to overwrite the active data. Other than promoting to the baseline data, a scenario can also be deleted, duplicated, or reset. Deletion removes both the scenario and its data, whereas reset erases the data in the scenario while still keeping the scenario for future usage. The duplicate option duplicates the selected scenario and creates a new one for further simulation exercises.

A scenario doesn't contain its own master data, and it shares the master data with the baseline scenario. Planners can create scenarios in the planning interface without any preconfiguration.

Figure 4.8 shows the scenario interface in the planning interface and an example of data displayed with multiple versions and scenarios.

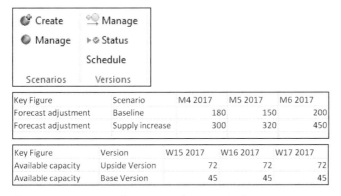

Key Figure	Scenario	M4 2017	M5 2017	M6 2017
Forecast adjustment	Baseline	180	150	200
Forecast adjustment	Supply increase	300	320	450

Key Figure	Version	W15 2017	W16 2017	W17 2017
Available capacity	Upside Version	72	72	72
Available capacity	Base Version	45	45	45

Figure 4.8 Scenario and Version in the SAP IBP Planning View

4.11 Reason Code

Reason codes are required to tag, share, and retrieve the information related to a change in the plan. Multiple reason codes can be configured in the SAP IBP environment. When a user changes some data in the planning view, he can select a reason code, provide an associated comment, and share it with an existing SAP Jam group. In this manner, the comment and reason code are published in the SAP Jam collaboration page for the team members in that particular SAP Jam group. Information in the SAP Jam collaboration page appears with a hashtag (#) and the reason code. Clicking on this provides all the comments related to this reason code. This is an efficient information-sharing mechanism; for example, if a sales manager adjusts the forecast for a market segment based on market information, the change can be tagged through a reason code like "Market intelligence input" with further comment and can be shared with the entire sales and marketing team related to the product segment. The data will be changed in real time through SAP IBP database changes, and the information will be shared with the relevant people in real time. If there are any further changes with this forecast with the same reason code, all the changes and comment information can be reviewed together through the # grouping functionality of the reason code. An example with system screenshot has been provided in Chapter 6, Section 6.2.3.

4.12 Global Configuration Parameters

Global configuration parameters are used to define default application settings used in SAP IBP that control system behavior. Global parameters can be used to make all charts and graphs available for public use or to restrict them for the user's authorization, for example. Global parameters are defined through parameter group, parameter name, and parameter value. Parameter group is provided as the standard part of the solution to control a particular application by maintaining the value for the parameter. Parameter name can be selected by the user while configuring the global parameter for a group. Information relevant to the parameter group is provided in Table 4.4.

Parameter Group	Solution Area	Control Areas
ANALYTICS	Analytical charts and dashboard applications	Access to charts, graphs, and default number of alerts display
COLLABORATION	SAP Jam integration	Enable the collaboration through the SAP Jam application
FORECAST	Statistical forecast	Forecast algorithm when some historical data is missing; allows whether a negative forecast is acceptable
HOME_PAGE	Dashboard	Default planning area of the SAP IBP dashboard

Table 4.4 SAP IBP Global Configuration Parameters

Parameter Group	Solution Area	Control Areas
INTEGRATION	Integration	Default planning area for integration, aggregation level, or integration; debug capability
MASTER_DATA_OP	Master data	Maximum number of records that can be displayed, downloaded, or uploaded
PLAN_VIEW	SAP IBP Excel planning view	Rules for concurrent data save and job execution, time series data deletion parameter, maximum row size in planning view, and display of rows with all null values
PLCNTRL	Control parameter	Supply planning simulation control and system timeout setting
SCENARIO	Simulation version	Maximum number of simulation versions allowed to be created in the system
SYSTEM	Default email for password reset	Number of days relevant for notification
TRANSPORT	Transport	Attribute and target group of transport

Table 4.4 SAP IBP Global Configuration Parameters (Cont.)

4.13 Snapshot Configuration

The snapshot application is used to save the values of a particular key figure at different points in time so that the changes in the value can be tracked over time. This can be highly useful in business scenarios and metrics related to demand sensing, schedule adherence, plan change tracking, etc. Figure 4.9 shows the snapshot configuration in the SAP IBP system.

SAP IBP can support a maximum of nine snapshots for a key figure. A snapshot key figure in the planning view appears with the key figure name, the suffix for snapshot, and the snapshot number. Snapshots are triggered through the planning operator and can be executed periodically. For example, a snapshot can be configured for a forecast key figure so that three snapshots are taken for the preceding three months. The forecast values for a product group or customer group can be analyzed over a period of time to understand the consistency and to take action if required.

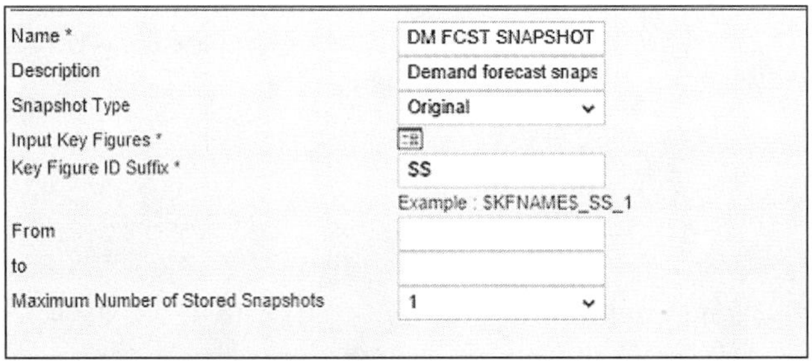

Name *	DM FCST SNAPSHOT
Description	Demand forecast snaps
Snapshot Type	Original ⌄
Input Key Figures *	▤
Key Figure ID Suffix *	SS
	Example : $KFNAMES_SS_1
From	
to	
Maximum Number of Stored Snapshots	1 ⌄

Figure 4.9 Snapshot Configuration

4.14 Summary

This chapter defined the concepts of the planning model and associated elements in SAP IBP. Basic elements covered include master data types, attributes, time profiles, planning areas, planning operators and key figure calculations. Also discussed were more advanced capabilities such as the creation of multiple planning versions, user-driven scenarios and key figure snapshots. You're now equipped with the knowledge required to build the solution in the SAP IBP system per your organization's supply chain infrastructure, design, and requirements. The next chapter will focus on step-by-step creation of the building block items.

Now that you understand the planning model and its entities, you're now ready to set up the SAP IBP system. This chapter will get into the details of system configuration for the SAP IBP planning models and its associated elements.

5   Configuring an SAP IBP System

The entities and components discussed in Chapter 4 need to be built into the SAP Integrated Business Planning (SAP IBP) system for use in the planning model. We highly recommend you complete a design document with the details of the planning entities before starting the system build and modeling. For system configuration, you can either copy the standard planning area provided by SAP or develop a planning model from scratch. It's recommended to start by copying a standard SAP planning area and then add further organization-specific objects to the copy. If using the copied planning area, further entities can be added into the model, including attributes, planning levels, key figures, and other objects. This chapter will cover the entities in detail so you can follow either approach.

Entities for the planning model can be configured in the system by using the information provided here. For the planning model creation and activation, we'll discuss the configuration and management of the most relevant elements, from managing planning attributes through deleting active objects.

5.1   Managing Planning Attributes

For attribute creation, from the SAP Fiori user interface, click the CONFIGURATION tile under the MODEL CONFIGURATION header. Click ATTRIBUTES or MANAGE ATTRIBUTE to open the attribute configuration screen (see Figure 5.1). The ATTRIBUTES tile under MODEL CONFIGURATION also opens the same screen. Before starting the configuration, you need the attribute design document with the attribute ID, description, data type, length, decimal (if relevant), and master data type association. Figure 5.1 shows the fields that need to be entered to create an attribute.

Click the ADD button to add the newly created attribute in the group, and then click the SAVE button to add the attribute to the database. Repeat this process to create all the required attributes in the SAP IBP system.

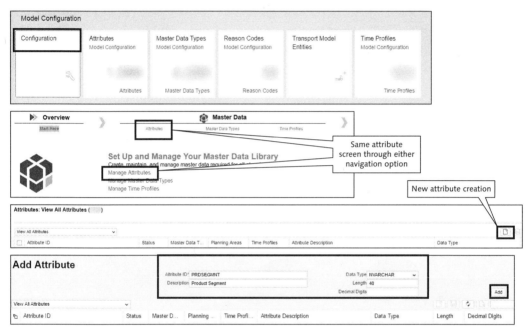

Figure 5.1 Attribute Creation Configuration Screen

5.2   Assigning the Master Data Type

After establishing the attributes, you must group them by the relevant master data type. Figure 5.2 shows the configuration tool used to create the master data type. The configuration buttons shown here exist in the same format for other elements, such as time profile, planning level, planning area, and key figure.

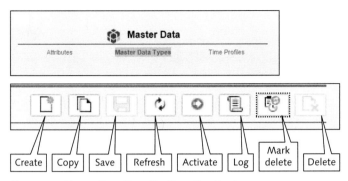

Figure 5.2 Master Data Type Configuration Tools

The configuration tool buttons perform the following functions:

▶ CREATE
This button creates the object. If clicked in the MASTER DATA TYPES screen, it creates a new master data type. A similar button accessed through time profile, planning area, planning level, and key figure creates a time profile, planning area, planning level, and key figure, respectively.

▶ COPY
This button is used to copy an existing element. A name is provided to the copied entity (e.g., master data type, time profile, or other objects), and the entity is edited further for usage in a model.

▶ SAVE
This button saves the object in the SAP IBP database.

▶ REFRESH
This button refreshes the screen and updates the status of the object.

▶ ACTIVATE
This button activates the data in the database and makes it ready for use in the planning model.

▶ LOG
This button shows the activation log and provides relevant information in case of any failure, so that action can be taken to resolve and correct the error.

▶ MARK DELETE
This button marks the entity for deletion. The same button can be used to reset the status if the object isn't entirely deleted (through activation after marking DELETE).

▶ DELETE

This button eliminates the object marked for deletion. Activation of the object is required to remove the object from the database totally.

To create a master data type, click the CREATE button, and give the new object a name. We recommend you put a three-letter prefix in the master data type name and use the same three-letter prefix in other relevant SAP IBP items. In the example shown in Figure 5.3, prefix ABC is used, and the technical name (ID), NAME, DESCRIPTION, and MASTER DATA TYPE are provided. For simple master data types, all the attributes for the master data are selected; key attributes for the master data type are also selected here.

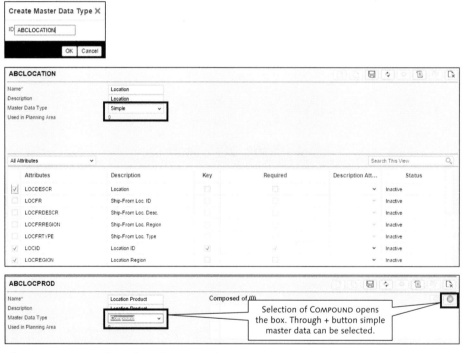

Figure 5.3 Creation of Simple and Compound Master Data Types

In the current example, the attributes are selected for location master data. The LOCID (location ID) attribute is marked as the KEY attribute for the master data type. From the CREATE MASTER DATA TYPE screen, a compound master data selection opens a table from which suitable simple master data types can be selected and added. The key attribute of a simple master data type is automatically chosen as soon as the simple master data type is added to form the compound master data type. Any other attribute required by the solution design can be added manually through the screen shown in Figure 5.3. The SAVE and ACTIVATION buttons can be used to write and activate the master data type in the database.

5.3   Creating Time Profiles

The time profile configuration screen is accessed through the CONFIGURATION tile or through the TIME PROFILES tile, both found in the MODEL CONFIGURATION group. The CREATE button is used to create a new time profile. You can assign a numeric value from 1 to 999999 for the time profile, but we recommend a three- or four-digit numeric value. For the DESCRIPTION, we recommend you use the same three-letter prefix used in the master data type, along with the associated time periods. Figure 5.4 shows a time profile creation with ID "400" and a DESCRIPTION of "ABC TP W M Q Y". The START DATE and END DATE of the time profile controls the relevance of the planning data in the past and the future. This time profile is created for a longer period than the planned time horizon for planning so that the associated time profile and planning area are used for an extended period of time after the initial solution configuration.

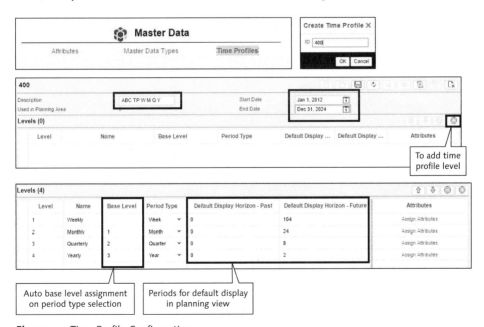

Figure 5.4 Time Profile Configuration

You can add the time profile level of the planning area by clicking the + button. You can select the period type from the PERIOD TYPE dropdown. You must start with the most granular level. In the time profile shown in Figure 5.4, the WEEK is the most granular level and hence appears in the first row. The system automatically creates base level values. If day is also a planning granularity level, then DAY will be selected as the first row (base level 0), and Week will get assigned as BASE LEVEL 1.

Other than the day, week, month, quarter, and year, the technical week is also supported as a planning period type in the time profile of SAP IBP. A technical week always starts on the first day of the month, and the next technical week will start from the identified fixed day. A normal week split in technical weeks is identified accordingly. For example, if TECHNICAL WEEK is used as the PERIOD TYPE, the base level value smaller than the week must be assigned.

The DEFAULT DISPLAY fields control the horizon as shown in the default planning view, for example, a value of 0 to 104 for the weekly bucket will display data from the current week to the next 104 week (about 2 years). If a value is populated for the past, say −6 for the week, then it will show data for the past 6 week also in the default planning view. Note that you can interactively change the periods of the planning view through the interactive screen. After performing maintenance on the time profile, save and activate it.

To use the time profile in the planning view, you must create the time periods for the time profile. Time periods for a particular time profile can be set up by uploading the time period data through the manual upload screen or by setting up an application job to create the time period automatically in the SAP IBP system. To load manually, the template for the time profile data load is generated from the DATA INTEGRATION tile of the ADMINISTRATOR section in the SAP Fiori launchpad of SAP IBP. To automatically create time periods, access the APPLICATION JOB TEMPLATE tile in the ADMINISTRATOR section. Use the CREATE TIME PERIODS FOR TIME PROFILES template with the same name you assigned for the time period, and then select the time profile level of the time period. Scheduling this job creates the time periods for the time profile, making it ready to be used in the planning view.

5.4 Defining Planning Areas

To configure the planning area from scratch, access the CONFIGURATION tile from the MODEL CONFIGURATION section, and click PLANNING AREA AND DETAILS, as shown in Figure 5.5. Click the CREATE button, and provide the name of the planning area in the pop-up screen. For the system implementation stage, we recommend you maintain multiple planning areas for configuration management, user testing, integration development, and training. You can use your naming convention to distinguish one area from another. We also recommend using the organization-specific three-letter prefix discussed in previous sections.

In Figure 5.5, ABCACTIVE is the name of the planning area. Multiple planning areas are synced from the copy functionality. The same functionality is also used to copy the standard planning area provided by SAP for the client's usage. Changes in the copied planning area can be performed to meet the requirements of the organization's supply chain planning and execution.

Figure 5.5 Planning Area Configuration

Figure 5.5 demonstrates the configuration options for the planning area. With the name, it's essential to select the time profile relevant for the planning area.

Storage time profile level should be chosen as the lowest time bucket of the time profile to allow the aggregation and disaggregation across the time period levels of the time profile. Supply Planning Enabled is selected if the supply planning must be executed through this planning area. The External Time Series Enabled indicator allows the near real-time integration of the key figures with the execution system as SAP ERP or SAP S/4HANA. The Change History Planning Area Enabled indicator may be selected to use the change history and snapshot functionality in the planning area.

Be aware that a high level of change history and snapshot usage can impact system performance. Planning horizon parameters must be maintained. The past and future buckets determine the planning horizon through the planning area. Note that this horizon works on a rolling time basis. The planning operator window is used to choose the planning operators relevant for planning in this planning area. The operators can be a SAP-provided standard operator or user-configured operator. An operator will be available for a planning area only if it's selected for the planning area through this configuration screen. Click the Save button to save the planning area after completing the configuration.

You must select the master data type and relevant attributes to make them part of the planning area. Only the selected attributes will be available for the creation of the planning level and for planning in the SAP IBP Excel planning view. Attribute categories Optional, Mandatory, or Calculated are selected in this configuration screen. Attributes that need to be used as the key figure in the planning area must be selected for their relevant box in the Key Figure column. Note that this box appears only for the attributes that are created as decimal data types. Attributes such as price or sourcing ratio after selection in the planning area will also need the Key Figure box selected, in order to be transformed into key figures. Figure 5.6 shows an example of attribute selection for the standard planning area SAP2.

Two options are available for the planning areacopy function: simple copy or advance copy. A simple copy creates every element except the master data type, time profile, and attributes associated with the source planning area. These items are built for the target planning area. The advance copy copies the entire set, including the master data type, time profile, and attributes associated with the source planning area.

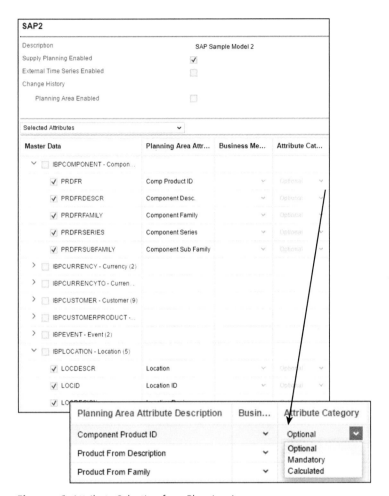

Figure 5.6 Attribute Selection for a Planning Area

A simple copy requires the name of the source planning area and target planning area. The source planning area already exists in the system, and the target area is the name assigned to create the new planning area. A copy can be performed as a merge or replace option. For an advance copy, because the master data type can also be copied, there is the option to change the prefix of the master data type while copying. For example, while copying the SAP2 planning area to create a new planning area through an advance copy, the source prefix "IBP" can be replaced with a new prefix for the newly created planning area. An advance copy also requires a new target time profile ID to be provided while copying.

5.5   Managing the Planning Level

The PLANNING LEVELS configuration screen is accessed by clicking the PLANNING LEVEL link on the CONFIGURATION tile under the MODEL CONFIGURATION header. Figure 5.7 shows the steps necessary to create the planning level. The technical name and description are provided to create the level. You will select the attributes of the master data type relevant for the planning level on the PLANNING LEVELS screen. Root attributes must be marked by checking the ROOT box for the attributes identified as the root for the planning level, per the solution design.

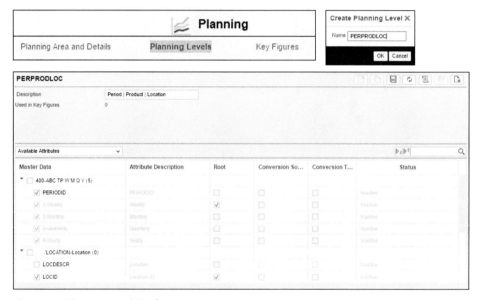

Figure 5.7 Planning Level Configuration

Refer to the SAP standard planning level available in the system for naming conventions. Table 5.1 shows some standard naming conventions for selecting the master data type at the planning level.

Object Type	Name in Planning Level
Period	PER
Product	PROD
Location	LOC

Table 5.1 Object Type and Recommended Name in the Planning Level

Object Type	Name in Planning Level
Customer	CUST
Component	CMP
Location to	LOCTO
Location from	LOCFR
Source (source ID)	SRC
Product family	PRODFML
Resource	RES
Currency from	CURR
Currency to	CURRTO
Substitute product	SPROD
Unit of measure from	UOM
Unit of measure to	UOMTO

Table 5.1 Object Type and Recommended Name in the Planning Level (Cont.)

After identifying all the attributes and root attributes of the planning level, click SAVE, and the next planning level can be created. You must create every planning level for the planning area one by one if the configuration has been done from scratch. If the planning area has been created by copying the SAP standard planning area, then the planning levels will also be copied, and you need only review the planning levels, change them per the solution design, and save them.

5.6   Using Key Figures

The KEY FIGURES screen is accessed by clicking the KEY FIGURES link on the CONFIGURATION tile under the MODEL CONFIGURATION header. A new key figure can be configured by copying an existing key figure or by creating it from scratch (see Figure 5.8).

To create a key figure from scratch, after clicking the CREATE button, provide the technical name (KEY FIGURE ID) and the BASE PLANNING LEVEL of the key figure in the pop-up that appears. In the next screen, provide the name, which will appear in the planning view to the user for this key figure. Select the AGGREGATION MODE, DISAGGREGATION MODE, and EDIT ALLOWED of the key figure per the solution design. If this is an alert key figure, select ALERT KEY FIGURE, and make sure to maintain the calculation for the same. If the planning area is relevant for planning and if the key figure is relevant for external data integration, maintain the setting for external key figure quantity (as discussed in Chapter 4).

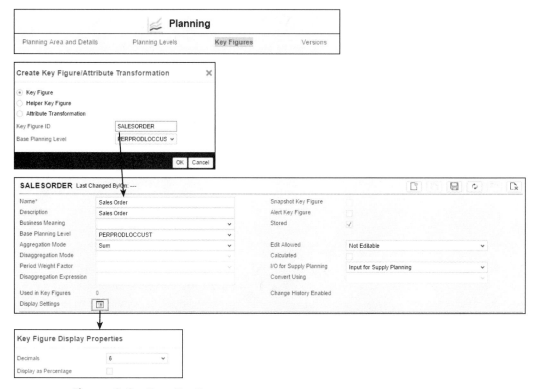

Figure 5.8 Creating a Key Figure

The CHANGE HISTORY ENABLED and SNAPSHOT KEY FIGURE checkboxes activate these functionalities in the key figure. Based on the nature of the key figure, mark the STORED or CALCULATED checkboxes to identify the key figure. If this will be used as input or output for supply planning (heuristic or optimizer), select the required functionality from the I/O FOR SUPPLY PLANNING dropdown. The number of decimals displayed in the planning view and whether the key figure needs to be displayed as a percentage can be identified as DISPLAY SETTINGS in the key figure. After maintaining the settings as mentioned here, the key figure calculation (discussed in the next section) needs to be built before saving the key figure.

5.7 Adding Calculation Logic to Key Figures

Calculations for the key figure must be added through the ADD CALCULATION button at the bottom of the KEY FIGURES screen. Refer to Figure 5.9 for the system representation. You can add a calculation using the + button on the screen. Every key figure needs a definition for the request level through the base level. Note that the data of the key figure are saved or calculated at the base level, and the request level can be any planning level higher than the base level. Other calculation levels and operators can be added per the solution design of a particular key figure. Key figure calculation logic was discussed in detail in Chapter 4, Section 4.7. Use the INPUT KEY FIGURE button to identify the key figures that will be used as input and/or stored values for the current key figure calculation. The FORMULA/GRAPH VIEW option is used to display the calculation graph. A light green color indicates that the stored value is used in the key figure calculation. The formula page is used for maintaining and editing the calculation, while the graph page can be used for the easy review and validation of the calculation logic.

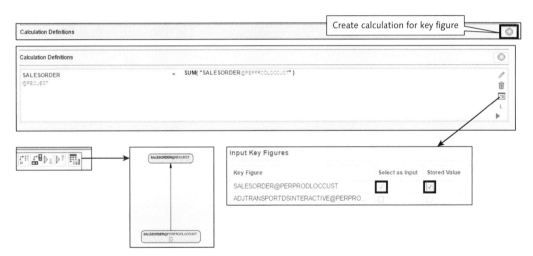

Figure 5.9 Building Key Calculations

5.8 Applying Planning Operators

To access the planning operator screen select the CONFIGURATION tile in the MODEL CONFIGURATION section. Then, under the group heading of MISCELLANEOUS SETTINGS, select the MANAGE PLANNING OPERATORS link. The system will display all the operator types and respective operators maintained in their groups. To edit an existing operator, click on the type and operator name. To create a new operator of a particular operator type, click the operator type in the left of the screen, and click the + button to add a new operator of that specific type. Figure 5.10 shows the steps in the system. Select the Interactive Mode, Batch Mode, and Filter Mode as appropriate for the planning operator. Maintain the operator parameters through Define Parameters links in the Parameters column. Click the Save button to save the planning operator after completing the configuration.

Figure 5.10 Planning Operator Management

5.9 Creating Reason Codes

Reason codes are set up in the system to keep track of the changes made in the planning view by the planners. During the solution design phase, we recommend you identify potential reason codes and the associated team members who may be changing the planning data in the planning view and may be interested in determining a trackable cause of this change.

To create a new reason code, access the reason code screen through the Miscellaneous Settings of the Configuration tile. As displayed in Figure 5.11, provide the REASON CODE ID and REASON CODE NAME after clicking the CREATE button. While performing a change in the planning view, the planner can select the possible reason code and the group to share this update in on the collaboration page. For ad hoc requirements of a new reason code, the planner can create a new code through the configuration screen as shown in Figure 5.11 and use the code through the Excel planning view while editing and saving the data.

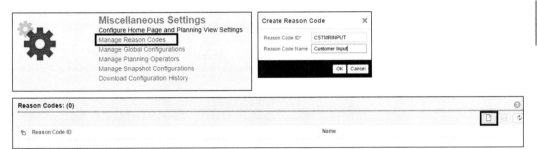

Figure 5.11 Reason Code Creation

5.10   Version Configuration

To use a planning version for an alternative or simulation plan, you must create it through configuration. A user may access the version creation screen by selecting VERSIONS accessed through the CONFIGURATION tile of the MODEL CONFIGURATION section. Click the CREATE button and assign the name of the version in the pop-up as shown in Figure 5.12. If the version is planned to work with its master data, check the VERSION-SPECIFIC MASTER DATA box. The relevant key figures must be selected in the version that will be used for the simulation plan. The VERSION-SPECIFIC KEY FIGURE checkbox allows using the key figure for information as well as editing in the version. If there are any key figures for which the baseline value will be utilized as a reference value in the version, then select the BASELINE KEY FIGURE box for the key figure. Click the SAVE button to save the version and make this available for planning.

Version usage for planning simulation requires further version management in the planning view. As shown in Figure 5.12, through the planning view, the planner can use the MANAGE button to copy the data from the base version to the simulation version for master data (if VERSION-SPECIFIC MASTER DATA is checked for the version configuration) and key figures. A filter can be applied if the copy needs to happen for a selected list of master data. This copy can be performed on demand or can be scheduled by the planner in the background. To review the version-specific planning data, the planner needs to access the new view or edit the view options to select the version for planning. Multiple simulation versions, with or without the base version, can also be selected if required for analysis.

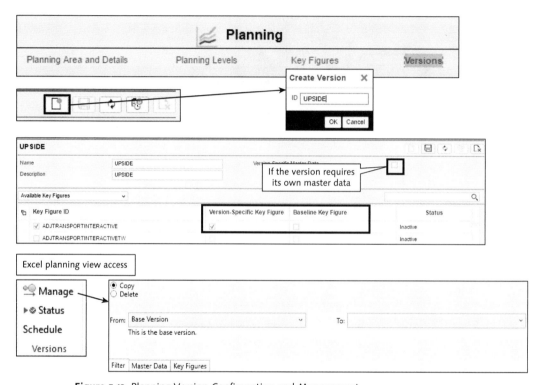

Figure 5.12 Planning Version Configuration and Management

5.11 Creating Scenarios

Planning scenario creation and management doesn't require system setup, and it's controlled through user action in the planning view. As shown in Figure 5.13, a new scenario can be created by clicking the CREATE button in the SCENARIOS section in the planning view. The changes performed by the planners in the current sheet are saved as the scenario data. The scenario data, along with other scenarios or base scenarios, can be compared, reviewed, and planned in one view by selecting the appropriate scenarios using the EDIT VIEW or NEW VIEW options in the planning view.

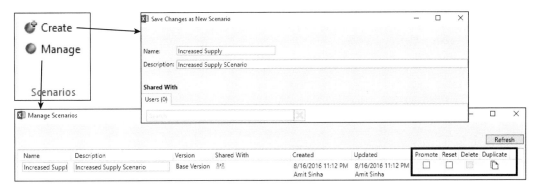

Figure 5.13 Scenario Creation and Management

Administration of the present scenarios in the system is performed through the MANAGE button in the SCENARIOS section of the planning view. Through the MANAGE SCENARIOS view, the following actions are performed:

▶ PROMOTE
Move scenario data to base planning data.

▶ RESET
Remove any changes made by the planners in the scenario without deleting the scenario.

▶ DELETE
Delete the scenario along with the data in the scenario.

▶ DUPLICATE
Create a copy of the scenario and data under a different name as a new scenario.

5.12 Managing Global Configuration Settings

To maintain global configuration settings, click MANAGE GLOBAL CONFIGURATIONS in the MISCELLANEOUS SETTINGS list accessed through the CONFIGURATION tile under MODEL CONFIGURATION (see Figure 5.14). Use the CREATE button to configure a new global parameter. The parameter group must be selected from the dropdown (see Chapter 4, Section 4.12, for more detailed information on parameter groups). Based on the parameter group, the parameter name will be available to select from the dropdown option of the parameter name. You must fill in the parameter value (see Figure 5.14). After the parameters are maintained, save them by using the SAVE button to make them effective in the system.

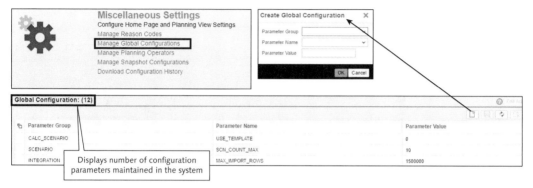

Figure 5.14 Global Configuration Value Management

5.13 Activating the Planning Model

After the configuration elements are completed, you need to activate the planning model to make them available for use. Planning model activation is mandatory for usage in the SAP IBP Excel planning view. The activation needs to follow a sequence and can be started by clicking the ACTIVATE button. Figure 5.15 shows both the ACTIVATE button and the ACTIVATE LOG button. We recommend you have only one object activation running at a time. The log displays any error, warning, and information for the activation process. An error is a hard stoppage of the object activation and requires a corrective action. Warning and information messages can be reviewed to understand if any action is required.

The planning model activation must follow this sequence:

1. **Activate the time profile.**
   To activate a time period, access the time period through the CONFIGURATION tile and click the required time period on the TIME PERIOD page. Click the ACTIVATE button to start the activation. Click the ACTIVATE LOG button, and use the REFRESH button on the log page to verify the activation result. The time profile activation validates the configuration definition provided in the time profile

along with the level dependencies and connection with a planning area. If the time period had been loaded for the time profile, then any change in the profile are validated for the present time period. If there are major variations in the time period, it's recommended to create a new time profile and assign it in the planning area, instead of changing the time profile and reactivating. A successful validation results in an active time profile; any error that stops the activation will be available through the activation log and will require action from the user to resolve it.

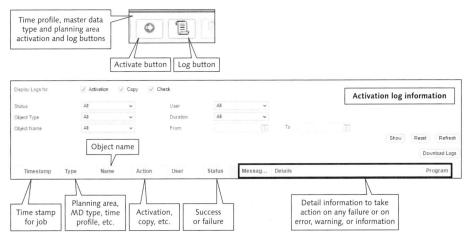

Figure 5.15 Planning Model Activation

2. **Activate the master data type.**
   The master data type is activated along with all the attributes associated with the master data. To activate a master data type, click the ACTIVATE button. Activation results can be checked through the activation log; a successful activation will activate this master data type and every attribute which is a part of this master data type. A master data type or a group of master data types can be activated through the MASTER DATA TYPE screen. Every master data type associated with a planning area can be activated while activating the planning area by selecting the option to include MASTER DATA TYPE during planning area activation.

3. **Activate the planning area.**
   Planning area activation activates the planning area along with the planning level, key figures, and versions associated with the planning area. Master data

and attributes assigned to the master data must be active prior to the planning area activation or must be activated together during planning area activation. The time profile associated with the planning area must be active before starting the planning area activation. Note that there aren't separate activations for planning level, key figure, and version; their activation is controlled through the planning area activation.

A planning area activation can fail if there are errors in the configuration of the objects associated with the planning area. For troubleshooting, it's suggested to review the error log and take action to resolve the issues. Following are examples of common errors and ways to resolve them:

▶ Concurrent runs: Only one activation task should be executed at a time. We recommend you check the activation log to make sure no further run is in progress before starting an object's (time profile, master data, or planning area) activation.

▶ Missing essential root attribute in the planning level: Make sure that the root attributes, essential for the calculation and aggregation/disaggregation across the levels, are added at the planning level.

▶ Dependent object activation: We recommend you activate the logical activation sequence following time profile, master data type, and planning area activation.

▶ Key figure calculation issues: Key figure calculation issues can have different root causes and hence may need an action based on the root cause. Some of the common examples of key figure calculation issues can be grouped as follows:

  – Incomplete calculation graph: Make sure the calculation graphs end in stored key figures (marked in green).

  – Missing calculation at request level: Create the request level calculation for every key figure. This isn't a mandatory requirement for helper key figures.

  – Number of planning levels in a calculation: The maximum number of planning levels used in a calculation should not exceed two. Note that a planning level that is stored and calculated is considered as two different levels. For those calculation scenarios, consider using a helper key figure.

  – Missing attribute in output key figure: Every attribute in the planning level for the output key figure must be included in the planning level of input key figures.

- Planning level subset: The output key figure planning level must be a subset of the input key figure planning level.

- Expression error: Check that the mathematical operators, parentheses, and other items are consistent for the calculation.

▸ Version: If a version has been configured in the system, it must have at least one key figure assigned to it.

▸ Editing while activating: Don't edit the planning area when activation is in progress.

▸ Timeout: Planning area activation can also fail based on a timeout, and a reactivation can help.

5.14 Deleting Active Objects

Active objects such as master data types, time profiles, planning levels, key figures, and planning areas can be deleted in the SAP IBP system if required, although the object deletion can only be accomplished by following the necessary logic and steps. To remove a time profile, it's essential that it's not attached to any planning area. To delete a particular object, you must first delete the objects in which this has been used.

For example, to remove a master data type, first the planning level that uses this master data type should be removed. Similarly, a key figure can only be deleted if it's not used as an input for another key figure. To delete an active object such as a time profile, master data type, planning level, or planning area, the sequence of deletion requires several steps. The first step is to check the dependency as explained previously. Then, the button to mark for deletion is selected for the object to be deleted. The same button can be used to remove this and to return to the original stage. This changes the status of the object to PENDING FOR DELETION. The activation of the object deletes and removes this from the system.

5.15 Summary

The planning model elements of SAP IBP and their configuration methods were discussed in detail in this chapter and the preceding chapter. System configuration in SAP IBP is much simpler, effective, and efficient based on the inherent design, solution completeness, and standard modeling parameters provided with SAP IBP. Concepts learned for model building are applicable for managing the planning processes (S&OP, demand, supply, response, and inventory optimization) in SAP IBP. We're now ready to discuss supply chain planning processes and their optimization through SAP IBP.

Sales and operations planning (S&OP) processes finalize the organization-wide plan for demand and supply. This chapter discusses S&OP, its associated subprocesses, and how to use SAP IBP to efficiently manage them.

6   Sales and Operations Planning with SAP IBP

A typical supply chain network consists of a complex structure of multiple parties such as suppliers, production plants, warehouses, distribution centers, and many other stock-keeping and order-processing facilities. Sales and operations planning (S&OP) allows the organization to work as an integrated team to finalize one plan for product and asset demand and supply. This chapter covers managing S&OP processes in an organization and using SAP Integrated Business Planning (SAP IBP) for sales and operations to design and execute this end-to-end integrated process with complete visibility and control.

In Section 6.1, we'll begin by looking at the primary objective of S&OP, expanding on our current definition. From there, in Section 6.2, we'll consider how to balance demand and supply through S&OP with the power of SAP IBP. Finally, in Section 6.3, we'll examine the details of using SAP IBP for sales and operations to manage and automate S&OP processes.

6.1   Objective of Sales and Operations Planning

S&OP delivers a single, central place where an organization's demand, supply, and financial plan come together. It consists of a set of business processes designed to finalize a unified demand and supply plan for an organization or business unit. Efficient management of the S&OP process generates the most profitable plan that matches projected demand with planned supply. S&OP helps organizations achieve high service levels and operational efficiency while reducing costs, all within the approved budget plan. This organization-wide operating plan is agreed upon and adopted by senior management, culminating in the allocation of required resources to achieve the plan's objective.

6.1.1 Sales and Operations Plan

When developing a *sales and operations plan*, collaboration is key. Individual teams may have different motivations when managing the demand and supply of an organization. For example, a sales manager may over-forecast the products at a customer fulfillment location to achieve a higher service level or request frequent production schedule changes based on the order dynamics; on the other hand, an operations manager may want to run large batches to maximize production efficiency. The finance department may be aiming for achieving the budget plan with efficient working capital management. An effective sales and operations plan takes all of these objectives into account and harmonizes demand, supply, inventory, finance, and strategic plans into one common organizational plan. It's important to understand the concept of planning decisions categorized as strategic, tactical, and operational.

Strategic plans are performed at a high level to determine the organization's goals and objectives for a typical horizon of 3, 5, or even 10 years. The *tactical* plan is a set of specific medium-term plans that enable decision-making to align operations with strategy and guide short-term plans. These short-term plans are categorized as *operational* plans that are executed in the day-to-day operations of the organization. The sales and operations plan is typically a tactical plan for a time horizon of 3 to 18 months. In many cases, this horizon can be as long as 24-36 months . A sales and operations plan is managed in the time interval of weekly, monthly, and quarterly buckets. Normally, S&OP is performed at the aggregate level to align demand with supply and capacity.

A tactical sales and operations plan is guided by the long-term strategic plan and can also bi-directioanlly impact the strategic plan with recommended adjustments. For example, for a recurring product allocation or capacity overload, management may make the decision to increase supply or capacity through a new investment and influence the strategic plan. S&OP drives the short-term operational plan through disaggregation from a weekly to a daily level which drives operations, such as order execution, production runs, and warehouse activities.

A balanced sales and operations plan can result in a highly efficient operations plan as a result of fewer short-term variations. For example, poor planning of a sales promotion or a lack of visibility for a planned machine shutdown in the operations plan can lead to drastic changes in the short term, resulting in lower service levels and increased costs. On the other hand, if the promotion and machine availability were planned in advance in the sales and operations plan, fewer short-term adjstments will be required during the promotion period, resulting in an optimum demand and supply situation.

6.1.2 Benefits of Sales and Operations Planning

S&OP processes deliver multiple benefits to organizations. They improve forecast accuracy and efficiency of new product introduction, optimize customer service rates, and minimize the service costs. In comparison, a traditional silo-based planning approach has multiple issues that impact the profitability of an organization. Table 6.1 compares the organizational behavior and process implications in a silo planning approach to the well-orchestrated S&OP approach.

Business Area	Outcome in Traditional Silo Planning Approach	Outcome in Well-Managed S&OP Environment
Sales plan	▸ Missed targets ▸ Missed sales opportunity caused by product shortages ▸ Poor service rate	▸ Sales plan achievement ▸ High product availability ▸ Excellent service quality
Production plan	▸ Schedule breakage ▸ Missed production plan attainment ▸ Firefighting mode to meet sales expectations ▸ Low resource utilization	▸ Schedule optimization ▸ Lower changes to production schedule leading to higher resource utilization and low cost ▸ Production target achievement
Finance/budget plan	▸ High variance between budget and actual results ▸ Missed revenue targets ▸ Hard to make strategic investments	▸ Budget plan attainment ▸ Achievement of agreed and approved revenue targets ▸ Information and visibility to make strategic decisions

Table 6.1 Comparison of the Traditional Silo Approach with the S&OP Approach

Business Area	Outcome in Traditional Silo Planning Approach	Outcome in Well-Managed S&OP Environment
Product development	▸ Higher cost of development due to misaligned sales, marketing, production, and operations ▸ Missed launch date and missed revenue targets	▸ Optimized product development process resulting in efficiency and effectiveness ▸ Achievement of planned launch date and revenue targets
Inventory management	▸ Inventory shortage and excess issue ▸ Loss due to inventory write-off and poor working capital management	▸ Optimum level of inventory to meet the demand at lowest cost ▸ Higher profitability through efficient working capital management
Relationships in sales, marketing, operations, and finance departments	▸ Communication gaps, blame for missed targets of one team citing responsibility of others ▸ Different teams working on different plans and motivation	▸ Collaborated and integrated team working together on one common goal ▸ Aligned motivation and plans for sales, marketing, operations, and finance teams

Table 6.1 Comparison of the Traditional Silo Approach with the S&OP Approach (Cont.)

For example, consider the case of an organization in which different business units perform their own separate forecasting, operations is not involved in the demand-supply alignment process, and finance works independently on the budget plan. This scenario will lead to high forecast error, lower service levels, poor asset utilization, and a missed budget plan. On the other hand, efficient S&OP processes enhance the effectiveness of sales, operations, supply chain, and finance teams to maximize the revenue and profitability of the organization.

6.2 Balancing Demand and Supply through Sales and Operations Planning

SAP IBP for sales and operations is an ideal application to manage S&OP processes, which can be performed in a highly efficient, effective, and collaborative manner. This is done through capabilities such as automation, collaboration, task control, and analytics.

Traditional enterprise systems and legacy planning systems aren't well equipped to support an efficient S&OP process. Even organizations with well-established S&OP business processes may miss out on the opportunity for business value due to gaps in their system's capability such as lack of computational power or consistency across planning levels, manual/fragmented process management, and broken collaboration. SAP IBP for sales and operations addresses these issues with cutting-edge capabilities to implement and manage S&OP processes. This delivers maximum value to the organization through an optimized demand and supply plan.

The crucial capabilities of SAP IBP for sales and operations that are instrumental to effectively operate S&OP are shown in Figure 6.1.

Figure 6.1 Crucial Capabilities of SAP IBP for Sales and Operations

In this section, we'll walk through some of the capabilities and features of SAP IBP for sales and operations.

6.2.1 Complete Scalable Model

SAP IBP for sales and operations is powered by a unified demand, supply, and financial data model. This model is populated by detailed master and transactional data elements from the execution system and enables integrated demand, supply, and financial planning and analysis.

S&OP is typically performed at an aggregate level, above the base planning level. For example, product ID represents the base level of product data. Grouping multiple products at higher levels such as product family or product group consitutes an aggregate level. S&OP is also typically performed in weekly or monthly buckets. Demand and supply matching can be performed at the aggregated monthly, quarterly, or yearly level. SAP IBP for sales and operations provides the ability to perform planning at different levels of aggregation, across multiple time horizons. Roll-up to the aggregated planning level is a built-in capability of SAP IBP, as is disaggregation down to more detailed levels. Data consistency is maintained across the levels while rolling up and down.

Figure 6.2 shows an example of planning across levels. Selection or deselection of a level initatates the aggregation or disaggregation while maintaining data consistency. For example, if a product group consists of ten different products, selecting the product group at a particular level dynamically sums up the forecast for individual products within each planning period. Now consider this scenario for a mid- to large-size organization with thousands of SKUs, hundreds of customers, and dozens of manufacturing and fulfillment locations. Performing these functions on a local spreadsheet or older technology in a reasonable amont of time is nearly impossible—SAP IBP for sales and operations can perform them in a matter of seconds.

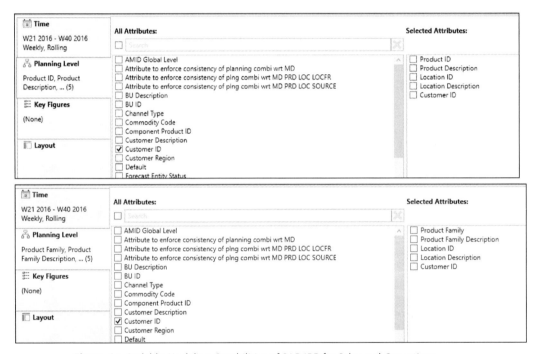

Figure 6.2 Scalable Modeling Capabilities of SAP IBP for Sales and Operations

Data updates and changes can be performed at different levels, and the system will take action to maintain the data consistency. For example, a forecast increase at the product family level will distribute the forecast down to the product level, while an increase at the product level will roll-up the forecast to the next level. This dynamic, scalable model supports decision making from the high-level executive analysis down to the lower level operations.

6.2.2 Scenario Planning

SAP IBP for sales and operation employs easy-to-use capabilities for real-time scenario planning. Because S&OP focuses on performing tactical planning to finalize the demand and supply plan, executing scenario planning with alternative scenarios is one of the most widely used and valuable features of the application. Users can, on the fly, create scenarios with real data to create alternatives, perform impact analysis, compare alternative scenarios, and promote a scenario as the final plan.

Scenario planning can cover a broad range of alternatives on decisions such as produce versus procure, enhancement of manufacturing capabilities, supply options for product allocation, promotion planning, new product introduction, and more.

Figure 6.3 demonstrates the scenario creation and management tool in SAP IBP. A *scenario* allows different values for the planning key figures and also helps in comparing them after execution of supply planning or other algorithms based on the assumptions in the scenario. Scenario functionality in SAP IBP also tracks the assumptions and changes to scenarios.

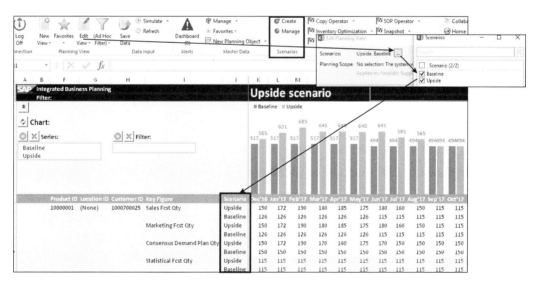

Figure 6.3 Scenario Review and Comparison

In this example, you can see how the SAP IBP Excel planning view shows the base planning data with the scenario data. You can choose the EDIT VIEW option to select the base data, a single scenario's data, multiple scenarios' data, or a combination of scenario data with base data. All the planning algorithms can be executed for the base as well as for multiple what-if planning scenarios. The results can be compared in one datasheet for identification of the best plan. With the click of a button, the best scenario can be promoted as the base plan for execution.

6.2.3 Collaboration

Considering that the most important word in any S&OP process is collaboration, SAP IBP for sales and operations has been enriched with very powerful collaboration features. SAP IBP provides multiple channels of collaboration, including planning views, data sharing, task assignments, information management, and decision-making processes. SAP IBP for sales and operations enhances collaboration among the S&OP process team members. Collaboration is widely used for the following elements:

▸ Process automation and control

▸ Planning collaboration

▸ Decision-making

▸ Information sharing

In the following sections, we'll look at each of these different applications in greater depth.

Process Automation and Control

The process automation and control feature in SAP IBP for sales and operations enables the collaboration between multiple teams to develop one plan. With SAP IBP, you no longer have to control and manage the processes through disconnected channels (emails, reminders, local sheets, etc.).

SAP IBP for sales and operations process modeling can be used to create multiple instances of the process. Multiple team members can be part of one process, and their responsibilities can be assigned and triggered through process automation. Because these processes are connected through the same database, SAP IBP provides real-time updates for every participant. Process modeling in SAP IBP is connected through the SAP Jam collaboration platform, which enhances its usability through dynamic information sharing.

Figure 6.4 shows an example of process modeling in SAP IBP for sales and operations. S&OP is represented as the integration of five different subprocesses with individual process and task owners. A *task* can be assigned to one or multiple persons who need to perform updates so that the next step can begin. The completion of the task in the tool updates everybody on the team and also starts the next related task. Considering that S&OP is a monthly and/or weekly process, process modeling is frequently used for managing the entire S&OP processes.

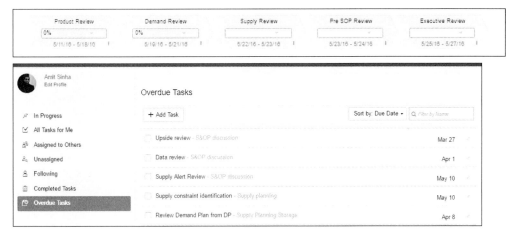

Figure 6.4 S&OP Process Modeling and Task Management

Planning Collaboration

A planner, while working on demand, supply, and inventory information, can share the planning views with colleagues and can request reviews and updates to the plan. The reviewer can update the plan and save the update to the base or scenario plan. They can also share unstructured feedback and recommendations via updates through SAP Jam.

Decision-Making

Many decisions are required to be made in a typical S&OP cycle. SAP IBP for sales and operations provides a channel to manage, track, and record these decisions in an easy-to-use and highly efficient manner. Decision-making can be supported by a formal process of *pool creation* or an informal process of *information sharing* and questions asked through group feeds that involve the team members required to make the decision.

Information Sharing

In addition to managing the feeds in SAP Jam, planning views are also integrated with the collaboration channel to maximize teamwork and transparency. The purpose behind an update in the planning view can be shared with the relevant group through the seamless integration of planning data and the collaboration channel.

6.2.4 Advanced Analytics

SAP IBP for sales and operations is supported through the advanced analytics applications of SAP IBP. Readily available and easily understandable analytics tables and charts support the organization's S&OP processes. These charts contain information regarding forecast error (location level, product group level, sales area level, etc.), profit projections, cost projections, capacity utilization percentages, and more. Relevant information is supported in multiple chart formats, and chart data can be controlled through the selection of planning objects and time periods. Figure 6.5 shows the chart types available in SAP IBP. We'll discuss this topic in detail in Chapter 14 and Chapter 15.

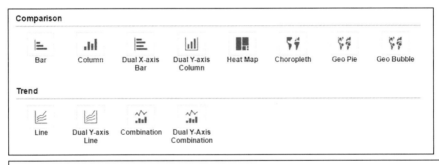

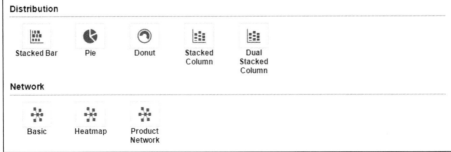

Figure 6.5 Chart Types in SAP IBP

6.2.5 Intuitive User Interface

SAP IBP technology interfaces with user groups through multiple channels and devices. SAP IBP for sales and operations has mobile capabilities and can be accessed through devices such as smartphones and tablets in addition to traditional desktops and laptop computers. This capability puts people, data, analytics, and collaboration together for finalizing the best sales and operations plan for the organization.

In this section, we looked at how SAP IBP for sales and operations helps to balance demand and supply planning processes. In the next section, we'll round out our discussion and look at the role SAP IBP plays in managing S&OP processes.

6.3 Managing Sales and Operations Planning Processes with SAP IBP

As previously discussed, S&OP includes a group of processes leading to the creation and finalization of a single demand and supply plan. Although these processes may have different names and levels of detail for different organizations, most organizations represent the processes as follows:

- Demand review
- Supply review
- Pre-S&OP meetings (or pre-S&OP review)
- Executive review

In this section, we'll look at each of these different processes and their associated tasks.

6.3.1 Demand Review

The objective of the *demand review* process is to generate an *unconstrained demand forecast* using the collective knowledge of the sales, marketing, finance, and demand planning teams. It utilizes the historical sales data, product lifecycle information, market intelligence, and the organization's financial plans to generate the unconstrained demand forecast. The demand review starts with the product review process and follows through steps to create and adjust the demand projections.

The following sections take an in-depth look at the subprocesses of a demand review.

Product Review

The *product review* process is based on identifying the relevant products and analyzing their market status through product lifecycle (PLC), new product introduction (NPI), and end of life (EOL) data. The product review process also analyzes the product development stages so that the lead time to launch the product can be factored in to the demand review. New product plans and the financial plan for new products, along with the current inventory, are provided as input for the forecast generation.

Demand Forecast

The *demand forecast* step is performed to generate the *base forecast*, which is based on historical sales data. When creating the demand projections, most organizations perform statistical modeling on the historical sales data to generate the forecast for the future. Sales data must be cleansed of any known outliers before being used as the input for statistical modeling. A sales promotion during last year may have increased the demand, or a natural calamity may have reduced the actual market demand; the impact of similar scenarios must be removed from the sales history before feeding this data to generate the forecast. SAP IBP for sales and operations can generate the forecast for the products through statistical modeling of historical data.

SAP IBP for demand contains additional features for generating a more accurate demand forecast and can be used to feed the demand forecast data to SAP IBP for sales and operations. Demand forecast models of SAP IBP for sales and operations are covered in Chapter 7, based on the system configuration, while the demand forecast generation in SAP IBP for demand is covered in Chapter 9.

Forecast Adjustment

The output of the demand forecast process is the base forecast, which can be analyzed at different aggregation levels in SAP IBP. The *forecast adjustment* step is dedicated to adjusting this forecast through market information and the organization's budget plan.

In SAP IBP for sales and operations, the forecast adjustment or override process can be divided into multiple subprocesses to be performed by different team members from the sales, marketing, finance, and supply chain groups. By using the highly flexible functionality of the SAP IBP planning views, a separate planning view can be created for the sales representatives at the sales rep, customer, and product level to analyze and adjust the monthly forecast. Any changes in the forecast quantity will be automatically aggregated and disaggregated through the planning levels. After completion of the sales representative forecast adjustment, the marketing team can further adjust the demand forecast based on planned events. Further adjustments or changes can be recommended by the finance team while reviewing the higher level demand plan alignment with the annual operating plan (AOP) of the organization.

Consensus Demand

The *consensus demand* plan step is performed to finalize the unconstrained demand forecast for the S&OP planning horizon. This finalization is achieved through consensus meetings led by the demand planner. Input for those discussions includes the updated plans from sales, marketing, supply chain, and finance as discussed in the previous section. An agreement is achieved on the most accurate representation of the market forecast for the organization. Completion of the demand review process is achieved with the unconstrained forecast as the end result. This can be analyzed at different levels of detail using the planning level and data aggregation/disaggregation functionality of SAP IBP for sales and operations. This agreed upon unconstrained forecast represents the demand plan of the organization for the supply review process.

6.3.2   Supply Review

The *supply review* aligns the overall supply plan with the unconstrained demand plan via rough-cut material and capacity planning. The review is performed through aggregated production, purchase, and transport capabilities of the organization.

Supply planning in S&OP is performed as an aggregated demand supply match to meet the required product demand through possible supply options of production, purchasing, inventory usage, and stock transfers.

The aim, input, and output of the supply review process are as follows:

▶ **Aim**
Meeting the demand by inventory, make, buy or delay strategies

▶ **Input**
  ▶ Unconstrained demand, production information, planning information (stock, lead time, procurement, and transportation information)
  ▶ Last month's performance, key performance indicator (KPI) review, and any action item

▶ **Output**
  ▶ Draft S&OP plan (constrained demand, supply, and inventory plan)
  ▶ Identified issues and opportunities in supply and inventory while aiming to plan for unconstrained demand plan

The goal of the supply review step is to determine the best possible supply option (or options) to meet the demand forecast. This step is performed when the draft sales and operations plan is created, which consists of the constrained demand plan, supply plan, and inventory plan. An organization meets the supply requirement through stock, production, or purchase scenarios. Figure 6.6 shows the input factors for creating the supply plan. SAP IBP for sales and operations models the input parameters and suggests the best supply option to meet the demand forecast.

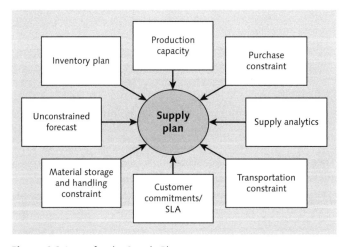

Figure 6.6 Input for the Supply Plan

Input parameters and their modeling in SAP IBP for sales and operations can be categorized as follows:

► **Unconstrained forecast**
Unconstrained forecast, finalized in the demand review step, is the major input for the supply plan. Due to the native integration of the planning model in SAP IBP, the unconstrained forecast is available in the supply planning model without any forecast release step or any further data transfer job.

► **Inventory plan**
Supply against demand forecast can be achieved through the available inventory of the finished product (for make-to-stock materials) or assembly or processing of the available stock of components (for make-to-order materials). The inventory plan influences the working capital of the organization and is impacted by the target service level, demand deviation, and forecast accuracy. SAP IBP for sales and operations is integrated with the execution system and has access to updated inventory levels which need to be considered while creating the supply plan.

► **Production capacity**
Most organizations have a finite production capacity, which determines the maximum output in a period (e.g., weekly, monthly, etc.). The production capacity of an organization is captured at the aggregated supply data for bottleneck resources in SAP IBP for sales and operations. The supply planning algorithms available in SAP IBP for sales and operations include the *heuristic* and *optimizer* algorithms:

  ► Heuristic algorithm: Creates the supply against the demand without considering any constraints; however, the result is available for review, and adjustments can be made through resource loading data. For example, a heuristic output can have the capacity loaded by more than 100% in a particular time period. Planners are alerted through the multiple exception handling features of SAP IBP and can take action to achieve a feasible supply plan and constrained forecast.

  ► Optimizer algorithm: Considers the supply capacity as a hard constraint with respect to the available capacity to produce. The planning output aims to maximize the profits for an organization while fulfilling the constraint. Any extra demand will be left unfulfilled.

▶ **Purchase constraint**
Supply constraints through procurement are mostly due to the purchase lead time and capacity of the supplier. Other constraints, like procurement, lot size, and periodicity are also possible. These limitations are mapped into SAP IBP for sales and operations so that the supply planning output considers these limitations while generating the supply plans.

▶ **Material storage and handling constraint**
Warehouse storage capacity and material handling capacity are mapped into the SAP IBP for sales and operations system for consideration while creating the supply plan.

▶ **Transportation capacity**
Transportation capability of an organization along with the capability and flexibility of the logistics partners can be considered in performing the feasible supply review for S&OP processes.

▶ **Customer commitments**
There may be some hard customer commitments or service level agreements (SLAs) for an organization, which must be considered in the supply plan when matching and generating supply against the unconstrained demand forecast.

▶ **Supply analytics**
SAP IBP for sales and operations generates the supply plan through a planning algorithm and available master data for the constraints. This supply plan algorithm needs to be adjusted and reviewed to identify the best possible option to meet the demand. To facilitate this analysis in the most efficient manner, you can use the analytics application of SAP IBP. Last month's performance data, action items, and relevant KPIs are available to the S&OP group members while creating the supply plans.

The supply review process is aimed at generating the rough-cut supply plan while checking the aggregate-level supply constraints. SAP IBP for sales and operations contains the resource data for planning against these constraints. SAP IBP contains multi-level bill of materials (BOMs) for in-house produced materials. The supply planning algorithm of SAP IBP explodes the material BOM to identify the dependent demand of the components and consider the lead time and any other planning constraints (lot size, safety stock, etc.) for the supply plan.

For the supply review process in SAP IBP for sales and operations, a supply planning run is executed with the supply data for inventory, purchase, production, material storage, and physical movement. The planning results are readily available in the system for review and further analysis.

In some cases, meeting the total unconstrained forecast may lead to overloading of resources (more than 100% of the capacity) or result in under-utilization for a particular time period. These cases require scenario analysis with an aim to maximize the profit potential. For example, an in-house product can be considered for procurement or an extra manufacturing shift can be planned in case of a mismatch where the unconstrained forecast can't be met through available capacity. On the other hand, in the event of under-utilization, a promotion can be considered to increase the demand of the product, which will result in the optimum loading of resources. SAP IBP for sales and operations provides an excellent scenario mapping functionality to perform the supply analysis. Different scenarios can be created on the fly and can be compared together for the cost and profit data.

The output of the supply review step is supply planning options with the analysis of the projected profit, replenishment percentage, constrained forecast, and issues and actions for different scenarios. The constrained demand forecast, along with the supply scenarios, comprise the draft sales and operations plan. The draft sales and operations plan is the input for the next step of the S&OP process called the pre-S&OP review.

6.3.3 Pre-Sales and Operations Planning Review

The *pre-S&OP review* step provides the first opportunity to compare the holistic demand, supply, and finance plan to the functional plans in previous steps in order to agree on a consensus plan. The draft sales and operations plan are discussed with representatives from sales, marketing, supply chain, operations, and finance to agree on the best option to present as the proposed plan for management review and approval. SAP IBP for sales and operations models the proposed S&OP plan and potential options to demonstrate the demand, supply and financial impact of different assumptions. Through dynamic scenario modeling, easily accessible analytics, and the SAP Jam collaboration platform, SAP IBP for sales and operations makes this step highly effective and efficient.

For scenario review and analysis, in the pre-S&OP step, the unconstrained demand and supply options are combined with insight from members of various teams to determine the best possible option. Because S&OP is a periodic process, a course correction is performed for plans through updated information and insight available during the current month's S&OP cycle. The built-in capabilities of *currency conversion* and *unit of measure conversion* are useful when generating and reviewing the sales and operations plan of an organization operating in multiple geographies using different currencies and units of measure to operate the business.

The collaboration capabilities of SAP IBP for sales and operations are widely utilized for the pre-S&OP review step. Discussion groups for the pre-S&OP step can be created in SAP Jam, and the collaboration can be performed through the live discussion, information sharing, document upload, and decision-making tools. Because the planning view updates are integrated with the collaboration feed, comparison sheets and plan updates can be shared with the entire group through feed messages. Proposed sales and operations plans can also have alternatives. In a short supply scenario, the pre-S&OP review can lead to two possible constrained demand plans resulting in either product allocation or a supply increase. A supply increase decision may have a strategic impact and require approval from managers and executives.

The output of the pre-S&OP process is the identification of the best demand and supply plan finalized through collaboration across different teams. This recommended plan is now ready for executive review and approval.

6.3.4 Executive Review

In the *executive review* step, the proposed sales and operations plan options are reviewed along with related issues and escalations to identify, finalize, and approve the best plan for the organization. The *committed sales and operations plan* contains the constrained demand plan, supply plan, and inventory plan for the S&OP horizon. Decisions on the committed plan are taken after analyzing the issues and opportunities as presented through the base plan and any other scenario comparison in SAP IBP for sales and operations.

The executive dashboard in SAP IBP provides the appropriate tools for executives to make a strategic decision when reviewing demand, supply, inventory, and financial plans.

Figure 6.7 shows an example of the executive dashboard in SAP IBP for sales and operations. This dashboard is presented with the current status of the S&OP

process, planning views, and performance indicators. The dashboard a highly customizable view and can be generated with the required information and analytics per the requirements of a particular organization's S&OP process and key factors. Analytics and the dashboard are covered in detail in Chapter 15.

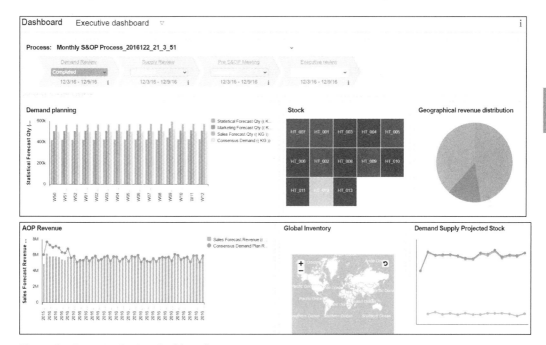

Figure 6.7 Executive Review Dashboard

Key decisions are made in the executive review process to identify the best way to meet the customer demand in conjunction with supply optimization and profit maximization. These decisions result in the committed sales and operations plan for the organization and provide one common set of numbers for demand and supply.

6.4 Summary

This chapter provided the details of business processes that constitute S&OP, and discussed the importance of the S&OP process to an organization. We also reviewed the capabilities of SAP IBP for sales and operation to manage, automate, and optimize the S&OP process. In the next chapter, we dive into the details of the configuration and usage of SAP IBP for managing the sales and operations process.

An organization implementing SAP IBP for sales and operations requires a system based on its business requirements, supply chain structure, and IT landscape. This chapter discusses the building and configuration of SAP IBP for sales and operations.

7   Implementing SAP IBP for Sales and Operations

The sales and operations planning (S&OP) process is the combination of demand consensus, supply planning, and matching aggregated demand with supply to identify and approve an organization-wide plan. This process is automated, supported, and organized within the application of SAP Integrated Business Planning (SAP IBP). A planning model is built and activated within SAP IBP for sales and operations. The first section of this chapter illustrates the steps you need to take to build the planning model. We then discuss the S&OP algorithms for demand and supply planning. We end the chapter by covering the planning views, alerts, and collaboration process for S&OP processes in SAP IBP.

7.1   Managing Master Data for Sales and Operations Planning

SAP IBP for sales and operations requires master data types and attributes that together define the entities of the supply chain network and product flow processes. (See Chapter 3 for detailed information on the master data elements relevant for S&OP.) In the standard model provided by SAP, there are two relevant planning areas applicable to S&OP in SAP IBP:

- ▶ **SAP2**
  This planning area is devoted to the S&OP process.

- ▶ **SAPIBP1**
  This unified planning area contains the objects applicable to S&OP in addition

to the objects for other planning processes like demand, supply, and inventory planning.

Figure 7.1 shows an example of a supply chain network. The network consists of suppliers (SP1 and SP2), a manufacturing plant (PL1), distribution centers (DC1 and DC2), and customers (C1, C2, and C3). Finished goods PR1 and PR2 are produced at the manufacturing location, stored at distribution centers, and from there supplied to customers. Finished materials PR1 and PR2 are manufactured at machine RES1 by using the components CP1, CP2, and CP3, provided by the suppliers. This network can be built in SAP IBP by creating the master data types and planning levels, and then assigning the key figures to perform the planning.

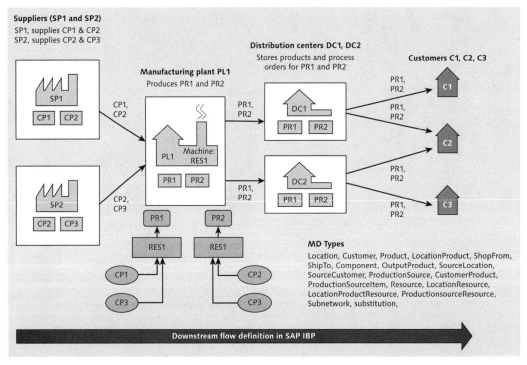

Figure 7.1 Representative Supply Chain Network Containing Master Data Types in SAP IBP for Sales and Operations

Demand for products PR1 and PR2 can be statistically forecasted by using the sales history for customers C1, C2, and C3. Through the demand review process, sales, marketing, finance, and supply chain teams agree on the demand plan and consider this as consensus demand. A supply planning algorithm is executed to plan the fulfillment taking into consideration the customer sourcing rule, location sourcing rule, and production requirements of finished materials and components. Requirement date and quantity of the demand determines the volume and dates of production, purchase, and stock transfer activities. The supply plan created by SAP IBP is reviewed and finalized for further analysis in the S&OP process. The output of the S&OP process in this example will then be finalized and approved mid-term as the demand and supply plan for products PR1, PR2, CP1, CP2, and CP3 to the customers (C1, C2, and C3). This plan has been generated by considering the network and resources of the organization as represented in Figure 7.1. A real supply chain network of even a small organization is much more complex than the illustrated example. However, a complex network is made of multiple simple units as explained here. Planning for a complex network is an extension of planning the simplified example.

Network structure and product flow are mapped to the master data types mentioned in Figure 7.1. The following summarizes the most important master data types in S&OP:

▶ **Location**
Maps the supplier, manufacturing, or packaging location, and any other internal location for material storage and movement.

▶ **Customer**
Maps the customers or customer groups relevant for S&OP.

▶ **Product**
Product scope for S&OP.

▶ **Location/product**
Product extended to locations for planning usage.

▶ **Customer/products**
Products extended to customer or customer group locations for S&OP.

▶ **Ship-from location and ship-to location**
Reference master data of location to map the shipping and replenishment locations.

▶ **Component and output product**
Reference master data of product to map the input component and output material of a bill of material (BOM).

▸ **Source location**
Replenishment rule for a product at a replenishment location with information on the supplying location. Sourcing rule, quota, and lot size parameters are used in the supply calculation.

  ▸ The source of supply rules are as follows:

   – Transportation (represented by T): If supplied from another location in the network.

   – Production (represented by P): If material is produced in-house, production data for the BOM and resource usage will be required.

   – Customer (represented by C): For a material to be supplied to a customer.

   – Unspecified (represented by U): Unknown supply source, accounts for the end of the network. For example, a component provided by a supplier is denoted by a "T" rule at the manufacturing location and by a "U" rule at the vendor location denoting end of network.

  ▸ Ratio of quota information: If a product can be provided by multiple supply locations (product CP2 at the PL1 location in Figure 7.1), the percentage quota adds up to 100 for the sourcing rule.

  ▸ Lot size information: Quantities in which a product must be produced to minimize set-up costs or other factors. Lot size controls the order quantities for production, purchase, and stock transfer. A lot for lot strategy matches the demand and supply quantity in an order, though a fixed lot, minimum lot, maximum lot along with rounding value provides the opportunity to plan further level of order quantities.

▸ **Source customer**
Product flow to the customer or customer group.

▸ **Production source**
Output material, source ID (BOM ID), and output quantity.

▸ **Production source item**
Source ID with the component materials and quantity for output quantities maintained in the production source.

▸ **Resource and resource/location**
Manufacturing, packaging, or other machines with availability information.

▸ **Location/product/resource**
Product association at the manufacturing plant with the resource used for manufacturing.

▸ **Production source/resource**
Production output quantity and resource unit requirement.

▸ **Subnetwork**
Divides the supply chain network into smaller subsets.

▸ **Product substitution**
For the product substitution rule.

Some of the attributes used in the master data types of S&OP can be categorized as time relevant and must be converted to key figures using the ATTRIBUTE AS KEY FIGURE functionality in SAP IBP. An attribute is converted into key figure by accessing the planning area screen through the MODEL CONFIGURATION tile. On this screen, the attribute in the master data group is accessed and you then select the KEY FIGURE checkbox. For example, for a time varying quota (supply quota for an internal location or quota for the customer) or a time varying component, usage in a BOM can be mapped with different values in different horizons by using a key figure for the attribute.

Upstream and downstream product flow directions are used in the SAP IBP network model. Downstream relates to the product flow from the supplier to an organization's locations to customers as shown previously in Figure 7.1. The product flow in the downstream direction is represented with some of the standard key figures in SAP models with the names added as downstream. Note this distinction, as this downstream definition can be opposite to the flow discussed in some of the standard textbooks on supply chain management. Understanding this representation in SAP IBP will avoid any possible confusion.

7.2 Building and Activating Sales and Operations Planning Models

After defining the master data type, you must generate the time profile and planning level for the S&OP model in SAP IBP. Key figures at different planning levels in SAP IBP models are used for performing S&OP. Planning area activation and proper operator settings prepare the SAP IBP planning model for data load and S&OP processes. See Chapter 4 and Chapter 5 on model configuration for details about the planning model objects. The following most important objects for the S&OP model will be discussed in the following sections:

▸ Time profile and planning level

▸ Key figures

▸ Planning area activation and related settings

7.2.1 Time Profile and Planning Level

Typical time buckets for S&OP can be week, month, or quarter. The daily bucket is normally not applicable for S&OP, as it's a mid-term operational planning process. Planning levels for S&OP are based on the key figures that will be used for the demand planning, supply planning, and collaboration. Table 7.1 contains the planning levels used in the standard S&OP model in SAP IBP.

Planning Level	Planning Level Name	Usage Example
PER	Period	Period-relevant calculation to identify past, present, and future periods
PERPROD	Period/product	For cost information and revenue data usage
PERPRODLOC	Period/product/location	For most of the demand, supply, and inventory information
PERPRODCUST	Period/product/customer	For customer price, revenue, and demand data
PERLOCRES	Period/location/resource	For a resource and its capacity information
PERPRODCUSTCURR	Period/product/customer/currency	Cost- and revenue-related data in the S&OP plan
PERPRODCUSTCURRCURRTO	Period/product/customer/currency/currency to	For generating and reviewing the plan in one monetary unit by using the currency conversion parameter
PERPRODFML	Period/product family	For plan and review at the aggregated product family level
PERPRODFMLCUST	Period/product family/customer	For forecasting the product family at a customer

Table 7.1 Planning Level Examples for SAP IBP for Sales and Operations

Planning Level	Planning Level Name	Usage Example
PERPRODFMLCUSTRGN	Period/product family/customer region	For aggregate planning at the product family and customer region levels
PERPRODLOCLOCFR	Period/product/ location/location from	For sourcing location information of a product at the replenished location
PERPRODLOCRES	Period/product/ location/resource	For product, location, and associated resource used for production or packaging
PERPRODLOCSRC	Period/product/ location/source	For component information to create a product at a location
PERPRODUOM	Period/product/ unit of measure	Assigning a unit of measure for relevant objects
PERPRODUOMUOMTO	Period/product/ unit of measure/ unit of measure to	For performing calculations for unit of measure changes so that the plan can be generated in one unit of measure

Table 7.1 Planning Level Examples for SAP IBP for Sales and Operations (Cont.)

The planning levels listed in Table 7.1 are used for defining the S&OP key figures.

7.2.2 Key Figures

The key figures used for performing S&OP in SAP IBP can be categorized by their usage nature and characteristics, as follows:

- **Input key figures to the planning algorithms**
  These are the key figures used in the demand or supply planning algorithms of SAP IBP for sales and operations. Examples include the consensus demand and the sales history, which are input key figures for supply heuristics and demand forecasting, respectively. Some adjusted key figures are used in SAP IBP for the S&OP model, for which a nonzero value is considered as a fixed value for the input or output of planning algorithms. Hence, if a value is maintained for an adjusted customer receipt key figure for a combination of period/product/ location/customer, this value is considered a fixed value for supply planning. An adjusted key figure can behave differently for different supply planning

algorithms such as heuristic and optimizer. For example, the adjusted demand key figure for a combination of period/product/location is considered a fixed value of the dependent demand of the product through heuristics, although the same isn't fixed for the supply optimizer algorithm.

▸ **Output key figures of the planning algorithm**
Demand and supply planning algorithms in SAP IBP for sales and operations generate planning results through multiple key figures. For example, dependent location demand for a product at a location shows the demand in a period calculated by the supply planning for a product at a location supplied from a ship-from location. Dependent demand is a key figure generated at the period/product/location level (without having a ship-from location as a planning level) as the sum of all the dependent demand (dependent customer demand, dependent location demand, and dependent production demand).

▸ **Collaboration or update key figures**
Normally, multiple key figures are required to support teamwork and cooperation. Sales and marketing professionals may require updated key figures for their team. This case may be true for finance and supply chain teams too. Consider the example of consensus forecast generation through the demand review process. A statistical forecast can be the output of the demand plan algorithm, and the key figures assigned to sales, marketing, finance, and supply chain teams can be used for the logic of generating the consensus demand plan.

▸ **Master data attributes as key figure**
As discussed in the previous section, master data attributes such as location sourcing ratio can be configured and used as key figures for time-varying values of these attributes.

▸ **Information key figures**
Information from other systems can be integrated with SAP IBP for the S&OP model. Up-to-date information can be used for updating the sales and operations plan. Examples include key figures such as supplier commitment and blocked stock. These aren't the direct input or output for the supply planning algorithms, but their visibility can help with the decision-making processes.

▸ **Calculation key figures**
Calculation key figures can be used by the system to perform the demand-supply planning algorithms, or they can be defined by the users for alert calculations. Projected inventory is an example of a system-generated key figure based on the total demand and total supply situation of a location/product combination.

▶ **Downstream and upstream key figures**
Usage of downstream and upstream key figures in SAP IBP helps with representing the product flow in downstream and upstream directions as discussed in Section 7.1.

▶ **Supply and receipt key figures**
Using supply and receipt key figures is important, and the terminology usage can confuse planners. In SAP IBP terms, a receipt represents a quantity that will be received at the location from another location; the supply is the sum of all the quantities that leaves a location to go to other sites.

Key figures relevant for business users and system configurators are listed in Table 7.2.

Key Figure	Technical Name	Usage
Actuals quantity	ACTUALSQTY	For actual historical data
Adjusted actuals quantity	ADJUSTEDACTUALSQTY	For performing any adjustment before using the statistical model for generating a forecast
Statistical forecast quantity	STATISTICALFCSTQTY	Statistical forecast value as generated from the SAP IBP model or for importing data from other systems generating forecasts
Sales forecast quantity	SALESFCSTQTY	For taking adjustment from the sales team
Promotion forecast quantity	PROMOTIONFCSTQTY	For adding promotion impact
Marketing forecast quantity	MARKETINGFCSTQTY	For collaboration with the marketing team
AOP quantity	AOPQTY	For mapping the annual operating plan (AOP) quantity
Demand planning quantity	DEMANDPLANNING-QTY	For adjustments by the demand planner
Consensus demand quantity	CONSENSUSDEMAND	Finalized demand plan through demand review collaboration for input to supply planning

Table 7.2 Key Figures Relevant for Business Users and System Configurators

Key Figure	Technical Name	Usage
Component coefficient	COMPONENT-COEFFICIENT	Time-varying component requirement for producing output material defined in a BOM or source ID
Production sourcing quota	PRODUCTIONRATIO	For assigning a time-based quota if multiple source IDs exist for producing a material
Location sourcing ratio	LOCATIONRATIO	For assigning a time-based quota for external receipt of a product at a location from another location
Customer sourcing ratio	CUSTOMERRATIO	Time-based quota for supplying materials to customers from the organization's locations
Exchange rate	EXCHANGERATE	Exchange rate value for currency conversion
Cost per unit	COSTPERUNIT	Product cost at a location, normally an imported value in SAP IBP
Fixed transportation cost	FIXEDTRANSPORTA-TIONCOST	Fixed cost rate for a product at a location to get it transported to another location
Transportation cost rate	TRANSPORTATION-COSTRATE	Variable cost rate at the period/product/location/location from level
Inventory on hand	INITIALINVENTORY	Inventory available in current period
Target inventory	INVENTORYTARGET	Target for supply planning, considering inventory optimization calculation
Dependent customer demand quantity	DEPENDENT-CUSTOMERDEMAND	Demand at a location for a product from a customer as calculated from supply planning algorithms following master data and independent demand key figures
Dependent production demand quantity	DEPENDENT-PRODUCTIONDEMAND	Demand calculated by supply planning for component requirements for production
Dependent location demand quantity	DEPENDENT-LOCATIONDEMAND	Demand of a product at a location from another location as calculated by supply

Table 7.2 Key Figures Relevant for Business Users and System Configurators (Cont.)

Key Figure	Technical Name	Usage
Dependent demand quantity	DEPENDENTDEMAND	Total demand for a product in a period at a location considering dependent customer demand, dependent production demand, and dependent location demand
Net demand quantity	NETDEMAND	Net requirement calculated by the supply planning after netting total demand, total existing receipt, inventory target, and initial stock on hand
Available resource capacity	CAPASUPPLY	Available capacity of a resource
Capacity requirement	CAPADEMAND	Required capacity of a resource as calculated by supply planning to meet the requirements
Capacity consumption	CAPACONSUMPTION	Capacity consumption of the resource with the current orders
Production receipt quantity	PRODUCTION	Proposed production calculated by the supply planning algorithm
Adjusted production quantity	ADJUSTED-PRODUCTION	Production receipt quantity as adjusted by the planner
External receipt quantity	RECEIPT	Receipt quantity at a location from other locations
Adjusted external receipt quantity	ADJUSTEDRECEIPT	External receipt quantity as adjusted by the planner
Total receipt	TOTALRECEIPT	Sum of all the receipt quantities for a product at a location
Constrained demand	CONSTRAINED-DEMAND	Constrained demand plan quantity as an output by supply planning at the period/product/location/customer level
Adjusted constrained demand	ADJUSTEDCON-STRAINEDDEMAND	Manual adjustment to the constrained demand quantity
Total constrained demand	TOTALCONSTRAINED-DEMAND	Total constrained demand quantity for a product in a period for a customer without replenishment location reference; used by supply planning uses with customer sourcing ratio to propagate the demand in the network

Table 7.2 Key Figures Relevant for Business Users and System Configurators (Cont.)

Key Figure	Technical Name	Usage
Projected inventory quantity	PROJECTEDINVENTORY	Projected inventory for a product in a period at a location by considering total demand and total receipt elements; system configuration possible to either consider or ignore the shortage in the last period

Table 7.2 Key Figures Relevant for Business Users and System Configurators (Cont.)

Note that the key figures discussed here represent a subset of the key figures in SAP IBP for sales and operations. For the detailed list, you can refer to standard planning model SAP2 of SAP IBP.

7.2.3 Planning Area Activation and Related Settings

The planning area for your SAP IBP for sales and operations model can be created from scratch or by copying the standard SAP planning area. The standard SAP planning areas that can be used for copying to create a baseline customer-specific S&OP area are SAP2 and SAPIBP1. We recommend you copy the standard planning area and then edit it following your organization's solution design. Whether you choose SAP2 or SAPIBP1 will be based on the planning solution scope in SAP IBP. If other planning modules such as demand, inventory, or supply are also in the planning scope of SAP IBP, then choose the unified planning area. However, if only S&OP and SAP Supply Chain Control Tower are in your scope, then the SAP2 planning area can be the base for the planning model.

You should consider using the standard SAP planning area SAP74 as the reference to create the planning model if both time series and order series planning models are in scope. Note that any of the standard planning area copies can be extended to enhance the solution to include other planning processes. Hence, the solution design and configuration of SAP IBP isn't restrictive in nature; it can be extended with time, business requirement change, organization maturity, and growth.

After adding the elements of master data type, time profile, planning level, and key figures, activation of time profile and master data is performed. Demand forecast generation and supply plan generation can be in the scope of the S&OP modeled by SAP IBP. The respective planning operator must be created and added in the planning area to perform these operations.

Operators that need to be created and added in the planning area per the solution scope are as follows:

- **Statistical forecasting: IBPFORECAST**
  Required to perform statistical forecast modeling. Available forecast algorithms are based on licensing of S&OP and licensing of SAP IBP for the demand solution.

- **S&OP heuristic: INFINITE-WITHOUT-SHORTAGE**
  Required to use the supply planning heuristic in the planning area.

- **S&OP optimizer: OPTIMIZE**
  Required to perform finite cost or profit optimized supply planning.

- **Quota calculation: COMPUTE-RATIOS**
  Required to generate a quota from the system through the optimized supply plan.

- **Local update: LOCAL**
  Required to locally analyze the impact of change on some of the key figures.

- **Check network heuristics: CHECK_MODE**
  Required to perform the planning run to check the data consistency across the supply chain and report the issues without changing any number.

With an active time profile, active master data types, and the correctly assigned planning operators, the planning area for your SAP IBP for sales and operations model is activated. See Chapter 4 and Chapter 5 for detailed steps for system build and data load.

7.3 Demand and Supply Planning for Sales and Operations Planning

S&OP also contains functionality related to demand review and supply review. SAP IBP for sales and operation can be used to map the demand review and supply review processes. Detailed configuration and application of the system are discussed in the following sections.

7.3.1 Demand Review Process Configuration

The demand review business process consists of generating a baseline forecast through statistical modeling and then leveraging the team's collaboration to finalize the demand plan known as the consensus demand plan. The SAP IBP system is used for mapping and automating both of these processes.

The statistical forecast quantity is generated in SAP IBP using actual history data as input, performing any data-cleansing activity and then executing the statistical model to generate the forecast value. SAP IBP is a highly sophisticated tool for generating the statistical forecast quantity. Although most of the advanced capabilities of preprocessing, forecast modeling, and post-processing are provided to users through the SAP IBP for demand license, SAP IBP for sales and operations includes basic statistical forecasting; advanced analytical forecasting capabilities are under the license of SAP IBP for demand.

> **Note**
>
> See Chapter 8 and Chapter 9 to learn how to use the SAP IBP demand planning solution. In particular, Section 8.3, Section 8.4, and Section 8.5 will provide a broader understanding of many of the concepts mentioned in this section.

We can compare the statistical forecasting capabilities in the demand module (advanced) and S&OP module (basic) as follows:

- Advanced statistical forecasting scope through SAP IBP for demand:
  - Preprocessing: Multiple methods for historical data cleaning.
  - Forecasting model: Wide variety of forecasting models with an option to automatically select the best method.
  - Post-processing: Multiple forecast error calculation algorithms and their applications.
- Basic statistical forecasting scope through SAP IBP for sales and operations:
  - Pre-processing: No system capability, only manual cleaning and adjustment of data.
  - Forecasting model: Limited forecasting models—moving average, single exponential smoothing, double exponential smoothing, triple exponential smoothing. Triple exponential smoothing can generate a forecast for a data set with level, trend, and seasonality behavior.
  - Post-processing: Only root mean square error (RMSE) forecast errors are available.

Note that the configuration for the forecasting model is controlled through the same objects, irrespective of whether you're using SAP IBP for demand or SAP IBP for sales and operations. The solution scope available to a client is entirely dependent on the product license (SAP IBP for demand, SAP IBP for sales and operation, or both) purchased by the organization. For a small organization with limited locations or products, the forecasting model provided in the S&OP solution can be a good fit; however, for a medium or large organization with multiple locations and a wide product range, forecast modeling through SAP IBP for demand may be a better fit.

7.3.2 Supply Review Process Configuration

The supply review process in SAP IBP uses a supply planning algorithm to generate the supply plan against the demand plan, followed by analysis and collaboration. Supply plan algorithms in SAP IBP for sales and operations are used for checking the network consistency and creating a supply plan considering the demand, the master data, and the value of key figures in the system. Algorithms are provided in the system as planning operators and can be accessed through the MODEL CONFIGURATION tile. Supply planning algorithms are grouped under the heading SCM (S&OP OPERATOR).

Figure 7.2 shows the navigation example from the system to access planning operators. Operators are accessed through the MANAGE PLANNING OPERATORS option under MISCELLANEOUS SETTINGS on the MODEL CONFIGURATION page. To create a supply planning operator for use in the planning area, access the group SCM, and create a new operator by clicking the + button. The planning operator ID will be assigned by the system, and you'll need to provide the operator NAME and DESCRIPTION. By selecting the INTERACTIVE MODE, BATCH MODE, and FILTER MODE checkboxes, you can determine the execution of the batch job and possibility of using a filter. Parameters for the planning operator are defined by clicking the DEFINE PARAMETERS option. The ALGORITHM_TYPE parameter determines the nature of the planning operator. For heuristic planning, the algorithm type INFINITE_WITHOUT_SHORTAGE is selected, as displayed in Figure 7.2. The SAVE button at the top right side is used for saving the created operator. The operator must be assigned to the planning area to make it available in the SAP IBP planning model.

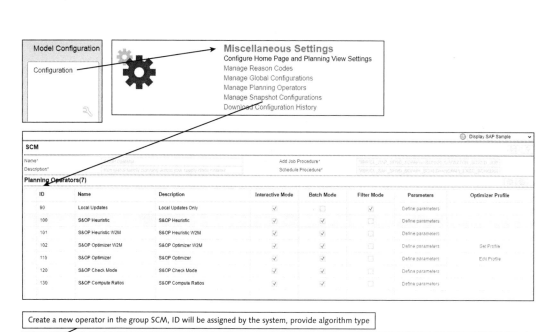

Figure 7.2 Operators in SAP IBP for Sales and Operations

The standard system algorithm types for the supply plan algorithms are as follows:

▶ **S&OP heuristic (INFINITE_WITHOUT_SHORTAGE)**
S&OP heuristic creates an infinite demand and supply plan for the product flow in the supply chain network without considering the resource capacity. In addition to not checking the resource capacity, it also doesn't consider the maximum values assigned to the stock level and production receipt. Projected inventory at a location after the S&OP heuristic can become negative because the material availability isn't checked by the system at the source location while meeting the demand at the destination location. As such, the supply plan created by the heuristic may be infeasible.

S&OP heuristic supply plan is widely useful in managing S&OP, even though it generates an infeasible plan. Value addition is based on the end-to-end visibility of possible issues in fulfilling the requirements finalized through the consensus demand process. Overutilization of resources, material shortages, and other exceptions are available for planners to review through alerts and planning views for taking the action to match demand with supply.

Although the S&OP heuristic doesn't consider the resource constraints and maximum value constraints as discussed previously, it does consider some of the constraints in the supply chain network as follows:

- Lead time maintained in the source of supply
- Manual adjustments (adjustments to key figure values by the planner is considered a hard constraint by the S&OP heuristic)
- Lot size policy and parameters, lot size value, and rounding value
- Quota distribution
- Minimum receipt key figure values

This constraint can result in shortages or excess inventory in the supply chain network; the exceptions can again be flagged in the SAP IBP system through alerts and analytics.

The S&OP heuristic works through demand propagation across the network. If demand is provided at the customer level, it is moved to the supply location through the master data source customer, and then on to the relevant production locations and suppliers through master data maintained for source location and source production. Based on the demand, available on-hand inventory, and available receipts in the system, the heuristic creates the net demand values for the products at a location that is required to be replenished by supply. The net demand value is supplied by production, purchasing, and transportation based on the master data and supply chain network modeled in SAP IBP. Projected inventory at a location is the net value of receipts and demands in a period. Through standard planning operator behavior, a shortage in the last time bucket isn't carried forward to the next bucket; hence, a shortage quantity in the last period doesn't impact the projected inventory for the current period. However, this behavior can be modified by using another parameter for carrying negative projected inventory (`CARRY_OVER_NEGATIVE_PROJECTEDINVENTORY`) and assigning the value of this parameter to `yes`.

- **S&OP optimizer (OPTIMIZE)**
  S&OP optimizer creates a finite optimized supply plan. Supply plan optimization is performed using cost minimization to achieve profit maximization or delivery maximization while meeting the customer demand. This is achieved by modeling the demand, supply, and cost functions through the mixed integer linear programming (MILP) method.

  S&OP optimizer can be modeled for either profit maximization or delivery maximization in the supply chain network. The supply optimization solution is highly data intensive; it requires multiple data sets to be able to create an optimized supply plan. Cost modeling of the S&OP optimizer in SAP IBP can be carried out either by assigning the values of the cost key figures or by using time-independent penalty costs. Cost modeling through key figures is done by providing the values of fixed and variable rates for customer transport, production, external receipt, and internal transport. The non-delivery cost rate can be provided to either map actual non-delivery costs or to maintain the system to minimize non-delivery. In the case of non-availability of detailed cost data through key figures, the relative penalty cost in the optimization profile can be used to optimize the supply.

Factors for the S&OP supply heuristic are provided through the optimizer profile maintenance in the planning operator screen. Figure 7.3 and Figure 7.4 show the configuration values for the S&OP optimization profile. The settings in different groups control the optimization calculation.

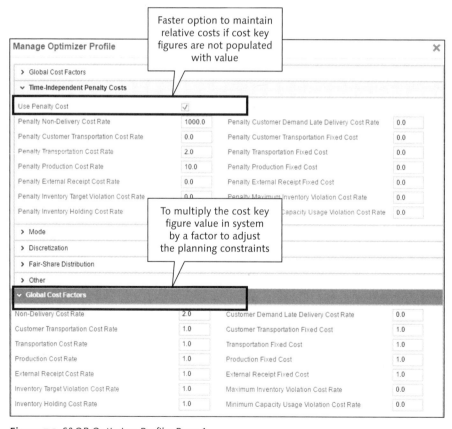

Figure 7.3 S&OP Optimizer Profile: Page 1

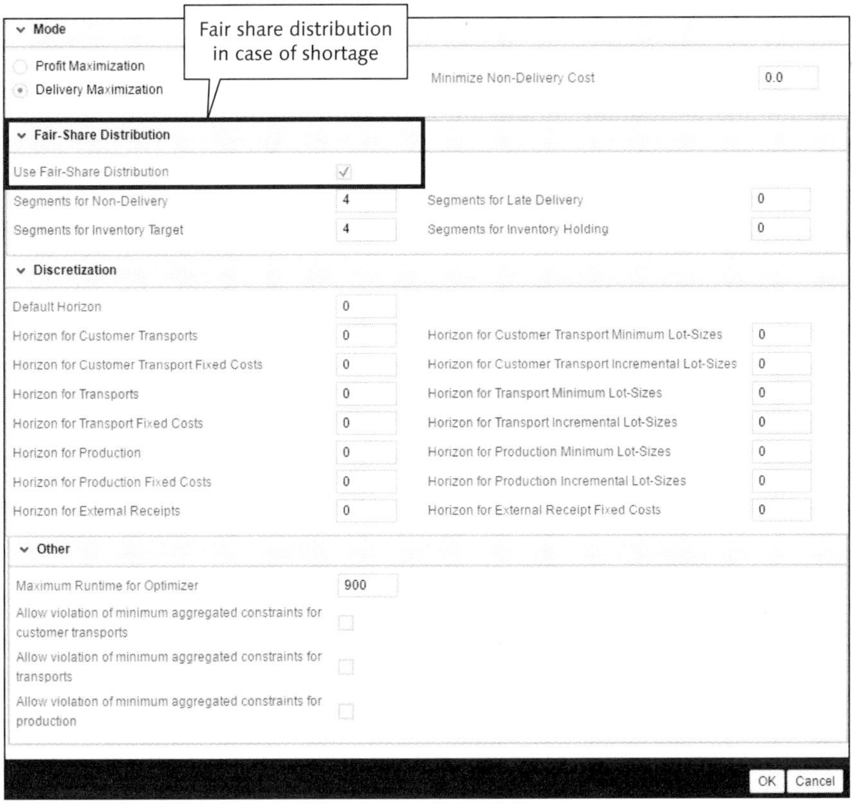

Figure 7.4 S&OP Optimizer Profile: Page 2

The most important settings are as follows:

▶ **Time-independent penalty costs**
   Default cost considerations for optimization calculation is through the cost
   key figures defined in the planning model. This setting of the optimizer profile
   provides an easier and faster approach to maintaining the relative costs, and
   the values maintained here supersede the key figure values. If the USE PENALTY
   COST box is checked as shown in Figure 7.3, then the S&OP optimizer ignores
   the key figure values and uses the values maintained for the calculations. Relative weights for production, purchase, transportation, and inventory holding
   are provided for optimizer consideration. Costs that are relevant for both
   fixed value and variable rates, for example, production costs, can have their
   respective values maintained. Violations for minimum capacity usage and
   maximum inventory quantity can also be assigned with the cost rate values.

▶ **Global cost factor**

If the planning model has the cost key figure values maintained for optimization calculation, then a quick adjustment to the cost of every product in the model can be made by using the global cost factor in the optimization profile. This cost change works as a quick lever to synchronize with changes in the business strategy. Therefore, a transportation cost rate increase can be adjusted for the optimization model by assigning a factor for the same. Alternatively, to avoid the non-deliveries, the non-delivery cost factor can be increased by providing a higher value.

▶ **Mode**

S&OP optimizer can be executed in either Profit Maximization or Delivery Maximization mode. The relevant mode is selected by choosing the radio button shown in Figure 7.4. The Delivery Maximization option allows maximizing the service level to the customer, even if it involves a relatively higher cost. Note that the profit maximization logic can make the decision not to meet the customer demand if the associated cost gets higher while fulfilling the requirement as compared to leaving the request unfilled. Delivery Maximization mode takes care of this by non-delivery cost. If the system configurator provides a value in the Minimize Non-Delivery Cost field, then this value is considered by optimizer as the cost of non-delivery for all the demand. However, for a blank value, the system calculates and uses a high non-delivery cost if Delivery Maximization mode is selected for the optimizer.

▶ **Fair share distribution**

In the case of a shortage situation, the optimization algorithm can calculate quantities to assign available material to one customer and not provide any at all to another customer. The cost of non-delivery to two customers due to partial shipment can be higher than the cost of non-delivery to one customer if all the available material is assigned to one customer, filling the requirement completely and not supplying any quantity to any another customer. Through the Fair Share Distribution checkbox in the optimization profile, fair share logic can be added to the supply planning optimization. In this case, the cost is calculated through segmented costs with the number of segments chosen in the configuration and not through normal cost rates. At least two segments are required for the fair share distribution. A value from 2 to 10 can be entered in the segment fields for the appropriate segment.

- **Discretization**
  Supply optimization requires considering discrete decisions while performing the modeling. This calculation is performance intensive; detailed discrete calculations may not be necessary for time periods far in future. For example, lot size and rounding values are much more important for supply planning consideration in the short-term to medium-term time frame, although it has less impact on the long-term horizon. The discretization parameters are used to control this. If a value is maintained for the default horizon, then the discrete decisions are considered by the optimizer only from the current period to the assigned period value. It's possible to maintain discrete horizons for individual decision parameters such as production, transportation, and external receipt, instead of maintaining a default value.

- **Performance and violation parameters**
  Performance and violation parameters are grouped under OTHER in the optimization profile. Maximum runtime in seconds can be assigned here, which controls the maximum runtime taken by the algorithm for calculating optimization results. For a complex model with abundant discrete decisions, the time taken by the optimizer can be very high, and we recommend you use a value here. The constraint in the system, which can be violated for optimized results, can also be selected here.

  The optimization profile with the assigned value is saved for the operator name. The operator is assigned to the planning area for the S&OP model and is available to execute through the interactive, batch, or filter modes per the configuration of the planning operator. Interactive mode allows the planners to perform the supply plan in the interactive mode of the Excel planning view. A batch mode allows executing the plan in a background batch job. The filter option enables the planner to add the master data filter under which the plan needs to be executed. Associated master data through the supply chain network are selected automatically. For a connected network, however, it's recommended to plan the entire network through the optimizer without any filter assignments.

- **Check network heuristic (CHECK_MODE)**
  Check network heuristic is used for checking the network consistency of the supply chain. It doesn't generate any supply, although it propagates the supply chain structure to check the master data and key figures. This heuristic generates the logs for any inconsistency and errors found in the network. It checks the customer source, location source, production source, associated quota, and infinite loop (cycle) in the planning network. It is highly recommended to use

this algorithm during the initial phase of data load to identify and take action on the inconsistencies. This algorithm should also be executed periodically in a live environment to make sure the supply chain network is consistent and error-free. Any issue identified must be resolved; organizations should strive for zero errors before using a heuristic or optimizer to generate the supply in a supply chain network.

▶ **Quota calculation or compute ratios (COMPUTE_RATIOS)**
Quota calculation can be used to generate the optimized quota from the system instead of assigning the same manually. A cost-optimized supply plan is first executed for the network, and then the quota calculation algorithm calculates the quota from the optimized plan and assigns the same in the outbound quota key figures. Through a copy job, the value from the outbound quota key figures is copied to the inbound quota key figures. As such, the system has the optimized quota value for further supply heuristic runs. Note that the optimizer calculation works through the MILP and doesn't consider quota as a constraint. On the other hand, quota is a restriction for the S&OP heuristic. This functionality provides the option to generate optimized quotas and reduces manual work for the same. However, if the quota in the business is driven from the corporate rules and agreements, then this may not be required for the supply planning but can be still performed for simulation and analysis.

▶ **Local update algorithm (LOCAL)**
Local update of the deficit, shortage, and projected stock key figures for a product location is done through this algorithm. This algorithm updates the three key figure values locally, but it neither updates the values of other product locations nor does it do any supply planning. Supply planning isn't performed through this algorithm, even if the demand has been changed from the last supply planning run.

Planning runs are executed in SAP IBP for sales and operations through either the SAP IBP Excel planning view by using the advanced category option or by running a batch job through the SAP Fiori view as discussed in Chapter 16, Section 16.2.

7.4 Planning Views and Alerts through Sales and Operations Planning

Plan review, adjustment, action on exception, and team discussion through the SAP IBP tool are relevant for all the sub-processes of S&OP. Therefore, the sub-processes—demand review, supply review, pre-S&OP, and executive review—are managed efficiently in SAP IBP for sales and operations.

The SAP IBP solution automates and supports end-to-end S&OP. In addition to planning algorithms for demand and supply planning, the plan review, collaboration, and plan finalization activities are performed in SAP IBP. Features used for performing these applications are as follows:

- **SAP IBP Excel planning view**
  Demand and supply plan review, including simulation
- **Process and task management**
  Work management with clear responsibility and due date
- **SAP Jam**
  Enterprise collaboration for S&OP
- **Alerts**
  Identification and resolution of exceptions
- **Analytics**
  Tool enabling S&OP decisions

The power of the SAP IBP system is based on integrated capabilities. For example, a plan update in the Excel planning view can be shared with an SAP Jam collaboration group, an exception condition generated by the change appears in the alert view, the resolution can be started in the integrated task page, and finally the resolution action can be analyzed from analytics and dashboards.

Every sub-process of S&OP can be automated and supported by a different planning view. For example, in the demand review process, a view can be created for sales professionals with only the key figures relevant to their work with the expectation that a sales manager will update the sales forecast for his product or customer group. Similar planning views can be maintained for marketing managers, finance managers, and demand planners to support the planning collaboration. Update logic can be configured in SAP IBP per the business requirements. For example, it's common to provide a rationale stating that if an update is performed for a key figure (e.g., sales forecast), refresh the demand plan with the updated value, or alternatively consider the statistical value. Similar logic can be defined for other collaboration scenarios such as agreeing on the scheme to generate consensus demand through the demand review process. Figure 7.5 shows an example of the demand review process from SAP IBP for sales and operations. In addition to statistical forecast quantity, sales, marketing, and demand planning, key figure values are used for finalizing the consensus demand of a product for a customer.

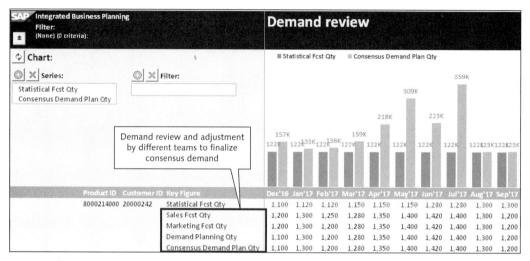

Figure 7.5 Demand Review Process in SAP IBP

During the S&OP review process, a highly desired capability for many of the organizations is to be able to perform planning simulations. In SAP IBP, a scenario is created by a planner on the fly; analysis can be conducted for the scenario without impacting the live data in the system. Figure 7.6 shows an example of scenario analysis in SAP IBP for sales and operations. In addition to baseline, the upside scenario is created by the user with a click of a button. Data for either simulation or base version along with the simulation version can be loaded for analysis. In the example, both baseline planning data and simulation data are being reviewed together for analysis and discussion of any possible upside adjustment of the demand plan.

A planned update can be shared with the planning group through the integrated collaboration capability. It can be associated with a reason code in the SAP IBP system. Detailed steps for reason code creation are discussed in Chapter 5, Section 5.9. Figure 7.7 shows an example of demand forecast adjustment in the Excel planning view and information sharing with the closed group named S&OP DIS-CUSSION. It also illustrates the update in the collaboration page as updated on the integrated SAP IBP environment. From the collaboration page, further tasks can be assigned to a team member if required.

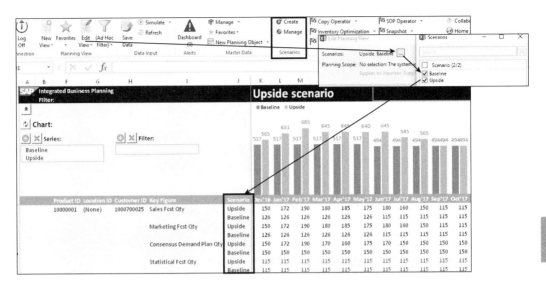

Figure 7.6 What-If Scenario Comparison for Demand Review

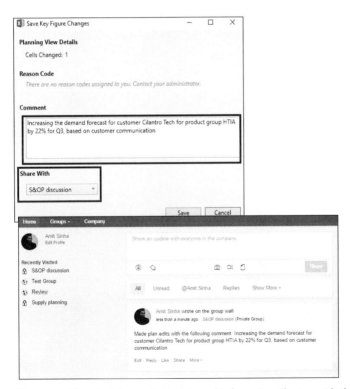

Figure 7.7 Planning View Data Update and Information Sharing with the Group

Similar planning views can be created for supply review, pre-S&OP review, and executive review processes. The planning views, planning levels, and key figures used in these views are highly customizable and can be configured specifically for an organization's business requirement. Figure 7.8 shows an example of the supply planning view in SAP IBP with supply and projected inventory key figures. Demand, supply, and projected inventory at aggregated and disaggregated levels are reviewed in the SAP IBP planning view. Available on-hand inventory, target stock, and projected inventory provide useful views of the demand, supply, and stock positions in the mid- to long-term horizon. Information obtained here is used for the supply review and pre-S&OP process.

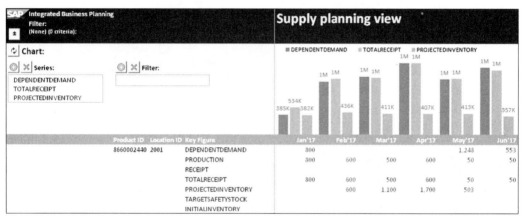

Figure 7.8 Supply Planning View for the Supply Review Process

A similar view is built in SAP IBP for sales and operations with the cost and revenue key figures. Through the currency conversion option of the edit planning view, cost and revenue numbers in one currency unit (e.g., USD or euros) are represented in the planning view and can be reviewed for alignment with your AOP.

Rough-cut capacity planning can be in scope for the S&OP process. For the planning review, the resource capacity and load can be represented in the specific planning view. S&OP heuristic planning has a higher probability of resulting in an overload situation as compared to the optimizer, which is a finite planning algorithm. The planning result shown in Figure 7.9 can be reviewed for an exception overload scenario by adjusting the plan for the supply review process. Figure 7.9 shows an example of a supply planning view with information on capacity load. The utilization percentage has been mapped with an alert key figure to become visible when the resource load is more than 90%.

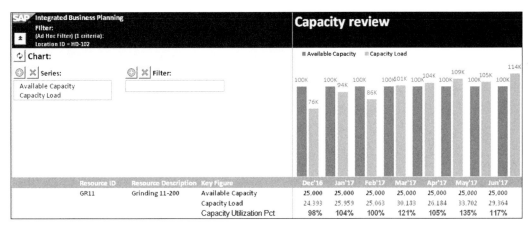

Figure 7.9 Capacity Review for the Supply Plan Review

Exception situation handling is performed in SAP IBP for sales and operations in the Excel planning view (as discussed earlier) and in the custom alert view. Custom alerts are displayed in the SAP Fiori planning view of SAP IBP and are included in the SAP Supply Chain Control Tower license of SAP IBP. Figure 7.10 shows an example of the custom alert screen as used for the S&OP planning review with the exception scenarios categorized as high, medium, and low severity. Through this top-level view, you get the detail of the alerts and can take the required action by accessing the integrated planning view, by creating an acting on a task, or by a mix of these activities. Configuration details for managing custom alerts are provided in Chapter 15, Section 15.7.

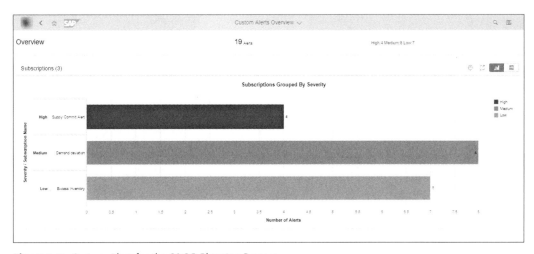

Figure 7.10 Custom Alert for the S&OP Planning Process

Analytics and ready reference information are critical when making S&OP decisions. In SAP IBP, custom dashboards are recommended for different subprocesses and roles. Figure 7.11 shows an example of the executive dashboard used in the executive review subprocess of S&OP for plan review, recommendations, and plan approval. Steps for creating this dashboard are discussed in Chapter 15, Section 15.3. Note that the dashboard also shows the example of S&OP process, task mapping, and control through SAP IBP.

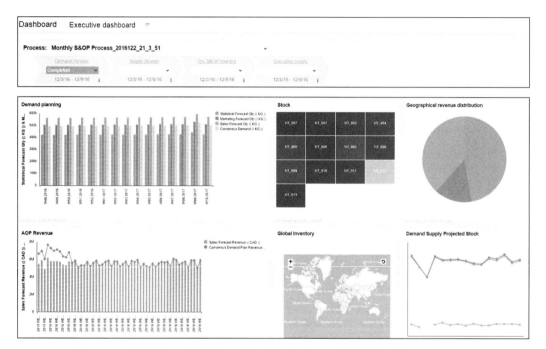

Figure 7.11 Analytics and Dashboard for Plan Review and S&OP Decisions

7.5   Collaboration

SAP SuccessFactors instance creation and SAP Jam setup are performed for the SAP IBP users to work on the integrated collaboration platform. Team collaboration is used for the S&OP processes for task management, option review, information sharing, and decision approval. Different groups of identified users can be made to support the subprocesses of demand review, supply review, pre-S&OP, and executive review. Widely used collaboration functionalities of the S&OP process include case discussion, task assignment, document sharing, and information regarding a plan update through a reason code. Figure 7.12 shows an example of an exchange of information and work collaboration in SAP IBP for sales and operations. For a potential sales increase, information is shared in S&OP DISCUSSION with team members, and a task is assigned to a relevant person for taking action by a due date.

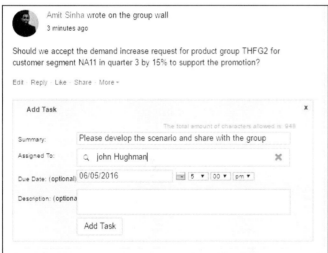

Figure 7.12 Information Sharing and Collaboration for the S&OP Process

There are multiple applications in the collaboration tool to enable the S&OP decision-making process. This can be through creating a discussion, asking a question, or creating a poll and requesting that people respond. Figure 7.13 shows a case of decision-making through polling. In this example, a planner has created a poll with possible options for the team members to respond by the assigned due date. Individual team members will vote to get their recommendation captured in a formal manner. Further discussion may be required within the team in addition to the poll. SAP IBP supports this through SAP Jam.

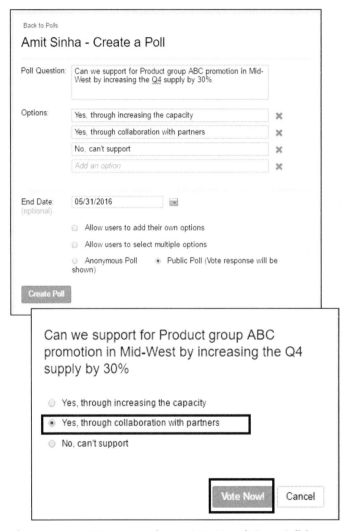

Figure 7.13 S&OP Decision-Making in SAP IBP with Team Collaboration

SAP Jam is useful for both individual work and group work. Individual or group pages can be selected from the home screen. Information sharing, liking, commenting, and updating are performed through the application. Figure 7.14 shows an example of the S&OP planner's group collaboration page in an organization. Update of a task or action in a plan can be shared with the team here. This application has tremendous benefits for the collaboration and decision-making processes of S&OP.

Figure 7.14 S&OP Process Collaboration in SAP IBP for Sales and Operations

7.6 Summary

SAP IBP for sales and operations is a highly effective and efficient tool for managing the S&OP processes of an organization. It provides end-to-end visibility and control of the subprocesses of S&OP and generates an efficient organization-wide mid- to long-term demand and supply plan.

SAP IBP capabilities are extended to end-to-end planning processes. Demand planning, response and supply planning, and inventory management are other applications whose value can be optimized through SAP IBP. This chapter and the previous chapter covered the details of S&OP processes and application of the SAP IBP for sales and operations planning process. Now we're ready to delve into the details of demand management applications through SAP IBP for demand.

This chapter explores the concepts of statistical forecasting, preprocessing, postprocessing, and collaboration for the demand planning process. Usage of statistical modeling along with cutting-edge applications for task management, analytics, and decision-making processes of SAP IBP for demand are discussed here for the finalization of the demand plan.

8   Demand Planning and Forecasting with SAP IBP

SAP Integrated Business Planning (SAP IBP) for demand provides capabilities to generate and manage demand forecasts for a short-term, medium-term, and long-term horizon. This allows you to create a baseline forecast for the full planning horizon by using the historical data and related inputs in a statistical forecasting model. Forecast accuracy for the medium term can be enhanced through the collaboration, data adjustment, and statistical model adjustment capabilities of demand forecasting in SAP IBP. Accuracy in the short term is improved by the demand-sensing capabilities of SAP IBP, which allow adjustments in the short-term forecast to achieve a demand-driven supply chain.

Table 8.1 provides a summary of the demand planning capabilities of SAP IBP for demand. In addition to traditional statistical models for forecast generation using historical sales data, SAP IBP for demand has been enriched with the advance modeling of predictive analytics, demand sensing, and promotion planning capabilities. Forecast modeling enables you to choose one or a combination of multiple statistical models to predict the forecast. Predictive analytics have autoregressive capabilities to identify the best fit model along with the relevant parameters of the forecast algorithm. Demand sensing uses the actual current order data, along with the recent history, to adjust the forecast for the short-term horizon. The promotion planning capability adds an option to either perform the promotion planning in the SAP IBP system or to integrate the SAP IBP system with an external promotion planning system.

SAP IBP for Demand Capabilities			
Traditional statistical forecast model	Predictive analytics for demand forecast	Demand sensing for short term forecasting	Promotion planning
▸ Statistical modeling ▸ Outliers detection in historical data ▸ Factors adjustments and forecast error for higher accuracy	▸ ARIMA model for auto regressive predictive modeling ▸ Pattern recognition mechanism for higher accuracy	▸ Demand driven forecast in short term horizon ▸ Actual data from present and recent past for automated demand adjustment	▸ History data adjustment by removing uplift ▸ Integration of external promotion system ▸ Promotion planning for future horizon

Table 8.1 Functional Overview of SAP IBP for Demand

In this chapter, we'll discuss the demand planning process of demand forecasting, demand finalization, and demand sensing processes. The demand forecasting process will be discussed in detail with preprocessing, statistical forecast generation, and postprocessing steps. Different statistical models and forecast error calculations are illustrated in this chapter. The collaboration process for demand plan finalization examples are discussed in SAP IBP through the demand plan process.

8.1 Demand Forecasting, Demand Planning, and Demand Sensing

Demand forecasting and demand planning processes are performed for baseline forecast generation and forecast adjustments to finalize the demand. A baseline forecast can be generated through a qualitative or quantitative approach. In the qualitative approach, the forecast is generated through the judgment and opinion of relevant people. This method is normally used for new products, in industries for which relevant historical data isn't available, or where historical sales aren't a good representation of futures sales. In the quantitative approach, past sales or shipment data is used for generating the baseline forecast. For most industries where products have relevant historical data, the quantitative approach is used for the demand forecast. Even for the new products, the sales history of a similar product can be used for generating the baseline forecast. After the baseline forecast is generated through the demand forecasting approach, collaboration of relevant teams finalizes the demand requirement or demand plan. The finalized demand requirement is also called a *consensus demand forecast*. The process of finalization of the demand requirement through forecasting and collaboration to generate the consensus demand is referred to as the demand planning process.

Figure 8.1 shows the process associated with the consensus forecast generation. Sales or shipment history data is collected through the execution system of the organization; some corrections in the historical data may be required to adjust the outliers due to any variation that may have impacted the data. The statistical forecast model is executed on the cleansed data to generate the baseline demand forecast. Further adjustment is performed through the collaboration process and for market information to finalize the demand forecast as the consensus demand forecast.

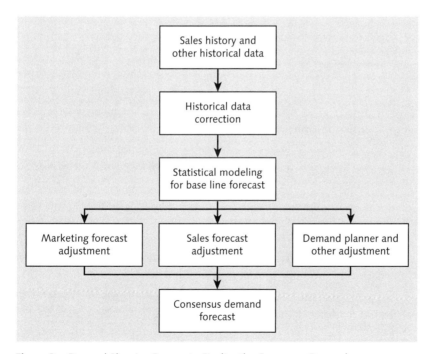

Figure 8.1 Demand Planning Process to Finalize the Consensus Demand

The consensus demand forecast in the short term is considered an input, along with the actual orders and recent history, to update the short-term forecast through the demand sensing algorithm. Figure 8.2 shows the process of short-term demand adjustment through the demand sensing approach. Demand sensing helps make the forecast more accurate and profitable by aligning the company's resources to the actual market demand. Short-term deviations in the market requirement are addressed well through the demand sensing approach. Demand sensing is performed at the detailed granular level with typical demand adjustments in daily and weekly periods for an average of two to six weeks.

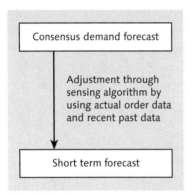

Figure 8.2 Demand Sensing Process for Adjusting Short-Term Forecasts

Table 8.2 lists further information and comparisons of demand planning and demand sensing capabilities. Note that the demand sensing process isn't an alternative but an extension of the demand planning process. Demand sensing is useful for industries with rapid changes to demand and relatively shorter lead time for order fulfillment. For those industry groups, the changes in market dynamics can be quickly incorporated into the short-term demand plan of the organization to align with the shift in the market. For example, demand sensing can be highly relevant for the fast moving consumer goods (FMCG) market in which a promotion can highly impact the sales numbers, and the order replenishment can be performed more quickly. However, for a high-tech company (a server manufacturer) with the component lead times in weeks (and sometimes in months), demand sensing in the short term for updating the requirement for the next few weeks is less relevant.

Relevant Factor	Demand Planning	Demand Sensing
Relevance	For almost every industry to predict the demand forecast through sales history and associated factors. Examples are across industry segments such as consumer goods, life sciences, high-tech, retail, manufacturing, auto, etc.	For industries that have high variations in demand patterns and for which demand is impacted heavily by changes in market conditions. Examples are FMCG and the retail industry. Demand sensing is an extension of the demand planning process to adjust the demand in the short term and is not an alternative.
Horizon	Short term, medium term, and long term (monthly and weekly buckets)	Short term (weekly and daily buckets)
Decision impacted	▸ Sales and operations planning (S&OP) plan ▸ Purchase plan ▸ Production plan ▸ Budget plan ▸ Partner management	▸ Deployment ▸ Packaging ▸ Order fulfillment ▸ Order confirmation ▸ Logistics execution
Input requirements	History data and demand influencing factors	Consensus demand, order information, point-of-sale data, and recent history

Table 8.2 Demand Planning and Demand Sensing Details

Demand Planning for a New Product

A new product introduced by the organization may need to be considered for demand planning to identify the potential market demand and supply planning processes. However, the absence of historical sales data for the new product restricts the usage of the statistical model in generating the baseline forecast value of the new product. As discussed earlier in this chapter, the qualitative forecast approach can be used to finalize the demand requirement of the new product. However, there may be another product (or a group of other products) in the supply chain network of the organization whose historical data can be referred to for generating the demand forecast of the new product. SAP IBP for demand supports the baseline forecast generation of a new product by referring to the demand history of a similar product.

To perform the statistical forecast of a new product, the Manage Product Lifecycle app of the SAP Fiori screen is used, and existing product references are provided to the planning object of the new product. In the statistical forecast model of SAP IBP, there is an option to select the product lifecycle and activate the new product forecasting in SAP IBP through a reference product. The forecast start date of the new product is chosen based on the market launch program of the product lifecycle. It's recommended to review the system-generated baseline forecast value by the sales, marketing, and planning teams to align on the demand and supply of the new product.

8.2 Performing Demand Forecasting and Demand Sensing

Demand forecasting and demand sensing activities in SAP IBP are performed in the SAP Fiori view and the SAP IBP Excel planning view. Figure 8.3 shows the steps for demand forecasting and demand sensing processes in SAP IBP.

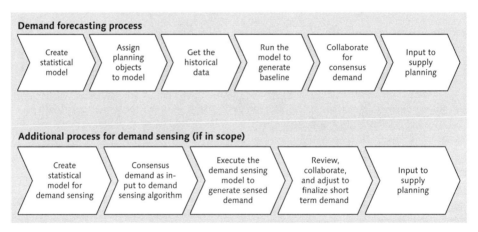

Demand forecasting process

Create statistical model ⟩ Assign planning objects to model ⟩ Get the historical data ⟩ Run the model to generate baseline ⟩ Collaborate for consensus demand ⟩ Input to supply planning

Additional process for demand sensing (if in scope)

Create statistical model for demand sensing ⟩ Consensus demand as input to demand sensing algorithm ⟩ Execute the demand sensing model to generate sensed demand ⟩ Review, collaborate, and adjust to finalize short term demand ⟩ Input to supply planning

Figure 8.3 Demand Forecasting and Demand Sensing Steps

As shown in Figure 8.3, the demand forecasting process starts with identification and creation of a statistical model in SAP IBP. The model is finalized by analyzing the historical data and model fit capabilities of SAP IBP. Historical data is provided as the input to the statistical model for generating the forecast. Any data cleansing or adjustment is performed for removing unusual or causal deviations. The generated baseline forecast value is reviewed, adjusted, and shared in SAP IBP with different teams to finalize the consensus demand as the final demand plan of the organization. This is used to drive the supply planning process of either S&OP or response and supply planning based on the system landscape and processes of the organization.

The demand sensing process requires further steps in addition to those described for the demand forecasting process. After creation of the statistical model for demand sensing, the consensus demand as finalized through the demand planning or S&OP process is provided as the input for the model. You execute the demand sensing statistical model to generate the sensed demand for the short-term horizon, typically 8 to 12 weeks. Review, adjustment, and collaboration in the SAP IBP tool are used for finalizing the short-term sensed demand as the input for the replenishment or supply processes.

There are many key figures that together perform the demand planning activities in SAP IBP. Understanding the following three data elements is required to get into the further details of the solution:

- **Input to forecast key figures (history key figures)**
  The input to the forecast is the sales or shipment history data that are considered as the input data for the statistical modeling. This data can be checked and adjusted for any causal deviation. Cleansed historical data at the correct planning level are used in the forecasting model to generate the ex-post and forecast values.

- **Ex-post forecast**
  The ex-post forecast is generated by the SAP IBP system in the historical time bucket through the statistical model. The ex-post forecast is the output of the statistical forecast model in the history horizon while considering a part of the history for generating the forecast. Hence, it provides the opportunity to compare the forecasted value with the actual value, to compare the forecast errors, and to find the best fit model.

- **Forecast**
  The forecast key figure is the output of the statistical model as the demand requirement for the future. Forecast key figures can be further adjusted through different adjustment key figures based on collaboration, market information, and planned promotion to derive the final demand known as the consensus forecast.

Figure 8.4 shows an example from the SAP IBP system in the Excel planning view representing the historical key figure (DELIVERED QTY ADJUSTED) and the ex-post forecast (EXPOST FORECAST QTY) as calculated by the forecasting algorithm of SAP IBP for demand.

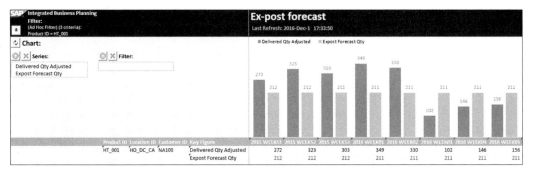

Figure 8.4 Adjusted Delivery Quantity and Ex-Post Forecast in SAP IBP

Demand forecasting in SAP IBP for demand is performed by modeling input to the forecast key figure, performing preprocessing steps to cleanse the history, selecting a model to generate the forecast, and then adjusting the forecast to finalize the consensus demand. You perform demand sensing in SAP IBP by using the consensus demand and real-time demand streams as input, executing a demand sensing algorithm, and adjusting the demand plan using the sensed demand. Forecast patterns, shipment patterns, and demand signal data patterns are analyzed by the system (open orders are also taken into consideration), allowing the system to sense the demand in daily and weekly buckets and update the demand forecast using the sensed demand for the short-term horizon.

Figure 8.5 shows the example of the DEMAND PLANNING view through statistical forecast and collaboration processes. In this example, the STATISTICAL FORECAST QTY is used as input by the demand planning, sales, and marketing teams to collaborate and finalize the demand plan as the consensus demand.

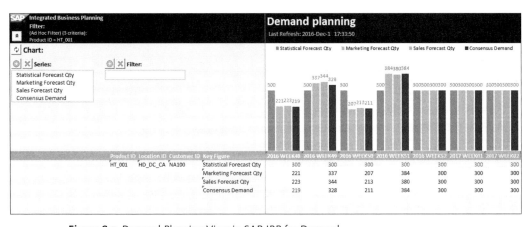

Figure 8.5 Demand Planning View in SAP IBP for Demand

The sensed demand example in short-term demand planning is represented by Figure 8.6. This is from the Excel planning view example of SAP IBP for demand. SENSED DEMAND QTY as calculated by the demand sensing algorithm can be reviewed and adjusted by the planner, and the adjusted value can be used as the final sensed demand or the short-term demand plan.

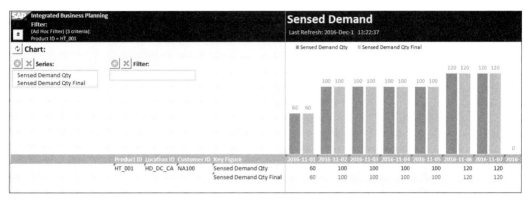

Figure 8.6 Sensed Demand in SAP IBP

8.3 Preprocessing for Demand Forecasting

Through pre-processing, historical data is cleaned for the outliers to feed into the model as the input to forecast. This process is performed in SAP IBP for demand to avoid unwanted influence of erroneous or causal data that are identified as outliers through the pre-processing model. If this step is ignored, then the abnormal deviation in the input data can distort the forecast. There are different methods and algorithms available in SAP IBP for demand to perform the preprocessing data correction. The following contains the detailed information on the preprocessing steps and associated algorithms in SAP IBP for demand:

▸ **Substitute missing values:**

  ▹ Application: Substitute missing values due to data missing in the history data, which can distort the forecast.

  ▹ Algorithm for forecast generation: Mean or median of the historical available data.

  ▹ Output property: Substituted missed value through mean or median value (see Figure 8.7).

▷ Usage notes: Algorithm can be used for both history and future forecast values.

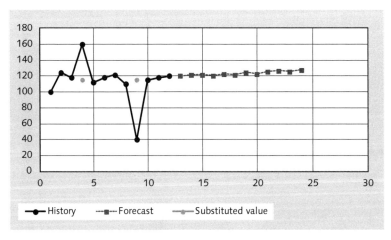

Figure 8.7 Missing Value Substitution

▶ **Outlier correction through interquartile range test:**

▷ Application: Identify the outliers and substitute them with the average value in the normal range.

▷ Algorithm for forecast generation: Correction of outlier value through mean, median, or tolerance values.

▷ Output property: Substituted missed value through mean, median, or tolerance values (see Figure 8.8).

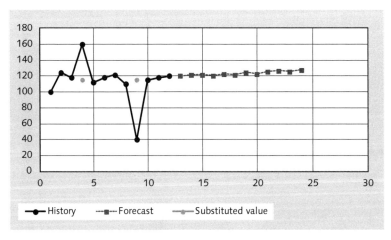

Figure 8.8 Outlier Correction through Interquartile Range Test

- ▸ Usage notes: Outlier values can either be considered or ignored during the substitution calculation.

- ▸ **Outlier correction through variance test:**

  - ▸ Application: Identify the outliers and substitute them with the average value in the normal range.

  - ▸ Algorithm for forecast generation: Correction of outlier value through mean, median, or tolerance values.

  - ▸ Output property: Substituted missed value through mean, median, or tolerance values (see Figure 8.9).

  - ▸ Usage notes: Outlier values can either be considered or ignored during the substitution calculation.

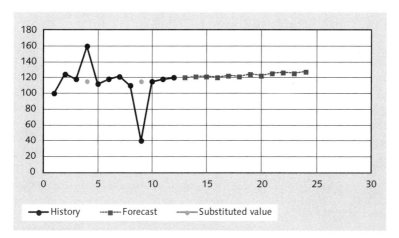

Figure 8.9 Outlier Correction through a Variance Test

- ▸ **Promotion sales lift elimination:**

  - ▸ Application: Remove the sales lift due to promotion while using the history for short-term demand sensing.

  - ▸ Algorithm for forecast generation: Sales history used for demand sensing is calculated based on the sales uplift due to promotion and consensus forecast.

  - ▸ Output property: Value substitution is based on sales lift and forecast (Figure 8.10).

▷ Usage notes: Value = Sales history × [Consensus forecast ÷ (Consensus forecast + Planned sales lift)]

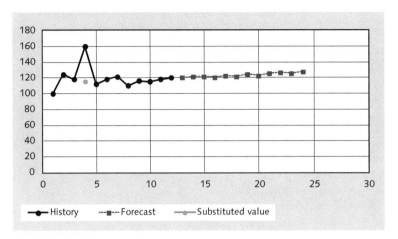

Figure 8.10 Promotion Sales Lift Correction for History Data

8.4 Forecasting

Through the forecast step, information provided to SAP IBP for demand to generate the demand forecast is as follows:

▸ Input key figure to forecast

▸ Ex-post forecast key figure

▸ Statistical algorithm selection

▸ Output key figure for forecast

▸ Utilization of multiple algorithms

Through modeling, relevant key figures can be assigned to input, ex-post, and output key figures. There are multiple forecast algorithms available in SAP IBP, which can be used to generate the forecast based on the properties of the historical data. Forecasting methods along with the associated factors can be assigned through the forecasting modeling in SAP IBP. There are multiple time series statistical models available to perform the demand forecast. In addition to the time series models, the predictive forecasting model is also available to generate the forecast in which the system calculates the factors for the best fit model. In the forecasting step, it's possible to use multiple models to generate the forecast. The final forecast can be an output of the weighted average of multiple models or by using the system's capability to choose the best fit forecast model based on the forecast errors or post-processing step.

The following details the relevant information for different forecasting models available for performing the demand forecast in SAP IBP for demand:

▶ **Simple average:**

  ▷ Application: Mature products with stable demand.

  ▷ Algorithm for forecast generation: Average of historical data for selected number of time periods.

  ▷ Output property: Constant forecast value for every future time bucket (see Figure 8.11).

  ▷ Usage notes: This is a simple algorithm with limited application.

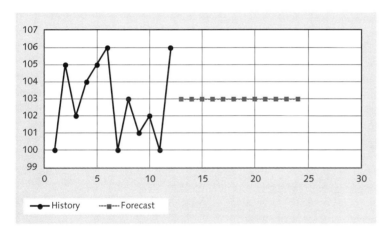

Figure 8.11 Simple Average Forecast

▶ **Weighted average:**

  ▷ Application: Mature products with stable demand; some time periods and seasons impact demand more than others.

  ▷ Algorithm for forecast generation: Usage of weighting factors for values of all periods.

  ▷ Output property: Constant forecast value for every future time bucket (see Figure 8.12).

▸ Usage notes: Forecast is based on the average value, while some time series values contribute more than others.

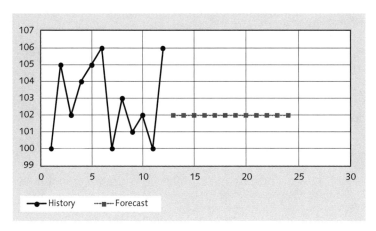

Figure 8.12 Weighted Average Forecast

▸ **Simple moving average:**

   ▸ Application: Sales forecast for mature products with stable demand.

   ▸ Algorithm for forecast generation: Average of last few periods of sales history.

   ▸ Output property: Constant forecast value influenced by the historical value of an identified number of periods (see Figure 8.13).

   ▸ Usage notes: Number of periods "m" is provided for the calculation.

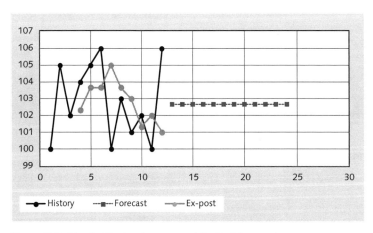

Figure 8.13 Simple Moving Average and Ex-Post Forecast

▶ **Simple moving average with extended calculation:**

   ▶ Application: Sales forecast for mature products with stable demand.

   ▶ Algorithm for forecast generation: Average of last few periods of sales history for first value of forecast, continuation of calculation with calculated forecast value.

   ▶ Output property: Time series value of forecast for future time buckets, for example, with a number of periods as three, for the first forecast value, the last three historical values are used. For the next calculation, the first forecast and last two historical values are used. For continuation of the time series forecast value, the last three forecasted values calculate the forecast value for the next time period (see Figure 8.14).

   ▶ Usage notes: The moving average concept is extended throughout the forecast horizon.

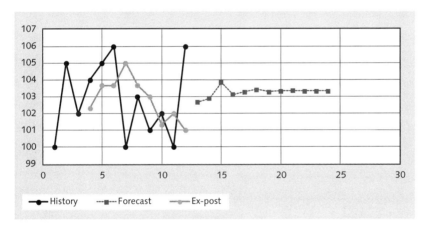

Figure 8.14 Simple Moving Average with Extended Calculation

▶ **Weighted moving average:**

   ▶ Application: Sales forecast of mature products with stable demand; demand is closer to the recent sales history than from the further past values.

   ▶ Algorithm for forecast generation: For the number of periods identified, the weighted average of those values predicts the forecasted value for the full forecast horizon.

   ▶ Output property: Constant forecast value for future time buckets (see Figure 8.15).

▶ Usage notes: The number of periods and the weighting factors for those periods are required for forecast value calculation.

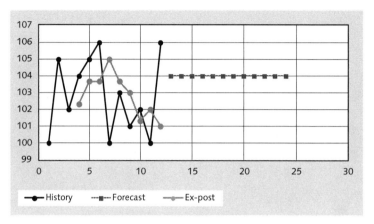

Figure 8.15 Weighted Moving Average and Ex-Post

▶ **Weighted moving average with extended calculation:**

▷ Application: Sales forecast of mature products with stable demand; demand is closer to the recent sales history than from the further past values.

▷ Algorithm for forecast generation: Weighted average of the last few periods of sales history for the first value of the forecast; continuation of calculation with calculated forecast value.

▷ Output property: Time series forecast values (see Figure 8.16).

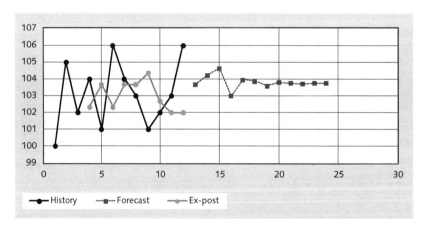

Figure 8.16 Weighted Moving Average with Extended Calculation

- ▹ Usage notes: The weighted moving average concept is extended throughout the forecast horizon.

- ▸ **Single exponential smoothing:**

  - ▹ Application: Mature products with stable demand; output is a constant value throughout the forecast horizon.

  - ▹ Algorithm for forecast generation: Historical data fluctuation is smoothed with weights that decrease exponentially over time.

  - ▹ Output property: Constant value for future buckets through exponential smoothing (see Figure 8.17).

  - ▹ Usage notes: The exponential smoothing factor is provided as α (Alpha coefficient) with a possible value from 0 to 1 and a normal value from 0.1 to 0.5. A relatively higher value provides more influence of recent historical value.

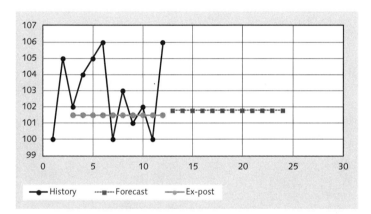

Figure 8.17 Single Exponential Smoothing

- ▸ **Adaptive response rate with single exponential smoothing:**

  - ▹ Application: Mature products with stable demand; output is a constant value throughout the forecast horizon.

  - ▹ Algorithm for forecast generation: Historical data fluctuation is smoothed with weights that decrease exponentially over time.

  - ▹ Output property: Constant value for future buckets with exponential smoothing and an updated alpha value (see Figure 8.18).

  - ▹ Usage notes: The smoothing factor α is calculated and adapted by the system for the ex-post forecast calculation and finally used for the forecast value calculation.

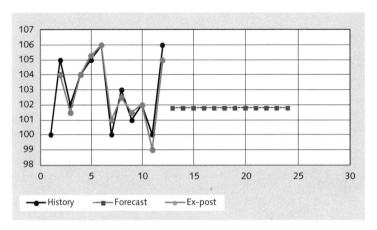

Figure 8.18 Adaptive Single Exponential Smoothing

▶ **Double exponential smoothing:**

▷ Application: Forecast for products in a growth or decline phase without seasonality.

▷ Algorithm for forecast generation: Historical data and trend data are exponentially smoothed for the baseline and trend line.

▷ Output property: Forecast is a trend line for future time buckets resulting from the level estimate and trend estimate of the double exponential calculation (see Figure 8.19).

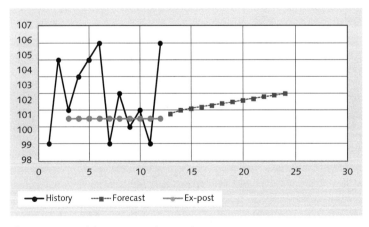

Figure 8.19 Double Exponential Smoothing

> ▸ Usage notes: Two smoothing factors—α (Alpha) and β (Beta) with possible values between 0 and 1 and normal values between 0.1 and 0.5—are used for the base value and trend smoothing lines.

▸ **Double exponential smoothing with trend dampening:**

> ▸ Application: Forecast for products in a growth or decline phase without seasonality; trend dampening with time for future values.

> ▸ Algorithm for forecast generation: Historical data and trend data are exponentially smoothed for baseline and trend line; the forecast trend is gradually eliminated.

> ▸ Output property: Forecast is a trend line for future time buckets resulting from the level estimates and trend estimates of the double exponential calculation (Figure 8.20). The forecast trend is eliminated through another smoothing factor.

> ▸ Usage notes: Along with α and β, another smoothing factor φ (Phi) is used for trend dampening. Possible values of φ range between 0.1 and 1; a higher value dampens the trend over a shorter period of time.

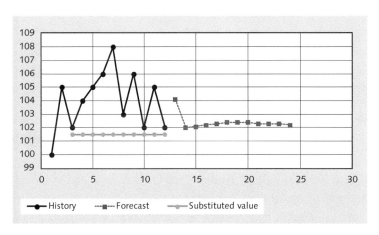

Figure 8.20 Double Exponential Smoothing with Trend Dampening

▸ **Triple exponential smoothing:**

> ▸ Application: Forecast for products in a growth or decline phase with seasonality.

▶ Algorithm for forecast generation: Historical data, trend data, and seasonality are exponentially smoothed for baseline, trend line, and seasonality behavior.

▶ Output property: Different forecast values for different future time buckets with trend and seasonality patterns in the forecast (Figure 8.21).

▶ Usage notes: There must exist at least two full seasons of demand data history. Along with α and β, another smoothing factor Υ (Upsilon) is used for seasonality. The normal value of Υ is between 0.1 and 0.5.

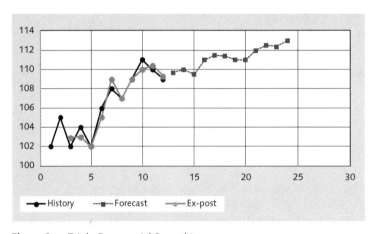

Figure 8.21 Triple Exponential Smoothing

▶ **Triple exponential smoothing with trend dampening:**

  ▷ Application: Forecast for products in a growth or decline phase with seasonality. The trend isn't expected to continue for a long time.

  ▷ Algorithm for forecast generation: Historical data, trend data, and seasonality are exponentially smoothed for baseline, trend line, and seasonality behavior. The trend dampening factor dampens the trend value.

  ▷ Output property: Seasonality, and trends along with trend dampening (Figure 8.22).

  ▷ Usage notes: Along with α, β, and Υ for baseline, trend, and seasonality smoothing, φ is used as the trend dampening factor to dampen the effect of the trend line.

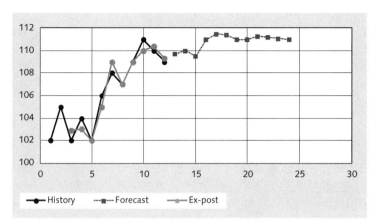

Figure 8.22 Triple Exponential Smoothing with Trend Dampening

▶ **Automated exponential smoothing:**

▷ Application: Can be used for a variety of product types that either have or don't have stable demand, trend, or seasonality.

▷ Algorithm for forecast generation: System automatically selects the exponential model and smoothing factors for forecast generation.

▷ Output property: The result can be a constant forecast, a trend forecast, or seasonal with or without trend (Figure 8.23).

▷ Usage notes: This is based on the SAP IBP solution capability to identify the best fit of the exponential model along with smoothing factors. Preferably, the history should have data for at least two seasons.

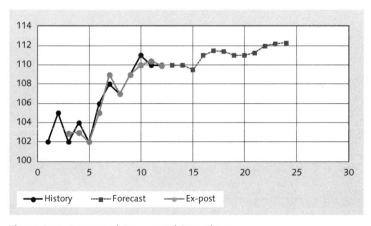

Figure 8.23 Automated Exponential Smoothing

► **Croston method:**

▻ Application: For demand forecast of products with intermittent demands.

▻ Algorithm for forecast generation: Ex-post forecast calculation and period with no demand between demand forecast is calculated to avoid distortion due to zero values in history.

▻ Output property: Output is a mix of forecasted and zero values for future time buckets. Buckets with positive values can have sporadic forecast or constant forecast (Figure 8.24).

▻ Usage notes: Sporadic forecast or constant forecast creation can be controlled through selection fields and α coefficient selection in the SAP IBP forecasting model. Selection depends on the product group and inventory holding preference.

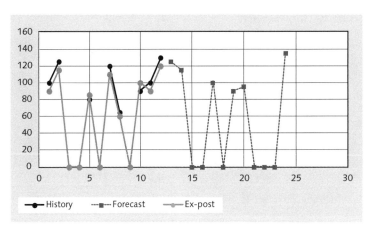

Figure 8.24 Croston Method

► **Multiple linear regression:**

▻ Application: For the products whose demand is decided by identifiable independent factors such as price, promotion, weather, etc.

▻ Algorithm for forecast generation: Forecast model based on cause-impact modeling of independent and dependent variables.

▻ Output property: Different forecasted values for different buckets based on the values of the independent variables (Figure 8.25).

▻ Usage notes: Historical values of sales and independent variables are used for ex-post forecast creation and multiplier value (coefficient) calculation in the model. These coefficients are used along with the predicted value of the independent variables to calculate the forecast.

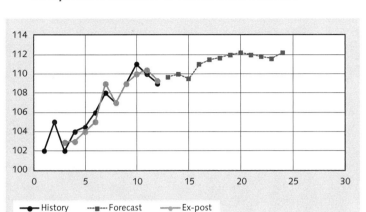

Figure 8.25 Multiple Linear Regression

8.5 Postprocessing and Forecast Error

The postprocessing step uses the forecast error to identify the best fit forecast model, taking into account the parameters of the model. The forecast error calculation uses the ex-post forecast value calculation through a statistical model and comparison of the value with the actual sales history. There are different types of forecast errors available in SAP IBP, and they are calculated through different formulas while using the ex-post and history values.

In addition to finalizing the best fit model for forecast generation, error measures as calculated in the postprocessing step can be used in the SAP Supply Chain Control Tower to generate the custom alerts and analytics for enhancing the forecast accuracy. Multiple forecast errors are available in SAP IBP for demand with different properties. One, or a combination of different forecast errors, can be used for the postprocessing step.

The available forecast error methods in SAP IBP are as follows:

▶ **Mean percentage error (MPE)**
MPE is calculated by the average of the percentage error from the actual value with the forecasted value. This is calculated through the percentage variation of the ex-post forecast with the historical value. The limitation of this approach is

that the deviation on positive and negative sides can offset each other for forecast error calculation and hence can hide the high values of erroneous forecasts if the deviations are distributed on both sides. However, due to the same property, MPE is a good measure of forecast bias. The equation is as follows:

$$MPE = \frac{1}{n}\sum_{t=1}^{n}\frac{V(t) - P(t)}{V(t)}100\%$$

- **Mean absolute percentage error (MAPE)**
  For MAPE calculations, the absolute percentage forecast deviation is calculated. Through this approach, the negative and positive deviations aren't offset, and absolute deviations are considered for the forecast error. Error consideration and forecast fit through this method helps in identifying the method for fitting the forecast line in data with high positive and negative deviations. The limitation of this approach is that it can't be used in the case of intermittent demand in which some of the time periods have zero actual sales history value. The equation is as follows:

$$MAPE = \frac{1}{n}\sum_{t=1}^{n}\frac{|V(t) - P(t)|}{V(t)}$$

- **Mean square error (MSE)**
  MSE is calculated by the mean of the square of the ex-post deviation from the actual historical value. It's similar in nature to the MAPE as the negative and positive deviations don't offset each other. For the unbiased variation, MSE helps in minimizing the variance in the forecast data. However, outliers in the data can heavily impact the effectiveness of this method. The equation is as follows:

$$MSE = \frac{1}{n}\sum_{t=1}^{n}(V(t) - P(t))^2$$

- **Root mean square error (RMSE)**
  RMSE is the square root of the MSE and is calculated by the square root of the average of the deviation squares. The RMSE forecast error method works through the deviation calculation and standard fit of the data. The square root of the data limits the impact of the outlier; however, this method is also more

useful for data with less bias and relatively higher deviations. The equation is as follows:

$$RMSE = \sqrt{\frac{1}{n}\sum_{t=1}^{n}(V(t) - P(t))^2}$$

▸ **Mean absolute deviation (MAD)**
MAD is the average value of the absolute deviations over a period of time. It's measured by the absolute deviation of the ex-post forecast from the actual historical value and through the average value of the result. It's not recommended for data with bias, but it can be an efficient fit for data with deviations in both directions or for events in which some of the actual values are zero. The equation is as follows:

$$MAD = \sum_{t=1}^{n}\frac{|V(t) - P(t)|}{n}$$

▸ **Mean absolute scaled error (MASE)**
MASE is a good fit for error calculation and forecast model fit in the data with seasonal and trend behavior. It's calculated while considering errors in a period, along with the calculation of the deviation of the actual value from one last period. It's one of the most versatile methods for forecast error calculations. The equation is as follows:

$$MASE = \frac{1}{n}\sum_{t=1}^{n}\left| \frac{V(t) - P(t)}{\sum_{i=2...n}\frac{V(i) - V(i-1)}{n-1}} \right|$$

▸ **Weighted mean absolute percentage error (WMAPE)**
WMAPE is calculated by dividing the sum of the absolute error by the sum of the historical value. The WMAPE calculation considers the magnitude of the actual data for the forecast error calculation and hence can be useful to model the scenarios in which different product groups have high deviations in the actual sales numbers. The equation is as follows:

$$WMAPE = \frac{\sum_{t=1}^{n}|V(t) - P(t)|}{\sum_{t=1}^{n}V(t)}100\%$$

In the represented formulas, the historical value, ex-post forecast value, period, and number of periods are represented as follows:

- $V(t)$: Historical value in period t.
- $P(t)$: Ex-post forecast in period t.
- n: Number of periods for which the ex-post forecast is calculated.

8.6 Promotion Planning and Management with SAP IBP for Demand

SAP IBP for demand has been enriched with the following functionalities of promotion planning:

- **Promotion uplift removal**
  You must remove the impact of a promotion from the historical data to cleanse the it before using the data for statistical modeling. Based on the historical promotion performance information, the history value can be edited with the available uplift, or the pre-processing algorithm can be used to identify and adjust the outliers for cleaning the promotion impact from the order history.

- **Promotion plan maintenance and usage in SAP IBP**
  The planned promotion uplift in the demand plan can be maintained directly in the SAP IBP system. The projected uplift value as a key figure is added to the forecast key figure during the consensus demand finalization process. The promotion uplift key figure must be aligned to the planning level of the forecast and consensus demand key figure to finalize the demand calculation after considering the impact of the promotion.

- **Integration with the promotion management system**
  Many organizations perform promotion planning in a separate trade promotion, customer relationship management, or related system. SAP IBP can be integrated through the SAP Cloud Platform to transfer the planned promotion uplift information from the external system to SAP IBP. Generally the promotion data in a customer relationship management or trade promotion system are maintained at the period level, the product/product group level, or the period, product/group, and customer level. However, for supply chain demand planning, location is an important planning level for the demand forecast. Hence, promotion split or disaggregation may be required to calculate the promotion

data in SAP IBP for demand at the same planning level as the demand forecast. After performing the promotion split or disaggregation, the final promotion uplift can be added to include the promotion plan in the final demand.

▶ **Promotion analysis**

The Analyze Promotions app provides detailed information and relevant analysis for promotion planning in SAP IBP for demand. This application can be used to analyze the promotion data with the source either from the external system or from local maintenance in SAP IBP. The following analyses and actions are possible through the Analyze Promotions app:

- ▷ Review promotion data as integrated from the external system.

- ▷ Apply a location split factor for promotion split and disaggregation.

- ▷ Include or exclude a promotion to forecast data for finalizing the demand.

- ▷ Engage in the promotion management collaboration process through SAP Jam integration or through sharing the information by adding notes to a promotion.

Figure 8.26 shows an example of the ANALYZE PROMOTIONS screen from SAP IBP for demand. It shows the detailed information on promotions, planned sales increase due to promotions, start time, end time, and other relevant information. Status information suggests whether the promotion sales impact is considered in the final demand plan. Additional notes can be added by the planner for a particular promotion event.

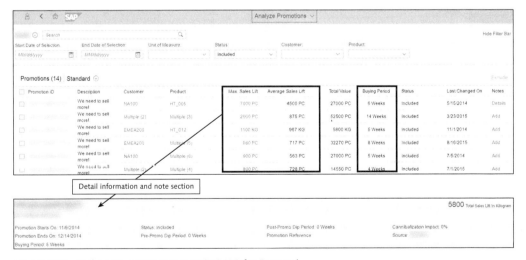

Figure 8.26 Analyze Promotions App in SAP IBP for Demand

8.7 Summary

The products and services requirements of the market on an organization are finalized through the demand planning process. The demand forecasting process is used to predict the demand for short-term, medium-term, and long-term horizons. Demand in the short term can be adjusted to align with the market realities through the demand sensing algorithms of SAP IBP. The pre-processing step is performed to clean the input data for the statistical model; the post-processing step focuses on minimizing the forecast errors by comparing the statistically modeled data with the actual data. Along with the sophisticated statistical models, and analytics, the collaboration and task management capabilities of SAP IBP are used for the demand planning process. With the knowledge you've gained regarding demand planning and SAP IBP for demand, you're now ready to get into the configuration details of of modeling the demand planning process.

This chapter delves into the details of the configuration steps for SAP IBP for demand for managing the demand planning processes. Configuration and application are discussed for both demand forecasting and demand sensing, along with the application of SAP IBP for the generation, review, and collaboration processes of the demand forecast.

9 Implementing SAP IBP for Demand

To implement SAP Integrated Business Planning (SAP IBP) for demand, you need to configure and update the system to the demand planning business processes and requirements. Figure 9.1 and Figure 9.2 display the configuration steps for executing the demand planning and demand sensing processes in SAP IBP for demand. These steps are further illustrated in detail in subsequent sections of this chapter.

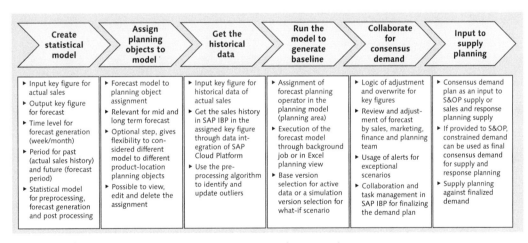

Figure 9.1 Demand Planning Process Mapping in SAP IBP for Demand

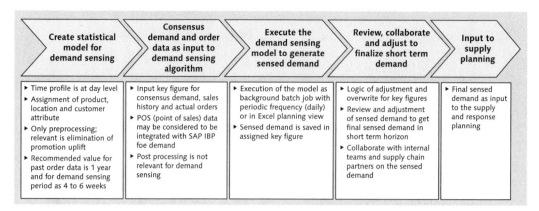

Figure 9.2 Demand Sensing Process Mapping in SAP IBP for Demand

This chapter discusses the steps required for implementation of demand forecasting, demand planning, demand sensing, and promotion planning in SAP IBP for demand. We start with the steps to build the planning area model to perform demand planning and demand sensing in SAP IBP. Forecast model build configuration is discussed for preprocessing, statistical modeling, and postprocessing steps of demand forecast generation. Execution of the demand planning run and plan review in the SAP IBP Excel planning view is discussed for the collaboration process in demand plan finalization. The promotion planning application in SAP IBP is discussed in the last section of this chapter.

9.1 Planning Model Configuration

Most of the planning objects discussed in Chapter 5 are relevant for the demand planning model. There are some specific configuration elements relevant to SAP IBP for demand, which need to be maintained for usage of the demand planning application, which we'll cover in the following sections.

9.1.1 Master Data Types

Master data types of product, location, and customer must be added to the planning model to be used for the demand plan. The key attributes in the model must be named as they are used in the standard SAP model (see Table 9.1). Other attributes of these master data types have the flexibility to be used as the ID and the description. If promotion planning is used in the demand planning application, you must also have the promotion master data with promotion ID (PROMO-TIONID) in the model.

Essential Master Data Type	Key Attribute in the Demand Planning Model	Attribute ID
Product	Product ID	PRDID
Location	Location ID	LOCID
Customer	Customer ID	CUSTID

Table 9.1 Essential Master Data Types and Attribute IDs for Demand Planning

Master data types production source, location source (transportation lane), and customer source are necessary for the supply planning to meet the requirements finalized by the demand plan. However, these specific master data types aren't directly relevant for demand planning.

9.1.2 Period Type

The period types relevant for demand forecasting are month and week. For the demand sensing application, you must have the time profile in week and day. Hence, if both demand forecasting and demand sensing are in scope, it's recommended to use the time profile with the month, week, and day levels. The additional time profile levels of technical week, quarter, or year can be selected if required for the planning process. Figure 9.3 shows the for standard SAP time profile used for demand model SAP6.

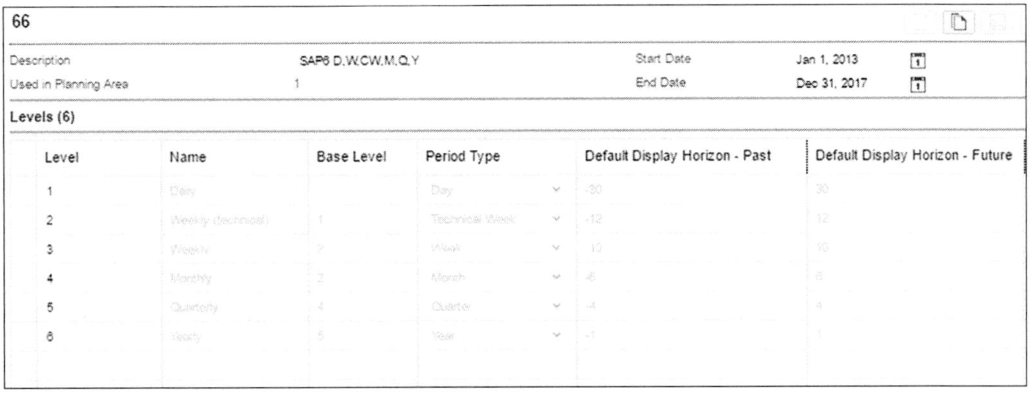

Figure 9.3 Sample Time Profile for Demand Planning

9.1.3   Planning Level

Many of the planning levels related to product, location and customer discussed in Chapter 4 are relevant for the demand planning application. The essential planning levels for demand forecasting and demand sensing are product/location/customer/week and product/location/customer/day consensus demand and sensed demand, respectively. The planning model elements for demand planning from the standard SAP planning models are SAP6 or SAPIBP1. SAP6 is delivered by SAP as a demand planning model, and SAPIBP1 is the unified planning model delivered by SAP. Figure 9.4 and Figure 9.5 show examples of planning levels provided in standard SAP planning models for demand planning and demand sensing capabilities.

Figure 9.4 Representative Planning Levels at the Week Level with Product, Location, and Customer

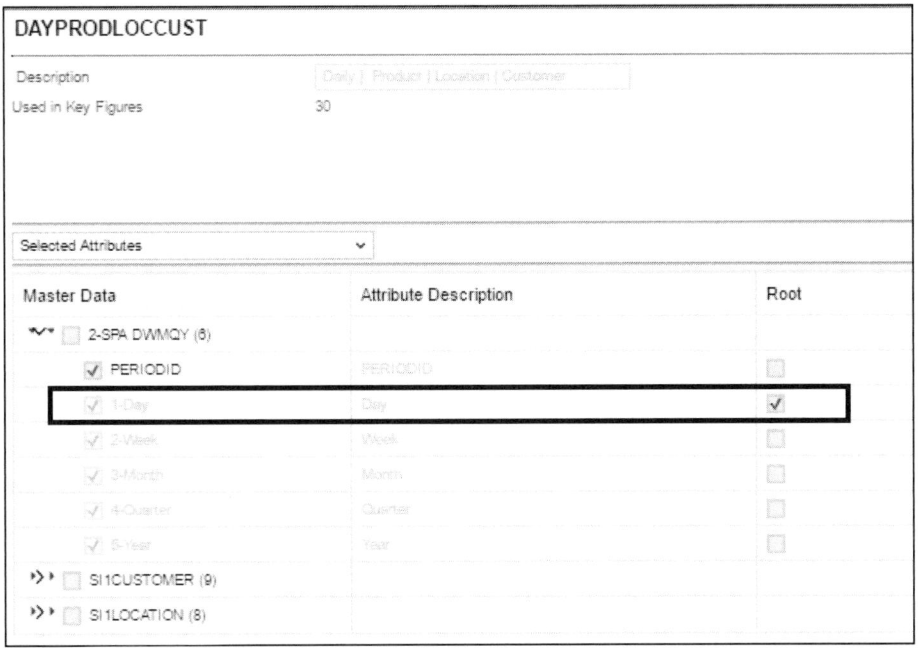

DAYPRODLOCCUST

Description   Daily | Product | Location | Customer

Used in Key Figures   30

Selected Attributes

Master Data	Attribute Description	Root
2-SPA DWMQY (6)		
PERIODID	PERIODID	
1-Day	Day	✓
2-Week	Week	
3-Month	Month	
4-Quarter	Quarter	
5-Year	Year	
SI1CUSTOMER (9)		
SI1LOCATION (8)		

Figure 9.5 Representative Planning Levels at the Day Level with Product, Location, and Customer

9.1.4   Key Figures

Key figures used in demand planning applications are for the input, output, and processing applications of demand planning and demand sensing processes. These key figures are related to the past order data, statistical model output, adjustments key figures, helper key figures, and the finalized demand plan. Table 9.2 shows the list of demand planning key figures that must be added in the planning model and that are crucial for understanding the demand planning application for SAP IBP.

Key Figure ID	Name	Level	Application or Logic
DELIVQTY	Delivered quantity	DeliveryDaily	Actual historical data of delivered quantity

Table 9.2 Important Key Figure Mapping and Information for Order and Data Mapping in Demand Planning

Key Figure ID	Name	Level	Application or Logic
ADJDELIVQTY	Adjusted delivery quantity	LocProdCustDaily also calculated at LocProdCustWeekly	Any adjustment in delivered (historical data) quantity before using in forecast model
STATISTICALEXPOST-FCSTQTY	Ex-post forecast quantity	LocProdCustWeekly	For mapping and calculating ex-post forecast
STATISTICALFCSTQTY	Statistical forecast quantity	LocProdCustWeekly	Output of statistical forecast calculation
SALESFCSTQTY	Sales forecast quantity	LocProdCustWeekly	For edit by sales team; if blank, statistical forecast can be copied
MARKETINGFCSTQTY	Marketing forecast quantity	LocProdCustWeekly	For edit by marketing team; if blank, statistical forecast can be copied
DEMANDPLANNING-QTY	Demand planning quantity	LocProdCustWeekly	Final adjusted or planned demand quantity; if no adjustment or blank value, sales forecast quantity can be copied
CONSENSUSDEMAND	Consensus demand (without promotion adjustment)	LocProdCustWeekly	If blank, demand planning quantity; otherwise value maintained for consensus demand quantity
PROMOUPLIFT	Promotion uplift	PromoProdCustCalWk	Promotion uplift without location information; a location split disaggregation required for usage in demand planning

Table 9.2 Important Key Figure Mapping and Information for Order and Data Mapping in Demand Planning (Cont.)

Key Figure ID	Name	Level	Application or Logic
PROMOLOCATION-SPLIT	Promotion location split	LocProdWeekly	To disaggregate promotion
PROMOSPLIT	Promotion uplift	PromoLocProdCustWK	Uplift due to promotion, which can be added to consensus demand
FINALCONSENSUS-DEMAND	Final consensus demand	LocProdCustWeekly	Adding promotion plan to consensus demand to finalize the consensus demand; also used by some organizations for final consensus demand as the copy of the constrained demand as output of the S&OP process
CONSENSUS-DEMANDREV	Consensus demand revenue	LocProdCustCurrWK	Consensus demand quantity with sales forecast price and currency conversion
REQQTY	Requested quantity	SalesOrderDaily	Requested sales order quantity
CONFQTY	Confirmed sales order quantity	SalesOrderDaily calculated at LocProdCustDaily	Sales order confirmed quantity
SENSEDDEMANDQTY	Sensed demand quantity	LocProdCustDaily	Sensed demand quantity calculated by system
ADJSENSEDDEMAND-QTY	Adjusted sensed demand quantity	LocProdCustDaily	For performing any adjustment in sensed demand

Table 9.2 Important Key Figure Mapping and Information for Order and Data Mapping in Demand Planning (Cont.)

Key Figure ID	Name	Level	Application or Logic
FINALSENSED-DEMANDQTY	Final sensed demand	LocProdCustDaily	Adding adjusted sensed demand to sensed demand to get final sensed demand
UOMCONVFACTOR	Unit of measure (UOM) conversion factor	ProdUomTo	UOM conversion factor (if relevant to plan with different UOM)
EXCHANGERATE	Exchange rate	CurrFromToDaily	Exchange rate for currency conversion
DEMANDPLANNING-QTYERROR	Demand planning forecast error percentage	LocProdCustLagMly	For mapping the forecast percentage error

Table 9.2 Important Key Figure Mapping and Information for Order and Data Mapping in Demand Planning (Cont.)

9.1.5 Planning Area, Model, and Planning Operator

To use the demand planning application in SAP IBP for demand, you must perform some necessary configurations in the planning area, planning model, and planning operator.

For the planning area, it's recommended to refer to the SAP standard planning area SAP6 or unified planning area SAPIBP1 for creating the planning area for demand planning. Some of the important settings required in the planning area are as follows:

▶ **Attribute, master data, and time period**
Maintain the relevant attribute, master data type, key figures, and time profile as discussed previously.

▶ **Change history enable**
For performing the demand sensing run, it's required to enable the planning area for change history by selecting the CHANGE HISTORY PLANNING AREA ENABLED checkbox.

▸ **Planning operator selection**

It's mandatory to select the forecast planning operator STATFORECASTING under the planning operator group IBPFORECAST for using the statistical models for demand forecasting and demand sensing. In addition to the forecast planning operator, some of the planning operators from copy, disaggregation, and advance simulation groups are also required to perform the calculations of the demand planning processes. Figure 9.6 show an example of the planning area settings and relevant planning operators for reference.

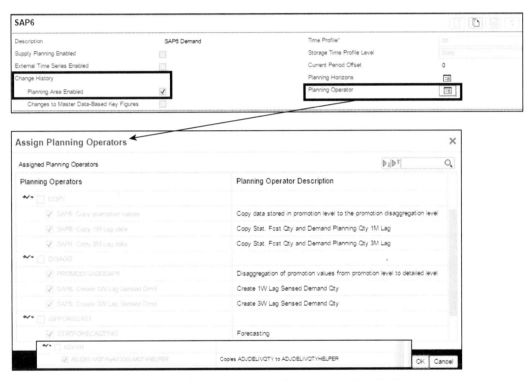

Figure 9.6 Planning Area Settings and Planning Operator for the Demand Application

For activation and usage of the model, time profile, master data, and key figures, make sure that the independent elements are loaded into the system before the dependent ones.

The recommended sequence for model building is as follows:

1. Time profile activation
2. Master data activation

3. Planning area activation

4. Upload of location (including supplier), product, and customer

5. Location product and customer product

6. Currency (optional)

7. Exchange rate (optional)

8. Unit of measure to (optional)

9. Unit of measure conversion (optional)

10. Sales order (for demand sensing)

11. Delivery (for demand sensing)

12. Promotion (for promotion planning)

13. Key figure data (delivered quantity, consensus demand, etc.)

If demand sensing is in scope, then a snapshot key figure must be configured in the planning model. Using the MANAGE SNAPSHOT CONFIGURATION option in the CONFIGURATION tile, a snapshot type of change history is created at the week/product/location/customer planning level. The demand planning quantity is selected as input for the snapshot before saving it. Note that snapshot creation in a planning area deactivates the planning area and requires a new activation after this configuration step.

9.2 Forecast Model Management

The Manage Forecast Models app in SAP IBP for demand is used to map the statistical model for demand forecasting, demand sensing, and forecast error calculation. In the following sections, we'll look at the configuration elements that are mapped in the app, as follows:

▸ General settings

▸ Preprocessing

▸ Forecasting

▸ Postprocessing

9.2.1 General Settings

You define the planning area assignment and the periodicity through the configuration in the GENERAL settings. Figure 9.7 shows the MANAGE FORECAST MODELS app under DEMAND PLANNER; it also displays an example of the configuration elements maintained in the general settings for a forecast model. The HISTORICAL PERIODS field refers to the number of periods in the past used for forecast generation; the FORECAST PERIODS field refers to the number of periods in the future for which the forecast is generated.

In addition to the TIME SETTINGS values, the MODEL NAME and DESCRIPTION fields are provided in the GENERAL settings tab.

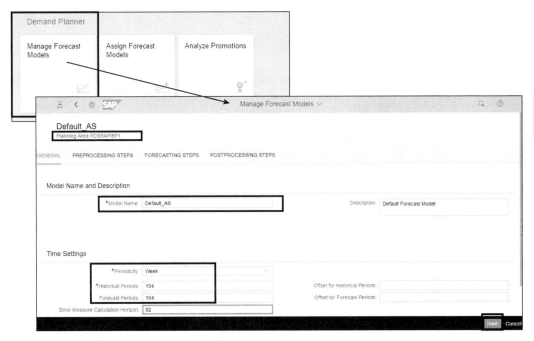

Figure 9.7 General Setting for the Forecast Model

9.2.2 Preprocessing

Configuration for the outlier data correction and missing value substitution is performed through the preprocessing step of the forecast model management. Figure 9.8 shows an example of the preprocessing step configuration. The OUTLIER DETECTION METHOD and OUTLIER CORRECTION METHOD are selected through the available algorithms. Input of the algorithm key figure selects the key figure of the actual sales history, which needs review and correction.

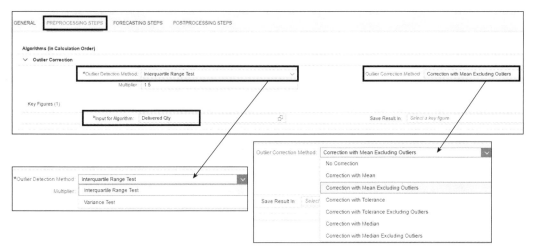

Figure 9.8 Preprocessing Step Configuration of the Forecast Model

There are two possible approaches to using this methodology in the planning process. Either the correction from the system is directly used as input for the forecast as an automated approach, or the suggested correction can be reviewed and adjusted manually before being using in the forecast model. To use the automated approach, the same forecast model can have the preprocessing and forecasting step with the corrected key figure selected as input for the forecast. To use the two-step approach, first the model can contain only the preprocessing step, and the output can be saved as a different key figure that can be used for review and adjustment. The adjusted value can be used as input to the forecast step through a second model with a forecasting step. The second model can also have the postprocessing step if desired for forecast error calculation.

9.2.3   Forecasting

Overall parameter and forecast algorithm selection for demand forecasting and demand sensing is performed in the forecasting step. See Figure 9.9 for the configuration elements of forecasting step.

Input and output key figures of the statistical model are provided here. The Ex-Post Forecast Qty key figure field is mapped to the ex-post information used for forecast value generation and error calculation.

The Add Forecasting Algorithm button is used to select the algorithm for demand forecasting or demand sensing. From a list of available algorithms, the relevant statistical model is selected for the demand plan.

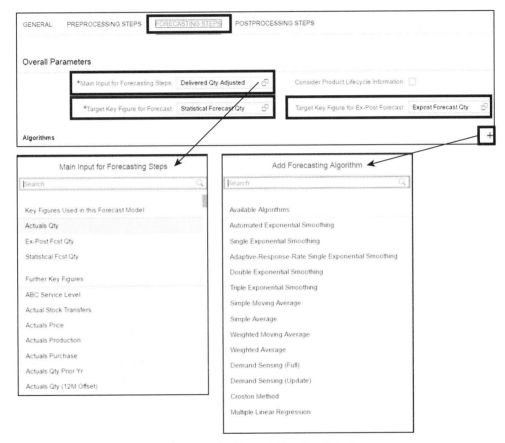

Figure 9.9 Forecasting Step Configuration for Key and Algorithm Selection

Figure 9.10 shows an example of a configured forecasting model, which can be used for forecast generation.

Figure 9.10 Forecasting Step: Perform a Demand Forecast with the Triple Exponential Method

To add and use multiple forecast algorithms for the statistical forecast genera-tion, you can use the + button in the FORECASTING STEPS screen. Utilization on the basis of best fit or weighted average value can be controlled through the METHOD field. A configuration example is shown in Figure 9.11. Through the dropdown menu options, forecasting algorithms are selected for a multiple fore-cast approach. In this example, the MEAN PERCENTAGE ERROR (MPE) value is used to identify the best approach for statistical forecast generation from the selected multiple methods.

For predicting sensed demand, the algorithm for demand sensing can also be added through the ADD ALGORITHM option in the FORECASTING STEPS screen. The input and output key figures must be selected as relevant for the demand sensing calculation. The only preprocessing algorithm relevant for demand sensing is PROMOTION SALES LIFT ELIMINATION. Figure 9.12 shows the algorithm configura-tion fields for forecasting.

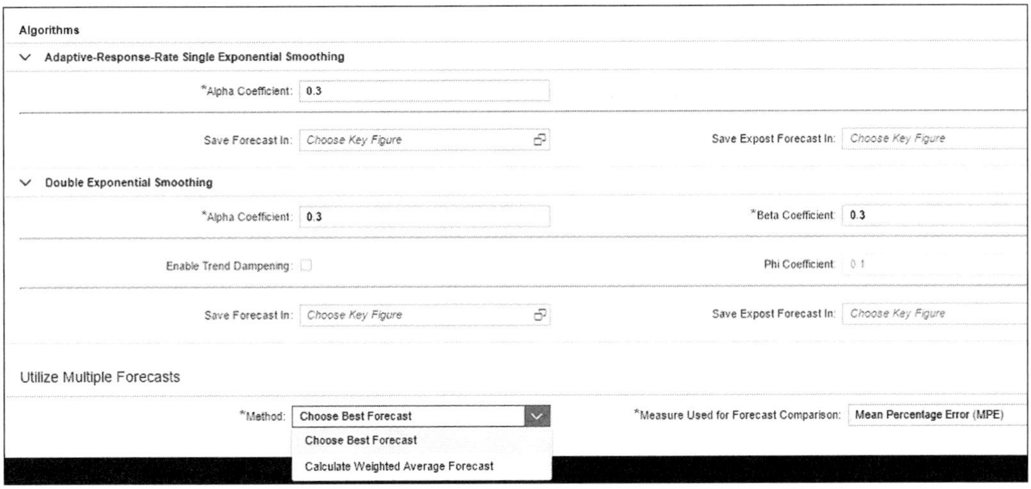

Figure 9.11 Usage of Multiple Forecast Algorithms

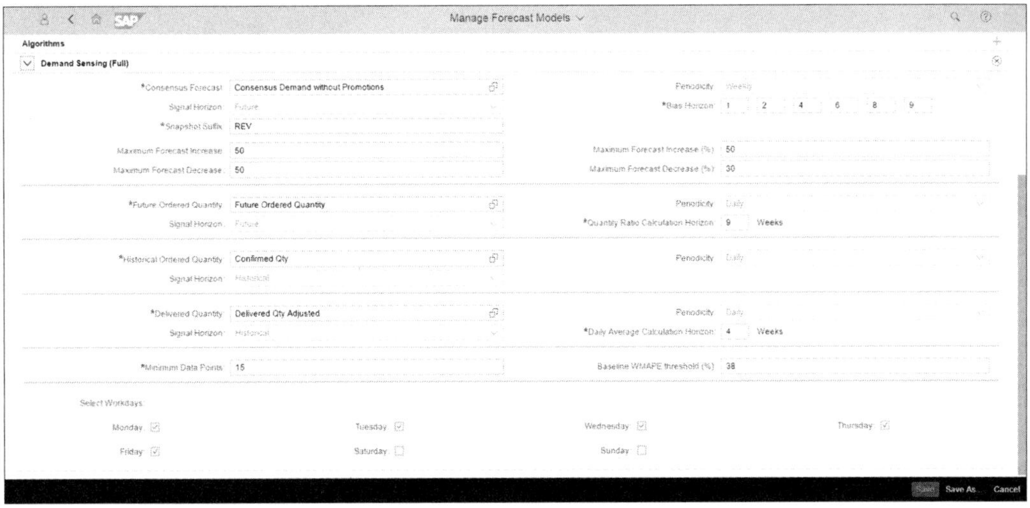

Figure 9.12 Demand Sensing Algorithm Configuration in Demand Forecasting

Key figures are mapped for the consensus demand (demand as finalized through the demand planning process), order quantity (for past and future), and delivered quantity. The SNAPSHOT SUFFIX field is the suffix created through the configuration.

Change history enabled and the snapshot key figure are systems requirements for performing demand sensing. The value of SIGNAL HORIZON is for assigning the time horizon for the demand signal in the demand sensing run. MAXIMUM FORECAST INCREASE and MAXIMUM FORECAST DECREASE parameters control the allowed deviations of sensed demand from the consensus demand in absolute and percentage terms. BIAS HORIZON is for assigning the recent weeks in the past for which forecast bias needs to be calculated and considered by the planning run. Workday selection for the week is performed to select normal working days; it's used by the system to disaggregate the weekly consensus demand into equal daily forecasts for workdays.

In addition to the *full demand sensing* algorithms shown in Figure 9.13, an *update demand sensing* algorithm is also available in SAP IBP for demand for calculating sensed demand. The update algorithm is relatively faster and is recommended to be executed every day after execution of the full demand sensing algorithm during the start of the week. The update algorithm doesn't require a bias setting and works with less input data elements and calculations.

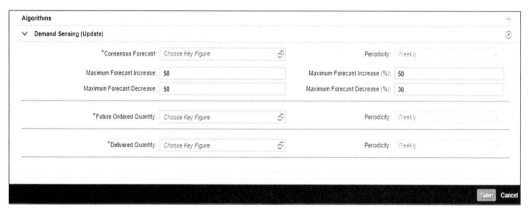

Figure 9.13 Update Demand Sensing Algorithm Configuration Fields

9.2.4 Postprocessing

Configuration for the forecast error measurement and relevant key performance indicator (KPI) for forecast error selection is performed through the postprocessing step of the Manage Forecast app. Detailed information and the application of different types of forecast errors are discussed in Chapter 8. Per the nature and data elements of the demand forecast, one error measure parameter or a combination of them can be selected through the configuration selection fields shown in Figure 9.14. Postprocessing is only relevant for the demand forecasting algorithms and isn't applicable for the demand sensing algorithms.

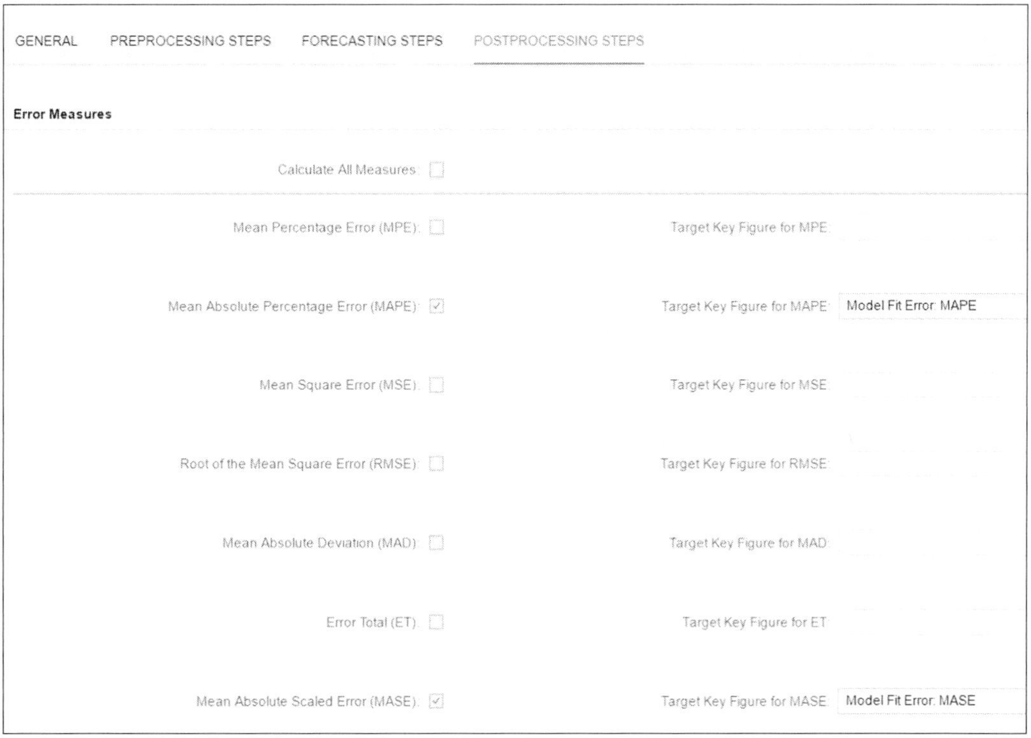

Figure 9.14 Postprocessing Step Configuration of Forecast Management

9.3 Promotion Planning

System configuration for promotion planning in SAP IBP for demand is either performed through integrating the external promotion system (e.g., the SAP trade promotion system or similar system) or by maintaining the promotion data directly in SAP IBP. Through either approach, the value for the key figure for promotion uplift (PROMOSPLIT) is populated in the SAP IBP system and is added into the final consensus demand to finalize the demand plan after considering the promotion plan.

The promotion key figures are added into the planning model for demand and are used for the promotion disaggregation to the promotion/customer/location/

product/customer/weekly planning level to be added into the consensus demand. Promotion information and its impact in planning is analyzed through the SAP IBP Excel planning view by selecting the promotion key figures or through the Analyze Promotions app. Figure 9.15 shows an example of promotion planning in SAP IBP for demand.

This application is accessed through the Analyze Promotions app in the DEMAND PLANNER header. By clicking a particular promotion row, detailed information about a promotion can be reviewed. There is also an option to add the information in the notes section for collaboration and task management in SAP IBP.

The PROMOTION ID, MAX. SALES LIFT, AVERAGE SALES LIFT, and BUYING PERIOD information is provided in the SAP IBP system for demand planning. The demand plan is updated with the planned promotion uplift value and is ready for further review. Any relevant information is managed and shared with the team through the detailed information and note section as shown in Figure 9.15.

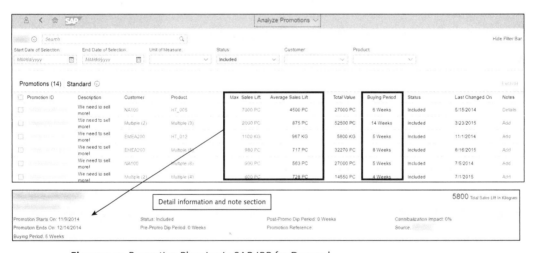

Figure 9.15 Promotion Planning in SAP IBP for Demand

9.4 Demand Planning Run in SAP IBP

Statistical forecasting algorithms can be executed in SAP IBP for demand through the Excel planning view. This can be manually executed on demand, can be scheduled as a one-time job execution, or can be modeled to be executed periodically as batch jobs. Mid-term and long-term statistical forecasts can be executed at the base planning level of the relevant key figures as well as at an aggregated level. However, short-term forecasting is run only at the product/location/customer level. While performing a mid-term or long-term forecasting, base or any simulation version can be used to either update the planning data or to perform the what-if simulation. Short-term forecasting through demand sensing can only be executed for the base level.

For execution of demand planning forecasting and demand sensing, the ADVANCED group in the Excel planning view is used for the STATISTICAL FORECASTING tab. Figure 9.16 shows an example of scheduling a demand forecasting planning run.

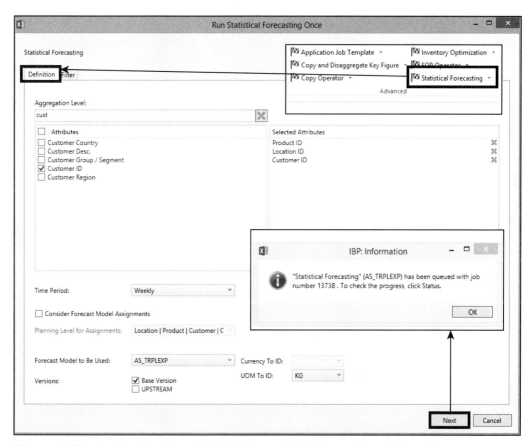

Figure 9.16 Planning Execution through Statistical Forecasting for Forecasting and Demand Sensing

In the same Advanced group, by using the Statistical Forecasting dropdown arrow, a status option can be selected to view the job execution status. In a planning environment, this job is usually scheduled on a periodic basis. Figure 9.17 shows an example of scheduling a recurring job. For end-to-end demand planning process support, a sequence of scheduling may be required for recurring batch jobs of planning runs and other runs for operators such as copy and disaggregation.

Figure 9.17 Periodic Recurring Job Scheduling in SAP IBP for Statistical Forecasting or Demand Sensing

9.5   Demand Planning for a New Product

Modeling a new product in SAP IBP for demand is done by creating the profile for the new product and then activating the Manage Product Lifecycle indicator in the forecast model (see Figure 9.18). The Consider Product Lifecycle Information indicator is checked in the forecasting step of the forecast model.

Configuration of the new product forecast is done by creating a profile accessed through the Manage Product Lifecycle app in the Demand Plan header. In the management of product lifecycle configuration, the new product and the reference product information is selected. More than one product can be configured

as the reference product, and a weighting percentage can be applied for generation of the forecast of the new product. OFFSET IN DAYS determines the period for
which the historical data is used. This information is helpful if the reference product was in phase-out mode and a certain period should not be considered. Therefore, for a value of 180 days for the offset, the last 6 months of historical data
won't be included when forecasting the new product.

Figure 9.18 New Product Demand Forecasting Model Configuration

Figure 9.19 shows the pop-up for the new product while creating a new profile.
Forecast START DATE, as displayed in Figure 9.19, represents the location and the
start date of the new forecast data. This forecast date is used to control the phase-
in date of the new product. After assignment of the values, the SAVE button is
used to save the profile. Assignment of a new product and reference products to
the forecast model will generate the forecast for the new product.

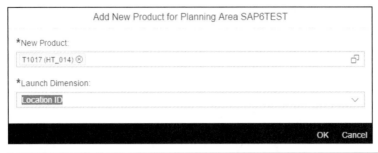

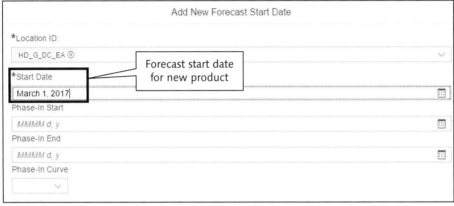

Figure 9.19 Assignment of Product, Location, and Forecast Start Date for the New Product

9.6 Planning Results

Demand planners use the Excel planning view of SAP IBP for reviewing, adjusting, and analyzing the demand plan. Multiple planning views can be saved or created on the fly to analyze the information through different key figures that are relevant for the demand planning application. The planning views are used to analyze historical data and statistical forecast data as generated by the SAP IBP system or as imported from any other legacy system. Figure 9.20 shows an example of the Excel planning view for data review and cleansing by considering the deviation range of plus or minus three standard deviation value. Through manual data adjustment, auto adjustment, or alert generation, the historical data can be cleansed to remove the outliers before using the past data in the statistical model of forecast generation

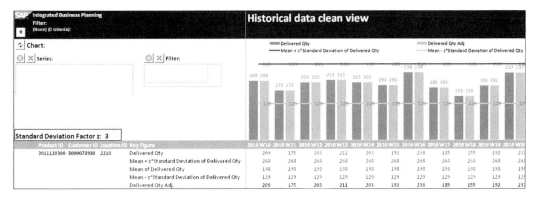

Figure 9.20 Historical Data Review and Clean View

Demand planning adjustments through collaborative demand planning, for example, with the sales and marketing team, is performed in the planning view, along with any adjustment to the promotion planning. Through inherent integration with SAP Jam, information related to the plan update can be shared with team members.

Figure 9.21 and Figure 9.22 show examples of demand planning views in SAP IBP for demand. Figure 9.21 shows the statistical forecast, along with the planning key figures relevant for the demand planner, the sales personnel, and the marketing team. Planning views, along with the collaboration process supported by SAP IBP, are used for finalizing the demand plan as a consensus demand. A similar planning view can be used for promotion planning through key figures for demand adjustments through planned promotion.

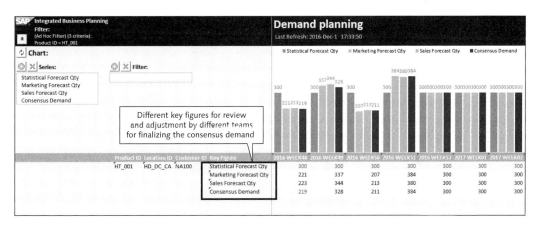

Figure 9.21 Demand Planning Views in SAP IBP for Demand: Part 1

Figure 9.22 shows an example of a product group for a customer region for demand planning quantity as input to the S&OP of the demand review subprocess. Quantities, revenue, and profit for demand planning, sales, marketing, and finance (annual operating plan, AOP) team in one view are represented for consideration and cross-team discussion.

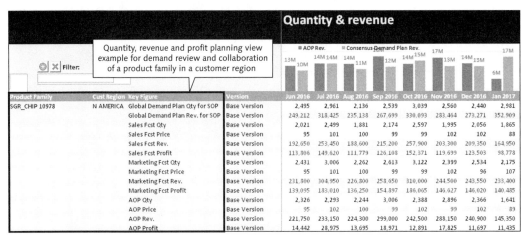

Figure 9.22 Figure. Demand Planning Views in SAP IBP for Demand: Part 2

Figure 9.23 shows another planning view with an example of demand sensing. It represents the short-term demand adjustment and finalization through short-term demand planning. The sensed demand key figure is calculated by the system, which can be adjusted based on the planner's input to finalize the demand and to achieve a demand-driven supply chain.

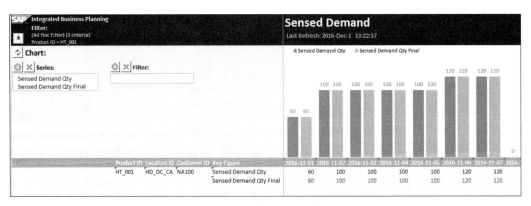

Figure 9.23 Demand Sensing in SAP IBP for Demand

In addition to the Excel planning view, the SAP Fiori view through the Analyze Promotions app is used to view and analyze promotions related to a specific set of master data as discussed in Section 9.3.

In addition to the Excel planning view and promotion analysis application, the Task Management app of SAP IBP is also used for collaboration to finalize the consensus demand and final sensed demand. This app is discussed in detail in Chapter 15, Sections 15.2 and 15.5. In the SAP IBP system, a task is created and assigned to the team members to manage the work item, to share the information, and to collaborate while working in one system with total visibility and one version of truth.

9.7 Summary

SAP IBP for demand is a sophisticated, and easy-to-use tool for managing the demand planning process. Statistical algorithms generate the forecast for short-term, medium-term, and long-term horizons. Configuration of SAP IBP for demand can be done by referring to the standard planning model provided by SAP. Mapping of a client's master data, business processes, and transactions is done through easily configured steps to generate an organization-wide demand plan. The generated plan is further adjusted and reviewed through a collaboration process supported by SAP IBP for end-to-end visibility and control of the demand planning process.

Customer demand finalized through the demand planning process is used for driving the supply through production, transportation, and purchasing. This chapter discusses the concepts of supply planning and response management business processes along with their modeling with SAP IBP for response and supply.

10   Response and Supply Planning with SAP IBP

The process of planning for fulfillment in the supply chain is called supply planning. It's performed to meet requirements such as anticipated customer demand, sales orders, or internal consumption. An organization fulfills customer demand through a combination of producing, purchasing, and transporting goods and services across the supply chain. This chapter will discuss the various supply planning approaches used to successfully execute these activities.

Supply planning is relevant for short-term, medium-term, and long-term horizons with special focus on the medium-term planning horizon. Long-term supply planning is aligned with sales and operations planning (S&OP), while the short-term supply planning works with response planning.

Response planning, on the other hand, focuses on reacting to market changes in the short term for the most desirable results. A variation of the actual event from the anticipated behavior requires a response management solution. The real demand of customers may vary from the forecast; a supplier's inability to supply a component or a transportation delay can disrupt the original supply plan. An effective response solution enables the organization to determine the best course of action in those scenarios. Therefore, response planning is a supply solution with a short-term horizon.

In this chapter we'll start with the overview of response and supply planning, followed by a discussion of the response and supply planning methodology. Building up the knowledge gained on supply planning in Chapter 6 (Section 6.3.2) and Chapter 7 (Section 7.3.2), we'll move into the discussion of rule-based response and supply planning with demand prioritization, supply confirmation, and allocation. The SAP IBP for response and supply application includes a highly valuable feature of gating factor analysis, which we'll discuss in a separate section. Finally, we'll analyze the planning view, simulation, and collaboration applications in SAP IBP for response and supply.

10.1 Response and Supply Planning Overview

Table 10.1 shows the supply planning solution in short-term, medium-term, and long-term horizons. Long-term supply planning is normally performed for 18 months to 5 years and is typically in a monthly horizon. This drives the strategic decisions of the organization for demand and supply. Decisions regarding capacity enhancement, product development, supplier selection, and network changes are examples of long-term supply planning. Mid-term supply planning decisions are operational in nature and generally performed in weekly buckets for a typical period of 6 weeks to 18 months. Operational supply planning of production, distribution, and procurement are performed for this period. Short-term supply planning or response planning is generally performed in daily buckets for a period up to 6 weeks.

Planning Horizon	Short Term	Medium Term	Long Term
Representative time bucket	Daily	Weekly	Monthly
Strategy level	Response	Operational	Strategic
Planning activity examples	▸ Adjust supply plan ▸ Respond to incoming customer orders for deviation from forecast ▸ Confirm sales orders ▸ Plan allocation for constrained supply	▸ Develop production, purchasing, and stock transfer plans against demand forecast and sales orders ▸ Forecast-driven replenishment plan ▸ Action for resolution of any predicted supply issue	▸ Mid- to long-term higher level supply plan ▸ Supplier collaboration ▸ Executive and intra-team collaboration to have one organization-level plan

Table 10.1 Supply Plan for Different Planning Horizons

The start of the response planning period is based on any frozen period. For organizations that follow a frozen period of a couple of days to a week, the response solution is relevant from the end of the frozen period to the end of the response solution horizon. For a frozen period of one week and response solution period of six weeks, the horizon of response planning will be from one week to six weeks. With no frozen period, the response solution horizon will be from current date to the end of the response planning horizon. Typical decisions for the response planning solution are adjustment of the supply plan, order fulfillment, and assignment of quotas.

For most industries, demand is volatile, lead time for product availability is higher than the required customer service time, and carrying inventory increases costs and reduces flexibility of the organization. These factors demonstrate the need for efficient response and supply planning. For organizations with a presence across the globe and a complex network structure of production plants, warehouses, suppliers, and customers, efficient response and supply planning is paramount for efficiently servicing their customers. An efficient response and supply solution enhances the profitability of the organization by adding value through the following:

- Higher service rate
- Lower inventory cost
- Alignment with business priorities
- Higher resource utilization

The lead time to procure and produce a material is higher than the anticipated time by the customer to receive the material after placing an order. Hence, supply planning in advance is crucial for an organization to be able to serve a customer with a higher service rate. This is true for both *make-to-stock* as well as *make-to-order* environments. For the make-to-stock scenario, ideally the material should be available in finished goods inventory before receiving the customer order; for the make-to-order scenario, required components should be available in the finished goods inventory to start the final assembly or manufacturing as soon as the customer order is received. At the same time, carrying inventory locks the capital, increases the cost, and reduces the flexibility of the organization. Therefore, serving the customers optimally and responding to the market realities against forecast becomes hugely important, and response and supply solution becomes the central nervous system of the organization.

Not all demands are equal for an organization, and you may be required to follow a prioritization rule when fulfilling orders. An efficient response and supply solution must be able to meet this requirement while aligning demand and supply because it increases the organization's success and profitability in the long run.

10.2 Supply Planning Methodology

The supply planning algorithm creates the supply plan for production, purchase, and stock transfer. It's driven by the master data of the supply chain network and the algorithm type identified for the supply plan. The master data that governs the supply planning solution are the production rule (driven by bill of material [BOM], resource, and recipe/routing), replenishment rule (driven by the sourcing logic or transportation lane), and network structure for the products (through production rule, transportation rule, or procurement rule). The master data topic for supply planning is discussed in detail in Chapter 3.

Some supply planning algorithms are as follows:

- Unconstrained supply heuristic planning
- Constrained supply optimization
- Supply, allocation, and response planning
- Deployment planning

Unconstrained heuristic supply planning and constrained supply optimization are the supply planning algorithms for time bucket planning. They are part of the planning operators of SAP IBP for sales and operation, and are covered in detail in Chapter 7. Optimization in order-based planning is currently on the product roadmap of the SAP IBP for response and supply is under development and is planned to be available in the year 2018. However, functionality-wise, it's similar to the optimization concepts explained in Chapter 7.

Supply, allocation, and response planning is the backbone of SAP IBP for response and supply. This is based on constrained supply, allocation, response, and order confirmation planning which are performed through two different planning operators:

- Supply and allocation planning
- Response and order confirmation planning

For supply, allocation, and response planning, there is an option to fulfill the demand through a prioritization sequence to meet the higher priority demands in case of constrained supply situations. The next section is devoted to the demand prioritization logic in SAP IBP for response and supply before going into the details of the planning logic mentioned here.

10.2.1 Demand Prioritization

Demand prioritization in SAP IBP is achieved through a prioritization rule, segments for the rule, and sorting logic within a segment. The elements used to calculate the demand prioritization are as follows:

- Demand prioritization rule
- Sorting condition in a segment
- Demand segments
- Review of demand sequence on defined priority

Figure 10.1 shows an example of the demand prioritization logic in SAP IBP through prioritization rule, segment creation, and sorting criteria. The prioritization rule is used to prioritize every demand element in a planning version or a subset of the elements based on certain selection criteria. There is at least one segment in every rule. Segments are the building blocks of the rule; a rule can have multiple segments with the sequence of the segments defined for their prioritization. A segment defines the selection criteria or condition for a demand element. Based on the selection criteria and property of a demand element, it is associated with a segment.

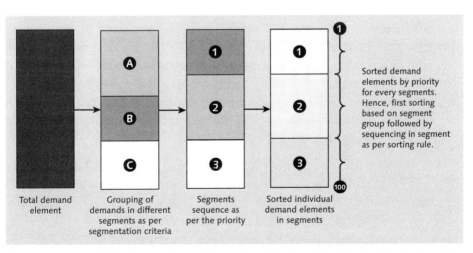

Total demand element | Grouping of demands in different segments as per segmentation criteria | Segments sequence as per the priority | Sorted individual demand elements in segments

Sorted demand elements by priority for every segments. Hence, first sorting based on segment group followed by sequencing in segment as per sorting rule.

Figure 10.1 Demand Prioritization through Segments and Sorting Criteria in the Prioritization Rule

For example, a segment can be created for a customer classification (e.g., customers classified as **Ⓐ**, **Ⓑ**, or **Ⓒ**), material categorization (e.g., materials categorized as group **❶**, **❷**, **❸**, etc.), material requirements planning (MRP) for demand type (e.g., MRP type VC for sales order, FC/FA for forecast, etc.), or any other segments based on the attributes defined for the master data elements. The planning system identifies the demand elements as part of the segment group and then sequences the segments per the sequence identified in the rule. Each segment has one or multiple sorting criteria for further sequencing of the demand elements within a segment. Hence, within a segment for customer group A, individual demand elements can be sorted based on attributes such as requirements date, order delivery priority, revenue, order entry date, etc. Sorting grouped with the segment identifies and ranks every demand element in the system in order of replenishment priority for the response and supply planning solution. Demand elements with the prioritization rank are available for review by the planners in the SAP IBP system. Based on the review, the prioritization rule can be edited to meet business priorities.

10.2.2 Supply, Allocation, and Response Planning

Rule-based response and supply planning in a constrained environment is achieved through supply allocation and response planning algorithms in SAP IBP for response and supply. Figure 10.2 shows the planning sequence and details for rule-based supply, allocation, and response planning. Prioritized demand through the prioritization rule and supply constraints (resource, material, supplier capacity, etc.) are the input for *constraint supply planning*. A constraint supply planning run is also known as a *constraint forecast run* in SAP IBP. The output of this planning run is a supply plan and a *constrained demand forecast*. A constrained demand forecast is generated using the prioritized demand and organization's ability to supply while considering the supply constraints. In a short supply scenario, the constrained demand forecast will be less than the unconstrained forecast, as shown in Figure 10.2.

In SAP IBP, the constrained forecast can be copied as the product allocation, which will limit the supply of a product against an order while considering the prioritized demand. A confirmation planning run, available as a separate algorithm in response and supply planning, re-plans the supply with the most recent prioritized demand and the product allocation. This planning run also performs the order confirmation. For any change in the demand and supply situation, the confirmation planning run re-creates the plan and confirms the orders. Therefore, the output of this complete cycle is the confirmed orders and the most preferred supply plan per the prioritization rule and organization's ability to supply.

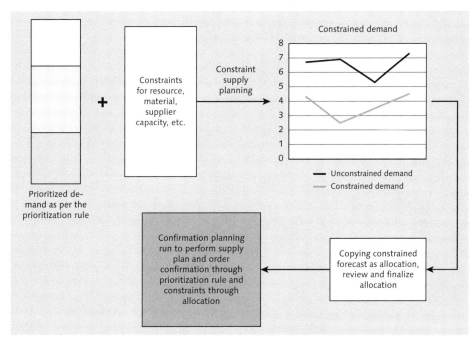

Figure 10.2 Supply Allocation and Response Planning with SAP IBP Response and Supply

10.2.3 Deployment Planning

Deployment planning is performed as short-term supply planning to supply the actual available material against open orders. This planning methodology matches demand elements with the existing supply. Deployment is normally performed only in the short term for the *actual product movement horizon*, typically from a couple of days to a week. Deployment planning can be grouped with the planning time fence or frozen horizon for supply planning. If adequate supply is available, then the deployment totally matches the demand elements with the supply elements. In a short supply scenario, fair share or other replenishment logic can be applied. The output of deployment planning is the confirmed order. As of SAP IBP 1611, deployment planning isn't yet part of the solution, although it's on the product roadmap and is expected to be available by mid-2018.

10.3 Forecast Consumption

Forecast consumption is a standard requirement and functionality of response and supply planning. In a make-to-stock scenario, a product is manufactured and is made available in inventory in anticipation of the customer order. After the sales order enters the SAP IBP system, it consumes the existing forecast first. This consumption is usually performed at either the period/product/location or period/product/location/customer level. The option of the planning levels gives the flexibility to either consider or not consider the customer while consuming the forecast.

Table 10.2 shows an example of forecast consumption with the logic of the consuming forecast in the same bucket against the requested sales order. Total demand of the material in a time bucket is the sum of the requested sales order and net forecast (unconsumed forecast) in the time bucket. Hence, if the requested sales order in a time bucket is less than the forecast, total demand in that period is the original forecast. However, if the sales order is higher than the forecast in a time period, the net demand is equal to the total number of requested sales orders.

Time Period (Months)	1	2	3	4
Unconstrained forecast	100	100	100	100
Requested sales order	60	120	90	110
Consumed forecast	60	100	90	100
Net forecast (unconsumed)	40	0	10	0
Total demand (sales order + forecast)	100	120	100	110

Table 10.2 Forecast Consumption with Consumption in the Same Time Bucket Only

10.4 Gating Factor Analysis

Gating factor analysis provides information on all the constraints that prevent fulfillment of a sales order on time. Gating factors are associated with the details of order elements in response and supply planning. An order may not be fulfilled on time due to limitations or constraints such as resource availability, material shortage, allocation, etc. The gating factor functionality in SAP IBP provides detailed information on the limiting factors so that the planner can analyze the issue in advance and take appropriate action.

Gating factor types and related information in SAP IBP for response and supply are shown in Table 10.3. This ready reference information in the system helps in the root-cause analysis on an unwanted scenario before the exception actually hits the demand and supply plan. This alert mechanism is highly useful in adjusting the plan to take the best possible action in the event of supply challenges.

Gating Factor Type	Gating Factor Information
Lead time	Procurement or stock transfer lead time
Resource	Production capacity availability of a resource
Projected stock	Stock level lower than the expected level to fulfill an order based on the demand and supply situation
Supplier constraint	Supplier commitment with the limit on the material supply in a horizon
Product allocation	Allocation finalized by the business in a supply shortage scenario
Supply chain model	Issue in supply chain model consistency and data elements

Table 10.3 Gating Factor Types in SAP IBP

10.5 Order Review and Analysis

Order review and analysis in SAP IBP for response and supply is performed at both the time-bucket aggregate level as well as at the detailed order-based level. Planning results in time-bucket aggregation are reviewed in the SAP IBP Excel planning view. Order-level reviews for the order confirmation, projected inventory, and gating factor analysis are performed in the SAP Fiori app of SAP IBP.

10.5.1 SAP IBP Excel Planning View

Even though the response and supply solution is based on the order-level planning, planning key figures of demand, supply, allocation, and net calculations can be reviewed in the time-bucket planning view. Based on the properties of a key figure, it may be available for review but not for editing. Key figure information that is normally relevant for response and supply planning in the Excel planning view includes demand forecast, allocation, constrained forecast, inventory, net demand, production, purchase, and projected inventory.

Figure 10.3 displays an example of the SAP IBP Excel planning view relevant for response and supply planning. The forecast, sales order, and allocation planning view example shows these key figure in the daily time bucket. Based on the solution requirement and nature of the organization's business, a weekly or monthly time bucket can also be considered for this review. The second example in the same figure shows the projected stock view, along with elements of total demand, total supply, and inventory information. Note that the key figures not relevant for change in the planning view are grayed out with a different background color than white.

Forecast, sales order, and allocation planning view example

Customer ID	Location ID	Material Number	Key Figure	12/05/2016	12/06/2016	12/07/2016	12/08/2016	12/09/2016	12/10/2016	12/11/2016	12/12/2016
10000012	2000	PR1_ABC	Allocation	100	100	50	40	100	100	100	100
			Allocation Adjusted				60				
			Allocation Consumed	50	100	50	40	0	0	0	0
			Allocation Final	100	100	60	40	100	100	100	100
			Allocation Remaining	0	0	10	0	100	100	100	100
			Forecast Constrained	100	100	50	40	100	100	100	100
			Forecast Unconstrained	100	100	100	100	100	100	100	100
			Sales Order (Confirmed)	50	100	50	40	0	0	0	0

Projected stock planning view example

Location ID	Material Number	Key Figure	11/16/2016	11/17/2016	11/18/2016	11/19/2016	11/20/2016
DC1	PR_AC2	Stock Projected	12	62	82	-18	0
		Initial Stock	0	0	0	0	0
		Total Demand	50	100	50	100	100
		Total Receipt	62	150	70	0	118
		Production (Planned)	0	0	0	0	0
		Production (Confirmed)	0	0	0	0	0
		Distribution Receipt (Planned)	0	50	70	0	118
		Distribution Demand (Planned)	50	100	50	100	100
		Distribution Receipt (Confirmed)	62	100	0	0	0
		Distribution Demand (Confirmed)	0	0	0	0	0
		Dependent Demand (Planned)	0	0	0	0	0
		Dependent Demand (Confirmed)	0	0	0	0	0
		Safety Stock	0	0	0	0	0

Figure 10.3 Forecast, Sales Order, Allocation, and Projected Stock Planning in the SAP IBP Excel Planning View

Figure 10.4 shows other examples of supply planning views in the SAP IBP Excel planning view for the response and supply solution. The capacity planning view is represented here, along with available capacity, consumption, and consumption percentage. The supplier planning view shows an example of the supplier's delivery plan and constraint.

Capacity planning view example

Location ID	Resource	Key Figure	11/15/2016	11/16/2016	11/17/2016	11/18/2016	11/19/2016	11/20/2016	11/21/2016	11/22/2016
PL1	MC1_PL1	Capacity Available	480	480	480	480	0	0	480	480
		Capacity Available (Adjusted)			400	320				
		Capacity Available (Final)	480	480	400	320	0	0	480	480
		Capacity Consumption	350	350	400	320	0	0	600	700
		Capacity Consumption (%)	73	73	100	100			125	146
		Capacity Consumption (Confirmed)	0	0	0	0	0	0	0	0
		Capacity Consumption (Planned)	350	350	400	320	0	0	600	700

Supplier plan and constraint example

Material Number	Supplier ID	Key Figure	11/17/2016	11/18/2016	11/19/2016	11/20/2016	11/21/2016	11/22/2016	11/23/2016
PR1_AGH	SUPPLIER1	Supplier Constraint	75	75	75	75	75	75	75
		Supplier Delivery (Confirmed)	60	55	50	0	0	0	0
		Supplier Delivery (Planned)	60	55	50	40	75	100	70
	SUPPLIER2	Supplier Constraint	120	120	120	120	150	150	150
		Supplier Delivery (Confirmed)	120	100	100	80	0	0	0
		Supplier Delivery (Planned)	120	110	100	80	150	200	140

Figure 10.4 Capacity and Supplier Plan in the SAP IBP Excel Planning View

Note that the planning view example discussed here is just for reference; based on the planning example in SAP IBP for response and supply, any combination of key figures can be added as part of the planning view for review and analysis purposes. Due to the inherent capability of SAP IBP to show the order series data also in the appropriate time bucket, the planning data review through the Excel planning view becomes highly useful for planners.

10.5.2 SAP IBP: SAP Fiori View

A lot of order-relevant planning information is reviewed through the SAP Fiori app view of SAP IBP for response and supply. The Demand by Priority app provides a detailed sequential view of the demand per the prioritization rule. The View Projected Stock app is used to analyze the projected stock of all materials in the supply chain. This analysis helps planners select the products with shortage potential as well as identifies the extra inventory in the supply chain that increases cost and reduces flexibility. This application has the option to review the demand and supply situation in the element view, periodic view, or chart format. Order confirmation information is analyzed through the View Confirmation app in SAP IBP. For a material, customer, and order information, details are available for the percentage confirmation, requested date, quantity, and delay in order fulfillments with date and quantity. Gating factor analysis, on the other hand, provides the root-cause analysis and the issues in the supply chain, which limits the customer order fulfillment on time.

Together, the SAP Fiori planning application view and SAP IBP Excel planning view provide detailed, end-to-end visibility, as well as easy-to-use and efficient tools to maximize the service level and minimize the waste in the supply chain through these cutting-edge planning applications.

The planning view apps you're most likely to use are as follows:

▶ Demand by Priority (Figure 10.5)

▶ Projected Stock (Figure 10.6)

▶ Order Confirmation (Figure 10.7)

▶ Gating Factor Analysis (Figure 10.8)

These views are highly useful for efficient planning and review purposes. Information represented in the views can be configured to display relevant data elements such as material, location, customer, quantities, and order number. For ready reference and quick usage, these views have been fortified by graphical representations and traffic light signals to represent the excess, shortage, confirmed, and not confirmed quantities.

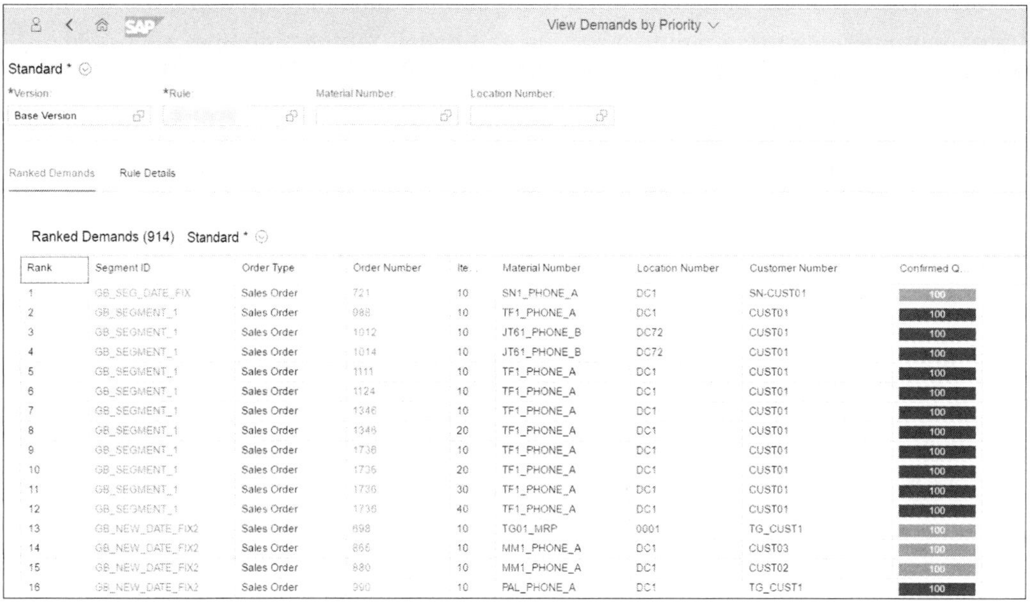

Figure 10.5 Demand by Priority App in SAP IBP for Response and Supply

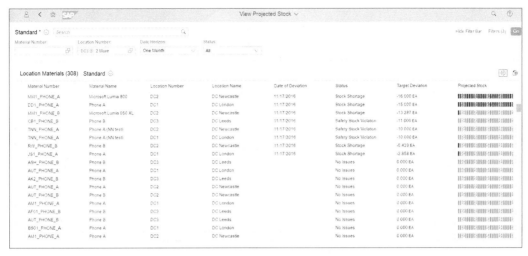

Figure 10.6 Projected Stock Analysis through the SAP Fiori App of SAP IBP for Response and Supply

Item	Customer Number	Requested D	Requested Q	Confirmed Q	Material Number	Location	Confirmed Percent	Unconfirmed Percent	Confirmed I%	On-Time Quantity	Delayed Quantity
10	CUST01	12/14/2016	5 EA	3 EA	FR1_PHONE_A	DC1	60 %	40 %	60 40	3 EA	0 EA
10	TG_CUST1	12/06/2016	100 EA	100 EA	TG2_PHONE_B	DC2	100 %	0 %	100	100 EA	0 EA
10	CUST01	12/02/2016	50 EA	50 EA	RW_PHONE_A	DC1	100 %	0 %	100	50 EA	0 EA
10	TG_CUST1	11/29/2016	100 EA	100 EA	TG2_PHONE_A	DC1	100 %	0 %	100	100 EA	0 EA
40	CUST08	11/28/2016	1000 EA	0 EA	HH01_PHONE_A	DC1	0 %	100 %	100	0 EA	0 EA
80	CUST08	11/28/2016	2000 EA	0 EA	HH01_PHONE_A	DC2	0 %	100 %	100	0 EA	0 EA
10	CUST05	11/24/2016	272 EA	272 EA	JV01_PHONE_B	DC2	100 %	0 %	100	272 EA	0 EA
30	CUST08	11/22/2016	400 EA	0 EA	HH01_PHONE_A	DC1	0 %	100 %	100	0 EA	0 EA
10	CUST02	11/21/2016	20 EA	20 EA	JV01_PHONE_A	DC2	100 %	0 %	100	20 EA	0 EA
10	CUST01	11/18/2016	20 EA	5 EA	KS1_PHONE_A	DC1	25 %	75 %	25 75	0 EA	5 EA
10	CUST05	11/18/2016	312 EA	312 EA	JV01_PHONE_A	DC1	100 %	0 %	100	312 EA	0 EA
10	TG_CUST1	11/18/2016	10 EA	10 EA	TG2_PHONE_A	DC1	100 %	0 %	100	10 EA	0 EA
30	CUST08	11/18/2016	900 EA	0 EA	HH01_PHONE_A	DC1	0 %	100 %	100	0 EA	0 EA
10	CUST01	11/17/2016	20 EA	20 EA	KS1_PHONE_A	DC1	100 %	0 %	50 50	10 EA	10 EA
10	CUST08	11/16/2016	100 EA	0 EA	HH01_PHONE_A	DC2	0 %	100 %	100	0 EA	0 EA
10	CUST03	11/14/2016	50 EA	50 EA	JV01_PHONE_A	DC1	100 %	0 %	100	50 EA	0 EA
10	CUST09	11/14/2016	462 EA	462 EA	JV01_PHONE_B	DC2	100 %	0 %	42.7 57.3	193 EA	259 EA
10	SN-CUST01	11/14/2016	50 EA	50 EA	SN1_PHONE_A	DC1	100 %	0 %	100	50 EA	0 EA
10	CUST01	11/11/2016	10 EA	10 EA	JV01_PHONE_A	DC1	100 %	0 %	100	0 EA	10 EA

Figure 10.7 View Order Confirmation App in SAP IBP for Response and Supply

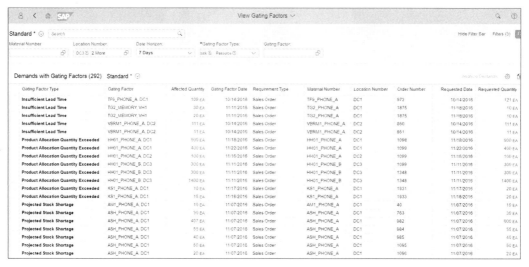

Figure 10.8 Gating Factor App in SAP IBP for Response and Supply

10.6   Order Simulation and Scenario Planning

Simulation in response and supply planning is used to perform the what-if analysis for a potential opportunity or risk scenario without impacting the live data in the system. The functionality in SAP IBP for response and supply allows simulating a sales order, constraints, creating a scenario, collaborating, and choosing the best possible action for supply.

The functionality for using the simulation and scenario can be grouped and discussed in sections, as follows:

▸ Simulation of sales order

▸ Scenario creation, analysis, and constraint management

▸ Collaboration, decision, and data update to the live system

10.6.1   Simulation of Sales Order

With the Simulate Sales Order app in SAP IBP, an additional sales order and its impact on the current demand and supply situation can be analyzed by the system.

The sales order for the material, delivery location, relevant customer, quantity requested, and priority can be created in the simulated environment. An added order in the system has an impact on the current demand and supply situation; based on this, the order confirmation for the created sales order as well as previous present orders in the system are affected.

The View Confirmation app shows the confirmation for the created sales order as well as any impact on the existing orders in the system. Product allocation information can also be reviewed and analyzed for the simulated environment. Based on the result displayed by the order addition in the simulated environment, along with the planner's expectation, either the simulation can be performed on the live data or further action on constraint review or scenario analysis can be carried out to identify the best option. SAP IBP provides a system-generated instruction sheet for the steps taken by the planner in the simulated environment so that the same actions can be performed for the live data if required. Detailed system steps for a sales order simulation can be found in Chapter 11, Section 11.6.

10.6.2 Scenario Creation, Analysis, and Constraint Management

A simulation in SAP IBP for response and supply can be saved as a scenario; a scenario with its inherent nature in SAP IBP can be further reviewed, edited, and shared with other users for performing further analysis. Data in the scenario can be reviewed, and based on the supply levers of the organization, it can be edited for impact analysis. For example, for a resource constraint, running an extra shift might be considered, whereas for a supplier constraint, an alternate supply option might be considered. Based on the possibility of a potential action for issue resolution, the action result (e.g., increased machine availability, higher allocation amount, etc.) can be updated in the scenario by updating the supply constraint. A further planning run can be performed for the scenario on the impact analysis in the what-if environment. Figure 10.9 and Figure 10.10 shows an example in which a sales order simulation is being saved as a scenario for further analysis. The data in the scenario can be analyzed through the Manage Version and Scenario app.

Figure 10.9 Sales Order Simulation to Scenario Creation: Part 1

Figure 10.10 Sales Order Simulation to Scenario Creation: Part 2

10.6.3 Collaboration, Decision, and Data Update to the Live System

A planner can share the scenario data with team members for collaboration and to determine the best course of action. Figure 10.11 shows how scenario information is sent to another user in the system for collaboration. The user can review and edit the information for further analysis. Following the result and impact analysis through order simulation and scenario, a decision can be made to take action against the market opportunity. Based on the result identified and agreed on through the simulation and scenario, an instruction sheet is automatically created by the SAP IBP system that can be downloaded by the user to perform the agreed-upon action in the system. Figure 10.11 shows an example of the instruction sheet as generated by the SAP IBP response system. Following the instruction sheet generated by the system, the data can be updated in the live system to make the simulation model part of active data element.

This capability maximizes the profitability from a potential opportunity while considering the impact and agreeing on the best possible option through real-time result analysis and collaboration.

Figure 10.11 Collaboration, Decision-Making, and Instruction Sheet

10.7 Summary

Supply against customer demand for an organization is created through production, purchase, or stock transfer activities. Supply planning is performed by considering the demand, current inventory, and sourcing rules. An agile supply network has the flexibility to respond in the short term against market realities through the capabilities of response planning. Supply planning algorithms, unconstrained heuristic planning, finite optimization, and rule-based supply planning are used in SAP IBP for response and supply to generate the supply plan. The response planning algorithm automatically performs order prioritization and product allocation, following the defined rule for creating the most suitable supply plan for the organization. Simulation and collaboration capabilities of SAP IBP are applied for further review and finalization of the supply plan.

Now that we have a good understanding of supply planning processes and the capabilities of SAP IBP for response and supply, the next chapter will discuss the details of how the system is configured to enable these capabilities and processes.

Response and supply planning in SAP IBP are modeled through the planning model configuration, algorithm selection, and data upload. This chapter discusses the SAP IBP system setup and usage for response and supply planning, as well as the details of rule-based supply planning and order response planning solution development in SAP IBP.

11 Implementing SAP IBP for Response and Supply

This chapter is focused on the implementation details for SAP IBP for response and supply. It covers the following end-to-end configuration elements:

- Basic configuration for response and supply planning in SAP IBP
- Integration for response and supply planning
- Planning area overview for SAP IBP for response and supply
- Demand prioritization configuration
- SAP IBP for response and supply management planning run
- Order simulation and scenario planning
- Planning review for SAP IBP for response and supply
- Gating factor analysis usage in SAP IBP

Let's begin by taking a look at some basic configuration for SAP IBP for response and supply.

> **Note**
>
> Before going into the settings for system building of SAP IBP for response and supply, it's important to note that the time series supply planning solution with unconstrained heuristic and cost-based optimization was covered in Chapter 7, Section 7.3. In this chapter, we'll focus on configuring the order series rule supply planning and order response and confirmation solution.

11.1 Basic Configuration

Configuration of response and supply planning is performed to select the scope and methodology of the response and supply solution. The configuration option is accessible through the MAINTAIN RESPONSE MANAGEMENT SETTINGS and MAINTAIN FORECAST CONSUMPTION PROFILES tiles available under RESPONSE ADMINISTRATOR (see Figure 11.1). The configurations of the MAINTAIN RESPONSE MANAGEMENT SETTING tile control multiple planning parameters.

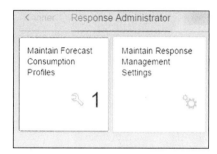

Figure 11.1 Configuration through the Response Administrator Screen

Figure 11.2 Configuration Elements of the Response Management Settings Screen

The configuration for the RESPONSE MANAGEMENT SETTINGS screen, as shown in Figure 11.2, can be illustrated through their groupings as follows:

▶ PLANNING AREA
Select the planning area relevant for the response planning solution. Any further configuration in this page is relevant to the assigned planning area.

▶ TIME PERIODS AND ATTRIBUTES
Provide the values for the DAILY PERIOD and WEEKLY PERIOD, as well as the key planning attributes for MATERIAL ID and LOCATION ID for usage in response planning. Other planning attributes for LOCATION TYPE, WORK CENTER, CAPACITY CATEGORY, and SUPPLIER ID can also be assigned and hence made available for the response planning solution.

▶ KEY FIGURE SEMANTICS
Assign the essential key figures created in the planning area to the key figure fields in the response solution for their consideration in the planning. The key figures that need to be mapped are listed in Table 11.1.

Key Figure	Usage in Response Planning
Forecast	Unconstrained forecast relevant for supply plan input
Constrained forecast	Possible supply considering the supply constraint
Product allocation	Key figure to provide input for product allocation; may be a copy of the constrained forecast
Safety stock	Stock quantity to be maintained as safety stock
Safety stock periodicity	Periodicity for time-based safety stock
Resource capacity	Capacity available for a resource
Resource capacity periodicity	For day or week, for example, available capacity per day or per week
Supplier constraint	Supplier constraint based on supplier commit
Supplier commit periodicity	Time bucket periodicity for supplier commit

Table 11.1 Key Figure Configuration Mapping for Response Planning

▶ SALES ORDER FIELD ASSIGNMENTS
Map the customer ID (CUSTID) attribute against the sales orders that will exist in SAP IBP.

▶ PLANNING LEVEL ASSIGNMENTS
Assign the consumption or allocation planning level in planning. Normally, the planning level for allocation or consumption is selected as either PERPRODLOC (period/product/location) or PERPRODLOCCUST (period/product/location/ customer) based on the requirement of not considering or considering the customer for allocation, respectively.

In addition to RESPONSE MANAGEMENT SETTINGS, the MAINTAIN FORECAST CONSUMPTION PROFILE, shown previously in Figure 11.1, is used for managing the planning level for forecast consumption. The forecast consumption profile needs to match one to one with the allocation profile. Figure 11.3 shows an example of a forecast profile in which the planning level is selected as period/product/location (PERPRODLOC).

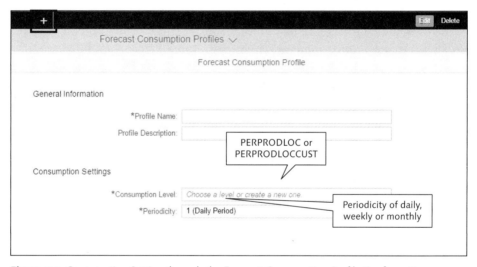

Figure 11.3 Consumption Setting through the Forecast Consumption Profile Configuration

11.2 Integration

Planning in SAP IBP is performed in time series and order series data models. In time series, planning is performed in the time bucket without detailed order or pegging-level information. On the other hand, order series planning is performed with detailed order-level information. Most of the planning elements in SAP IBP, such as sales and operations planning (S&OP), demand planning, supply planning, and inventory optimization are performed as time series data. Response planning is performed at the order series level.

Integration with an execution system for a time series model is achieved using the SAP Cloud Platform. For an order series model, real-time integration is achieved through SAP HANA smart data integration (SAP HANA SDI). Detailed information on this topic is presented in Chapter 3.

Order series data can also be viewed or analyzed in the time series format of SAP IBP. Order series data that are transferred to SAP IBP through external integration can be viewed in time buckets in the SAP IBP Excel planning view; these read-only data can't be edited in the time series planning view. Figure 11.4 shows an example of sales order data available in response management which can be reviewed in the relevant time bucket in a time series. The assignment of the time bucket along with the aggregation of the orders occurs dynamically in the time series view. Any edits to the time series key figures in the Excel planning view by the planner are available in the response data area immediately. This sync of the time series and order series models is the core of the integrated demand, supply, and response solution of SAP IBP.

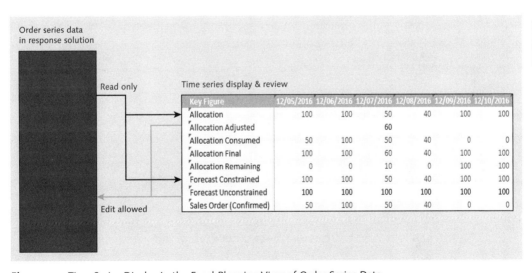

Figure 11.4 Time Series Display in the Excel Planning View of Order Series Data

11.3 Planning Area Overview

The SAP7 planning area is provided by SAP to support the response and supply solution. Aggregated orders for response planning are available in time buckets of days and weeks. Customers may copy the SAP7 planning area and can perform the required edit to use this for the response and supply solution.

Relevant key figures added for this solution area in the SAP7 planning area are represented in the following list (additional notes are provided for key figures that require further explanation):

- **Allocation**
  Allocation suggested by the planning run in a constrained supply situation.

- **Allocation adjusted**
  Allocation manually edited by the planner.

- **Allocation final**
  Final allocation number for the confirmation planning run.

- **Allocation consumed/allocation remaining**

- **Forecast unconstrained**
  For unconstrained forecasts as finalized by SAP IBP for demand or SAP IBP for sales and operations, or any other legacy system used for demand finalization. This key figure is mapped in the RESPONSE MANAGEMENT SETTINGS for consideration by the response planning solution.

- **Forecast open**
  Represents the open forecast by reducing the sales order quantity from the unconstrained forecast. If the sales order quantity exceeds the unconstrained forecast, then the value for the forecast open key figure is zero.

- **Forecast constrained**

- **Total demand**

- **Requested sales order/confirmed sales order**

- **Delivery output**

- **Dependent demand (planned)/dependent demand confirmed**

- **Distribution demand planned/distribution demand confirmed**

- **Distribution receipt planned/distribution receipt confirmed**

- **Production confirmed/production planned**

- **Production receipt**
- **Total receipt**
- **Initial stock**
- **Stock projected**
- **Stock in transit**
- **Safety stock planned**
  Time-based safety stock is mapped as the SAFETY STOCK (PLANNED) key figure in SAP IBP. This can be an output from SAP IBP for inventory if the SAP IBP solution is used for inventory optimization. Otherwise, it can also be managed by users in the Excel planning view.
- **Safety stock master data**
  Safety stock value as maintained in the material master data.
- **Safety stock**
  Safety stock for the planning run, based on the value maintained in master data or as the time-based planning value in the planning view.
- **Supplier constraint**
  Supplier's capacity to supply is mapped as the supplier constraint key figure in the response management solution for finite supply planning while considering the supplier's ability to supply. The value of the key figure is provided by the supplier through the collaboration process and is used in the response and supply solution as a material constraint.
- **Supplier delivery planned/supplier delivery confirmed**
- **Capacity available/capacity available adjusted/capacity available final**
- **Capacity consumption planned/capacity consumption confirmed**
- **Total capacity consumption**
- **Capacity consumption (%)**

11.4 Demand Prioritization Configuration

Demand prioritization rules and associated logic are configured in the system by accessing the RULES FOR DEMAND PRIORITIZATION tile under ACCOUNT PLANNER. In the following sections, we'll cover these steps to create and assign the rules:

- Creating rules with a segment sequence
- Maintaining segments
- Sorting conditions in segments
- Viewing demand by priority

11.4.1 Rule Creation and Segment Sequence

Rules for demand prioritization are accessed through the RULES FOR DEMAND PRIORITIZATION tile. Figure 11.5 shows the system page for configuring the rule. The NEW RULE button is used to create the rule.

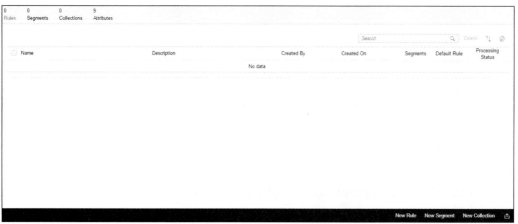

Figure 11.5 Rules for Demand Prioritization Configuration

Figure 11.6 shows the system screen for new rule creation in which the NAME and DESCRIPTION are provided for the rule. From this screen, segments in the rule can be created. In the SEGMENTS section of the screen, the NEW button is used to a new segment for this rule, and the ADD button is used to select a previously defined segment for usage in the rule.

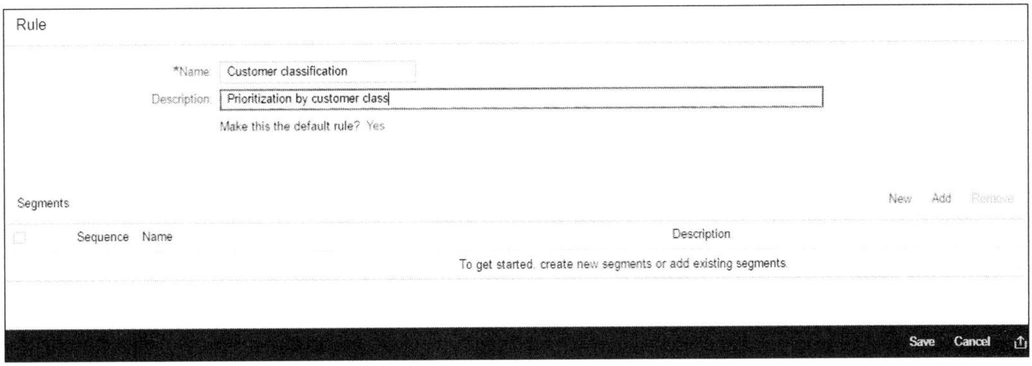

Figure 11.6 Rule Creation Screen for Supply Planning

11.4.2 Segment Definition and Segment Condition

Using the segment definition screen, the selection criteria are provided to identify the demand for prioritization. SAP IBP provides its segment configuration options through the system-suggested user-selection dropdowns. Figure 11.7 shows an example SEGMENT condition screen; attribute parameters and relational logic are available through the dropdown options. Multiple arguments can be made as one segment condition through the use of OR and AND conditional arguments. Users can start entering a string value and use the system prompts and expressions to complete the logic. This logic needs to be aligned with the master data in the system.

For example, the material requirements planning (MRP) type for the sales order is represented as VC in the master data, so a segment condition such as MRP_TYPE = VC can be used to select all the demand for sales orders. As another example, if the customer classification is maintained in the master data as A, B, and C based on the required service level quality, a segment condition on customer classification can be defined accordingly.

> **Note**
>
> For a detailed description of the operations using the editor, refer to the standard SAP help documentation on the SAP HANA rules framework guide at *https://websmp107.sap-ag.de/~sapidb/012002523100011424872016E/SAP_HRF1_08_DevImpGuide_v1.pdf*.

Figure 11.7 Segment Definition

11.4.3 Sorting Condition of a Segment

A sorting criteria is defined to sort the demands within a segment. Sort attributes are available to select from a dropdown menu; either the ASCENDING or DESCENDING condition is selected to further sort the orders in a sorting group. The sort sequence aligns the order priorities for the sorting. In the example shown in Figure 11.8, the first sorting group is based on the delivery priority in ascending order. If the delivery priority is maintained in the system, SAP IBP will aim first to fulfill the orders with a higher delivery priority. After completion of this sorting, the second sorting is performed on the requested date of the demand. The SAVE AS COLLECTION button can be used to save the collection of sort attributes to be used in a different segment.

Through demand prioritization configuration, one segment can have multiple sorting attributes, and one rule can have multiple segments. Figure 11.9 shows an example of a demand prioritization rule with two segments. Demand is prioritized for the first segment and sorting condition before being prioritized for the second segment and associated sorting condition. Whenever a segment is changed by a user, the system triggers a job to update the rules in which the segment has been used.

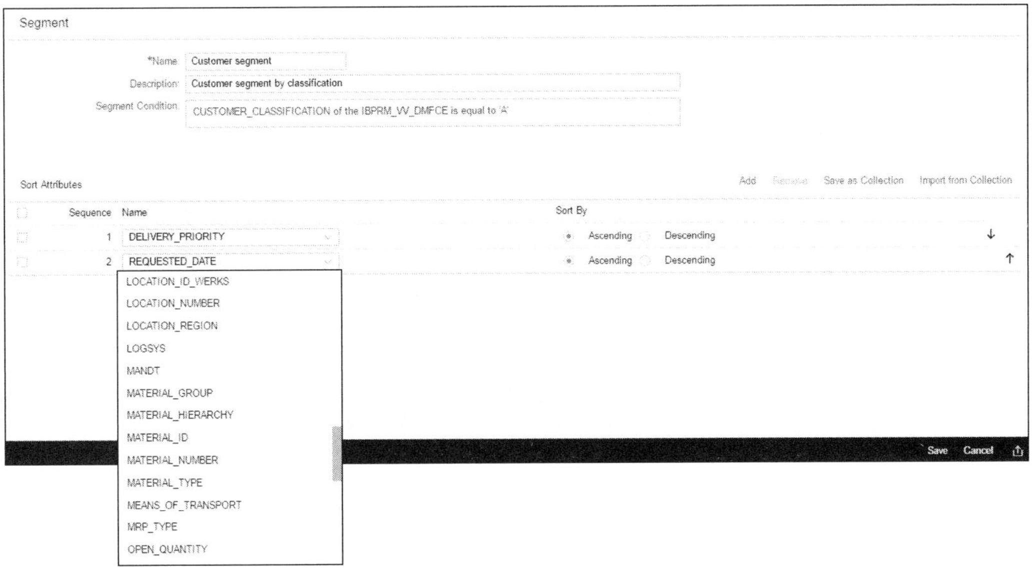

Figure 11.8 Sorting Attributes in a Segment

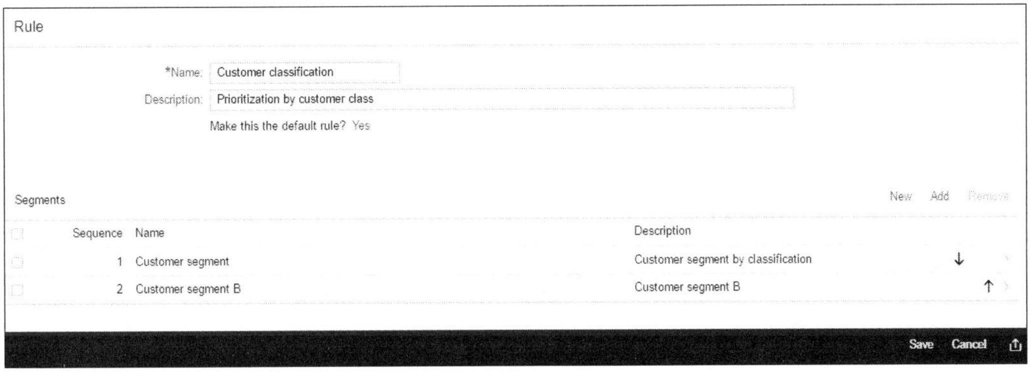

Figure 11.9 Example of a Rule with Two Segments

The update status is available through the information as a *processing status* on the RULE screen. A new planning run or generation of prioritized demand list should only be performed after the processing is completed and the PROCESSING STATUS isn't displayed as UNDER PROGRESS. Figure 11.10 shows the PROCESSING STATUS information in the demand prioritization rule.

| | 1 | 2 | 0 | 9 | | | | | |
| | Rules | Segments | Collections | Attributes | | | | | |

	Name	Description	Created By	Created On	Segments	Default Rule	Processing Status
	Customer classification	Prioritization by customer class	Amit Sinha	11/10/2016, 18:39:28	2		

Figure 11.10 Processing Status Information in the Demand Prioritization Rule

11.4.4 View Demand by Priority

The View Demand by Priority app in the ACCOUNT PLANNER provides a prioritized list of demand elements. It assigns a rank for demand elements per the demand prioritization rule. You must select a VERSION and a unique RULE to access the list of prioritized demands. The list can be limited by selection of materials and locations by using the relevant fields on the selection screen. Figure 11.11 shows the selection screen and an example of a prioritized demand list. The attributes of the list can be selected by the user through the configuration screen from the available options. Information on the covered quantity through the available supply is represented with the percentage number as well as the green and red traffic signals.

Standard *

*Version	*Rule	Material Number	Location Number
Base Version			

Ranked Demands   Rule Details

Ranked Demands (914) Standard *

Rank	Segment ID	Order Type	Order Number	Ite...	Material Number	Location Number	Customer Number	Confirmed Q...
1	GB_SEG_DATE_FIX	Sales Order	721	10	SN1_PHONE_A	DC1	SN-CUST01	100
2	GB_SEGMENT_1	Sales Order	998	10	TF1_PHONE_A	DC1	CUST01	100
3	GB_SEGMENT_1	Sales Order	1012	10	JT61_PHONE_B	DC72	CUST01	100
4	GB_SEGMENT_1	Sales Order	1014	10	JT61_PHONE_B	DC72	CUST01	100
5	GB_SEGMENT_1	Sales Order	1111	10	TF1_PHONE_A	DC1	CUST01	100
6	GB_SEGMENT_1	Sales Order	1124	10	TF1_PHONE_A	DC1	CUST01	100
7	GB_SEGMENT_1	Sales Order	1346	10	TF1_PHONE_A	DC1	CUST01	100
8	GB_SEGMENT_1	Sales Order	1348	20	TF1_PHONE_A	DC1	CUST01	100
9	GB_SEGMENT_1	Sales Order	1736	10	TF1_PHONE_A	DC1	CUST01	100
10	GB_SEGMENT_1	Sales Order	1736	20	TF1_PHONE_A	DC1	CUST01	100
11	GB_SEGMENT_1	Sales Order	1736	30	TF1_PHONE_A	DC1	CUST01	100
12	GB_SEGMENT_1	Sales Order	1736	40	TF1_PHONE_A	DC1	CUST01	100
13	GB_NEW_DATE_FIX2	Sales Order	898	10	TG01_MRP	0001	TG_CUST1	100
14	GB_NEW_DATE_FIX2	Sales Order	865	10	MM1_PHONE_A	DC1	CUST03	100
15	GB_NEW_DATE_FIX2	Sales Order	880	10	MM1_PHONE_A	DC1	CUST02	100
16	GB_NEW_DATE_FIX2	Sales Order	990	10	PAL_PHONE_A	DC1	TG_CUST1	100

Figure 11.11 View Demand by Priority Based on a Defined Rule

11.5   Response and Supply Management Planning Run

Configuration of the response management planning run is performed through the APPLICATION JOBS RESPONSE PLANNING tile under GENERAL RESPONSE PLANNER. Figure 11.12 shows the configuration details required. Templates can be chosen from the JOB TEMPLATE dropdown to select a planning run for the constrained forecast run, confirmation run, or gating factor analysis run. The SCHEDULING OPTION field is used to start the job immediately or at a set time as a one-time execution or as a periodic recurrence execution. Selection of the demand prioritization rule is mandatory for the constrained forecast and confirmation run, although the rule isn't relevant for the gating factor analysis run.

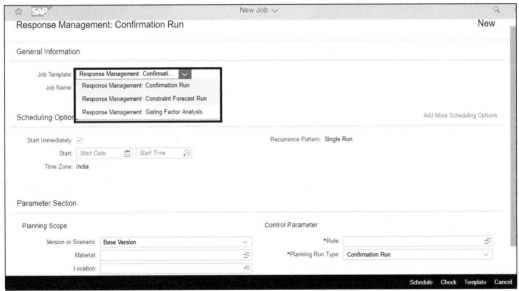

Figure 11.12 Jobs for Response Management Planning

Configuration elements for individual runs are performed through the Application Job Template app, including creating a new template for the response management planning run. Figure 11.13 shows the system example. The user enters the JOB TEMPLATE NAME in the GENERAL INFORMATION section as displayed in Figure 11.13. In the example in Figure 11.13, RESPONSE_CONFIRMATION RUN is selected. The PARAMETER SELECTION options shown in Figure 11.14 are used to provide the RULE and PLANNING SCOPE through the VERSION OR SCENARIO, MATERIAL, and LOCATION fields. A specific set of master data can be provided for MATERIAL and/or LOCATION, or it can be left blank if all the planning data is in scope. It's recommended to provide the location master data in this configuration by selecting the locations through the interactive screen that appears when you click the two-squares button at the end of the LOCATION field (see Figure 11.14).

The configuration of the constraint forecast planning run and the gating analysis planning run follows similar steps. These planning runs can be selected by using the Application Job Templates app. The PLANNING SCOPE information is provided via the RULE, VERSION, MATERIAL, and LOCATION values.

Figure 11.13 Response Management Planning Run Configuration through the Job Template App: Part 1

Execution of the three response planning runs is discussed in the following subsections.

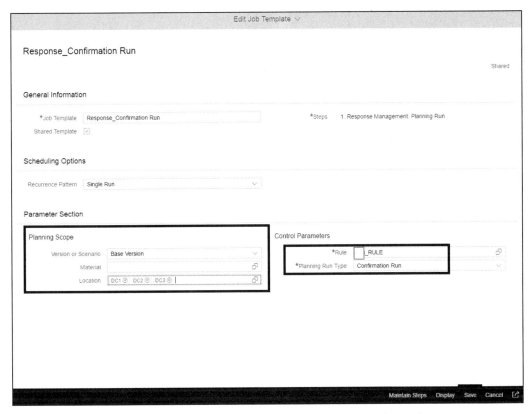

Figure 11.14 Response Management Planning Run Configuration through the Job Template App: Part 2

11.5.1 Constrained Planning Run for Product Allocation and Supply Plan

A feasible supply plan based on forecast and supply constraints is created using a constrained planning run. The demand elements, prioritization rules, and supply constraints are the input for this planning run. The output of the planning run is the *constrained forecast* key figure. Figure 11.15 shows an APPLICATION JOBS example to perform the constrained forecast planning run. RULE is selected in this screen to consider the demand prioritization for planning the supply. The job can either be executed for a limited set of material and location master data combination or for every material and location in the base version. Recurrence of the job can be automated by selecting a Recurrence Pattern in the Application Jobs configuration screen.

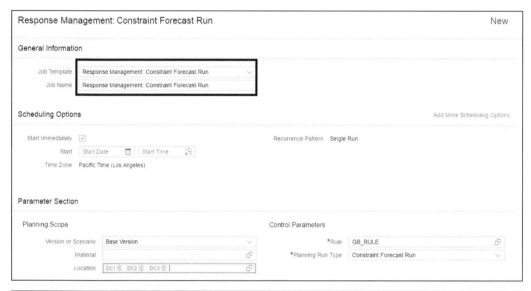

Figure 11.15 Constrained Forecast Planning Run

The constrained forecast generated through the constrained forecast planning run can be copied as the allocation key figure. The SAP standard planning copy forecast allocation operator (COPYFORECASTTOPAL) can be used to copy the constrained forecast key figure to the allocation key figure. The basic requirement of this copy is that it must be at the same planning level as the constrained forecast and product allocation key figures. This copy job can be executed in the background or foreground in the Excel planning view. This copy job should be scheduled to follow the constrained forecast planning run. Figure 11.16 shows an example of the planning view with the constrained forecast key figure as generated by the planning job and allocation key figure as populated by the copy job. The adjusted allocation key figure is used to manually adjust the allocation based on the planner's input.

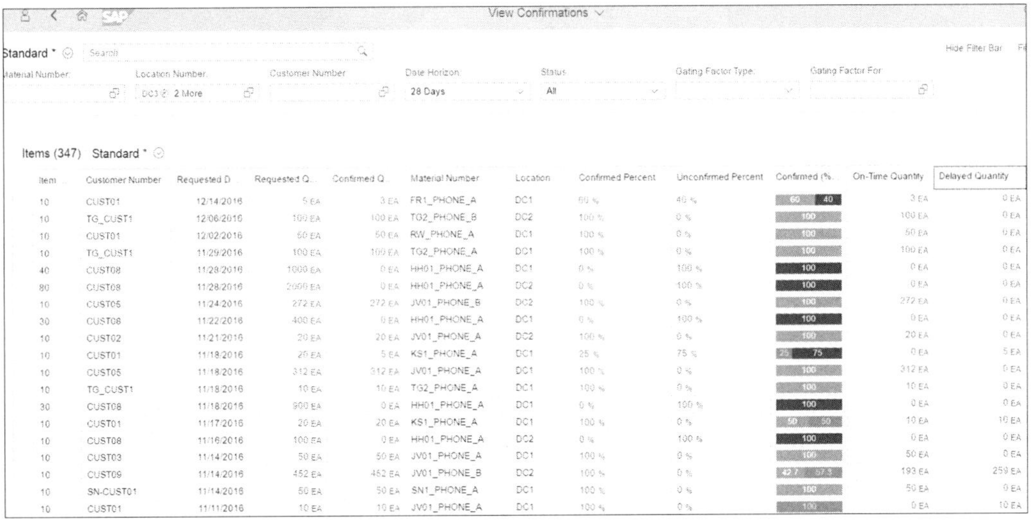

Figure 11.16 Planning Result Output of the Constrained Forecast Run

11.5.2 Confirmation Planning Run

By using the Response Management: Confirmation Run app, you can perform supply planning, order rescheduling and order confirmation in a single step. The system creates a short-term supply plan based on the prioritized demand and constrained supply. The product allocation and rules for demand prioritization allow planning for the restricted supply against the prioritized order. The constraints considered in the confirmation run include product allocations, resource capacities, supplier commit quantities, and materials. Figure 11.17 provides an example of the order confirmation display in SAP IBP, which shows the status after the most recent confirmation planning run. Orders that aren't confirmed can be further analyzed for required action using the Gating Factor Analysis app. Gating factor analysis is covered in more detail in Section 11.8.

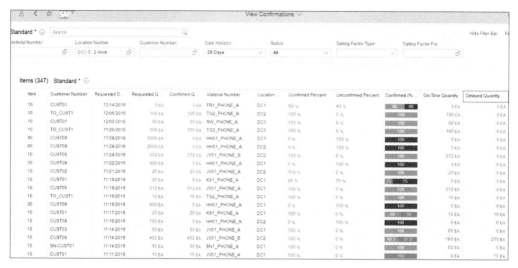

Figure 11.17 Sales Order Confirmation Information in SAP IBP after the Confirmation Planning Run

11.5.3 Response Management: Gating Factor Analysis Run

Through the APPLICATION JOBS FOR RESPONSE MANAGEMENT tile, you can choose GATING FACTOR ANALYSIS from the JOB TEMPLATE dropdown. The analysis can be performed for a version or a scenario and can be further limited for the execution by selecting master data objects of LOCATION and MATERIAL.

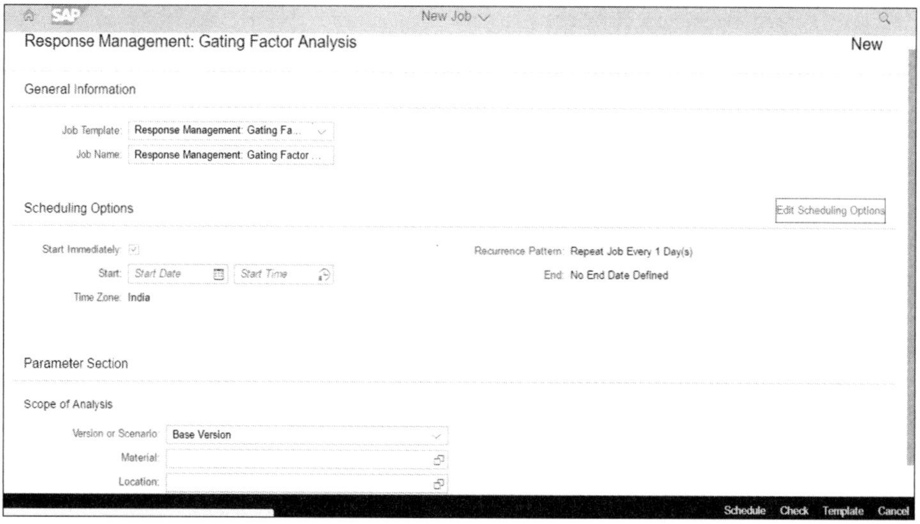

Figure 11.18 Gating Factor Analysis Run

The SCHEDULING OPTIONS settings are used to execute this on a periodic basis. We recommend you schedule the gating factor analysis run after the confirmation run; this will allow the system to use the most recent update on the issues that limit the order confirmation. Figure 11.18 shows an example of a gating factor analysis planning run.

11.6 Order Simulation and Scenario Planning

The Simulate Sales Order app is used for sales order simulation and what-if analyses. A pop-up screen enables you to add the information on material, location, customer, quantity, and date. Order priority can also be provided if relevant. Figure 11.19 and Figure 11.20 display an example of the sales order simulation. Clicking the START SIMULATION RUN button plans the sales order in a simulated environment without impacting the planning data in the active version. In the top yellow bar, an option appears to save this simulation as a scenario for further analysis and for sharing with other users. Through a scenario, the supply-constrained data can also be changed for key figures of supplier constraint, materials, resource constraints, etc. The response planning run for the scenario can be executed to update the demand and supply in the simulated environment.

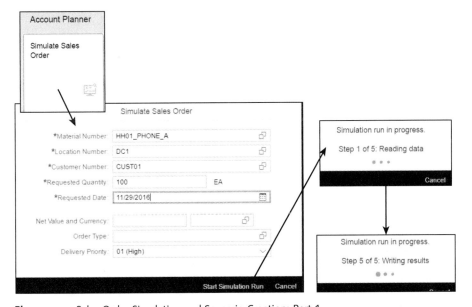

Figure 11.19 Sales Order Simulation and Scenario Creation: Part 1

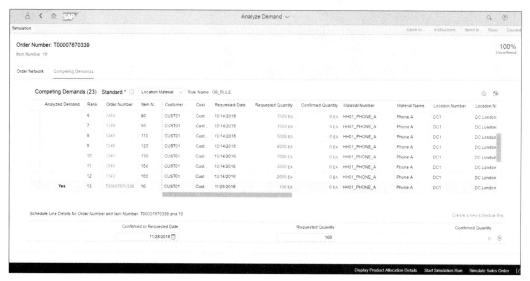

Figure 11.20 Sales Order Simulation and Scenario Creation: Part 2

An instruction sheet can be generated from the system detailing the manual data edits performed for the order simulation and scenario. This instruction sheet can be used to update the data in the base version if the changes performed in the simulated environment can be achieved and result in a better plan.

11.7 Planning Review for Response and Supply

The data review for response and supply planning is performed in the Excel planning view and in the SAP Fiori app of SAP IBP. The planning area relevant to the response and supply planning application contains the response and supply relevant key figures that can be reviewed in the planning view. A planner can select the key figures relevant to the response and supply plan representing demand, supply constraints, allocation, projected inventory, and so on.

In addition to the Excel planning view, response and supply planning results can also be reviewed through the SAP Fiori via the following apps:

- View Projected Stock
- View Confirmation
- Gating Factor Analysis

The View Projected Stock app provides the information on the projected inventory by considering the demand and supply situation along with the details of stock, requirement, and receipt elements. Figure 11.21 shows an example of the VIEW PROJECTED STOCK report. There is an option to limit the result for only shortage or safety stock violation cases. Results can be generated for every material location combination or for a closed list as provided in the input screen. Traffic light color-coding graphics enhance the ease of use for this view. The View Confirmation app planning view has already been discussed earlier (Section 11.5.2), and there is a separate dedicated section next on the Gating Factor Analysis app (Section 11.8).

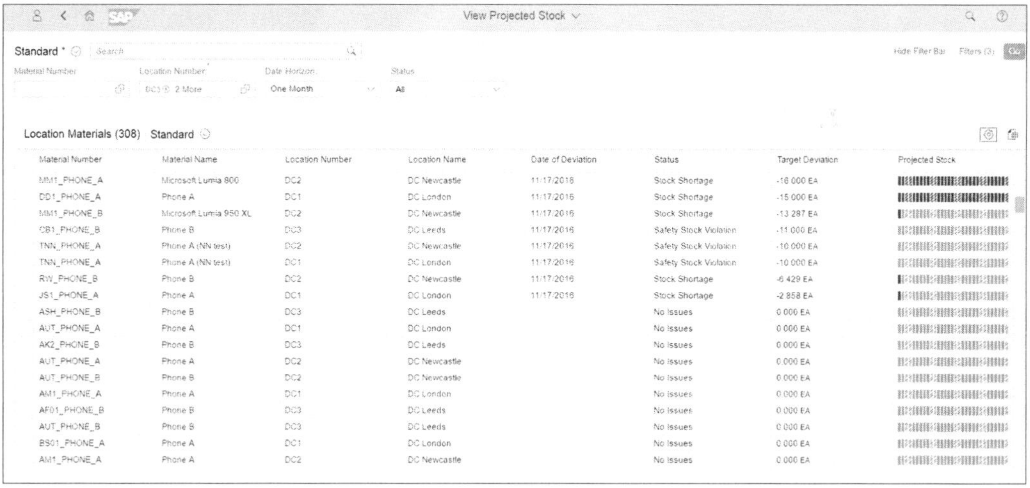

Figure 11.21 View Projected Stock Display for the Response and Supply Solution in SAP IBP

11.8 Gating Factor Analysis

The Gating Factor Analysis app provides information about the constraints that don't allow fulfillment of an order. The gating factor can be analyzed through the VIEW GATING FACTORS and VIEW CONFIRMATIONS tiles under SUPPLY PLANNER and ACCOUNT PLANNER, respectively. As shown in Figure 11.22, material, location, time horizon, and gating factor type can be selected to limit the result for the analysis. Detailed results displayed as the potential issue can be resolved by the planner, or other action can be taken to minimize the impact through early detection and resolution.

Figure 11.22 View Gating Factors Selection Screen

Figure 11.23 and Figure 11.24 show an example of the gating factor as displayed by the SAP IBP system. Here, the system displays that a product allocation doesn't allow fulfillment of an order. By clicking the ANALYZE DEMANDS button, you'll get further details to allow root-cause analysis of the supply issue for the order.

Gating Factor Type	Gating Factor	Affected Quantity	Gating Factor Date	Requirem...	Material Number	Location Number	Order Number	Ite	Requested Date	Requested Qua...
Product Allocation Quanti...	HH01_PHONE_A DC1	900 EA	11/18/2016	Sales Order	HH01_PHONE_A	DC1	1098	30	11/18/2016	900 EA
Product Allocation Quanti...	HH01_PHONE_A DC1	400 EA	11/22/2016	Sales Order	HH01_PHONE_A	DC1	1095	30	11/22/2016	400 EA
Product Allocation Quanti...	HH01_PHONE_A DC1	1000 EA	11/28/2016	Sales Order	HH01_PHONE_A	DC1	1348	40	11/28/2016	1000 EA
Product Allocation Quanti...	HH01_PHONE_A DC2	100 EA	11/18/2016	Sales Order	HH01_PHONE_A	DC2	1099	10	11/18/2016	100 EA
Product Allocation Quanti...	HH01_PHONE_A DC2	2000 EA	11/28/2016	Sales Order	HH01_PHONE_A	DC2	1348	80	11/28/2016	2000 EA
Product Allocation Quanti...	HH01_PHONE_B DC3	300 EA	11/11/2016	Sales Order	HH01_PHONE_B	DC3	1099	20	11/11/2016	300 EA
Product Allocation Quanti...	HH01_PHONE_B DC3	300 EA	11/11/2016	Sales Order	HH01_PHONE_B	DC3	1348	20	11/11/2016	300 EA
Product Allocation Quanti...	HH01_PHONE_B DC3	1400 EA	11/11/2016	Sales Order	HH01_PHONE_B	DC3	1349	60	11/11/2016	1400 EA
Product Allocation Quanti...	KS1_PHONE_A DC1	10 EA	11/17/2016	Sales Order	KS1_PHONE_A	DC1	1931	10	11/17/2016	10 EA
Product Allocation Quanti...	KS1_PHONE_A DC1	15 EA	11/18/2016	Sales Order	KS1_PHONE_A	DC1	1933	10	11/18/2016	20 EA
Projected Stock Shortage	AM1_PHONE_A DC1	10 EA	11/07/2016	Sales Order	AM1_PHONE_A	DC1	40	10	11/07/2016	10 EA
Projected Stock Shortage	ASH_PHONE_A DC1	30 EA	11/07/2016	Sales Order	ASH_PHONE_A	DC1	763	10	11/07/2016	30 EA
Projected Stock Shortage	ASH_PHONE_A DC1	497 EA	11/07/2016	Sales Order	ASH_PHONE_A	DC1	982	10	11/07/2016	600 EA
Projected Stock Shortage	ASH_PHONE_A DC1	55 EA	11/07/2016	Sales Order	ASH_PHONE_A	DC1	984	10	11/07/2016	55 EA
Projected Stock Shortage	ASH_PHONE_A DC1	40 EA	11/07/2016	Sales Order	ASH_PHONE_A	DC1	985	10	11/07/2016	40 EA
Projected Stock Shortage	ASH_PHONE_A DC1	50 EA	11/07/2016	Sales Order	ASH_PHONE_A	DC1	1095	10	11/07/2016	50 EA
Projected Stock Shortage	ASH_PHONE_A DC1	20 EA	11/07/2016	Sales Order	ASH_PHONE_A	DC1	1096	10	11/07/2016	20 EA
Projected Stock Shortage	ASH_PHONE_A DC1	35 EA	11/07/2016	Sales Order	ASH_PHONE_A	DC1	1097	10	11/07/2016	35 EA
Projected Stock Shortage	ASH_PHONE_A DC2	7 EA	11/07/2016	Sales Order	ASH_PHONE_A	DC2	784	10	11/07/2016	7 EA
Projected Stock Shortage	ASH_PHONE_A DC2	15 EA	11/07/2016	Sales Order	ASH_PHONE_A	DC2	785	20	11/07/2016	15 EA

Figure 11.23 Gating Factor Analysis and Analyzed Individual Demand Analysis: Part 1

Figure 11.24 Gating Factor Analysis and Analyzed Individual Demand Analysis: Part 2

11.9 Summary

The SAP IBP for response and supply solution is configured by defining the planning model with master data, key figures, and time profiles. Time series supply planning for heuristic and cost optimization solutions is configured by using the supply solution of SAP IBP for sales and operations. The order series planning solution for rule-based supply planning, allocation, and order confirmation planning is configured in SAP IBP for response and supply. Prioritization rules are defined with segments and sorting criteria to provide the order-ranking parameters. Supply planning and order confirmation happens according to this defined logic. Prioritized demands and supply issues are available for planners to review through SAP Fiori app planning views. The SAP IBP Excel planning view is used for reviewing and collaborating on demand and supply key figures.

Now that we have thoroughly covered the key SAP IBP capabilities for demand and supply planning we will move into the very important topic of inventory planning.

This chapter introduces inventory management and discusses the motivation for maintaining optimal inventory levels in a supply chain network. Different types of inventories and the factors that impact inventory levels are covered, along with using SAP IBP for inventory in performing inventory optimization in a supply chain network.

12 Inventory Management with SAP IBP

The previous chapters have focused on some of the more commonly employed levers in supply chain planning—demand, supply, and capacity—whose interrelationships are clear and direct. A change in demand triggers a predictable adjustment to supply whose timing and level depend on the type of response employed. The reverse is also true when companies look for new sources of demand to consume excess supply or capacity. The greater the variability of demand, the more challenging it becomes to maintain the appropriate level of supply. The same can be said for supply, which can also exhibit variability that can negatively impact how demand is fulfilled.

The impact of variability is amplified as supply chains increase in complexity as measured by the number of interconnected nodes and materials that flow through them. This extended deviation is commonly known as the *bullwhip effect*, the primary symptom being increased supply chain costs driven by excess inventory, which is often accompanied by subpar customer service. SAP Integrated Business Planning (SAP IBP) for inventory addresses this problem with a unique and powerful set of capabilities for determining the optimal level of inventory investment across the supply chain while simultaneously achieving higher levels of service.

In this chapter, we'll discuss the role of inventory in a supply chain network, along with different inventory types. We'll then explore the inventory optimization calculations and related analytics, followed by a dive into SAP IBP applications for inventory optimization in a supply chain network.

12.1   Why Hold Inventory?

To state the obvious: holding inventory in a supply chain network incurs costs, which consumes working capital. This capital could have been invested in other parts of the business for a better return. Inventory holding increases total costs due to storage costs, warehouse costs, and associated handling costs, so it has a negative impact on net revenue and profit. In addition to working capital and extra costs, inventory in the network increases the risk of pilferage, products obsolescence, and reduced product development flexibility.

Even after being well aware of the drawbacks of holding inventory, almost every organization across the globe keeps inventory in its supply chain network. The main reason for holding inventory is to address demand and supply variations. It's impossible to have 100% forecast accuracy and no variations in procurement, production, and transportation activities in an organization's supply chain. To deal with demand and supply deviations, inventory is kept at the locations of the network. This applies to both *make-to-stock* and *make-to-order* planning scenarios.

The difference between the two is that in the make-to-stock scenario, inventory management is done at the finished material level (in addition to semifinished and raw materials), but in the make-to-order planning scenario, inventory management is done at the component level before the decoupling point. A decoupling point determines the stage after which the activities occur only after receiving a sales order. For example, for a heavy machine manufacturer, assembly operation can be a decoupling point; that is, the machine is assembled based on the sales order details. However, it's important to hold the inventory of the components that may be used in the final assembly. For example, in a scenario in which there was no inventory available for any of the components before a sales order, the activities to procure the components, production (of any in-house component), and final assembly could take months or even years.

Therefore, to meet the customer demand in a reasonable time frame (per sales contracts and planned service level for the customers), it's necessary to hold the inventory in the supply chain.

After agreeing to keep the inventory in the network, another essential question becomes how much inventory an organization should hold in the network.

This question is complicated by the adverse implications of inventory holding and the complexity of modern organizations. A medium to large organization can have a network of dozens of locations (suppliers, warehouses, production plants, distribution centers, cross-docks, customers) that manage thousands of materials. For an optimized flow of the material to avoid any bottleneck and to meet the expected service level from the customer, an inventory optimization process is performed.

The aim of inventory optimization is to meet the expected customer demand while maintaining the lowest level of inventory possible in the supply chain network. Extra inventory in the supply chain is managed by identifying the quantity as *safety stock inventory*. The service level represents the percentage of customer orders filled on time. Figure 12.1 shows the conceptual relationship of the safety stock quantity with the achieved service level. Note that with the increase in the safety stock quantity, the service level increases. However, it also increases the total cost to meet the customer requirement and hence has a negative impact on profitability. For every organization, it's important to balance this relationship to achieve an optimum level. The quantity that achieves the expected service level at the minimum cost is the optimum amount of inventory in the network. This quantity may be different for different stock keeping locations and must be calculated based on multiple factors related to demand and supply variations and the interdependence of locations in the supply chain network.

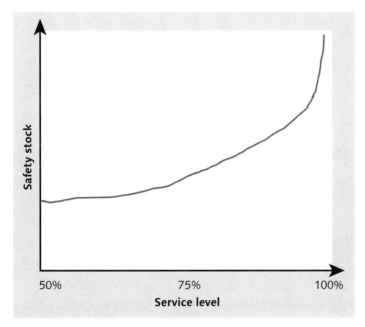

Figure 12.1 Safety Stock and Service Level Representation

Sophisticated inventory optimization algorithms can be applied to determine the required inventory quantity at every location for an organization. SAP IBP for inventory is equipped with advanced features to determine the optimum level of the inventory position by considering the demand variation, supply variation, interdependence of network, and expected service level to maximize the profitability of the organizations and help to achieve the required service levels at the lowest cost.

12.2 Inventory Types and Usage

Inventory types in a supply chain network can be broadly categorized into two different groups: those based on the product property and those based on the inventory optimization calculations. These categories are used for activities involving product movements, material storage, and inventory planning.

12.2.1 Inventory Types Based on the Product Property

Inventory in a supply chain network can be categorized based on product properties such as the following:

- Raw material inventory
- Semifinished or work-in-progress inventory
- Finished goods inventory
- Maintenance, repair, operations (MRO) inventory

Raw materials are the components typically provided by suppliers; these components are used for the assembly or manufacturing operations as a direct input for creating finished goods. Semifinished material inventory represents work-in-progress quantity. As the materials move across the production or assembly process, they are stored in temporary state before being used for the final product. For example, a car manufacturer may buy gears as raw material from a supplier, use them to assemble a gear drive assembly, store the assembly as the semifinished materials, and finally use this semifinished material to assemble a car.

In SAP IBP, this is managed with the production source and production source item (bill of material [BOM] and components) master data. Finished goods inventory is the stock of the finished sellable materials. For a make-to-stock planning strategy, finished goods are produced in advance and are kept in inventory in anticipation of a customer's order; whereas in a make-to-order planning strategy, finished goods are manufactured (per the customer specification) only after receiving a confirmed sales order from a customer.

MRO materials are the indirect materials used by the organization. They aren't used as the direct component input in the production process, but they support production or other processes of the organization. A relevant example is the inventory maintained by the maintenance team for a possible machine breakdown.

12.2.2 Inventory Types Based on Inventory Planning and Optimization

For inventory optimization calculations and for holding the inventory level, inventory can be classified as follows:

▶ **Safety stock**
Safety stock is maintained in the supply chain network to avoid stock-out conditions due to demand and supply uncertainty. The aim of safety stock isn't to be used for replenishment but to provide a cushion for the exceptional scenario. Figure 12.2 shows the ideal condition in which cycle stock isn't dipping into safety stock, and hence, safety stock maintains the target value.

▶ **Cycle stock**
Cycle stock is the average amount of inventory required to meet customer demand. As represented in Figure 12.2, with replenishment of an order, cycle stock is at its highest level, and its value decreases with the consumption against demand. During the review period, a new order may be placed to match the actual inventory position against the target inventory position. Delivery of material against the open order increases the value back to the highest level of cycle stock.

▶ **Pipeline stock**
Pipeline stock represents the materials on order that are physically not yet received. Hence, the quantity of pipeline stock depends on the demand quantity and order processing lead time.

▶ **On-hand inventory**
On-hand inventory is generally represented as the physical inventory available within the organization. Hence, it's the sum of safety stock and cycle stock at the

present time. For inventory projection in the future, current on-hand inventory along with the future demand and supply quantity (in addition to pipeline stock) are considered.

▶ **Target inventory**
Target inventory or target inventory position at any time represents the quantity expected for a material at a location. While performing supply planning with the consideration of safety stock, on-hand inventory, and any open order, target inventory is used for creation of any new replenishment order.

Figure 12.2 shows the inventory types in the supply chain network for inventory planning.

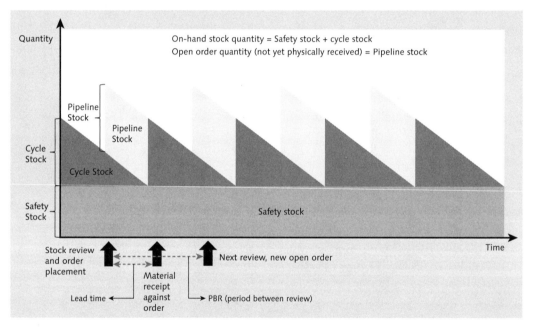

Figure 12.2 Inventory Types for Inventory Planning in the Supply Chain Network

Due to the demand and supply variations, it may be possible that operations of the organization require digging into the safety stock and may also result in a stock-out situation when the safety stock is consumed before the next replenishment. Figure 12.3 shows an example of exception scenarios due to demand and supply variations. During the first variation, due to late replenishment of cycle stock, the safety stock quantity is used. During the next shortage case, the material isn't received even after consuming the safety stock amount, and thus increases the possibility of a stock-out situation.

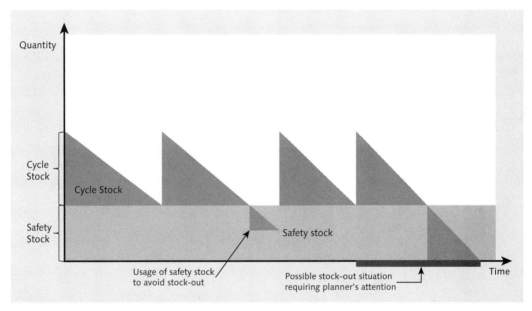

Figure 12.3 Safety Stock Usage with Demand and Supply Variations

The advantage of integrated planning with SAP IBP is that it first optimizes the situation to minimize the stock-out percentage at the lowest cost using planning algorithms. Alerts and exception scenarios can update the planners in advance about the possible stock-out situation so that action can be taken by the planner to avoid and manage this situation.

12.3 Inventory Planning and Related Analytics

The negative impact of poor inventory management on company performance can be quite profound, including reduced cash flow, increased working capital investment, and ultimately decreased shareholder value. In response to this, a growing number of companies have been adopting various techniques for optimizing inventory. These techniques are based on calculating the right level of safety stock and target inventory calculations for supply planning.

To understand the inventory optimization calculations discussed in Section 12.4, you should first take a look at some concepts related to the supply chain network, service quality, and relevant analytics, as discussed in the following sections.

12.3.1 Supply Chain Network and Inventory Optimization

A supply chain network is a structured grouping of multiple locations through which the product flows to the end customer. Different types of materials related to inventory planning were discussed in the previous section with the identification of raw materials, work-in-progress, finished goods, and MRO materials. It's essential to understand the different location types that are used for inventory optimization calculations. The locations are usually referred to as *nodes* in the supply chain network for inventory optimization purposes. In this chapter, nodes and locations are used interchangeably.

The following are the location types used for network mapping and inventory analytics:

- **Location type based on customer connection**
  A location is considered a customer-facing node if it directly replenishes a customer location. A non customer-facing node is a location that feeds an organization's internal locations, or internal nodes. A location that both feeds a customer and is an internal location is called a hybrid node.

- **Location types based on inventory holding capacity**
  Locations are categorized as *stocking nodes* or *non-stocking nodes* based on their ability to hold inventory. Hence, a distribution center or the warehouse where inventory is stocked and is issued to either a customer or to an internal location is considered a stocking node; however, a location such as a cross-dock doesn't store inventory and is called a non-stocking node. For inventory optimization calculations, safety stock is considered only at the stocking node locations.

- **Location types based on an operations property**
  Locations in a supply chain network are categorized as supplier, processing plant, warehouse, nonstocking node, and customer. A processing plant may contain the BOM master data for performing the inventory calculations of the component based on the finished material demand.

Figure 12.4 shows an example of location types in a supply chain network for inventory optimization. Note that a hybrid warehouse holding the inventory is connected to the customer as well as the internal location.

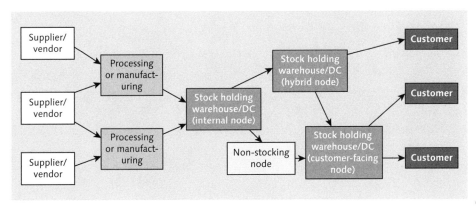

Figure 12.4 Nodes for Inventory Optimization in SAP IBP

12.3.2 Basic Concepts and Analytics for Inventory Optimization

To gain a deeper understanding of inventory optimization and the relevant calculations, it's essential to understand some basic concepts of supply chain management and inventory planning, as follows:

- Service level analytics
- Normal distribution and statistical probability
- Forecast error calculation
- Demand lag
- Supply variation calculation
- Sequential and cross-over order delivery types

Service Level Analytics

The service level represents the percentage of customer orders fulfilled. For inventory optimization, there are two possible analytics calculations widely in use:

▸ **Fill rate**
Fill rate represents the percentage of customer demand quantity met on time.

▸ **Available in full**
Available in full, also known as on time in full (OTIF) measures the percentage of the orders fully satisfied on time.

To understand the calculation, see Table 12.1, showing the customer demand and the supply made by an organization.

Date	Week 1	Week 2	Week 3	Week 4	Total for Month
Demand quantity, customer C1, product P1	100	120	110	120	450
Supply quantity, customer C1, product P1	100	120	100	120	440

Table 12.1 Demand and Supply Quantity in a Month for the Service Rate Calculation

For the demand and supply example given in Table 12.1, service levels can be calculated as follows:

▸ Fill Rate = (Total supply ÷ Total demand) × 100 = (440 ÷ 450) × 100 = 97.78%

▸ Available in full, OTIF = (Number of completely filled orders ÷ Total number of orders) × 100 = (3 ÷ 4) × 100 = 75%

Available in full, it should be noted, ultimately is a binary condition, producing either a 1 (completely satisfied order) or 0 (incomplete order). Selection of fill rate or available in full is based on the organization's financial and operational goals, industry segment, and customer contracts.

Normal Distribution and Statistical Probability

When you have a large amount of data, its distribution follows the normal curve. This concept is based on the *central limit theorem* and is used widely in statistics. The details of the statistical concept and the central limit theorem are out of the scope of this book; however, basic knowledge of the concepts is required to understand inventory optimization calculations.

For inventory optimization calculations, data for demand deviation and lead time variations follow a normal distribution. Figure 12.5 shows an example of normal distribution illustrating the percentage of data elements with the deviation ranges. Hence, for a normal distribution, there is 68% probability that a data element is within one standard deviation from the mean value. A standard deviation is the statistically calculated deviation of the data values from the mean value with the calculation provided in this section.

For safety stock calculations, the service factor or "Z value" is used for an associated service level. In a classic formula, the service factor is multiplied by the standard deviation to calculate your safety stock (more on this in Section 12.4).

A service factor of zero means that there is no safety stock. In this case, 50% of the demand cycles will be filled by the cycle stock, as shown in Figure 12.5.

For a Z value of 1 (i.e., one standard deviation), 50 + 34 = 84% of the demand cycles will be filled. Thus, the service rate probability with a Z value of 1 will be 84%.

Following the same logic, a service level probability with a Z value of 2 results in a service rate probability of 98%, as 50 + 34 + 14 = 98%.

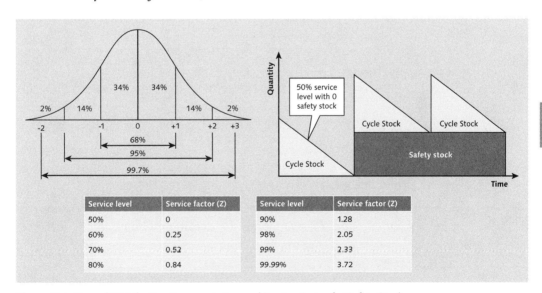

Figure 12.5 Normal Distribution Representation and Service Factor for Safety Stock

Mean, standard deviation, and coefficient of variance are calculated as follows:

- Mean: $\mu = (X1 + X2 + X3 + \ldots + Xn) \div n$

- Standard deviation: $\sigma = \sqrt{\dfrac{1}{n}\sum_{i=1}^{n}(x_i - \mu)^2}$

- Coefficient of variation: $CV = \sigma \div \mu$

For an illustration, consider the example of a supplier lead time for the past 24 weeks as represented in Table 12.2.

Week *n* Values	1	2	3	4	5	6	7	8	9	10	11	12	13	14	15	16	18	19	20
Lead Time (Days) *Xi* Values	14	13	14	12	13	14	14	13	15	15	15	14	14	14	13	13	15	16	13

Table 12.2 Data Value Example for Deviance Calculation

Thus, in this example, the following is true:

- Mean: $\mu = (X1 + X2 + X3 + \ldots + Xn) \div n = 264 \div 20 = 13.2$

- Standard deviation = 1.1610

- Coefficient of variation: $CV = \sigma \div \mu = 1.1610 \div 13.2 = 0.088$

The calculation logic of mean, standard deviation, and coefficient of variance is used for the inventory optimization calculation.

Forecast Error Calculation

For forecast error or demand deviation calculations, forecast value is compared with the actual sales data for every period. Calculated mean, standard deviation, and coefficient of variation of the forecast error are used for the safety stock and inventory calculations.

Forecast error can be calculated as the average mean absolute deviation or as the standard deviation.

Demand Lag

Variance reduction for demand and supply increases the efficiency of business operations. As discussed in previous chapters, fewer last-hour adjustments in demand, purchasing, and production processes help increase production efficiency and lower costs of operations. Along with the variation volume, time of change is also important. Some organizations allow changing the forecast value in the short-term horizon, although it creates a wrong impression of the forecast accuracy and impacts the effectiveness of sales and operations planning (S&OP).

For example, a change of demand forecast performed today for next week may show a higher forecast accuracy based on greater visibility of the incoming sales order and hence a better match with the projected demand. However, this change may result in significant changes in purchasing, transportation, and production, resulting in production schedule disruption, premium freight expense, and unfilled orders.

To control the process of last-minute forecast adjustments and to use a more realistic forecast error value for inventory calculation, demand lag is used. A lag represents the gap between the current period and the forecasted period. Lag X version of the forecast is the forecast that was generated X periods ago. Hence, if the forecast is performed in the weekly buckets, a forecast with lag 4 shows that this forecast value was maintained four weeks ago, and a forecast with lag 1 is one week old. SAP IBP can use the lag attribute with the forecast to measure the forecast accuracy and a demand variation calculation for an expected period of the forecast.

Supply Variation

Supply variation is used for the supply processes involving purchasing, production and transportation. The variation is calculated for the operations' lead time. Mean, standard deviation, and coefficient of variance can be calculated with the actual values of the lead times for usage in the inventory calculation.

Sequential and Cross-Over Order Delivery Types

Delivery types of the orders can be sequential or cross over. This is true for production, purchasing, and transport orders. In sequential delivery types, orders are processed on a first-come-first-serve basis, and a delay in one order delays subsequent orders based on the sequential nature. On the other hand, in a cross-over delivery system, a delay in an order may not impact other orders because the subsequent order can be delivered first instead of a delayed order. Delivery type is used for advanced safety stock calculations. A sequential order delivery type provides a more conservative approach to safety stock calculation.

12.4 Inventory Optimization Calculations

Inventory optimization calculations in a supply chain network are performed to calculate the recommended level of safety stock, level of cycle stock, and the target inventory position.

To understand how this works, it's useful to examine the major drivers of supply chain variability. On the demand side, there are escalating customer expectations about product features, quality, and availability. There is also increasing competition resulting in downward pressure on demand and shortening product lifecycles. Finally, changing demographics and emerging economies shift purchasing power across regions and open new channels and markets. All of this combines to make the task of the demand planner quite challenging, which is why forecast accuracy rarely exceeds the 70–80% range.

From a supply perspective, there are variable vendor and manufacturing lead times, transportation delays, capacity and material constraints, and growing product complexity. These factors create a situation where supply becomes unpredictable, causing planners to compensate with increased inventory buffers to mitigate the risk of shortages. In response to this, companies often initiate across-the-board inventory-reduction programs based on financial targets without regard to the operational aspects of the problem. While these programs sometimes deliver benefits in the form of reduced costs, these are often short lived and at the expense of other important metrics such as customer service. Over the years, various techniques have evolved to better manage inventory investment. These include coverage rules of thumb, inventory classification, and single-stage safety stock planning. Again, these techniques all can provide limited benefits when applied to simple situations but fall short when conditions of high demand, supply variability, and network complexity are present.

Calculation of the inventory target is based on the nature of the network, as follows:

▸ **Single-stage network**
  A single-stage network is mostly used as a simplified representation of a supply chain network unit for inventory calculation. It represents a customer and a customer-facing stocking node, and it can have another internal location that replenishes the customer-facing node.

The service level for the customer, average forecast, forecast error, lead time for material flow, and period between review are used for calculating the safety stock and target inventory position at the customer-facing node.

▶ **Multi-echelon network**
A multi-echelon network—a more realistic representation of a real supply chain network—is a complex structure with a multi-level product and location network. In addition to the multiple nodes, this network also requires the BOM information to calculate the recommended stock values for components based on the finished good demand. The nodes in a multi-echelon network can be customer-facing, internal, hybrid, processing plant, stocking, or nonstocking.

Figure 12.6 shows examples of single-stage inventory optimization and a multi-echelon network.

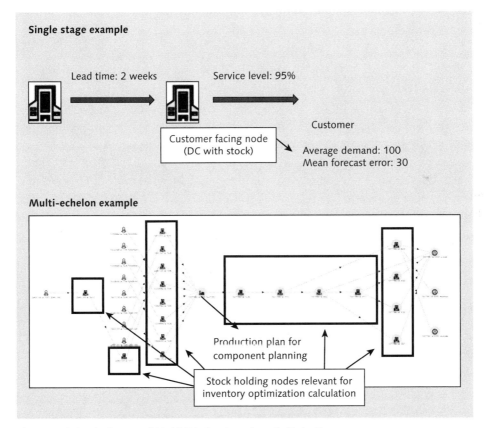

Figure 12.6 Single-Stage and Multi-Echelon Inventory Optimization

For single-stage inventory optimization, safety stock and target inventory position can be calculated as follows:

- Safety stock = Service level factor (Z) × Absolute forecast error × SQRT (Lead time + PBR)
- Target inventory position = (Lead time + PBR) × Average demand + Safety stock

Therefore, for the example displayed in Figure 12.6, the calculations would run as follows:

- Safety stock = 1.65 × 30 × SQRT (2 + 1) = 86
- Target inventory position = (2 + 1) × 100 + 86 = 386

For the multi-echelon example, calculations become much more complex due to multiple nodes (mix of internal and customer-facing), component requirement calculations, lead times, service factors, and order delivery types.

> **Note**
>
> SAP IBP for inventory uses a multi-echelon approach to calculate and optimize inventory targets based on the internal characteristics of the network as well as extrinsic factors.

On the the demand there are forecast errors, forecast bias, product seasonality, and product variability; on the supply side there are manufacturing lead times, batch sizes, supplier lead times, and supplier reliability. There are also service levels, not only to the end customer but between the various nodes, such as between plants and distribution centers. The SAP inventory optimization algorithm takes all of these factors into account in calculating inventory targets for every material/location combination in the network by usage category (safety, cycle, prebuild). The result is a time-phased material positioning plan that balances inventory investment with service levels across the entire network.

Figure 12.7 illustrates the relationship between inventory investment and service levels. The plot of current performance indicates a high investment in inventory relative to the current service level, which is approximately 92%. The curve shows how this performance can be improved by a properly segmented and optimized inventory policy.

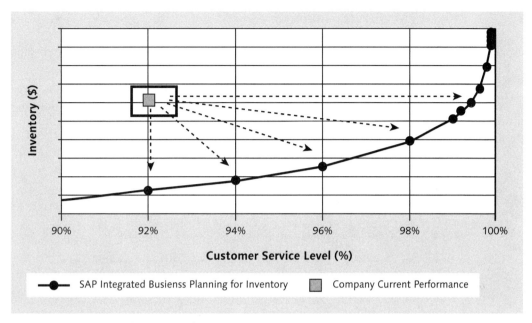

Figure 12.7 Inventory and Service Levels

While it may seem counterintuitive, this approach won't always recommend a reduction in inventory. In some cases, based on demand/supply variability or desired service levels, an increase of safety stock level may be recommended for a given material/location combination over a certain time period. This is known as "fixing the mix" of inventory. Fixing the mix refers to performing inventory optimization for each item at every location to meet the service requirement at the lowest cost; however, the output can be increased stock requirements for a few materials and decreased value of others. Overall, the network becomes leaner and the service level is increased with a fix-the-mix approach to inventory optimization. This is achieved through the detailed calculation and consideration of the product/location level in SAP IBP.

> **Note**
>
> The example here is for reference purposes to understand the concepts of inventory optimization calculations. The actual calculations used in SAP IBP are highly sophisticated and the property of SAP; the details of the calculation algorithm aren't in the scope of this text. For a business and technical user, understanding the input and output is required (as discussed in this and the next chapter) for using the inventory optimization in SAP IBP.

12.5   SAP IBP for Inventory

SAP IBP for inventory uses a combination of stochastic modeling and multistage planning to optimize inventory targets across the supply chain. The foundation of this solution is a complete, end-to-end model of the supply network that represents the material flow through every node from the end customer back to the source of supply.

In the following sections, we'll discuss SAP IBP for inventory applications in network visualization, inventory analytics, and planning views used for inventory optimization.

12.5.1   Network Visualization and Inventory Calculation

SAP IBP for inventory represents the supply chain structure, nodes, and product flow through network visualization charts. The nodes in the model can be any location, including manufacturing plants, distribution centers, and even customer or supplier locations. Each has associated with it a set of materials that flow through it. Each material can be represented by different forms of inventory such as raw, semifinished, or finished goods. They can also be represented by various uses of inventory, such as safety, cycle, or prebuilt stock. Each of these buckets of inventory will have a quantity associated with it that will vary over time. The lines that connect the nodes indicate that there is a demand and supply relationship between them, with an associated lead time that will also vary over time and by material. SAP IBP for inventory can map a highly complex network as represented here and can perform the inventory calculations for recommended stock levels.

The benefit of this model is that it provides a holistic picture of the complex interrelationships that drive material requirements across the supply network. The other important aspects of the problem are the material-specific characteristics that come into play.

12.5.2   Sales, Inventory, and Operations Planning and Analytics Applications

One of the key benefits of the SAP IBP architecture is that it enables seamless end-to-end cross-functional processes. One example of this is sales, inventory, and operations planning (SIOP), which combines the disciplines of S&OP and inventory optimization to produce a better plan. A good S&OP process can by itself be very effective at profitably balancing demand and supply based on given parameters. However, these parameters may not fully take into account supply chain variability. The stochastic optimization approach employed by SAP IBP ensures that both demand and supply variability are part of this balancing process. The following scenario is an illustration of how this works in practice.

Figure 12.8 shows a typical SIOP dashboard that provides an overview of the current situation, as well as some important details. Across the top is a process flow indicating the current status of the monthly SIOP cycle, in which the IBP DEMAND REVIEW has been completed and the IBP SUPPLY AND INVENTORY REVIEW is about to begin. In the middle section are a geographic view displaying the current overall stock coverage situation and a network view that represents the locations most impacted by the latest demand plan. The large red bubble on the geographic view indicates higher than expected inventory levels in the European region. This is confirmed by the heat map at the bottom showing projected inventory while the bar chart indicates supply shortages for specific materials. It's readily apparent from this dashboard that there are inventory imbalances that need to be addressed.

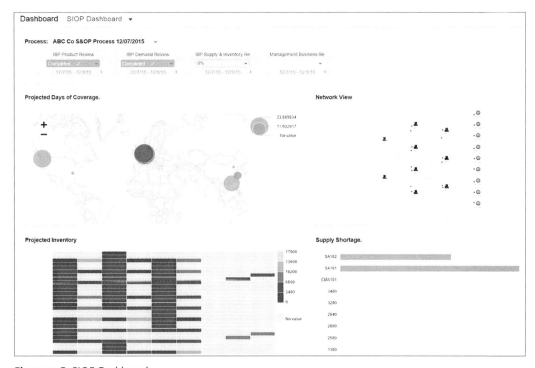

Figure 12.8 SIOP Dashboard

To investigate the situation further, the planner drills down to analyze the projected inventory plan for several product families. Figure 12.9 shows weekly projected days of coverage for three product families. Series 300 seems to have an extremely high value relative to the other families, which could be the result of a number of factors and needs to be brought back into line.

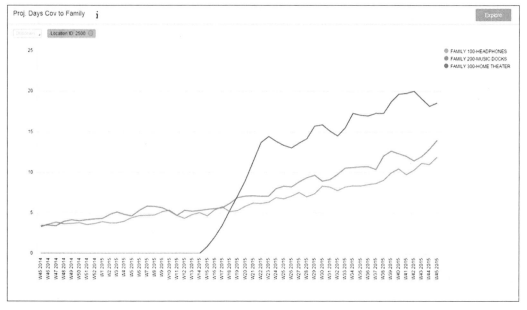

Figure 12.9 Projected Days of Coverage

12.5.3 Planning Views for SAP IBP for Inventory

To further analyze and to take action on the inventory management, the planning view functionalities of SAP IBP are used. The planner will access the Projected Inventory planning view shown in Figure 12.10. In this view, they can see some crucial details about these products, including target stock value, budget stock value, and service levels. These are only a small sample of the vast number of key figures that can be used to manage inventory investment. In this case, the first two are calculated, while service level is an input. One possible approach, although certainly not the only one, would be to adjust the service level for Series 300 from 95% to 93% and let the multistage inventory optimizer create a new inventory investment plan. This is an example of the discussion earlier in this chapter of striking a balance between inventory investment and service level and would most likely be done in a simulation mode to evaluate the impact before proceeding.

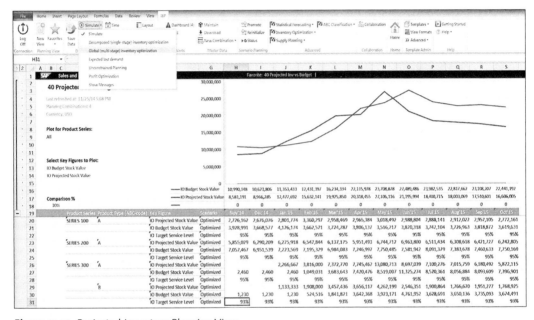

Figure 12.10 Projected Inventory Planning View

The scenario wraps up with another dashboard (Figure 12.11) that visually depicts the new situation after the inventory optimization run.

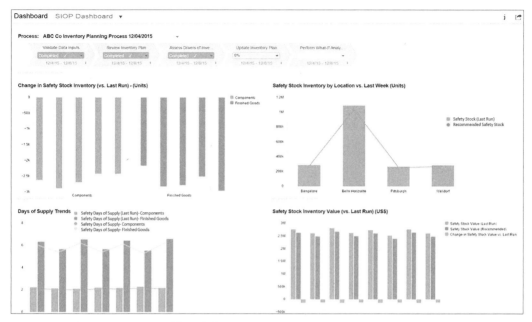

Figure 12.11 SIOP Dashboard after Inventory Optimization

Across the top is the INVENTORY PLANNING PROCESS subprocess flow indicating that the new plan has been reviewed and is ready for implementation. The upper-left bar chart shows the recommended change in safety stock quantities for components and finished goods, whereas the one on the lower right shows the total change in safety stock value. The other two charts illustrate safety stock by location and days of coverage trends. The planner can clearly see that the inventory situation has improved, and the SIOP process can continue, or they can run additional scenarios with different assumptions to see if the results can be further improved. It should be noted that while this scenario is focused on a certain set of products and locations, inventory optimization is a global process that delivers benefits across the entire supply chain. This combination of powerful optimization capabilities and real-time scenario analysis enables companies to dramatically improve working capital efficiency through better inventory positioning.

12.6 Summary

Even though storing inventory ties up working capital and reduces profit, it's crucial to hold inventory in the supply chain network in order to meet customer demand in a reasonable time. The inventory optimization process determines optimum target stock levels which meet these service level requirements at minimum cost. SAP IBP for inventory calculates these targets in a complex network using highly sophisticated inventory optimization algorithms.

After understanding the principles of inventory management, and the capabilities of SAP IBP for inventory, we're ready to delve into the details of configuring SAP IBP for inventory in the next chapter.

This chapter teaches you how to configure and set up SAP IBP for inventory for inventory optimization. Equipped with the knowledge and understanding of the inventory optimization concepts in the preceding chapter, you're now ready to look into the details of system build and usage of SAP IBP for inventory.

13 Implementing SAP IBP for Inventory

SAP Integrated Business Planning (SAP IBP) for inventory optimizes the inventory of the products in the supply chain to meet your target service levels. It calculates the inventory targets to achieve your service level goal at the period/product/ location level based on the actual data such as forecast error, demand variation, supply variation, and network structure of the organization's supply chain.

Using SAP IBP for inventory to perform inventory optimization and analytics requires you to model your organization's supply chain. This chapter illustrates how to create the network charts, build a planning model, and execute inventory optimization in the network through SAP IBP for inventory.

13.1 Building Network Visualization

Network visualization shows the supply chain network with the associated elements in a graphical chart display. The SAP IBP system automatically creates the chart by using the master data and key figure information provided to the system. In the following sections, we'll look at information on configuration and usage of the network visualization chart in the following areas:

- Nodes in the network
- Chart types
- Essential master data

13.1.1 Supply Chain Nodes

Inventory in a supply chain network is always associated with a location or as being in transit between two locations. As mentioned in Chapter 12, these supply chain network locations are referred to as nodes in SAP IBP. Hence, a supplier, a distribution center, a manufacturing plant, and a customer are all examples of nodes. Typical material movement in a supply chain network happens from the supplier node to the customer node while going through manufacturing and distribution center nodes, which may or may not hold inventory. The flow of material and the connection of the nodes are entirely dependent on the supply chain and product structure of an organization.

Node properties are assigned to the location master data in SAP IBP for inventory. Master data for this feature are organized as follows:

▶ Master data type: Location

  ▶ Attribute: Stocking node type (STOCKINGNODETYPE)

    – Stocking node: S

    – Nonstocking node: N

13.1.2 Chart Types for Network Visualization Display

Visualization of the supply chain network in SAP IBP for inventory can be performed using three different chart types that show varying levels of network information through associated data:

▶ **Basic network chart**
This chart shows the end-to-end inventory flow in the supply chain network.

▶ **Heat map network chart**
In addition to inventory flow, this chart shows the heat map for one key figure. The key figure that appears first in the selection is used for generating the heat map.

▶ **Product network chart**
In addition to inventory flow as displayed in the basic chart, a product ID can be filtered to show the movement of the product with associated components. Other products that share the components of the filtered product automatically are selected for the chart display.

13.1.3 Master Data Elements for the Network Visualization Chart

To be able to represent the supply chain network of the organization, it's critical to provide the basic master data elements to the SAP IBP system. These master data elements and their attributes are used to generate the network chart. The data elements required depend on the type of network visualization chart. For example, a product network chart requires source production and production source item master data to display the product component relationship in addition to location, product, and customer master data types.

The available master data types in the planning model whose information is relevant for generating the network chart are shown in Table 13.1.

Master Data Type	Attribute
Location	Location ID, location type, location region
Customer	Customer ID, customer group
Product	Product ID, product series, product family, product subfamily
Component	Product from ID
Location product	Location ID, product ID, stocking node type, service level type
Location from	Location from ID, location from region, location from type
Source location	Location ID, location from ID, product ID, transportation ratio, delivery type
Source customer group	Customer group, location ID, product ID, market segment
Source production	Location ID, product ID, source ID, production ratio, source type, production delivery type, output coefficient
Production source item	Source ID, product ID (for component), source item ID, component coefficient

Table 13.1 Essential Master Data Types and Attributes for the Network Visualization Chart

For an active model with master data attributes and generated key figures, the network chart can be created in SAP IBP by opening the Analytics app and selecting the CHART TYPE as NETWORK. For more details on the analytics features of SAP IBP, see Chapter 15.

Figure 13.1 shows the chart type area for a network chart along with an example of a network visualization chart. You must select the CHART TYPE as NETWORK, choose the PLANNING AREA, and provide the GROUP BY conditions of the master data types and attributes. Additional filter data can be provided to filter the selection of chart generation in the FILTER DATA area. For example, a product ID filter will generate a product chart. The network represented in Figure 13.1 shows the end-to-end supply chain network of the organization.

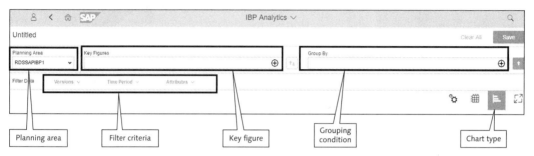

Figure 13.1 Network Visualization Chart in SAP IBP for Inventory

Different icons are used in the chart to represent various parties, including suppliers, manufacturing nodes, warehouse nodes, non-stocking nodes, and vendors. Figure 13.2 shows the component network with the processing plant, output material, and components by displaying a product network chart. Key figure values in the chart can be displayed by hovering the chart area at the nodes or arc of the network.

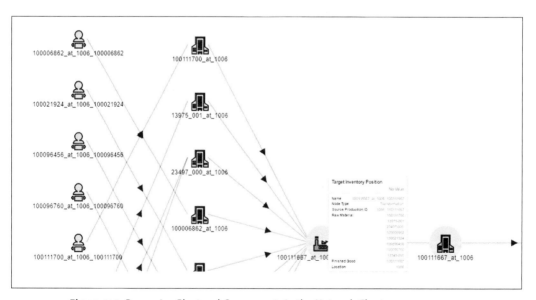

Figure 13.2 Processing Plant and Components in the Network Chart

13.2 Modeling Inventory Optimization

Inventory optimization can be modeled in SAP IBP using the standard planning models provided by SAP. The planning area dedicated to inventory optimization, SAP3, or the unified planning area, SAPIBP1, can be copied and edited. In addition to demand and supply information, the inventory optimization algorithm requires stock and order data from the execution system. Demand and supply data can be made available in SAP IBP if you're using SAP IBP for demand and SAP IBP for response and supply. Otherwise, SAP IBP will need to connect with the legacy systems being used for demand and supply. Stock, order, master data, and other execution system data can be transferred to SAP IBP by integrating the SAP-based execution system or any other legacy system using the SAP Cloud Platform.

> **Note**
>
> A number of topics covered in Chapter 5 will help you when creating your planning model for inventory optimization.

In addition to the topics covered in Chapter 5, additional information specific to inventory optimization is necessary to create your planning model, as follows:

▶ **Time profile**
The time profile used in the standard SAP3 planning area contains week, month, quarter, and year. Storage of data is performed at the lowest planning level: week. SAP IBP for inventory can also support technical week by configuring a time profile with technical week as a planning level and using a week weight factor in the time profile value. If technical week is used, then the data storage level will be technical week. Aggregation and disaggregation of inventory optimization key figures can be performed through the time levels in SAP IBP. It's required to provide the time bucket level in the inventory optimization (IO) operator to assign the time level at which inventory optimization calculations are performed in SAP IBP.

▶ **Master data**
The inventory optimization solution requires a minimum set of master data types and associated attributes. Many attribute values (e.g., stocking node type in the location master data) are only relevant for the inventory optimization solution and hence must have a value assigned for planning through SAP IBP for inventory. To avoid errors due to a missing value, the SAP standard solution has the uses a default value if there is a blank value in some parameters. It's

recommended that you understand and use the values relevant to the organization's supply chain network while managing the network in SAP IBP through the following master data types:

▶ **Customer master data type**
The customer ID and customer group attribute should be used with their values populated in the model.

▶ **Location master data type**
Attributes relevant for the location master data type of the inventory solution are as follows:

- Location ID

- Location region

- Location type (assign whether the location represents a supplier, production plant, distribution center, etc.)

- Latitude and longitude value (maps the location with global coordinates)

▶ **Location from**
Reference master data of location is used in the source location master data to create the network.

▶ **Product master data**
Along with product ID and description, stocking properties of the products are required in the inventory solution. Attributes such as product series, product family, and product subfamily can be added in the product master data. In addition to product, component master data types are also added if components of a bill of materials (BOM) are also in scope.

▶ **Source customer group**
The source customer group master data type is used to assign a group of customers with the product, fulfillment location, and planned target service levels. Attributes of the source customer group for inventory planning are as follows:

- Customer group: Group name with different customers for the same products supplied from the same location at one planned service level target.

- Product ID: Product that can be supplied.

- Location ID: Fulfillment location.

- Target service level: Used to assign the target service level; for example, for a 95% service level, the assigned value will be 0.95.

▶ **Location/product**

Inventory optimization parameters for a product at the storing and fulfillment location are provided through the master data attributes of location/product. Important parameters that control inventory calculations are as follows:

- Service level type: Assign F for fill-rate and A for available-in-full service level policy. Note that the service level percentage is part of the source customer group master data, which follows the policy for the percentage of the type assigned as the service level type in the location/product master data.

- Stocking node type: Assign S for the location that can hold inventory and N for the non-stocking node type for the location that doesn't store inventory. Safety stock calculation is performed only for the stocking node, although the non-stocking node is considered part of the network in the computation algorithm.

- Periods between review (PBR): The review period can be assigned for inventory review and business actions.

- Minimum and maximum internal service level: This is the exact value of the service level for internal locations (locations not supplying to a customer) and is calculated by the SAP IBP for inventory algorithm based on the assigned service level for the customer. However, minimum and maximum service levels can be assigned through values of these attributes to be considered by the inventory optimization calculation.

- Safety stock policy: Safety stock policy F (FCFS [first come first served]) can be assigned to put all demand streams at the highest service level. This is the default setting for the inventory optimization calculation. Divide (D) can be assigned to calculate safety stock values for each demand stream independently and then add them together. Safety stock calculation for an independent demand stream only can be performed through assigned value I (independent for safety stock policy).

▶ **Location source master data**

Location source master data is used for creating the network from the collection of locations. Product, location-from, and location attributes of master data control the products that can move from the assigned source to the target location. Attributes relevant for inventory level calculation are as follows:

- Lead time

- Lead time variability (coefficient of variance [CV] for the transport lead time)

- Sourcing quota and time series indicator to assign the sourcing rule

- Lot size values (through attributes minimum and incremental lot size)

- Transportation shipment frequency per week

- Transportation delivery type (S for sequential delivery and C for allowed cross-over delivery)

▸ **Source production master data**

In source production master data, source ID, product ID, and location ID control the BOM name, output product, and the manufacturing location information, respectively. Inventory optimization attributes for the source production master data type are as follows:

- Production lead time

- Production lead time variability (assigned through production lead time CV)

- Minimum production lot size and incremental lot size

- Production shipment frequency per week

- Production delivery type (S for sequential and C for allowed cross-over delivery type)

▸ **Production source item**

Production source item master data contains the attributes of the source ID with the components and quantity of the components. For multi-echelon inventory optimization calculations, the production BOM is decomposed for calculating the component requirements and related recommended inventory targets.

▸ **Lag**

Master data type lag is used with the attribute name lag for the time period parameter of the forecast value.

▸ **Currency, currency-to, and exchange rate**

Currency, currency-to, and exchange rate master data types are used for the cost values when assigning a currency and for performing the currency conversion in SAP IBP for inventory calculations and planning views.

▸ **Location/product/currency**

Location/product/currency master data is used for assigning the attribute information of *cost per unit* for a product at a location for inventory optimization calculation.

13.3   Forecast Error Calculation

Forecast errors can be calculated in the SAP IBP system for usage in the inventory planning calculation. To calculate the forecast error, you must create a forecast error calculation profile in SAP IBP for inventory. The profile for forecast error is created by accessing the MANAGE FORECAST ERROR CALCULATIONS tile under INVENTORY PLANNER. Figure 13.3 shows an example of the tile and new profile creation page from the SAP IBP system.

Along with the PROFILE NAME and PROFILE DESCRIPTION, PLANNING AREA and CALCULATION LEVEL are selected for the forecast error calculation. The PERIODICITY OF CALCULATION LEVEL setting selected in the profile controls the time level used for the inventory planning calculation. Select the USE LAG checkbox if lag in the forecast will be used for the forecast error. If USE LAG is selected, then the planning level should also have lag master data type in the selection.

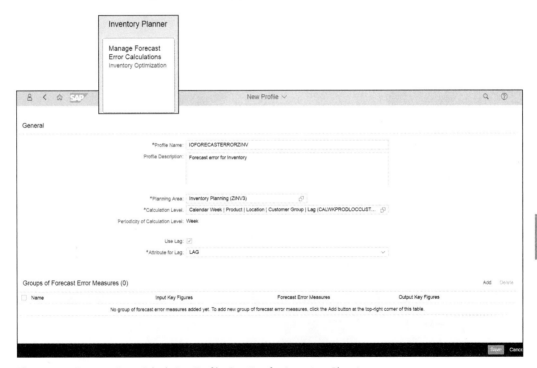

Figure 13.3 Forecast Error Calculation Profile Creation for Inventory Planning

In the forecast error profile screen, the input value is provided in the Sales History Key Figure and the Forecast Key Figure fields (see Figure 13.4). Assigned key figures are used to calculate the deviation of the forecast value with the actual sales. The Time Periods in the Past is chosen for the time relevance level of the calculation. In the example shown in Figure 13.3 and Figure 13.4, the calculation level is Week and the time period is "52"; therefore, the values of the forecast key figure and sales history key figure for the last 52 weeks will be used for calculating the forecast error. In the Output Settings of the profile, key figures are assigned for calculated CV and forecast error values.

Figure 13.4 Input and Output Settings for the Forecast Error Calculation Profile for Inventory Planning

After assigning the parameters in the profile, click the Save button to save the forecast error profile, which can be used for calculating the forecast error. Figure 13.5 shows an example of a forecast error profile in SAP IBP for inventory. This profile is used in the planning operator to calculate the forecast error. Execution of the operator through the SAP IBP Excel planning view or through a background job calculates the forecast error. The output of the calculation is used as an input for the inventory planning calculation.

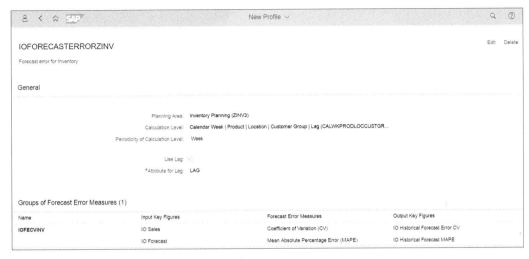

Figure 13.5 Forecast Error Profile for Inventory Planning

13.4 Input-Output Data Objects and Key Figures

Inventory optimization in SAP IBP for inventory is performed by using the actual demand and supply information along with the business rules to serve the customer. Figure 13.6 shows a representation of the input information to the inventory optimization tool, along with the output of the algorithm regarding expected service levels and recommended inventory positions.

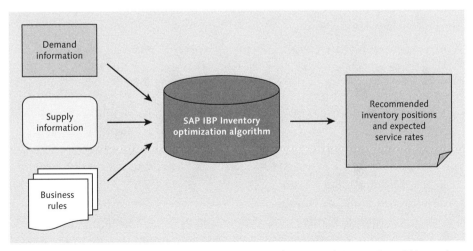

Figure 13.6 Modeling SAP IBP Inventory Optimization with Input and Output Data Objects

Recommended inventory positions as calculated by SAP IBP for inventory are used as an input for SAP IBP for response and supply as the inventory targets in supply planning calculations.

In the following sections, we'll look at both the data used as input for inventory optimization as well as the data that are output by the inventory optimization engine.

13.4.1 Input Data for Inventory Optimization

As displayed in Figure 13.6, input data for inventory optimization calculations can be grouped as follows:

- **Demand-related key figures**
  Actual sales history, demand forecasts, and forecast errors are the required inputs to determine demand deviations in the inventory planning algorithm. This information is fed into the inventory calculation through the key figures at the week/product/location/customer group planning level. In the technical names, prefix "IO" is used in the key figures for inventory optimization. A copy operator can be used to generate the value of these key figures while referring to the key figure data from SAP IBP for demand.

  Demand-related key figures used in inventory optimization modeling are as follows:

  - IO Sales (IOSALES): Historical sales quantity.

  - IO Forecast (IOFORECAST): Weekly forecast of a product at a location for a customer group.

  - Inventory Forecast Error CV (IOFORECASTERRORCV): Forecast error of a product at a location for a customer group.

- **Supply-related key figures**
  Supply-related key figures are provided to the inventory optimization calculation for parameters related to production, purchase, transportation, and storage. Values that are maintained as the master data attributes are converted to key figure values via the ATTRIBUTE AS KEY FIGURE option in SAP IBP modeling. Supply-related parameters are as follows:

  - **Production parameters**
    Production relevant parameters with respect to sourcing quota, lot sizes, lead times, and so on are provided as the input for the inventory optimization

calculation. These values are relevant for target stock calculations because they impact the quantity and time of the supply elements. Supply information for production is provided to the inventory optimization engine at the week/product/location/source planning level. Production rule key figures provided as input to inventory optimization are as follows:

– Production output coefficient (OUTPUTCOEFFICIENT): Output coefficient value in BOM.

– Production sourcing quota (PRODUCTIONRATIO): Sourcing quota for a produced product at the week/product/location/source planning level.

– Production minimum lot size (PMINLOTSIZE): Minimum lot size for a system-generated plan or production order for a produced product.

– Production incremental lot size (PINCLOTSIZE): Incremental lot size that determines the lot size and rounding value.

– Production lead time (PLEADTIME): Lead time in weeks, which can have both absolute and fraction values.

– Production lead time variation (PLEADTIMEVARIABILITY): CV for production lead time.

▸ **Purchase and transportation parameters**
Purchase and transportation parameters control material movements from one location to another in the supply chain network. Information is used for these parameters through the key figures defined at the week/product/location/location-from planning level. Hence, the input to the inventory optimization algorithm is for a product at a location that is being supplied by another internal (plant, distribution center, warehouse, etc.) or external (supplier) location.

The purchase and transportation key figures used as input to the inventory optimization algorithm are as follows:

– Sourcing quota (LOCATIONRATIO): Quota defined for procurement.

– Transportation lead time (TLEADTIME): Transportation lead time in weeks, which can be an absolute or fraction value.

– Transportation lead time variability (TLEADTIMEVARIABILITY): CV of transportation lead time in weeks, which can be an absolute or fraction value.

– Transportation minimum lot size (TMINLOTSIZE): Defines the minimum quantity for a system-generated transport or purchase requisition.

- Transportation incremental lot size (TINCLOTSIZE): Together with minimum lot size, defines the rounding value for transport and purchase orders.

For production and purchase, another relevant parameter for inventory calculation is unit cost for production or purchase. This is provided to the inventory optimization calculation through a key figure: standard unit cost (COSTPERUNIT). This key figure is the same for both the production and purchase materials and is defined at the week/product/location/currency planning level.

▶ **Storage parameters**
Storage parameters for the target inventory calculation are provided through the inventory holding cost rate key figure (INVENTORYHOSLDINGCOSTRATE). This represents the percentage value of the cost per unit and hence helps the calculation of production, purchase, and storage for meeting the target service level.

▶ **Business rules and requirements**
Business rules are provided for expected service levels and different stock requirements. The master data described in Section 13.2 provides the supply chain structure, nodes connectivity, location types, and attribute values for inventory planning.

Information for the service level is relevant at the week/product/location/customer group planning level. This gives the flexibility to aim for different service levels for different products and customer group selections. Different time periods may also be assigned to various service levels at a fulfillment location for a customer group and product combination.

Stock requirements information is relevant at the week/product/location planning level. Different fulfillment rules for minimum stocking requirements, service level targets, and so on can be assigned for different product/location combinations.

The business rules and requirement key figures for the inventory optimization calculation are as follows:

▶ Target service level (TARGETSERVICELEVEL): Target service level input for product, location, and customer group.

▶ Minimum internal service level (MININTERNALSERVICELEVEL): Minimum value of the service level at an internal node.

▶ Maximum internal service level (MAXINTERNALSERVICELEVEL): Maximum value of the service level at an internal node.

▸ Periods between review (PBR): Period in weeks for replenishment reviews.

▸ Minimum stock requirement (IOMINIMUMSTOCKREQUIREMENT): Minimum inventory at a customer-facing or retail location due to contractual, business, or legal requirements.

13.4.2 Output of the Inventory Optimization Engine

The output of the optimization algorithms used in SAP IBP for inventory are the recommended stock levels and expected service levels, along with some additional information. Many of the calculated output key figures, such as recommended safety stock, target inventory position, and so on, are used as the input for the supply planning algorithm to determine the requirements generated by the inventory engine. Other information generated, such as average service level, average working capital inventory, and so on, is used for analytics and management reporting. The output key figures from SAP IBP for inventory, relevant for business users, are as follows:

▸ **Recommended safety stock (RECOMMENDEDSAFETYSTOCK)**
This is the calculated safety stock quantity in a weekly bucket for a product at a location. This is at the week/product/location level and is not referred to a customer group.

▸ **Target inventory position (TARGETINVENTORYPOSITION)**
This is the calculated target inventory position at the week/product/location level.

▸ **Average service level (AVGSERVICELEVEL)**
This is the average of customer and internal service levels in a weekly bucket for a product at a location.

▸ **Fill rate or nonstock-out probability (AVAILABLEINFULL)**
This is the probability value of serving orders in full quantity for a product in a time period at a fulfilling location against the orders from a customer group.

▸ **Reorder point (ROP)**
This is the calculated threshold quantity for the replenishment trigger.

▸ **Expected lost customer demand (LOSTCUSTOMERDEMANDMEAN)**
This is the quantity of possible lost sales when the demand is more than the target service level coverage. This quantity may require a planner's action such as expedited shipment, collaboration, adjustment, etc.

- **Propagated demand (PROPAGATEDDEMANDMEAN)**
This is the propagated demand for a product at a node (location).

- **Average cycle stock (IOAVGCYCLESTOCK)**
This is the average inventory of a product in weeks at a location to cover the demand between shipments.

- **Average cycle stock value (IOAVGCYCLESTOCKVAL)**
This is the value of average cycle stock inventory.

- **Target cycle stock (IOTARGETCYCLESTOCK)**
This is the target inventory of a product in weeks at a location to cover the demand between shipments.

- **Target cycle stock value (IOTARGETCYCLESTOCKVAL)**
This is the value of the target cycle stock.

- **Average pipeline stock (IOAVGPIPELINESTOCK)**
This is the average quantity of on-order inventory that hasn't yet been received.

- **Average pipeline stock value (IOAVGPIPELINESTOCKVAL)**
This is the cost of the average on-order quantity that hasn't yet been received.

- **Target pipeline stock (IOTARGETPIPELINESTOCK)**
This is the target quantity of the pipeline stock.

- **Target pipeline stock value (IOTARGETPIPELINESTOCKVAL)**
This is the cost of the target on-order quantity that has not yet been received.

- **Merchandising stock (IOMERCHANDISINGSTOCK)**
This is the extra inventory quantity in addition to the safety stock, cycle stock, and pipeline stock to provide a cushion to meet the minimum stocking requirements.

- **Merchandising stock value (IOMERCHANDISINGSTOCKVAL)**
This is the value of the merchandising stock.

- **Average on-hand stock (IOAVGONHANDSTOCK)**
This is the calculated average amount of inventory at a location.

- **Average on-hand stock value (IOAVGONHANDSTOCKVAL)**
This is the value of the average on-hand stock quantity.

- **Average inventory position (IOAVGINVENTORYPOSITION)**
This is the average amount of inventory, including on-hand and on-order, reduced by order backlog.

▶ **Average working capital inventory (IOAVGWORKINGCAPITAL)**
This is the cost of the average inventory position.

13.5 Planning Operators for Inventory Calculation

Inventory planning is performed by configuring the planning operators for specific calculations, assigning them to the planning model (planning area), and executing the run using a planning job.

To create the planning operator, under MISCELLANEOUS SETTINGS, in the configuration section, click MANAGE PLANNING OPERATORS.

The planning operators for inventory calculations are as follows:

▶ **Forecast error calculator, algorithm type: FORECAST_ERROR**
The forecast error calculator algorithm calculates the error value with the provided input value of the forecast and sales order and assigns the error values to the identified output key figures.

▶ **Single-stage inventory optimization, algorithm type: SINGLE STAGE IO**
Single-stage inventory optimization is used to optimize inventory for each customer-facing location locally in a decomposed manner. It's more applicable for running in simulation or for performing a run after a multistage run.

▶ **Global multi-echelon inventory optimization, algorithm type: MULTI STAGE IO**
The multi-echelon or multistage inventory optimization algorithm optimizes the global network, involving every product and location in the network.

▶ **Expected demand loss, algorithm type: LOST SALES IO**
Expected demand loss calculates the expected lost demand quantity based on the planned service level and recommended safety stock values. A global multistage inventory optimization run must be executed before calculating expected demand loss quantity through this operator.

▶ **Calculate target inventory components, algorithm type: IO_DETERMINISTIC**
The target inventory component algorithm supports more granularity by calculating the quantity for different inventory types that determine the target inventory position. It calculates the ROP along with the cycle stock, pipeline stock, merchandising stock, and average inventory position.

After the planning operators are defined, they must be added into the planning area for inventory optimization. Activation of the planning area makes the operators available to execute in the planning runs.

13.6 Performing and Reviewing Inventory Optimization

An inventory optimization planning run is initiated either through the SAP IBP Excel planning view or through the SAP Fiori interface batch job. The planning results are viewed and adjusted by planners in the Excel planning view. Custom alerts and dashboards for inventory planning are also used for end-to-end visibility.

13.6.1 Executing Planning Runs

Planning runs for inventory optimization are usually performed through a scheduled application job to calculate the desired target inventory position and safety stock values for the products in the network. The results of the calculation are fed as an input to supply planning, which also can be a scheduled background job. Detailed steps to create and schedule an application job are covered in Chapter 16, Section 16.2.

Figure 13.7 shows the example of a new job creation for inventory optimization. OPERATOR TYPE, PLANNING AREA, and OPERATOR ID are selected for a job. The schedule time of the job is controlled via the EDIT SCHEDULING OPTIONS button. You must copy jobs to generate the forecast value (IO forecast key figure) and the sales history (IO sales history key figure) value from their source key figures, as well as execute the forecast error calculation, before executing the global inventory optimization job represented in Figure 13.7.

In addition to executing the inventory planning run as a background job, you can also perform the same task in the Excel planning view. Figure 13.8 and Figure 13.9 show an example of executing a forecast error calculation job and the weekly schedule of global multistage inventory optimization run. In Figure 13.8, the example shows the execution of the forecast error calculation in the SAP IBP Excel planning view. This job can be executed interactively or periodically scheduled. Figure 13.9 shows the execution of the multistage inventory optimization calculation. The example shows the option of using a WEEKLY recurrence (periodic) job to perform the calculation.

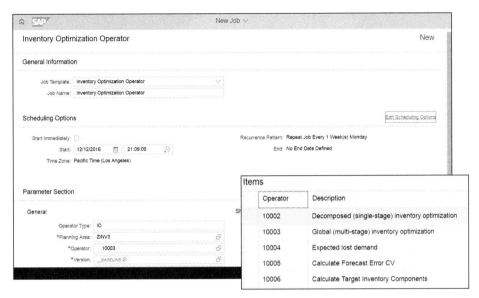

Figure 13.7 Application Job Creation Example for Inventory Planning in SAP IBP

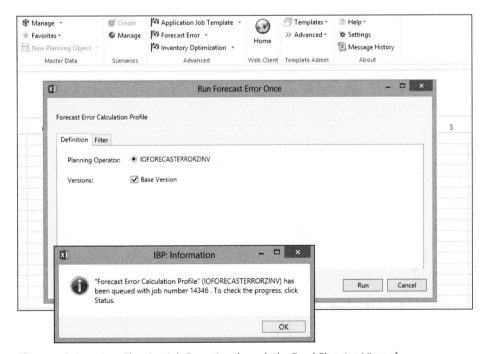

Figure 13.8 Inventory Planning Job Execution through the Excel Planning View of SAP IBP: Part 1

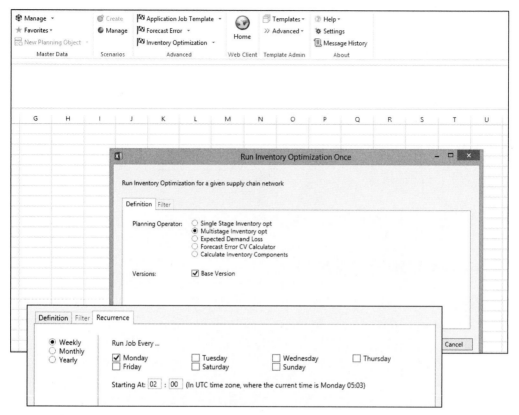

Figure 13.9 Inventory Planning Job Execution through the Excel Planning View of SAP IBP: Part 2

13.6.2 Review Inventory Optimization

Inventory optimization results produced by SAP IBP are available in the SAP IBP Excel planning view for you to review and update the data before they are used in supply planning. In addition to the Excel planning view, the SAP Fiori view is used to analyze and review the custom alerts, analytics, and dashboards of inventory planning and optimization.

Excel Planning View

The recommended stock values output of inventory planning are part of the input for the supply planning algorithm. The results generated by the optimization algorithm should be reviewed by the planner in the Excel planning view. After the review and any necessary adjustments, the plan is saved in the Excel planning view. In addition to the "live" plan, simulations can also be performed in the Excel planning view to adjust the numbers, execute a planning run, and review the results.

You can create specific planning views for inventory planning, analysis, and review with the key figures relevant for a role. Planning views can be created for forecast error values and the recommended safety stock level. Multiple planning views with required filters can be created in SAP IBP for roles such as inventory planner, supply planner and inventory manager.

Figure 13.10 and Figure 13.11 show an example of an inventory planning view. Figure 13.10 shows the data for the IO forecast, recommended safety stock, and target inventory position key figures for planner review. Figure 13.11 also contains the information on forecast error values, target service levels, and stock-out probabilities for the product, location, and customer group selection. By using the currency conversion functionality of SAP IBP and cost data in the system, inventory monetary values (current and projected) and related cost values can be displayed in the SAP IBP Excel planning views.

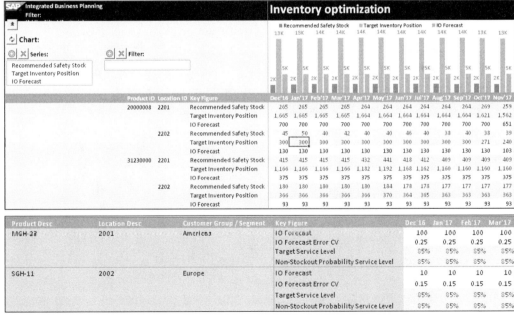

Figure 13.10 SAP IBP Excel Planning View for Inventory Planning: Part 1

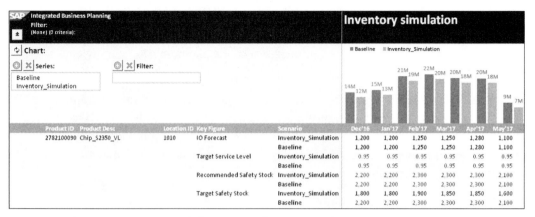

Figure 13.11 SAP IBP Excel Planning View for Inventory Planning: Part 2

The SAP IBP simulation capability is widely used in inventory planning and optimization. In Figure 13.10 and Figure 13.11, a scenario was created with the name INVENTORY_SIMULATION. The recommended and target safety stock values for the active planning version and the simulation scenario for what-if analysis have been represented in the example. Different planning simulations can be performed in this view for further optimization by considering potential opportunities and risks. You can edit the data in the simulation view and execute planning operators to simulate the effect of the adjusted planned inventory levels. Based on the analysis, review, and adjustment of the scenario data, a decision can be made to update the target inventory value.

The SAP IBP Excel planning views are also used to display the planning alerts or exceptions related to inventory positions. Supply shortage alerts and excess inventory alerts for inventory planning are among the most useful in SAP IBP. To build the alert scenario in the Excel planning view, an alert key figure is configured with the required business logic. In the example in Figure 13.12, the projected inventory key figure is used for the logic, and an alert will be generated whenever the projected inventory is negative.

The shortage can be configured with a different logic by using the recommended safety stock value in comparison with projected inventory. In addition to shortages, excess inventory situations can also be flagged as the exception scenario alert. In Figure 13.12, the logic used is as follows: if the projected inventory is more than 30% of the recommended safety stock value, then an alert will be generated. The exception scenarios shown by the alerts are used by the planners to take appropriate action.

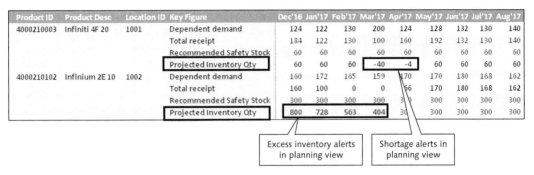

Product ID	Product Desc	Location ID	Key Figure	Dec'16	Jan'17	Feb'17	Mar'17	Apr'17	May'17	Jun'17	Jul'17	Aug'17
4000210003	Infiniti 4F 20	1001	Dependent demand	124	122	130	200	124	128	132	130	140
			Total receipt	184	122	130	100	160	192	132	130	140
			Recommended Safety Stock	60	60	60	60	60	60	60	60	60
			Projected Inventory Qty	60	60	60	-40	-4	60	60	60	60
4000210102	Infinium 2E 10	1002	Dependent demand	160	172	165	159	170	170	180	168	162
			Total receipt	160	100	0	0	66	170	180	168	162
			Recommended Safety Stock	300	300	300	300	3	300	300	300	300
			Projected Inventory Qty	800	728	563	404	30	300	300	300	300

Excess inventory alerts in planning view   Shortage alerts in planning view

Figure 13.12 Shortage and Excess Inventory Alert in SAP IBP Planning Views

For example, in the shortage situation in Figure 13.12, the possibility of an increase in production or supply from a contract manufacturer can be evaluated. If it's not possible to increase the supply, then the customer can be made aware in advance to work together on improving the plan. The excess supply alert is used to make the organization leaner by identifying ways to use the excess stock. For example, excess inventory at a node can be redistributed to other nodes where the inventory can be consumed, or it can be managed through controlled production of the item. Another approach is to work with the sales team to offer a promotion designed to convert the unwanted stock into revenue.

Custom Alerts, Analytics, and Dashboards

Along with the Excel planning views, the custom alerts, analytics, and dashboard capabilities of SAP IBP are widely used for inventory planning.

Custom alerts in SAP IBP can be categorized as low, medium, and high, for example. The alert logic for the inventory exception scenarios of shortage and excess is defined by the planner; a dynamic view of the alerts is available in the SAP Fiori interface of SAP IBP. Figure 13.13 shows an example of a custom alert with different shortage and excess scenarios defined as high-, medium-, and low-priority alerts. The configuration of a custom alert is covered in detail in Chapter 15, Section 15.7.

The SAP IBP dashboard can be used for managing the inventory planning processes. A dashboard can be created solely for inventory optimization tasks and related analytics, or inventory planning processes can be integrated with other planning processes. Figure 13.14 shows an example of an inventory review dashboard integrated with sales, inventory, and operations planning (SIOP) processes. Tasks for inventory, network charts, and related analytics are displayed in the dashboard, which is generated with the real-time system data that provides a window into the planning situation, along with the details from the Excel planning view. The configuration steps to create a dashboard are discussed in Chapter 15, Section 15.3.

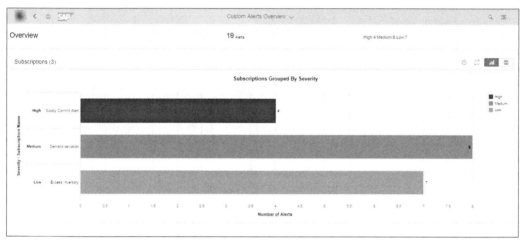

Figure 13.13 Custom Alerts in SAP IBP

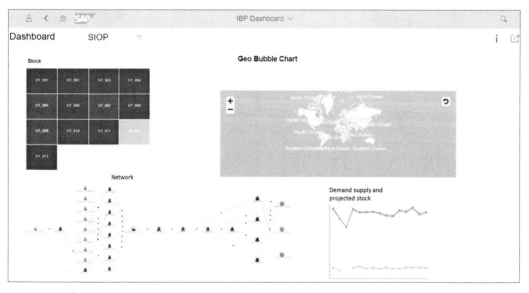

Figure 13.14 Inventory Review Dashboard of SAP IBP

13.7 Summary

SAP IBP for inventory optimizes material storage in the supply chain network to achieve expected service levels at minimum cost. Standard planning models for inventory optimization have been provided by SAP, which can be referred to when building customer-specific supply chain networks and inventory optimization solutions. While sourcing the forecast and actual stock information from the execution system, the inventory solution calculates the target inventory levels by using highly sophisticated algorithms that optimize the entire network as connected units for demand and supply. Planning views and the analytics application are used for planner review and action.

Now that we have covered the full set of SAP IBP planning applications, the next chapter will focus on the SAP Supply Chain Control Tower, which provides the planner with end-to-end visibility, analytics, and performance management capabilities.

SAP Supply Chain Control Tower provides end-to-end visibility, real-time monitoring, and real-time control of supply chain networks. In addition, users can identify, evaluate, and take action on the problems and opportunities in the supply chain. In this chapter, we'll discuss the details of supply chain analytics and how to use SAP Supply Chain Control Tower to enhance the performance of the organization.

14 SAP Supply Chain Control Tower

Most of the focus of the preceding chapters has been on the very powerful advanced planning capabilities of SAP Integrated Business Planning (SAP IBP). The people who deal directly with these applications are the professional demand, supply, and inventory planners who need to make critical decisions that can have a major impact on their company's supply chain performance. These professionals are faced with the following questions:

▸ How do we know if our decisions are in fact having the desired effect?

▸ How do we improve upon them in the next planning cycle?

▸ How can other people in the organization who aren't directly involved in these planning processes take a look at these results?

▸ How can data from other parts of the company, or even from outside the company, be combined with planning data to provide an end-to-end view of the digital supply chain?

The SAP Supply Chain Control Tower has been designed to address these questions. But before we dive in to discussing that, we'll start with defining supply chain analytics and its usage for enhancing the performance of a supply chain network. Then we'll discuss in detail the usage of SAP Supply Chain Control Tower as the analytics and central control system of the supply chain planning processes. We'll understand the key performance indicators (KPIs) of the supply chain and their usage with standard definitions and applications. We'll also discuss the SAP

Supply Chain Control Tower dashboard, process management, and alerts to illustrate end-to-end visibility, control, and corrective action.

14.1 Supply Chain Analytics and Dashboards

Analytics in business refers to the usage of data to derive information for decision-making, and then analyzing the decision impact for continuous improvement.

Figure 14.1 shows an example of an analytics cycle. The available data is converted into information that guides the appropriate action. The results of the action are analyzed to make a decision or course correction. This process is a virtuous cycle that keeps the organization on the path of continuous improvement.

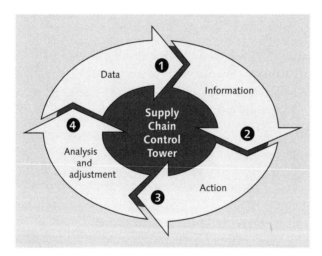

Figure 14.1 Analytics Cycle for Continuous Improvement

Supply chain analytics organizes information for a more efficient, profitable, and resilient supply chain network. Any organization's network is full of relevant data that can be converted into information for managing and controlling the supply chain. The direct applications of supply chain analytics are in demand management, supply planning, inventory optimization, and reacting to market dynamics.

Analytics in the broad sense is used for multiple purposes such as performance reports using historical data, predictive analysis for future events, end-to-end visibility of business events (e.g., exceptions), and tools to control these events. The supply chain is one of the richest areas from which to generate value through analytics.

SAP IBP contains robust analytical capabilities that are used in demand, supply, and inventory planning applications. Visibility, control, and performance parameters of supply chain analytics are part of the SAP Supply Chain Control Tower solution in SAP IBP.

The SAP Supply Chain Control Tower enables planners to identify and evaluate problems and opportunities in the supply chain network. It provides a channel to take action through collaboration and task management. Supply chain KPIs are readily available through custom reports and dashboards. Along with end-to-end visibility and monitoring with real-time data, custom alerts and analytics help you make decisions that manage risk and leverage opportunities.

The built-in dashboards of SAP IBP provide a single place for end-to-end visibility and control of the supply chain. These can be built and customized by the end user for their particular role and process. The use of dashboards is pervasive throughout SAP IBP. The applications consume and generate massive amounts of data, and dashboards are used to translate this data into useful information. Such dashboards tend to be application- or case-specific regarding demand, inventory, and supply situations.

SAP Supply Chain Control Tower dashboards are much broader in scope, often combining data from multiple applications to provide a global view of supply chain conditions. In addition, SAP Supply Chain Control Tower provides different means of representing data, including geographical, network, and chart views. Figure 14.2 is a good example of this type of dashboard. It contains the process flow, the demand planning analytics, inventory with global distribution, and the heat map. It also contains the summary information of demand supply match and annual operating plan (AOP) revenue number.

All of this information reflects the latest situation as of the last planning run or underlying transaction, providing a near real-time view into the overall health of the supply chain. In addition, these graphics are interactive, meaning that the user can drill down to additional information, paving the way for root-cause analysis and problem resolution, which will be covered in more detail later in Section 14.4. Finally, this is just one example of a dashboard that has been configured to meet the needs of a particular role or user. A virtually infinite number of such dashboards can be created by the end user without requiring any special technical skills.

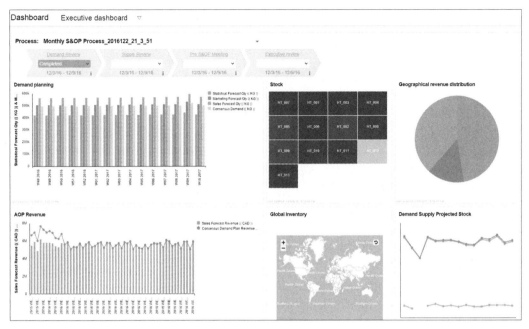

Figure 14.2 SAP Supply Chain Control Tower Dashboard

14.2 SAP Supply Chain Control Tower Alerts

As mentioned in the previous section, some SAP Supply Chain Control Tower dashboards contain interactive views that can guide the user from insight to action. This can be done via the use of alerts, which indicate a potential supply chain disruption. Similar to dashboards, the end user defines the business rules and logic that trigger an alert condition, as well as how the alert is presented in the application. These alert conditions can be based on any key figure in the system and for any time horizon. There is also a filtering capability so that alerts can be displayed based on priority. This combination of capabilities provides a high degree of supply chain visibility and control.

Figure 14.3 is a good example of such an alert, which could easily have been accessed from the planner's dashboard. On the left side is the alert list that provides a description and the underlying data that has triggered each alert, which, in this case, is deviation of consensus demand with statistical forecast. This is one of the unique capabilities of SAP IBP, in that it has the ability to represent both operational and financial metrics for any key figure.

Selecting one of the alerts, you can see more detailed information to help you better understand the situation. In the main view bar graph, you can see the potential excess inventory and write-off risk for a particular time period, along with the product and location in question. Further investigation would likely show the type of inventory (safety stock, cycle stock) that comprises the excess. This type of drilldown helps you make better decisions on how to resolve the issue. This will be discussed further in the following section.

Figure 14.3 SAP Supply Chain Control Tower Alerts

14.3 Integration with Other Systems

SAP Supply Chain Control Tower, is designed to be used in conjunction with the other SAP IBP planning applications as an overarching analytics solution. Figure 14.4 shows the SAP IBP solution landscape along with other solution areas. Connecting arrows illustrate how the individual solutions integrate with SAP Supply Chain Control Tower to deliver real-time visibility, analysis and control.

In addition to the planning components of SAP IBP, the SAP Supply Chain Control Tower can also be connected to the organization's operational systems to collect information regarding supply chain execution. These systems include order execution, purchasing, transportation, and any other system that would be considered relevant for supply chain visibility and control.

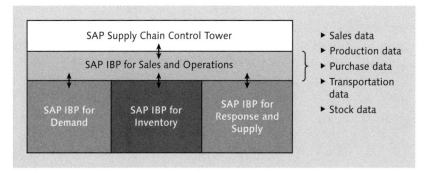

Figure 14.4 SAP Supply Chain Control Tower in the SAP IBP Landscape

14.4 Root-Cause Analysis and Resolution

After you've fully investigated and understood the issues in the supply chain network, such as material shortage, resource overload and excess inventory, there are several tools at your disposal to resolve these issues. One option is to use an SAP IBP application, such as inventory optimization, to evaluate one or more scenarios. In the example discussed in Section 14.2 regarding safety stock alerts, this may involve testing the impact of different safety stock parameters on inventory investments to see if a better result can be achieved. These scenarios can be run iteratively and independently of the *live plan* where the different results can be compared and evaluated. The scenarios and comparisons can also be shared with an expanded group of users via the integrated collaboration capabilities of SAP Jam, where stakeholders have the opportunity to comment and make recommendations on the best path forward (see Figure 14.5).

After a final decision has been agreed upon, the responsible planner can set up a SAP Supply Chain Control Tower case that describes the situation and proposed resolution, and assigns actions, or tasks, to the appropriate individuals to execute the decision (see Figure 14.6). This might involve performing a final inventory optimization run and updating the product master data record with the desired inventory targets. After it's completed, the task is updated, and the case is considered closed. This simple example demonstrates how SAP Supply Chain Control Tower can seamlessly orchestrate the resolution of a potentially costly supply chain problem.

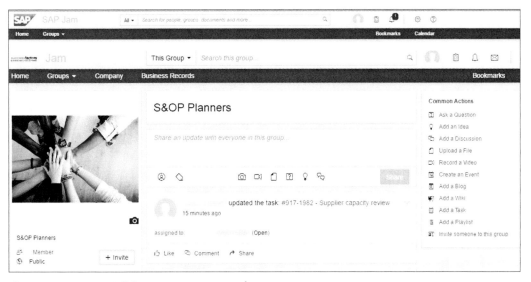

Figure 14.5 SAP Jam Collaboration

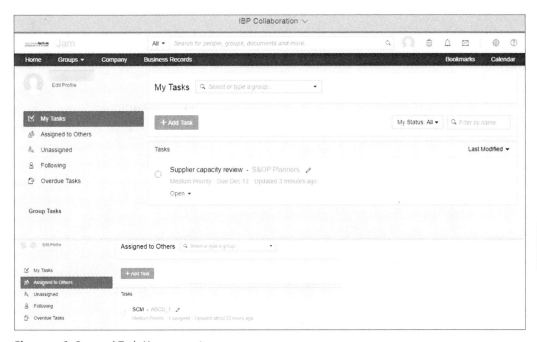

Figure 14.6 Case and Task Management

Of course, inventory issues are just one set of problems that SAP Supply Chain Control Tower is able to address. If we go back to our dashboard (refer to Figure 14.2), we recall that there was information regarding demand, supply, and production that might provide insight into other potential issues. For example, the graphic on the upper right indicates that there are imbalances in demand and supply over time. You may want to drill down and investigate further to see which products are affected. You can then run scenarios, that show the relationship between constrained demand and volume, revenue, and profitability for a given product.

Another example is shown in the geographic view where the size and color of the bubbles are indicative of potential production issues across regions. Here again, you can drill down to the product level to investigate any issues such as resource constraints or material shortages. Assuming the connection to the execution system is available, you can drill as deep into the network as required to identify the problem, even as far back as the material supplier. This type of end-to-end network visibility demonstrates the real power of SAP Supply Chain Control Tower.

14.5 Analytics and Key Performance Indicators

So far, we've discussed how the SAP Supply Chain Control Tower can leverage data from across the extended supply network to help identify and resolve specific operational issues that occur on a daily basis. The next issue is how to leverage this same data from a longer-term perspective to help avoid these issues in the future and continuously improve performance.

To address this issue, SAP Supply Chain Control Tower provides a framework for defining, calculating and analyzing KPIs. These KPIs can be historical in nature, such as the percentage of orders delivered on time in full (OTIF) for the past three months. The supporting data is collected in SAP IBP from the various planning and transactional systems. The underlying calculation is generated as a percentage, which is then displayed in a dashboard, perhaps in red to reflect a negative trend. You would have the ability to further investigate this KPI using the same drilldown capabilities as in the example discussed in Section 14.4 on root-cause analysis.

For example, you can see which products, orders, and locations are contributing to this negative trend to help identify the root causes, such as material shortages, production issues, or capacity constraints. With this information, you can use the same powerful planning tools to simulate different approaches to resolving the issue. You can, for example, add capacity, increase production, or adjust inventory policies. The aforementioned case and task management capabilities can then be used to execute the decision.

This example illustrates how historical data is used to improve future supply chain performance using metrics such as OTIF. A similar approach can also be utilized to project future performance using current planning data and adjusting those plans based on the results. A good example of such a forward-looking KPI is projected days of coverage, which compares the current supply plans and inventory positions to projected demand to determine if there is sufficient supply to cover the market demand. The results of the calculation can be displayed as a number in a dashboard, with any trends highlighted, allowing you to investigate the issue and develop and execute a solution. The primary difference here is that most of the required data resides in the planning model, so there is less dependence on transactional systems, thus improving response time and flexibility.

Figure 14.7 illustrates the type of dashboard we've been referring to. Note that this is a combination of historical and forward-looking KPIs and that this particular dashboard is very inventory and supply oriented. Of course, this content is completely customizable by the end user and could contain KPIs that are more demand- or even finance oriented, or any combination of categories. Another important point is that the SAP Supply Chain Control Tower comes packaged with a large number of predefined KPIs that can be used immediately, and includes all required key figures and calculations. This packaged set also includes a number of standard metrics from the Supply Chain Operations Reference model (SCOR), which is the de facto industry standard model for supply chain management. As of the SAP IBP 1702 release, there are approximately 50 predefined metrics delivered, a number that is growing with each subsequent release of SAP IBP. A full list of these KPIs is shown in Table 14.1.

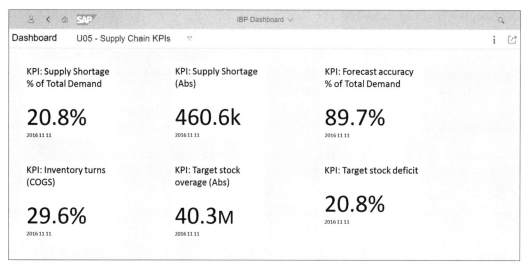

Figure 14.7 SAP Supply Chain Control Tower KPIs Dashboard

SCOR Perfect Order Fulfillment (20 KPIs)	SCM Inventory (17 KPIs)	SCOR Cash-to-Cash (12 KPIs)
Delivery item accuracy (L3)	Target stock deficit (% of location product)	Inventory turnover ratio
Delivery item accuracy (L2)	Target stock deficit (absolute)	Cost of goods sold (COGS)
Delivery item accuracy order (L3)	Target stock deficit (number of location product)	Annualized COGS
Delivery item accuracy order (L2)	Target stock overage (% of location product)	Annual average inventory cost rate
Delivery date accuracy (L3)	Target stock overage (absolute)	Inventory value
Delivery date accuracy (L2)	Target stock overage (number of location product)	Inventory days of supply based on annual COGS
Delivery date accuracy order (L3)	Safety stock deficit (% of location product)	RM (raw material) inventory quantity value
Delivery date accuracy order (L2)	Safety stock deficit (absolute)	WIP (work in progress) inventory value

Table 14.1 SAP Supply Chain Control Tower KPIs

SCOR Perfect Order Fulfillment (20 KPIs)	SCM Inventory (17 KPIs)	SCOR Cash-to-Cash (12 KPIs)
Delivery location accuracy (L3)	Safety stock deficit (number of location product)	FG (finished good) inventory value
Delivery location accuracy order (L3)	Safety stock overage (% of location product)	FG (finished good) inventory in plant
Delivery location accuracy (L2)	Safety stock overage (absolute)	FG (finished good) inventory outside plant
Delivery location accuracy order (L2)	Safety stock overage (number of location product)	
Delivery quantity accuracy (L3)	Supply shortage (% of location product)	
Delivery quantity accuracy (L2)	Supply shortage (absolute)	
Delivery quantity accuracy order (L3)	Supply shortage (number of location product)	
Delivery quantity accuracy order (L2)	Supply shortage (% of total demand)	
Orders delivered in full items level	Projected days of coverage	
Orders delivered in full order level		
Orders delivered on time item level		
Orders delivered on time order level		

Table 14.1 SAP Supply Chain Control Tower KPIs (Cont.)

In addition to the standard KPIs, SAP Supply Chain Control Tower enables you to create customized metrics, either using the delivered content as a starting point or adding new key figures and calculations to the model. This provides the ultimate in flexibility and control with regard to performance management and improvement.

Supply chain KPI selection for continuous improvement of an organization depends on the business processes, planning scope, and process maturity of the organization. In the following sections, we'll take a look at the most used KPIs for the supply chain for consideration of their enablement with the SAP Supply Chain Control Tower.

14.5.1 KPIs for Order Fulfillment and Service Quality

In the areas of order fulfillment and service level, the following are the most relevant KPIs:

- **OTIF (on time in full)**
  OTIF is the percentage of orders fulfilled on time with full quantity in a period as compared to the total orders in that period.

  The OTIF measurement is strict in nature as this is based on a binary result of order fulfillment with values 0 or 1. Therefore, for an order quantity of 100 to be delivered on March 15, 2017, if the delivery was made for a smaller quantity (say 95) or if it was late, then order fulfillment is considered as 0. So, if in a week of orders, one order was delivered with a partial quantity, and the other three orders are delivered on time with full quantity, then the OTIF will be 75%.

- **Fill rate**
  Fill rate is the percentage of the quantity delivered in a time period from the total quantity of orders placed.

  Part quantity is considered for calculation of fill rate. Hence, if for a month, against 5 orders of 100 quantity each with a total requirement of 500, the total supply in the month is 480, then the fill rate is $(480 \div 500) \times 100 = 96\%$.

- **Backorder**
  Backorder represents open sales orders for which the delivery is still pending. Backorders can be obtained as open sales order line items in the order execution system that have crossed due date, and there is no delivery block or billing block in the system.

14.5.2 KPIs for Demand Forecasting

In the area of demand forecasting, the following are the most relevant KPIs:

- **Forecast accuracy**
  This KPI measures percentage accuracy of forecasts by comparing with actuals. The ratio of absolute difference between the actuals and forecast and the actuals is computed as an error in the forecast:

  $(1 - \{|A_t - F_t| \div A_t\}) \times 100$ where

  F_t = Forecast value for period t

  A_t = Actual sales for period t

▶ **Forecast bias**

This provides the information on whether the forecast is getting biased on one side (either positive or negative represented by over-forecasting or under-forecasting, respectively).

The ratio of aggregated difference between actuals and forecast for the last six months and the aggregated actuals is computed as bias in the forecast:

Forecast bias = $(\sum(A_t - F_t) \div \sum A_t) \times 100$

t = 1 to 6 (prior months)

A = Actual sale units

F = Forecasted units

Forecast bias KPIs can be represented as a chart in the SAP Supply Chain Control Tower.

▶ **Forecast fidelity**

Forecast fidelity checks the changes performed in the demand forecast in the short-term period. Lag functionality of SAP IBP is used to save the values of the forecast at different periods to compare with the final forecast values.

In the following formula, Forecast for a time period "t" is represented by F_t, and *n* represents the time lag for the data:

Forecast fidelity percentage (lag 1) = $((F_{t(n)} - F_{t(n-1)}) \div F_{t(n)}) \times 100$

Forecast fidelity percentage (lag 2) = $((F_{t(n)} - F_{t(n-2)}) \div F_{t(n)}) \times 100$

Forecast fidelity percentage (lag 3) = $((F_{t(n)} - F_{t(n-3)}) \div F_{t(n)}) \times 100$

14.5.3 KPIs for Supply, Response, and Transportation

In the areas of supply, response, and transportation, the following are the most relevant KPIs:

▶ **Days of coverage**

Days of coverage represents the number of days of projected supply based on total demand.

▶ **Percentage resource capacity utilization (for bottleneck resource)**

Percentage resource capacity utilization represents the time consumed by the planned and confirmed production order from the total resource availability time.

- **Production achievement percentage**
  Production output percentage can be calculated for an individual resource, a group of resources for a plant, or for an entire organization. It's the ratio of actual output quantity with the production capacity quantity.

- **Supply shortage**
  Supply shortage represents the shortage of material availability in current and future periods as compared to the total demand of the product. Supply shortage is generally considered for periods of 1 month, 3 months, 6 months, and 12 months for tactical and operational decisions. Shortages in further long-term horizons can be used for strategic decisions.

- **Schedule disruption**
  This measures the number of production/process orders that had their start date changed at the last minute (e.g., within the past three days of the planned start date) against the total number of production/process orders in a month.

- **Premium freight percentage**
  Premium freight percentage represents the number of deliveries made by an exceptional premium route (e.g., an air route) as compared to the total number of deliveries made.

- **Sourcing performance**
  Sourcing performance represents the percentage of OTIF sourcing. It gives the percentage measure of the number of purchase order line items delivered OTIF against the total number of purchase order line items.

14.5.4 KPIs for Inventory

In the area of inventory, the following are the most relevant KPIs:

- **Inventory turn**
  This represents how many times a company's inventory is sold and replaced in a year. It can be calculated by dividing the total cost of goods sold in the past 12 months by the current inventory value. Some organizations use the total sales revenue of the past 12 months instead of cost of goods sold for the calculation.

- **Non-moving inventory**
  Inventory value of the products with inventory more than a certain period of time (e.g., 6 months old) and for products with inventory and no demand forecast for a certain period in the future (e.g., next 6 months).

▸ **Inventory at risk**
Inventory at risk represents the inventory with an associated batch set to expire in the near future, for example, in the next 15 or 30 days.

▸ **Inventory value**
Monetary value of the product-wise, location-wise, and organization-wise inventory. This can be generated individually for raw material, semifinished, and finished material inventory.

Many of these KPIs are readily available in the SAP Supply Chain Control Tower, as represented in Table 14.1. Others require the key figure configuration and calculation in SAP IBP using data from SAP IBP or connected systems.

14.6   The Future of SAP Supply Chain Control Tower

SAP is making a major investment in solutions that enable the digital supply chain. The SAP Supply Chain Control Tower is an important part of this strategy. In the following sections, we'll look at several topics that will likely be addressed in the near future.

14.6.1   Supply Chain Segmentation

With the increasing emphasis on customer-centricity through omnichannel retail, many large enterprises must manage multiple supply chains that serve different markets and customers. Each of these supply chains have different characteristics with regard to demand, supply, and cost, and thus each requires unique planning and fulfillment approaches. For example, companies in consumer-driven industries, such as electronics and apparel, commonly sell their products through both retail and consumer direct channels. These channels require different demand forecasting techniques, inventory policies, and distribution methods, as well as a comprehensive approach to measuring performance. The flexible modeling and metric definition capabilities of the SAP Supply Chain Control Tower lend themselves very nicely to this type of *supply chain segmentation*, which will be supported by a new set of KPIs as follows:

▸ Total cost to serve (costs)

▸ Vendor perfect order fulfillment (reliability)

▸ Order fulfillment cycle time (responsiveness)

- ▸ Return on supply chain fixed assets (asset management efficiency)
- ▸ Upside supply chain flexibility (agility)
- ▸ Upside/downside supply chain adaptability (agility)

These KPIs reflect different categories of performance and can be used to measure the individual performance of each supply chain segment to drive continuous improvement.

14.6.2 Supply Chain Collaboration

In Chapter 1, the idea of the sharing economy in the industrial world was discussed, which is reflected in increasing emphasis on collaboration across the network, and with suppliers, contract manufacturers, logistic service providers, and other partners. It was noted that networked companies tend to outperform their peers with regard to revenue and profitability. SAP Supply Chain Control Tower will be a key enabler of collaboration by providing connectivity with SAP's business network, allowing critical information to be exchanged between connected enterprises in a secure manner. Collaboration scenarios such as supplier-managed inventory, contract manufacturing, and collaborative forecasting will be supported, which will drive the SAP IBP applications with real-time data. In addition, complete visibility across the extended network will support real-time alerting, analysis, and issue resolution between business partners.

14.6.3 Digital Operations and Internet of Things

As the march of Internet of Things (IoT) and Industry 4.0 move inexorably forward, the lines between planning and execution will become increasingly blurred. Industry 4.0 refers to the digitization of manufacturing and logistics processes using data from connected devices (including IoT). The assets that power our factories and the products they manufacture will be connected to digital platforms that will enable enterprises to have access to live data, raising the meaning of real-time to new levels. The nature of planning itself will evolve from a periodic to a more continuous process where decisions on issues such as what demands to fulfill, where to deploy products, and what materials to use can be made more quickly and accurately than ever before. This is where the real power of SAP Supply Chain Control Tower can be demonstrated, the original concept of which was modeled after the set of protocols and technologies that allow aircraft to safely navigate around crowded airspace. The SAP Supply Chain Control Tower of the future will provide its subscribers with tools that allow them to successfully navigate through the increasing complexity of the environment in which they operate as never before.

14.7 Summary

The use of analytics in managing and controlling the supply chain network delivers tremendous benefits and keeps the organization on the path of continuous improvement. SAP Supply Chain Control Tower is a highly configurable and easy-to-use analytics tool for end-to-end visibility and control of supply chain activities. The included analytics, dashboard, alert, task management, and performance improvement capabilities are highly relevant for modern supply chain. Now, you're ready to get into the configuration details of SAP Supply Chain Control Tower as a SAP IBP solution, which we'll cover in the next chapter.

End-to-end visibility and control in a supply chain network for continuous improvement is enabled by the SAP Supply Chain Control Tower in SAP IBP. This chapter gets into the details of the system usage and configuration for developing an effective analytics solution.

15 Implementing SAP Supply Chain Control Tower with SAP IBP

Using the SAP Supply Chain Control Tower for end-to-end visibility, collaboration, and planning action requires system integration and configuration. Usage based on the roles and responsibilities of the supply chain personnel is supported by customized analytics, dashboards, and alerts. Most of the configurations are performed by the end users. However, the initial integration to source the data elements from multiple systems into SAP Supply Chain Control Tower needs to be completed by the implementation team. This initial system setup and configuration requires business skills in addition to the technical skills necessary to integrate and use the information elements.

Enterprise data relevant for the SAP Supply Chain Control Tower may exist in different environments such as execution systems (e.g., SAP ERP or SAP S/4HANA), partner management systems (e.g., SAP Customer Relationship Management [SAP CRM]), special process management systems (e.g., SAP Transportation Management [SAP TM]), or any legacy system. System integration and data flow needs to be completed during the SAP Integrated Business Planning (SAP IBP) implementation before making the SAP Supply Chain Control Tower ready for usage by the planners. Data integration from other systems to the SAP Supply Chain Control Tower can be achieved either through the SAP Cloud Platform or SAP HANA smart data integration (SAP HANA SDI).

After receiving data from different systems, the SAP Supply Chain Control Tower processes the data using key capabilities such as analytics, dashboards, collaboration, custom alerts, key performance indicators (KPIs), and the Excel planning view, which require basic system customization. This chapter will focus on the customization of these elements.

Most SAP Supply Chain Control Tower applications are accessed through the individual customizable tiles or apps. These apps are grouped under GENERAL PLANNER and ALERTS headers, as displayed in Figure 15.1. A planner's access to the information through the app can be controlled through the roles and responsibilities extended in the SAP IBP system.

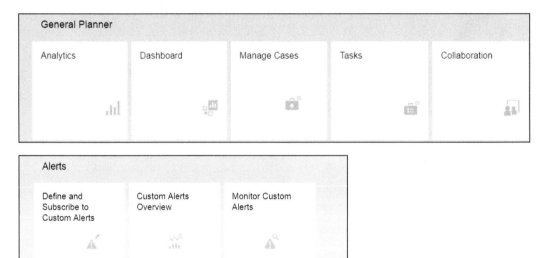

Figure 15.1 SAP Supply Chain Control Tower Tiles

15.1   Analytics Application

The Analytics app under GENERAL PLANNER opens a page that shows every chart created and available in the SAP IBP system. Chart name, chart type, creator name, and created date information are available on this screen. Detailed information for an individual chart can be displayed by clicking the row of the chart.

The drilldown functionality in SAP IBP charts allows you to get into the details through dropdown options. To support the drilldown levels, you have to provide the possible drilldowns through group and filter data. This adds the feature to analyze the chart and further investigate the data through drilldowns for different attributes. To further analyze the chart through new grouping and filtering conditions, click the EXPLORE button at the top-right corner of an analytics screen.

A new chart can be created by clicking NEW CHART on the SAP IBP analytics screen. Figure 15.2 shows an example of a new chart creation. The planning area is selected through the PLANNING AREA dropdown displaying all the active planning areas. When the planning area is selected, all the relevant key figures become available for selection. One or multiple key figures can be selected based on the business analytics requirement.

For example, it may make sense to display total demand, total supply, and projected inventory key figures for projected inventory analysis. Most of the time, grouping the information on factors such as time (e.g., analysis of data in a weekly or monthly horizon) or other parameters (e.g., location geography, product group, customer segment, etc.) is provided for in the customized analytics applications.

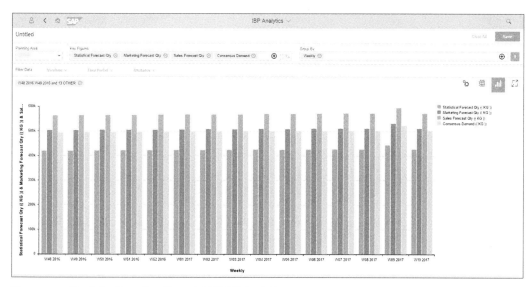

Figure 15.2 Chart Configuration through SAP IBP Analytics

Further customization for a planner is achieved through filtering the data. This filtering is performed through three parameters, as follows:

- Versions
  This is used to analyze the data for an active or simulation version.

- Time Period
  Instead of analyzing the complete planning horizon, a focused time period should be selected for the analytics purpose. For example, sensed demand analytics may be relevant for the next two to four weeks in daily buckets; on the other hand, supply plan analytics can be relevant for the next six months in weekly buckets. This focused information for a particular chart is available through the Group By option and Time Period filter selection. SAP Supply Chain Control Tower has the feature to make the time period rolling in nature to prevent the obsolescence.

- Attributes
  This option is used to filter the analytics data for certain objects. Hence, specific supply chain network information can be selected and displayed via this option. For example, a product group, location geography, or customer name/segment can be selected as the filter condition so that the analytics will be relevant only for the filtered conditions.

  Note that the detailed analysis through grouping and filtering is easy to use and can be performed by the end user without any major configuration requirements. This makes the SAP Supply Chain Control Tower highly usable in a typical business environment.

Different chart types such as bar, line, pie, network, heat map, and so on are supported by SAP Supply Chain Control Tower. A particular chart type can be selected based on the nature of the data elements and the analytics business requirements. See Figure 15.3 for the detailed list of the charts supported by the SAP Supply Chain Control Tower.

In the analytics configuration displayed previously in Figure 15.2, the Save button is used to save the chart with a name so that it will be available for the planner's usage. The data in the analytics are dynamically accessed when a chart is accessed by the user in SAP IBP. A saved chart is available for analysis through the SAP IBP analytics application. Figure 15.4 shows an example of a column chart, and Figure 15.5 shows an example of a heat map.

Figure 15.3 Analytics Options through Different Charts in SAP Supply Chain Control Tower

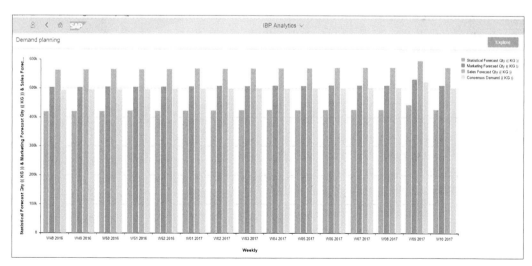

Figure 15.4 Analytics in SAP Supply Chain Control Tower: Column Chart

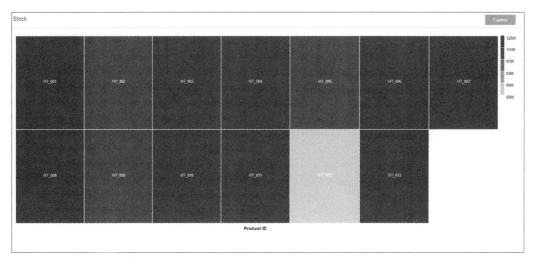

Figure 15.5 Analytics in SAP Supply Chain Control Tower: Heat Map

15.2 Process Modeling

Process modeling is accessed and configured through the Process Modeling app under ADMINISTRATOR. In addition to being used in SAP Supply Chain Control Tower, process modeling is used for managing and collaborating with other planning applications in SAP IBP. The available process templates, along with the owner names, are displayed in summary form on the first page of process modeling. An instance of an available process template can be created by choosing the CREATE INSTANCE option to start the process. Related activities will be kick-started per the information configured in the process.

A new process is created using the ADD button on the SAP IBP PROCESS MODELING page shown in Figure 15.6. On this screen, the information to be provided for a process creation is shown as an example. The TEMPLATE NAME is provided for creation of a process template; individual steps of the process can be added through the ADD button in the STEPS area.

Figure 15.6 Process Modeling and Application

For every step, the step owner, reviewer, participant group, and SAP Jam group are provided. DURATION controls the planned time to complete the process, while RELATIVE START DAY is relevant for the number of days from the instance creation date to the kick-start the process. Every step must have at least one task and a task owner. This information is provided in the process step through the ADD TASKS option. Information discussed here is relevant for every step of the process.

The SAVE button saves the process template for further usage, editing, or instance creation. The SAVE AND CREATE INSTANCE option saves the process template, creates an instance, and makes the process open and live in the SAP IBP system for further actions from the task and process owners. Information regarding the work and progress can be shared through the SAP Jam collaboration group assigned in the steps. The different steps of a process can be assigned to different SAP Jam groups for progress tracking and focused collaboration.

15.3   Dashboard Creation

The dashboard functionality is accessed through the Dashboard app under General PLANNER. If there is a default dashboard assigned to a user, the analytics associated with the default dashboard are available to review as soon as the user accesses the application. These analytics are always updated with the current data in the system.

The CREATE NEW DASHBOARD option in the dashboard dropdown can be used to create a new dashboard. The new dashboard page displays all the charts and process model available in the SAP IBP system. Note that the analytics summary information is independent of the planning areas, and all the charts and process models irrespective of the assigned planning areas are available to be selected through the standard ADD button on the screen. After the relevant processes and charts are added, the SAVE button is used to save the dashboard with a name.

Figure 15.7 shows an example of an executive dashboard, which has been created through selection of the S&OP process instance, and multiple analytics charts are aligned to the work area of the executive. This is highly customizable analytics information in one place with the option to navigate further into every analytic through the EXPLORE option. Display can be further controlled by either adding or removing the analytics, or by changing the height and width of a particular item. A user can have access to multiple dashboards, and one dashboard can be assigned to multiple users.

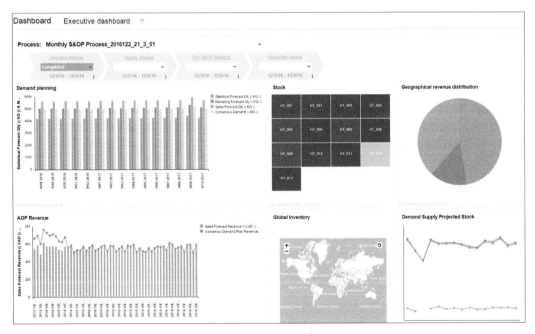

Figure 15.7 Dashboard in SAP Supply Chain Control Tower

15.4 Key Performance Indicators

One of the unique and widely used advantages of the SAP Supply Chain Control Tower is that it contains standard performance measurement parameters. Performance parameters are provided with their standard data elements (key figures) and associated calculations to readily generate the analytics through a plug-and-play approach.

Analytics performance parameters in SAP Supply Chain Control Tower are delivered through key figures defined as KPIs. The KPIs (discussed in detail in Chapter 14, Section 14.5) are provided in the standard SAP model of the SAP Supply Chain Control Tower in planning area SAP5 and in the unified planning model, SAPIBP1. Copies of the standard SAP model or key figures as defined in these standard models can be referred to for generating the analytics information. Analytics information through KPIs can be generated for past, present, and future time periods with the current and dynamic data in the system.

Numerous of KPIs are provided in the standard system; however, it's advisable to select and use the KPIs that are aligned to the business requirement, industry nature, and available data elements to map the input of the KPI. Figure 15.8 shows an example of one such KPI with the performance parameter known as inventory turnover ratio (INVTURNOVERRATION). Inventory turnover measures the number of times inventory is sold in a year; it's calculated by cost of goods sold divided by average inventory value. Note that the formula is already delivered in the standard SAP key figure definition. As soon as the input key figures are mapped with the data objects, the KPI is available in the SAP Supply Chain Control Tower.

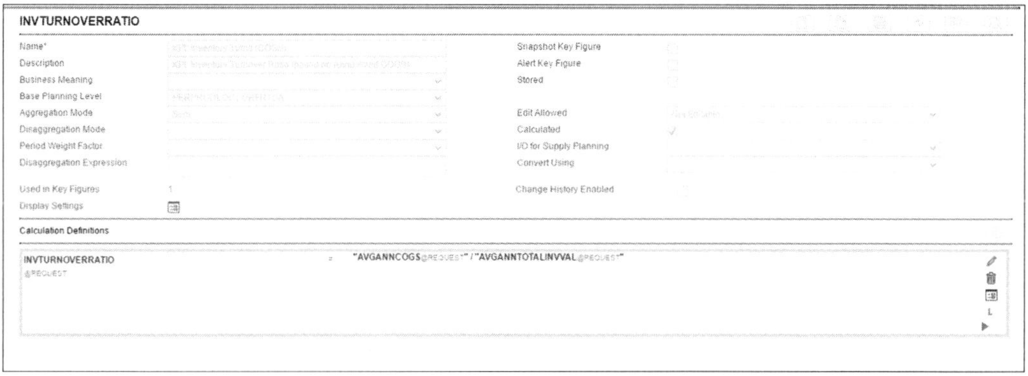

Figure 15.8 KPI Calculation in SAP Supply Chain Control Tower

This functionality adds two excellent values in the supply chain transformation projects as compared to previous technology. First, it exponentially reduces the implementation time in identifying, developing the logic, and delivering the objects in a typical business intelligence project. Second, instead of a static report with old data, the analytics generated through SAP Supply Chain Control Tower show the performance parameters in different time horizons, with live data in the format most easily understandable and usable by the planners.

After the identified KPIs are mapped and activated in the SAP Supply Chain Control Tower system, they can also be added in a dashboard for easy analysis. Based on the roles and responsibilities, different combinations of KPIs can be selected for generating different dashboards. Figure 15.9 shows an example dashboard with a combination of KPIs for a supply planner.

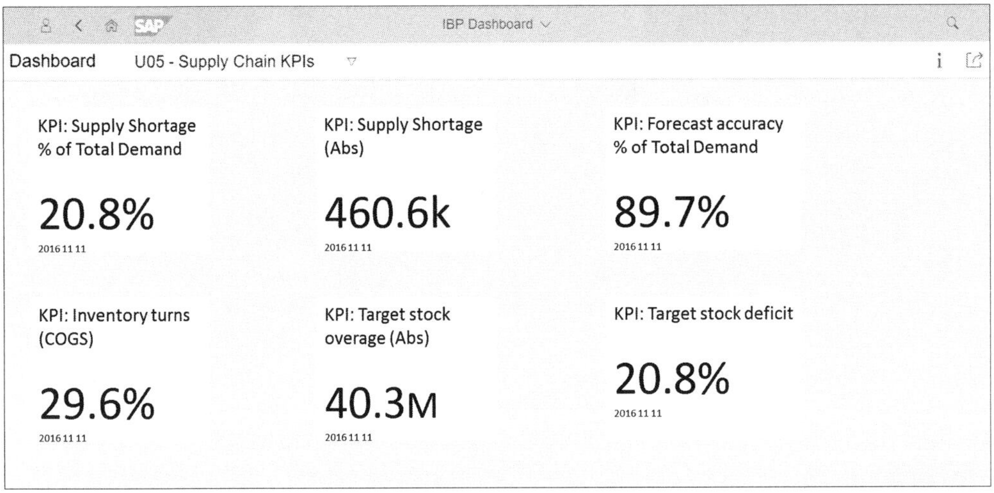

Figure 15.9 SAP Supply Chain Control Tower KPI Dashboard

15.5 Case and Task Management

Cases and tasks are used in SAP IBP for managing the work in a collaborative and trackable environment. These are the standard features that require basic steps from end users for creation, assignment, and control of the work objects.

Objects in the SAP Supply Chain Control Tower can be assigned to different groupings and can be made relevant to a closed group of people through the category and user-group applications of SAP IBP. The Manage Categories app and the User Groups app are provided under ADMINISTRATOR. The steps to create a new category and to create a new user group are illustrated in Figure 15.10.

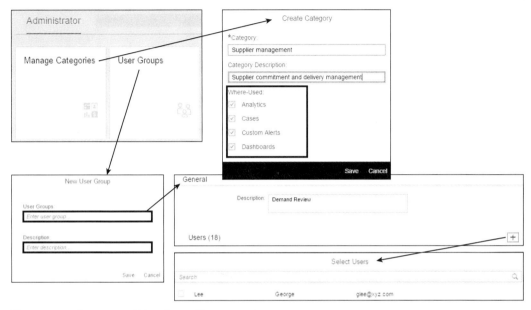

Figure 15.10 Category and User Group Management

The name and description of a new category are provided along with the relevant assignment of the category to analytics, cases, custom alerts, and dashboards. A category can be relevant for one or multiple applications; saving it with the selection will make it appear in the dropdown menu of the assigned application. For a new user group, after providing the name and the description for the group, users can be added by using the + button to assign a checkbox to the users from the active user list displayed by the system. After the categories and user groups are available in the system, they can be used for the case and task application of SAP IBP.

Case management is performed through the Manage Cases app under GENERAL PLANNER. Open cases can be edited to assign a user, add a comment, or close the case. A new case can be created by using the CREATE button. See Figure 15.11 and Figure 15.12 for an example of a new case creation, case management, and responsible team member assignment.

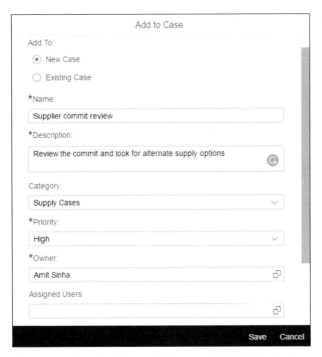

Figure 15.11 Case Creation and Assignment in SAP IBP: Part 1

For a new case, a name and description are provided. Information elements provided to create a case are as follows:

▶ NAME
Case name.

▶ DESCRIPTION
Case description.

▶ CATEGORY
Can be a planning or process area. It must have been created in advance; available categories are available to select through the dropdown option.

▶ PRIORITY
HIGH, MEDIUM, or LOW values; based on the case priority for review and action.

▶ OWNER
Case owner.

▶ ASSIGNED USERS
User from whom the action is expected.

- Assigned User Groups

  User group from which the case can be assigned. The user group must be created in advance; active user groups in the system are available to select through the dropdown.

- Due Date

  Due date for the case.

The Save button creates and saves the case in the Manage Cases app and makes it an open case. A comment can be provided in the case by the users, and further individual assignment can be performed to the case as shown in Figure 15.12.

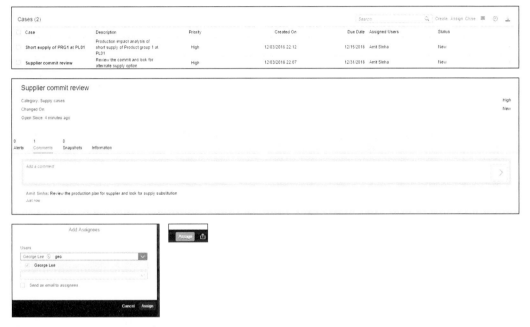

Figure 15.12 Case Creation and Assignment in SAP IBP: Part 2

Tasks in the SAP IBP system are managed through the Tasks app under General Planner. This app opens the task list page for the user and displays the tasks assigned to the user. A new task can be created by clicking the Add Jam Task button represented by +. A task is related to a process and a process step as defined in the Process Modeling app. The relevant data for the process, process step, and due date for task completion are provided while creating a task.

An example of task creation and management is shown in Figure 15.13. Through the task management feature, a comment can be added to share the information with the assigned group. Any additional users can be added via the ADD USER TO TASK option shown in Figure 15.13 using the + sign. To communicate that the action has been taken to close the task, simply selecting the radio button next to the task name strikes through the task name and changes the status of the task to CLOSED. The update happens dynamically to the process step associated with the task.

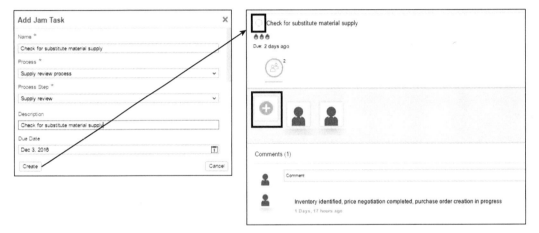

Figure 15.13 Task Management in SAP IBP

15.6 Collaboration

The Collaboration app is available under GENERAL PLANNER in SAP IBP, and it's relevant for most of the planning processes. Hence, in addition to SAP Supply Chain Control Tower, other SAP IBP planning applications also use the Collaboration app and associated functionalities.

SAP Jam, an enterprise social media application, is accessed through the Collaboration app. Figure 15.14 shows an example of the collaboration page. It provides different pages and information feeds for the user's home page and for the groups a user has been associated with. In the same page, information about open tasks and any notifications can be accessed through the application buttons. Figure

15.14 shows an example of a news feed for a closed group named S&OP PLAN-NERS. Activities of the group, such as a task update and assignment, appear as the information feed. It's possible for the users to share an update that can then be liked, commented on, or shared by other users. Hence, the information feed is added to other relevant personnel of the organization.

Figure 15.14 Collaboration and Enterprise Social Media Action in SAP IBP

Multiple other work-related actions can be performed through SAP Jam. On the right side of Figure 15.14, you can see a list of common action items. Some of the actions you can take are as follows:

- Start a discussion
- Ask a question
- Create a pool to make the decision based on user votes
- Upload a file for sharing the information with the closed group
- Add a task and assign it to a person for taking an action
- Add a wiki/blog/discussion
- Invite a new team member to join the group

Task collaboration and management can be performed through the SAP Jam home page by accessing the MY TASKS and ASSIGNED TO OTHER options, as displayed in Figure 15.15. An existing task can be modified or a new task can be added and assigned through this application. These activities are performed through buttons (e.g., a pencil symbol for EDIT, dropdown options to change the status, etc.), as displayed in Figure 15.15.

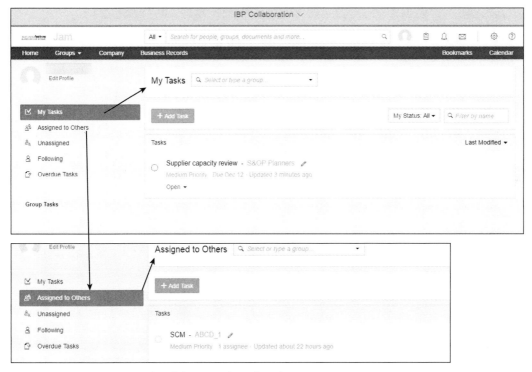

Figure 15.15 Work Collaboration through Task Assignment in SAP Jam

15.7 Custom Alerts

Custom alerts in SAP IBP have three dedicated apps for defining and subscribing to alerts, getting an overview of custom alerts, and monitoring exception scenarios. These apps are available under ALERTS in SAP IBP (see Figure 15.16).

Figure 15.16 Alerts Apps in SAP Supply Chain Control Tower

15.7.1 Defining and Subscribing to Custom Alerts

Custom alert creation, rule definition, and assignment to users are performed through the Define and Subscribe to Custom Alerts app. See Figure 15.17 and Figure 15.18 for the customization options while defining and subscribing to a custom alert.

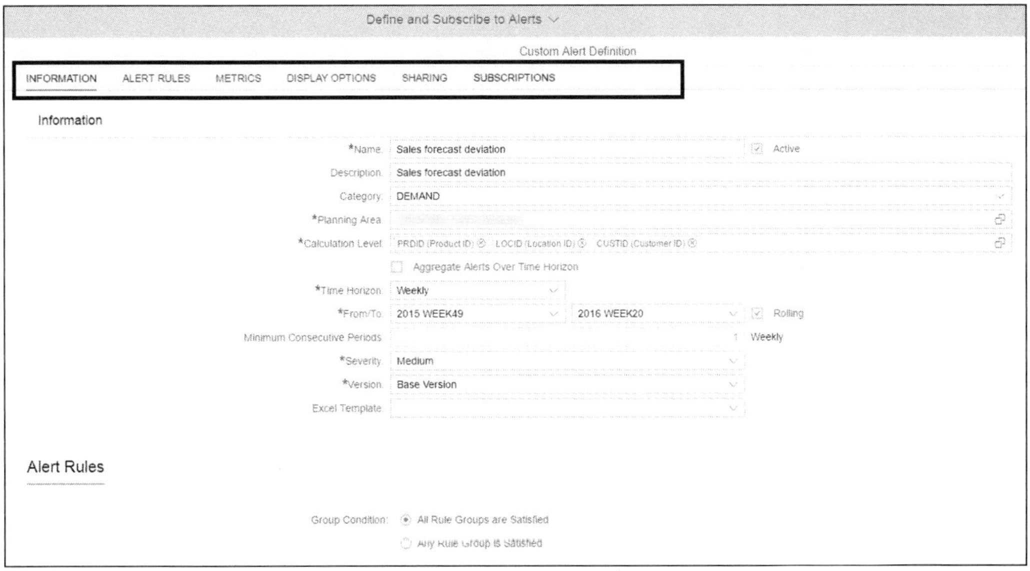

Figure 15.17 Custom Alert Definition and Rule Creation: Part 1

Figure 15.18 Custom Alert Definition and Rule Creation: Part 2

Figure 15.19 shows the metrics, display, sharing, and subscription configurations while defining an alert.

Figure 15.19 Custom Alerts Display, Sharing, and Subscription

The configuration items for defining an alert are as follows:

▸ NAME
Alert name.

▸ DESCRIPTION
A description of the alert's function.

- CATEGORY
  Alert category, selected from the dropdown. Only the categories previously created in the system with relevance indicated as ALERT are available to select in this screen.

- PLANNING AREA
  Associated planning area to fetch the data.

- CALCULATION LEVEL
  Parameters to perform the calculation for the alert generation, for example, PRODUCT ID, PRODUCT GROUP, LOCATION ID, CUSTOMER ID, CUSTOMER SEGMENT, and so on. The calculation for checking the alert condition will be performed on these levels.

- TIME HORIZON
  Horizon for calculation and display, for example, DAILY, WEEKLY, MONTHLY, and so on.

- FROM/TO
  Controls the time period for displaying the alerts in the screen.

- SEVERITY
  Alert severity level; select HIGH, MEDIUM, or LOW.

- VERSION
  For base or simulated version.

- ALERT RULES
  Calculation details for identifying the cases for which alerts need to be displayed.

- METRICS
  The key figure that needs to be shown in alert analytics.

- DISPLAY OPTIONS
  Chart type and other related parameters.

- SHARING
  Shares the alerts with other users.

- SUBSCRIPTIONS
  Only the users who are subscribed to an alert will have the particular alert displayed on their overview and monitor page. A user can be subscribed to the alert by using the + option in the subscription group, as shown in Figure 15.19.

After completing the configuration elements of an alert, the SAVE button is used to save the alert. This feature works dynamically in nature with real-time data.

Hence, as soon as a user is subscribed to an alert, the screen for the user is updated with the newly added or subscribed alert.

15.7.2 Custom Alert Overview

The Custom Alert Overview app shows the summary or overview of all the alerts a user is subscribed to, including the number of alerts and the current status of those alerts. Alerts are represented with their priority categorization.

Figure 15.20 shows an example of a custom overview screen for a planner representing high-, medium-, and low-priority alerts, along with the alert counts. This is a ready reference analytics sheet for a planner that helps in determining which items require the planner's attention based on criticality. In addition to a chart format, the ALERT ANALYTICS screen can be represented in a tabular format by selecting the radio button for the table. The CUSTOM ALERTS OVERVIEW screen is integrated with the detailed monitoring screen, so selecting a chart area or table row opens the details for monitoring and taking actions for exceptional conditions (alerts).

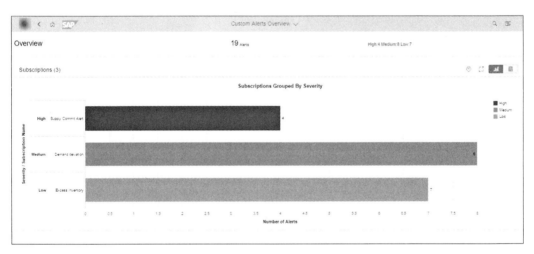

Figure 15.20 Custom Alert Overview

15.7.3 Monitoring Custom Alerts

Detailed information on the alerts for a particular user can be accessed through the Monitor Custom Alerts app under ALERTS. Users also come to this page when they drill down through the ALERT OVERVIEW screen. Figure 15.21 shows an example of the MONITOR CUSTOM ALERTS screen in SAP IBP.

Figure 15.21 Monitor Custom Alert in SAP IBP

Some of the important information elements associated with an alert as displayed on this screen are as follows:

- Alert name
- Metrics
- Master data, aligned to the selected calculation level in the alert definition
- Quantity and unit of measure
- Severity
- Shared with users and groups

By using chart and table buttons, information about an alert can be represented in either chart or table format.

Based on the analysis of the exception situation, a planner may have to take an appropriate action for an alert. Multiple action items for the alerts are integrated through the Monitor Custom Alerts app, as shown at the bottom of Figure 15.21. A planner can take the action on the alert directly by navigating through this page.

The available action options are as follows:

- SNOOZE
  An alert can be temporarily deactivated from appearing in the active part of the

Monitor Custom Alerts screen by using the Snooze option. As soon as an alert is snoozed, it moves out from the active list and joins the snooze list for the user. An alert can be snoozed indefinitely, to a particular date, or with the condition to reactivate the alert if any data changes happen for the relevant master data. The Snooze alert list can be displayed by selecting the header for the Snooze option in the left side of the screen. A snoozed alert can be reactivated by clicking the Activate button on the Monitor Custom Alerts page of a snoozed alert.

▶ Go to Excel
Navigation to the SAP IBP Excel planning view with the relevant planning level, key figure, and master data selection for the alert is possible by with this option. Detailed data analysis with the Excel planning view or through an edition of the planning view is performed through the Excel planning application. A data element (key figure) can be edited and saved if required to solve the exception condition represented by an alert.

▶ Go to Analytics
Clicking this option opens the SAP IBP Analytics page displaying the chart, along with the key figure, group-by, and filter data condition selections already performed for the alert. Additional analytics can be performed to analyze the situation to determine the best possible action.

▶ Add to Case
This option assigns an alert to the identified responsible person to take an action for the exception scenario. A new case can be created or an existing case can be updated for taking an action for the alert. Through the same screen, the responsible person and due date can be provided.

▶ Share in SAP Jam
This is available to discuss the exception scenario with a group through a group feed in the collaboration process. Comments to be shared with the group can be added before sharing the information. Based on the nature of the exception, a task may be created and assigned through the SAP Jam collaboration application for further action.

15.8 Summary

The SAP Supply Chain Control Tower solution of SAP IBP enables end-to-end visibility, real-time monitoring, analytics, exception management, and task control capabilities in a supply chain network. This is delivered through the analytics, dashboard, tasks, alerts, and collaboration tools that are part of the standard SAP Supply Chain Control Tower solution as a component of SAP IBP. This is achieved through easy-to-use configuration and applications.

We have now covered all the SAP IBP applications in detail. The next chapter will cover how these applications and their related processes can be fully integrated using the unifed planning area.

For an organization with different planning processes for S&OP, demand, supply, and inventory, integration of the planning processes and data management is paramount for optimizing the supply chain network as one integrated unit. This is achieved by using a unified planning area in SAP IBP.

16   Unified Planning and User Roles

In SAP Integrated Business Planning (SAP IBP), a unified planning area has been provided to build an end-to-end supply chain planning solution. For end-to-end planning, multiple planning activities must be performed in the correct sequence, which can be enabled through the application jobs functionality in SAP IBP. Different planners with different responsibilities must have system access with the correct authorization, which is maintained in SAP IBP system through user roles. This chapter discusses these three elements: unified planning area, application jobs, and user roles.

16.1   Unified and Integrated Planning Areas

SAP has delivered standard planning areas and objects for supporting all areas of the SAP IBP solution. In addition to standard individual planning areas for different planning solutions, a unified planning area has also been provided for building an integrated solution with shared master data and key figures. We will cover two standard planning areas in the following sections: *unified time series planning* and *integrated time series and order series planning*.

16.1.1   Unified Planning Area: SAPIBP1

SAPIBP1 is the planning area for supporting the integrated planning solution and is referred to as the unified planning area. It supports the following applications as one planning unit:

- ▸ **SAP IBP for sales and operations**
  This application supports demand review, supply review, collaboration, and finalization of the sales and operations (S&OP) plan.

- ▸ **SAP IBP for demand**
  This application supports demand forecast, promotion plan, demand plan, and demand sensing.

- ▸ **SAP IBP for inventory**
  This application is used for single and multi-echelon inventory optimization.

- ▸ **SAP IBP for response and supply**
  This application is used for time series supply planning involving supply heuristics and supply optimization.

- ▸ **SAP Supply Chain Control Tower**
  This application supports analytics, visibility, and task management.

The unified planning area is also the foundation of the Rapid Deployment Solution (RDS), a standard offering by SAP to map end-to-end planning applications supporting strategic, tactical, and operational plans. Through the RDS offerings, configuration documents, test scripts, planning processes, and planning views are provided by SAP that can be used by the customer as a base to start with. This offering helps in the faster delivery of the first working model in the client environment. Note that the aim of RDS isn't to restrict the solution scope of SAP IBP but to provide a set of accelerators that the customer can use for a faster planning model realization.

> **Note**
>
> As of February 2017, the unified planning area supports only time series-based planning, not order series planning. For unified planning modeling of time series and order series applications, the solution is provided through another standard planning area (SAP74) which is discussed in Section 16.1.2.

The standard unified planning area contains the properties for integrated demand and supply planning to support end-to-end planning. The time horizon maps day, technical week, week, month, quarter, and year. Figure 16.1 shows the time profile as provided in the unified planning area. Multiple planning operators for supporting different functionalities are added to the planning model.

Figure 16.2 shows the system example of copy, simulation, disaggregation, I/O, forecast, and SCM operator assignment in the unified planning area.

Unified and Integrated Planning Areas

12							
Description		W2M SPA D TW W M C		Start Date		Jan 1, 2011	
Used in Planning Area		1		End Date		Dec 31, 2020	

Levels (6)

Level	Name	Base Level	Period Type	Default Display Ho...	Default Display Ho...	Attributes
1	Day		Day	-730	730	Assign Attributes
2	Week (technical)	1	Technical Week	-130	130	Assign Attributes
3	Week	2	Week	-104	104	Assign Attributes
4	Month	2	Month	-24	24	Assign Attributes
5	Quarter	4	Quarter	-8	8	Assign Attributes
6	Year	5	Year	-2	2	Assign Attributes

Figure 16.1 Time Profile in the Unified Planning Area

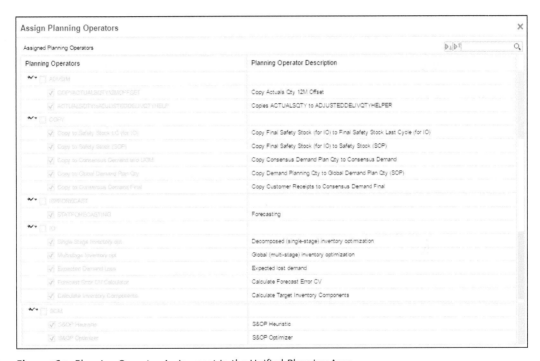

Assign Planning Operators

Assigned Planning Operators

Planning Operators	Planning Operator Description
ADVSIM	
COPYACTUALSQTY12MOFFSET	Copy Actuals Qty 12M Offset
ACTUALSQTYtoADJUSTEDDELIVQTYHELP	Copies ACTUALSQTY to ADJUSTEDDELIVQTYHELPER
COPY	
Copy to Safety Stock LC (for IO)	Copy Final Safety Stock (for IO) to Final Safety Stock Last Cycle (for IO)
Copy to Safety Stock (SOP)	Copy Final Safety Stock (for IO) to Safety Stock (SOP)
Copy to Consensus Demand with UOM	Copy Consensus Demand Plan Qty to Consensus Demand
Copy to Global Demand Plan Qty	Copy Demand Planning Qty to Global Demand Plan Qty (SOP)
Copy to Consensus Demand Final	Copy Customer Receipts to Consensus Demand Final
IBPFORECAST	
STATFORECASTING	Forecasting
IO	
Single-Stage Inventory opt.	Decomposed (single-stage) inventory optimization
Multistage inventory opt	Global (multi-stage) inventory optimization
Expected Demand Loss	Expected lost demand
Forecast Error CV Calculator	Calculate Forecast Error CV
Calculate Inventory Components	Calculate Target Inventory Components
SOM	
S&OP Heuristic	S&OP Heuristic
S&OP Optimizer	S&OP Optimizer

Figure 16.2 Planning Operator Assignment in the Unified Planning Area

Figure 16.3 and Figure 16.4 show examples of planning level and key figures provided in the unified planning model. We recommend you navigate through the planning model of the unified planning area for detailed information on the objects.

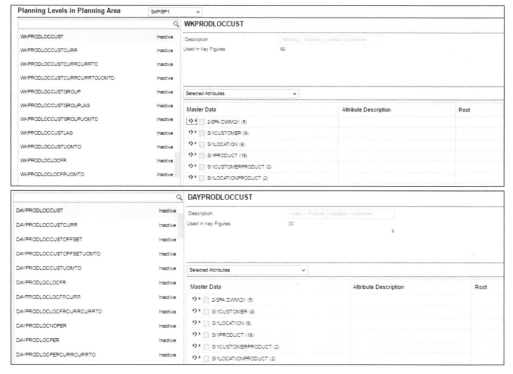

Figure 16.3 Planning Level Example from the Unified Planning Area

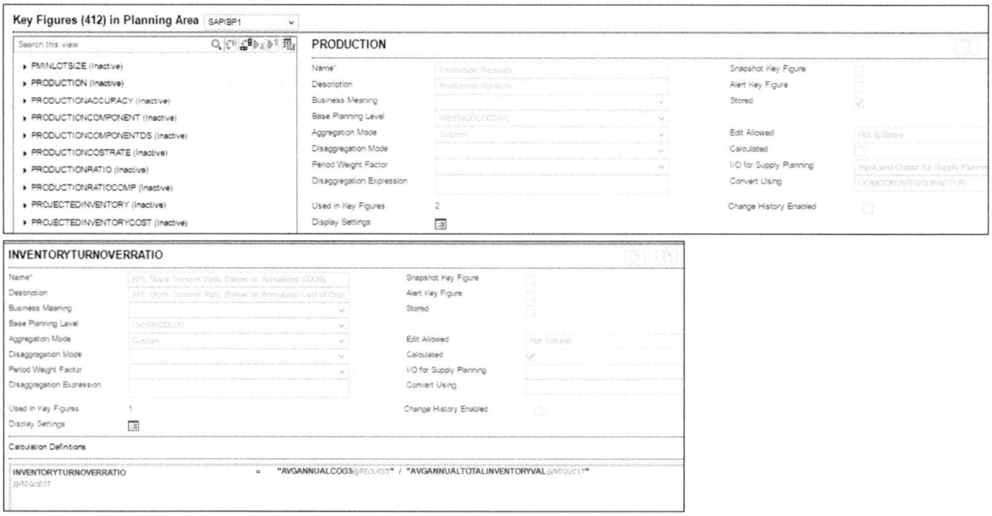

Figure 16.4 Key Example from the Unified Planning Area

While copying the unified planning area to create a user-specific planning area, it's possible to either copy the entire planning area or copy a subset of the planning area based on the planning process scope of SAP IBP.

Filters can be applied for a partial copy of the unified planning area, SAPIBP1, for the following planning processes and areas:

- S&OP and supply planning
- Demand planning
- Demand sensing
- Inventory optimization
- Supply chain control tower

The advanced copying functionality of the planning area copy is used to perform the partial copy. The resulting copy while using the filter contains a subset of the integrated planning area and hence keeps the model light with only contents relevant to the user's planning process in SAP IBP.

16.1.2 Integrated Planning Area for Response and Supply: SAP74

The SAP74 planning area is provided by SAP as a standard planning area to combine the response and supply planning solution (planning area SAP7) with S&OP (planning area SAP4). This provides the flexibility to run time-based S&OP with order-based response planning on the same set of master data.

Planning objects such as attributes, master data, and key figures provided by integrating planning area SAP74 can support S&OP algorithms (both heuristic and optimizer) and response and supply algorithms (constrained forecast, order confirmation, and gating factor). The storage time profile level for this planning area is day, and the time profile has the attributes of day, week, technical week, and month.

Data in the integrated planning area must be integrated with the SAP execution system using the SAP HANA smart data integration (SAP HANA SDI) functionality to make them available to use for both time series and order series planning.

16.2 Application Jobs

Supply chain planning for an individual planning application (demand planning or supply planning) or integrated planning process (integrated S&OP, demand, supply, and inventory planning processes) requires multiple planning operations to be performed in the correct sequence. In SAP IBP, you can schedule a planning job (e.g., executing a planning operator, copying a key figure to another key figure, or any other activity) and execute multiple operations in sequence through the application jobs functionality.

Application job functionalities in SAP IBP can be accessed via multiple apps under Administrator, General Planner, and General Response Planner, as shown in Figure 16.5. In the upcoming sections, we'll take a look at the following items:

- ▸ Application job templates
- ▸ Application jobs
- ▸ Application logs

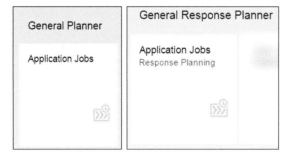

Figure 16.5 Apps Related to Application Jobs in SAP IBP

16.2.1 Application Job Templates

The Application Job Templates app is used to review the standard job templates provided by SAP and to create or edit customer-specific application job templates. It contains the collection of application jobs available in SAP IBP. Figure 16.6 and Figure 16.7 show the application job template page. Origin information on this page shows whether the job template has been provided by SAP (Global), was created by a user for sharing with others (Shared), or has been created by a user for private use (Private). A job template can be created, saved, and scheduled through this application job template. An application job template can have multiple planning steps defined for it through the Maintain Steps option in the Configuration page. There are multiple Scheduling Options to make it a one-time execution or a recurrence job with the defined recurrence schedule, as displayed in Figure 16.6 and Figure 16.7. An available template can be accessed through the Application Job app for further processing, as will be discussed in next section.

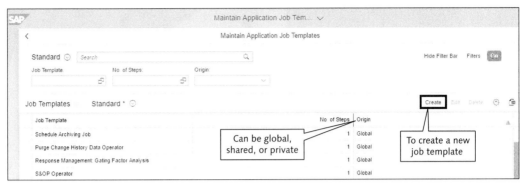

Figure 16.6 Creation and Scheduling Option of the Application Job Template: Part 1

Inventory planning — New

General Information

Job Template:	Inventory planning	Number of Steps:	2
Job Name:	Inventory planning		

Scheduling Options

Add More Scheduling Options

Start Immediately: ☑		Recurrence Pattern:	Single Run
Start:	Start Date	Start Time	
Time Zone:	Pacific Time (Los Angeles)		

Steps

Step No.	Step Name
1	Inventory Optimization Operator
2	ABC Operator

Scheduling Information

Start Immediately:	☐
Start:	12/04/2016 20:00:00
Time Zone:	(UTC-08:00) Pacific Time (Los Angeles)
Recurrence:	☑
Recurrence Pattern:	Weekly
Every:	1 Week(s)
On:	1st Day -1 Day(s) First
Sunday ⊗	
End:	None

Figure 16.7 Creation and Scheduling Option of the Application Job Template: Part 2

16.2.2 Application Jobs

The Application Jobs app is used in SAP IBP for creating, scheduling, sharing, monitoring, and canceling application jobs. This app can be found under GENERAL

PLANNER and GENERAL RESPONSE PLANNER for usage in time series and order series applications. Application jobs for response planning are specific to order series in SAP IBP response and supply; the app in the GENERAL PLANNER section is used for all other planning function applications.

Figure 16.8 shows an example of an application job creation for response planning. An application job takes the primary feed from the application job template; only the jobs defined in the template can be accessed and used through the application jobs page. Through this application, parameters for the job can be provided to execute this as a custom run. In SCHEDULING OPTIONS, whether the job will be executed once or needs to be a recurrent job is configured. The application job functionality provides the information on the job execution status with start time, end time, and duration. A pending job can be canceled through the option provided on this page by clicking the CANCEL button displayed in Figure 16.8. The information about the execution status is available at the summary level through this application. Detailed information about the job is accessed through the application logs, as discussed in the next section.

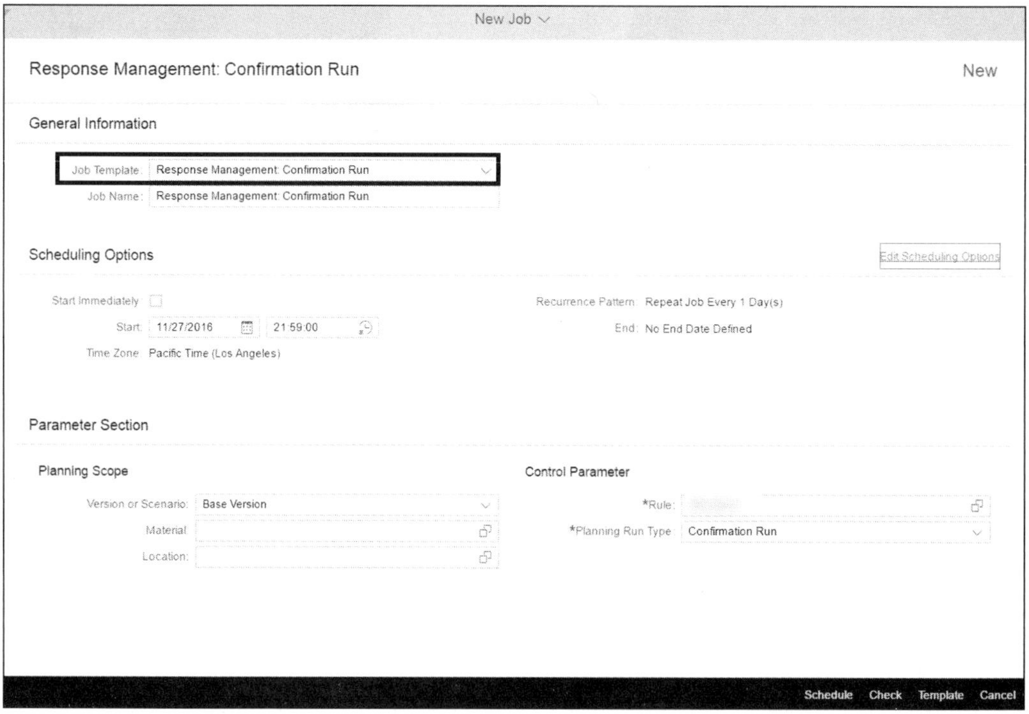

Figure 16.8 Application Job in SAP IBP

16.2.3 Application Logs

The Application Logs app is used to monitor the application logs from job scheduling and any other SAP IBP application. It shows the logs at summary as well as at the detail level (see Figure 16.9). Through the user selection fields, log reports can be generated by using parameters such as date range (CREATED BETWEEN), planning area (AREA), and user (CREATED BY). Through the displayed log report, detailed information about the particular job schedule can be obtained via the drilldown selection option. The SEVERITY column displays the status of individual job unit execution as INFORMATION, WARNING, or ERROR. Application logs are a widely used tool by the system administrator.

Figure 16.9 Application Log of SAP IBP

For optimizing the system resource, it's recommended to delete the old logs in the system by creating an application job template for deleting the log and then scheduling the job on a recurrent basis. Figure 16.10 shows an example of the job to delete the application log. Deletion criteria can be selected to provide the parameters in terms of time, area, and user data while performing the deletion. We recommend you use the OLDER THAN (DAYS) field to execute the deletion job.

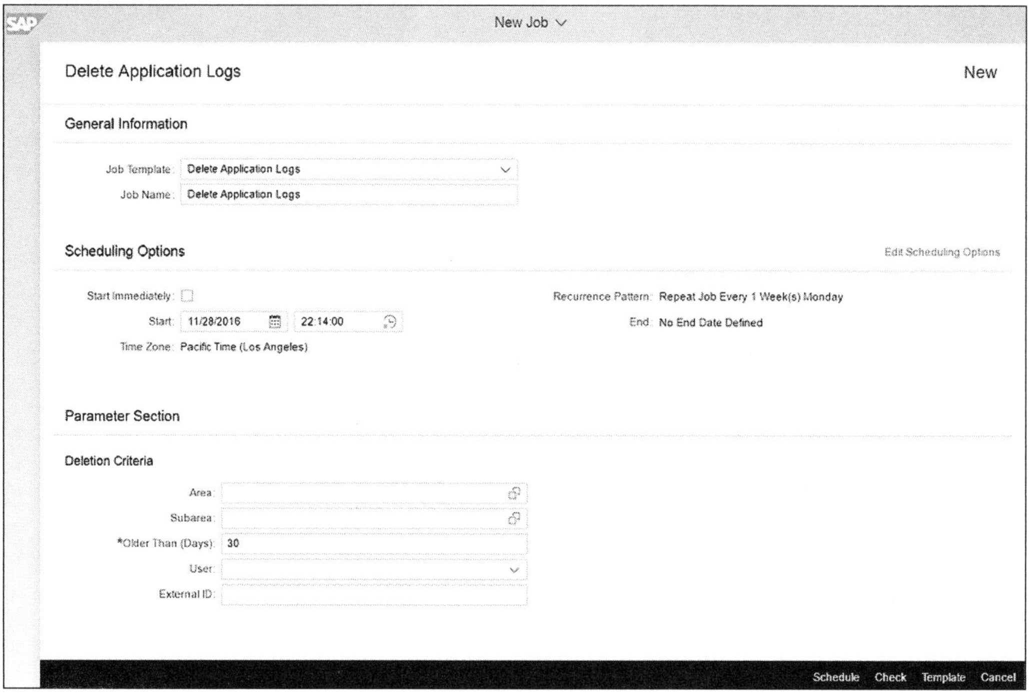

Figure 16.10 Deletion of Application Job Logs

16.3 User and Business Roles

Users of SAP IBP need to have the correct access and authorization to perform their tasks in the system, which is handled through user management and business roles management in SAP IBP. Figure 16.11 shows a high-level overview of the steps required in SAP IBP for user creation, business roles creation and assignment, user group creation, and providing the expected system authorizations.

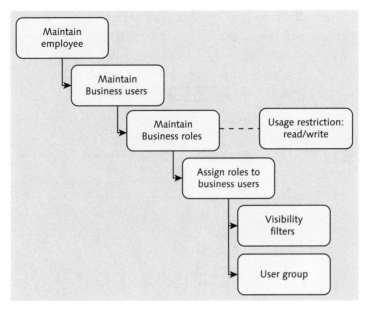

Figure 16.11 User and Business Role Management in the SAP IBP System

In the following sections, we'll look at the individual steps required to perform these tasks.

16.3.1 Maintaining Employees and Business Users

Your first step when providing an individual access to SAP IBP is to create the system user as an employee of the organization. The information elements of the employee master data, provided and saved in the system through the Maintain Employee app under EMPLOYEE MASTER DATA, are as follows:

- Name
- Employee number
- Contact: email ID and phone number
- Access validity period

After saving the information for the new employee, you must map the employee as a new business user. This is performed through the Maintain Business Users app under IDENTITY AND ACCESS MANAGEMENT. After you click OK on the CREATE

NEW BUSINESS USER screen, the new business user data is created and saved in SAP IBP. See Figure 16.12 for an example of the configuration steps in the system to create an employee and assign it as a new business user.

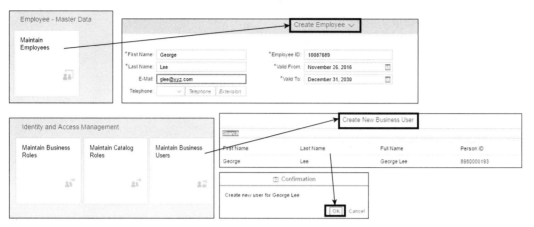

Figure 16.12 Maintain Employee and Business User in SAP IBP

16.3.2 Maintaining Business Roles

The SAP IBP system is delivered with multiple predefined business catalogues for business roles. The catalogues are organized by planning process and system management functions. For example, the BASIC PLANNING TASKS catalog has the authorizations for a set of planning tasks, including review and modification of planning data, and scheduling of planning jobs such as statistical forecasting, inventory optimization, and data integration.

Business roles in the system are maintained by selecting these catalogues. The process of business role selection can be done through the business catalogue or through the business role template. Figure 16.13 shows examples of both maintaining a new business role through catalogue and maintaining the role through the standard role template (a demand planner, inventory planner, supply planner, etc.). Using the template can make it easier for the role definition because the standard catalogues for the business roles are already added there. After maintaining the business role, restrictions in terms of data access and data change authorization are provided. Figure 16.13 shows giving read and write authorization to the role demand planner by selecting the business catalogue forecast model.

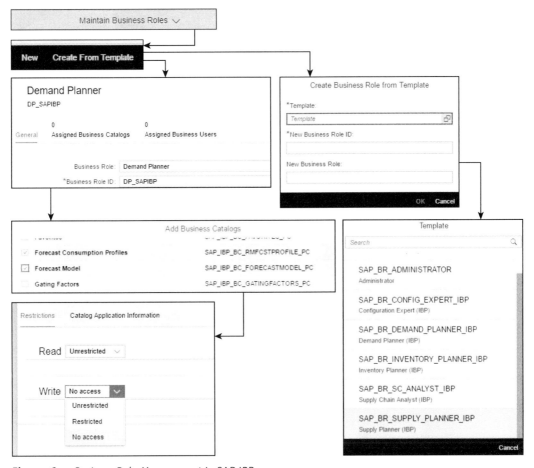

Figure 16.13 Business Role Management in SAP IBP

To restrict the specific planning area and data access, the general restrictions functionality of the business role application can be used. Through general restriction,
a controlled role can be created for the planning area, master data, planning operator, and so on. The visibility filter is one of the most widely used restriction tools
for business user roles. Through the visibility filter, a set of master data objects
can be assigned to a filter name, which can then be assigned to a role. Figure
16.14 shows the creation of a visibility filter to provide access to data related to
only one location in the supply chain. Then, through the business role application
of general restriction, the visibility filter can be added in the role.

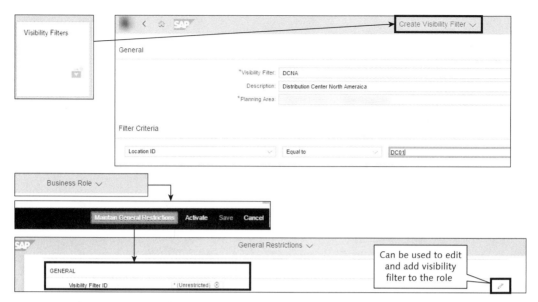

Figure 16.14 General Restrictions and Visibility Filter in a Role

16.3.3 Role Assignment

After a business user has been created in the system and the business roles for performing the planning function are defined, assignment of the role to the business user can be performed through easy mapping. A business user can get assigned one or multiple business roles per the roles and responsibilities of the individual in the organization. Figure 16.15 shows the system configuration example of giving the supply planner read and write role to the new user named George Lee.

16.4 User Group Creation

A user group in SAP IBP is used to perform the collaborated planning operations in a team and for sharing the information with a closed list of business users. User groups are created through the User Groups app under ADMINISTRATOR. After the user group is created, it can be edited to add the business users through the ADD (+) option shown in Figure 16.16. Multiple user groups can be created for collaboration between different individuals to work on a team. One user group contains multiple members, and one member can be a part of multiple user groups.

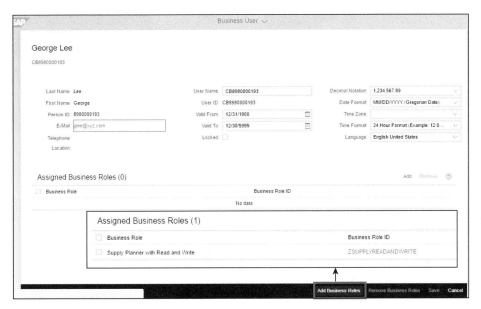

Figure 16.15 Business Role Assignment to the Business User

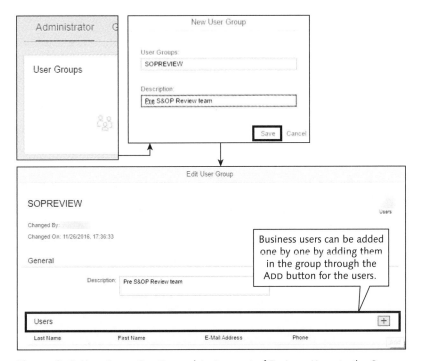

Figure 16.16 User Group Creation and Assignment of Business Users to the Group

16.5 Summary

The integrated supply chain planning solution can be configured by referring to the unified planning area model provided as part of the standard SAP IBP solution. The unified planning area model or a subset of the planning model can be copied for an organization's planning model configuration. System usage is controlled by extending required authorizations to the user profiles. Automated planning in SAP IBP can be managed through a set of batch jobs, which can be scheduled for execution based on the property and planning sequence requirement. The SAP IBP solution features of the unified planning area, roles management, and batch job application capabilities widely enhance the usability of the tool in mapping the supply chain network and making it efficient and easy to manage.

Armed with a complete understanding of the advance modeling and planning capabilities of SAP IBP, in the next chapter we will turn our focus to the agile implementation methodology that has become the de facto standard for achieving rapid time to value.

The era of the waterfall implementation approach is over with the advent of fast, cloud-based, digital-focused, and sleek new-breed technologies such as SAP IBP. The new agile implementation approach emphasizing periodic deliverables, faster time to market, and more alignment with customers' requirements is ideally suited for SAP IBP solution delivery.

17 Implementation Methodology

The expected value realized from a supply chain planning project depends to a great degree on the success of the project implementation. Project success is governed by the implementation methodology, vision, and action of the project team. With supply chain planning and SAP Integrated Business Planning (SAP IBP) project implementation, one size fits all doesn't apply. It's paramount for the business leaders, consulting partners, and technology teams to identify the best possible approach for a particular organization by considering the solution vision, organization culture, scope, and customer's expectations.

For a long time, the waterfall and ASAP project management methods have been the go-to approach for SAP systems development and solution implementation. With the launch of cloud-based products (e.g., SAP IBP), and global discussions on a faster approach, the newer *agile methodology* is more suited for delivering higher values to business in general and the supply chain in particular.

Note that this may not be an either-or situation; a blend of traditional and agile approach can be used by an SAP IBP client if the organizational and environmental factors require it. The project team and business leaders are expected to have the knowledge of the project implementation methodologies to identify and finalize the best option.

In this chapter, we'll discuss project implementation methodologies in detail, starting with an overview of an SAP IBP implementation, before moving on to specific information on the three main implementation approaches: the classic waterfall method with ASAP, the agile methodology, and the agile add-on for the

ASAP methodology. We'll close out the chapter with a discussion of sprint delivery and the necessary team framework, as well as some recommendations for your SAP IBP implementation.

17.1 SAP IBP Project Implementation

When considering an SAP IBP implementation, you should always start with the business value or perceived business value. The value in supply chain activities of an organization can be rated on their efficiency, service quality, cost, flexibility, and profitability. The perceived values can be achieved through business process improvement and most probably an efficient planning system with a sophisticated algorithm providing end-to-end visibility and control in a collaborated and easy-to-use environment.

After a business requirement or desired value is identified, you can begin looking at SAP IBP solution mapping. We recommended you analyze in detail the different planning processes of sales and operations planning (S&OP), demand, supply, response, inventory, and overarching supply chain analytics. Because SAP IBP is the end-to-end planning solution, it can be used for any or all of the planning processes. Solution scoping needs to be performed per your requirements, current status, and goals of the organization. The implementation approach of the selected solution is then discussed and finalized based on evaluating such factors as business requirement, solution scope, implementation team, timelines, and any environmental factor.

Another important factor that influences the timelines and project approach of SAP IBP projects is the data and system architecture of the organization. Considering the broad scope of supply chain planning, which requires execution, master data, and other system and data integration with SAP IBP, the integration work items must be considered for their alignment with the SAP IBP project plan.

The agile approach is widely used for SAP IBP project implementation, which is supported by its features that enable faster-working models; however, time-tested ASAP and the recently developed agile add-on to ASAP can also be considered for the implementation of SAP IBP.

17.2 Project Implementation Methodologies

For SAP IBP system implementation, the most widely used project implementation approaches, from oldest to newest, are as follows:

▸ Waterfall and ASAP methodology

▸ Agile methodology

▸ Agile add-on to ASAP methodology

17.2.1 Waterfall and ASAP Methodology

The waterfall methodology is the traditional approach to software development, which follows a linear path of completion of different phases with gating criteria for every phase. You create deliverables during every phase, and, at the end of the phase, a quality check is done to make a decision regarding starting the next phase of the project. Figure 17.1 shows an example of the waterfall approach with its phases and deliverables.

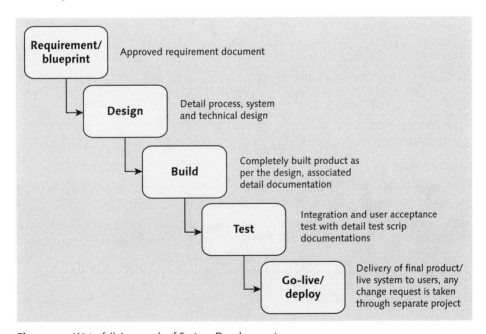

Figure 17.1 Waterfall Approach of System Development

The different implementation phases of the waterfall approach are as follows:

▶ **Requirement/blueprint phase**
In the requirement collection or blueprint development phase, business requirements are gathered, reviewed, and finalized. The finalized requirement is approved for the system build, test, and delivery. Any change in the requirement is managed through a well-defined scope change or change-request process. The deliverable for this phase is an approved requirement list.

▶ **Design phase**
Business process documents, along with detailed functional and technical design documents, are finalized in the design phase. This involves multiple discussions with the stakeholders while considering the business requirement document as the guide. System fit-gap analysis is performed for the business requirement and standard system features. Analysis of the gap and design of the technical work requirement is carried out in this phase. The approved versions of the design documents are the deliverables of this phase; a quality gating factor check is done on the mentioned deliverables.

▶ **Build phase**
The actual system build is executed in the build phase of the project. Build work is guided by the functional, system, and technical design documents finalized during the preceding phase. Any change due to system limitation and new findings requires reopening the design document, along with discussion and approval of the same. Unit tests are performed by the build team while creating the individual elements of the system. At the end of this phase, a fully built system aligned with the approved design is available for testing. Deliverable and quality gate of this phase are based on the system build completion as designed.

▶ **Test phase**
Testing of the unit, string, and integrated systems is performed in the test phase by the user representative of the business. This is controlled through formal test scripts and test completion documents. The last phase of the test phase includes user acceptance testing (UAT). Successful documentation of test results and success of the UAT is the quality gating criteria for the test phase.

▶ **Go-live and deployment phase**
Final cutover and delivery of the system is performed at go-live. A new live system requires initial support from the project or identified support team for helping the users while using a newly delivered system. Further changes and improvements are planned in a live system through a well-defined change control and continuous development approach.

Note that the delivered system is totally based on the requirement finalized in the first phase. Therefore, this approach is best used in a stable environment that has fixed requirements. The expectation is that requirements can be identified and finalized well in advance of starting any build work. Advantages of this approach are well-controlled phases and detailed documentation. Higher-level disadvantages are the lack of flexibility and longer time to deliver.

The ASAP approach is a blend of the waterfall approach developed by SAP over a period of time, based on the work performed with thousands of SAP system customers. This was the go-to project management approach for SAP system implementations for many years. Figure 17.2 shows the project phases of the ASAP project implementation approach, along with the deliverables of the respective phases. Deliverables of the project phases are quality check gating factors for the phases.

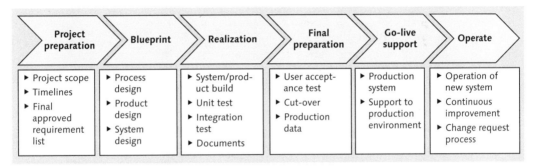

Figure 17.2 ASAP Methodology Approach

The different phases of the ASAP methodology are as follows:

- **Project preparation**
  Solution scope and project timelines are finalized in the preparation phase. Requirement gathering, discussion, and finalization are performed to get the approved business requirement list for the solution. This approved requirement list is the detailed solution scope of SAP; any change in this requires a discussion and approval process.

- **Blueprint**
  The detailed design for business processes, IT processes, system configuration, and technical development design is finalized and approved in the blueprint phase. Fit-gap analysis for standard SAP functionality with the requirement of any custom enhancement is performed and approved in this phase. Deliverables of this phase are the detailed design documents and system build plan.

▶ **Realization**

The realization phase for the SAP system is where you build and test your system. System configuration and technical coding aligned to the approved design are performed in this phase. Unit testing of individual elements, followed by string testing of one integrated unit followed by integration testing of the totally integrated system is done in this phase. Test results may require some development modification, which can be done and documented through the defined approach of the project. Integrating both build and test as one realization phase provides extra flexibility to act on the test results.

▶ **Final preparation**

Final preparation is aimed at getting users' approval for the production environment through completed and documented UAT. System cutover activities and data transitioning are performed in this phase. The SAP production system is ready for users at the end of this phase.

▶ **Go-live support**

Through go-live, the SAP system is delivered to the business and IT users for performing different activities required by the organization. This system is aligned to the requirement captured in the first phase of the project. Support to a newly delivered production environment is provided by the project team or specially built support team.

▶ **Operate**

The operate phase is aimed at operating the business and generating the value as planned for the project and SAP system. Continuous improvement in the system and changes in the live system are planned through a defined change management process.

17.2.2 Agile Methodology

Unlike the waterfall approach, which is linear in nature, the agile methodology follows an iterative approach to meeting the objective by going through multiple product models. The agile project management approach has been proven to work as a fast, flexible, successful, and efficient method for delivering and developing software products.

> **Note**
>
> The agile methodology has its roots in the "Agile Manifesto" published in 2001. Thinkers and management gurus Jeff Sutherland, Ken Schwaber, Hirotaka Takeuchi, and Ikujiro

Nonaka have been the leaders in developing the framework of agile methodology and popularizing this with organizations for software development cycles.

Figure 17.3 shows the different steps of the agile project management approach. An agile approach can be delivered through various methodologies; Scrum, discussed in detail in Section 17.3, is the most widely used and most applicable to SAP systems.

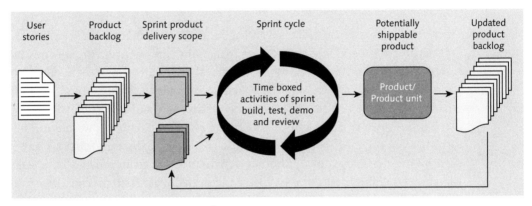

Figure 17.3 Agile Implementation Approach

As represented in Figure 17.3, the agile project starts with user stories. User stories are high-level business requirements provided by the users (end customers of the system). Different from the waterfall or ASAP methodology, these user stories capture the requirements for high-level story format (may be in bullet or paragraph format) and aren't the detailed list of specific business or system requirements. The agile approach assumes that not all requirements will be known while starting the project; it provides the flexibility with the end product and welcomes the change.

User stories are used to create product requirements called product backlogs. The product backlogs are prioritized based on the factors most relevant to customers. Customers are expected to be closely connected with the project team to provide regular feedback. The solution development phase is divided into multiple cycles called sprints. Sprints are the time-boxed efforts to work on the prioritized product backlogs to deliver potentially shippable products. The output of every sprint as referenced by potentially shippable products is the product or part of the product that can be used by the customer. After a sprint completion, the product backlog is again reviewed based on the feedback of the customer and remaining items in the product backlog as scope. This cycle is continued multiple times, leading to the final product delivery while working collaboratively with the customers from the very start of the project.

One of the biggest advantages of the agile implementation approach is the faster delivery of the first model of the product. It has been experienced time and time again that a working system in the hands of the customer provides new outlooks that enable tremendous improvements. Through the agile approach, the model delivery time is greatly reduced.

Figure 17.4 compares the waterfall and agile approach of a first product or system delivery to customers. In a waterfall approach, the first time a customer uses the system may be after 9 to 12 months for a typical SAP project. However, in an agile approach, the working model of the system is available for customer usage within 4 to 8 weeks of the project start. It has been shown in multiple SAP projects that most of the customers use only a part of the solution. Some of the solution features (maybe the most complex ones that required maximum effort) are never used by the customers, or a different variation of the feature could have been valuable. Providing a working model in the initial phase helps correct the scope of the product (the SAP IBP system in our case). Application of this with the prioritized product backlog results in the most relevant solution features delivered in an expedient and efficient manner. Based on the efficiency gained, the total project timeline and effort in an agile approach is lower as compared to the time and effort for the waterfall approach.

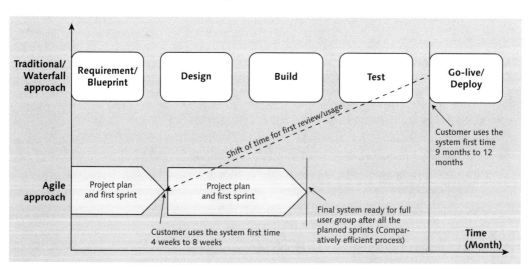

Figure 17.4 Product Delivery Approach Comparison in the Waterfall and Agile Approaches

Solution flexibility in the agile approach is obtained using the sprint method. An agile approach welcomes the change and doesn't expect that all the requirements are known in advance of building the solution. Solution delivery to the customer helps in updating the requirements aligned to the business expectations and value areas.

The agile approach is based on the lean principle of reducing process waste. The project team pursues only the activities that add value to the end customer. The lean work is controlled by working on the prioritized user requirements and a lean documentation, which is done to add the value and isn't a detailed, time-consuming documentation activity for the sake of it. Some care needs to be taken for the industries (e.g., pharmaceutical) that require detailed documentation. For those cases, however, documentation is considered a value add activity and part of the prioritized product backlog.

Planning for an agile approach is performed through a simple burnout chart as shown in Figure 17.5. Based on the product backlog, tasks and their required efforts are planned. Efforts and tasks are divided into different sprint cycles. With the completion of sprints, the chart progresses as displayed in Figure 17.5, as both the remaining efforts and remaining number of tasks decrease. Actual progress is tracked on the planned completion line, and any adjustment is performed as required. Because the tasks are reviewed, and the product backlog is updated after every sprint, the agile approach expects some level of flexibility with the project timelines. This can be controlled by planning for different project phases and by focusing on requirements according to their priority for the customer.

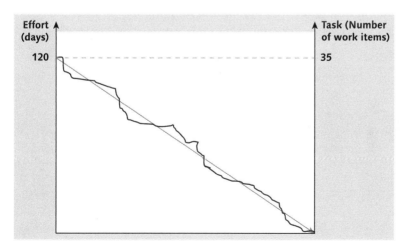

Figure 17.5 Burnout Chart for the Agile Approach

> **Note**
>
> The software development principle of the "Agile Manifesto" can be reviewed by the user for better understanding of the crux of the agile approach. You can find the 12 principles of the agile manifesto at *http://agilemanifesto.org/principles.html.*
>
> These principles are generally considered to be the guiding philosophy of agile project delivery.

17.2.3 Agile Add-On to ASAP Methodology

With the advent of the new-breed cloud-based digitally equipped SAP products and recent research on project management approaches, SAP has updated the ASAP project implementation approach with an agile add-on. This provides the benefits of using the agile approach in the framework of the ASAP approach.

With the agile add-on, the traditional project phases of the ASAP methodology are merged into the agile implementation phases. Figure 17.6 outlines this method. The benefit of this approach is to capture the advantages of the agile methodology by aligning the phases of traditional ASAP methodology.

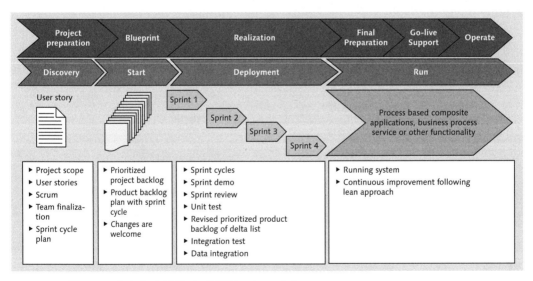

Figure 17.6 Agile Add-On to ASAP Implementation

The phases of the agile add-on to ASAP map as follows:

- **Project preparation → Discovery phase**
  The project preparation phase of the ASAP methodology is called the discovery phase in the agile add-on to ASAP. This phase defines the project scope through building the team and completing the user stories for the requirements. Planning the sprint cycles and the timelines of system delivery is finalized in this phase.

- **Blueprint → Start phase**
  Prioritized product backlog is an output of the start phase for assigning the scope of the first sprint and planning the scope and tasks for the remaining sprint cycles. Different from the traditional ASAP methodology, changes are welcome and are discussed after completion of every sprint cycle and before the start of the next sprint cycle.

- **Realization → Deployment**
  The deployment phase is the collection of sprint cycles for product delivery. It contains the subphases of sprint start, work completion, sprint demo, review, and product completion. Testing is done as part of the sprint cycles; the potentially shippable product is built after every sprint, and users review the product or SAP system environment. Product backlog for the next sprint is updated based on review comments. In this approach, the system at the end of the sprint is still with limited customers and isn't getting used as a productive environment of the organization. After completion of all the sprints and data uploads, the system gets ready for production system usage in a live environment.

- **Fine preparation, go-live support, operate → Run**
  The last three phases of the ASAP approach are grouped together as the run phase in the agile add-on to ASAP. Final activities of data load and related work items are performed to deliver the live environment to customers. The assigned support or project team provides support to the live environment. Guided by the continuous cycle of improvement, further work activity for enhancing the system can be planned by the stakeholders.

Note that the example discussed here provides a live environment at the end of every planned sprint. Although this isn't a restriction, the add-on to ASAP methodology can also work with a different flavor in which the SAP system is delivered for productive usage after the first or after the initial set of sprints.

17.3 Sprint Delivery and Team Framework

As mentioned in Section 17.2.2, Scrum is the most widely used method for the agile project approach. The Scrum method is based on the following guiding principles:

- **Scrum approach of team management**
  A Scrum team is usually a collection of three to nine cross-skilled individuals. A Scrum team is a self-managed team with two identified leaders as the product owner and Scrum master. Other people in the team are the team members delivering on work objects.

  The product owner owns the responsibility of product delivery and communicates with customers, senior executives, and managers in addition of the Scrum team members. The product owner manages the product backlog and performs the prioritization for dividing the scope of the solution for shorter solution development time horizons (sprints).

  The *Scrum master* guides the process of solution development per the sprint scope and cycle. In the SAP IBP project implementation, this person can also be the supply chain planning solution architect or solution leader. While working with the product owner and Scrum team, the Scrum master navigates through the process for successful delivery of the solution.

- **Work plan and sprint cycles**
  Based on the product backlog and assigned priorities, the most critical requirements for a working model are identified for working in a time-boxed approach called a sprint. Identified requirements are delivered as the solution scope of the sprint cycle. Solution development and testing activities are performed as sprint items. The working model is presented to the customers through a sprint demo. Feedback is collected through sprint reviews, and the working system model is either delivered to the customer for usage, or the customer review feedback is used for further work plan aligned with the updated product backlog.

- **Waste elimination**
  The agile approach supports the lean principle of waste elimination by stressing only the items that add value to the customers. Any activity that doesn't add direct value to the customer is removed from the scope. This waste elimination with an early product model highly enhances the efficiency of the project delivery. This eliminates the effort spent on unwanted or low-priority requirements and unnecessary documentations.

17.4 Implementation Recommendations

Every organization's supply chain network, products, planning processes, existing data architecture, and culture is unique. As such, there is no fixed implementation formula for SAP IBP. However, there are recommendations for best practices that should be considered for enhancing the success of the SAP IBP project implementation.

Based on our experience, the maximum value of the SAP IBP implementation is achieved when the implementation is guided by the supply chain transformation goals and associated business requirements. We recommend that you consider an SAP IBP product implementation as both a business and IT exercise driven by transformation or value-creating goals. Based on the identified value areas, a supply chain planning transformation road map is recommended to be finalized, which can have all of the planning processes (S&OP, demand, supply, response, inventory) or a subset of the same. Irrespective of the planning process chosen, analytics must be added into the scope, which can be either driven by the SAP Supply Chain Control Tower or the analytics functionalities of the individual planning processes of SAP IBP. Along with the selected processes, the timeline is another highly important factor.

An analysis is required to decide on either working on all the planning processes together or following an approach sequence for the planning process implementation plan, for example, going live with the first S&OP and demand planning, followed by supply, response, and inventory. Again, there is no set formula for this; the scope and sequence needs to be finalized for an organization based on factors such as business requirements, identified value areas, current infrastructure, process maturity, data availability, data accuracy, budget, team's availability, strategic integration, and so on.

While selecting the project implementation approach, we recommend you use either the agile approach or the agile add-on to ASAP methodology for the SAP IBP implementation. Based on the solution maturity achieved by SAP IBP and the standard planning models delivered by SAP, it's highly feasible to build a basic model during the initial weeks of the project. Using an iterative approach for the initial planning model aligns the planning solution to the business requirement and solves the most important problems. Having a planning system in the early phase of the project helps the planning and relevant team members (sales, marketing, finance, production, etc.) adjust the requirements to enhance the overall value, profitability, and efficiency.

413

Even if a planning solution was perfect, the project could still fail to achieve value due to poor data quality. It can't be stressed enough to religiously work on the input data quality in terms of its scope and accuracy. Hence, in addition to planning the phases of the project for the SAP IBP solution, project planning is required for data flow for both input and output data from the SAP IBP planning system. Because the automated data transfer channel may take time to be developed, consider using the manual data load functionality of the SAP IBP model for the initial model build activity if required.

Assuming that agile or agile add-on to ASAP is selected as the project implementation approach for the SAP IBP solution implementation, there are guidelines to consider for solution implementation:

► **Team structure**
Build small cross-skilled teams empowered to make decisions. A team size of two to nine people is suitable for every planning area of SAP IBP. Team members are recommended to work full-time, devoted to the project activity. Every skill required for the success (business, IT, and SAP IBP) of the project must be represented by the team members.

The SAP IBP implementation team must have an identified product owner who is responsible for delivering the product and who communicates closely with stakeholders such as customers, executives, managers, and so on. The product owner owns the product backlog and performs the prioritization for the iterative solution delivery.

The product owner tells the team what needs to be done, but questions regarding how it will be done and how much time it will take are answered by the implementation team. The implementation team should be self-driven, which means it may or may not have the assigned solution leader or solution architect. The solution leaders help navigate the parts of the solution as an integrated unit. The team can also decide to not select a solution leader and work together for building the solution model on the product backlog plan. Every team is recommended to have an assigned Scrum master, managing the sprint activities and timelines.

► **Communication and collaboration**
Agile team members should be in constant communication, though long meetings should be avoided. Every morning, a short (typically 15 minutes) stand-up meeting can be planned to discuss the activities. The activities discussed by the team members are based on yesterday, today, and tomorrow, that is, sharing what the person did yesterday, the person's aim for today, and the plan for tomorrow, along with any roadblock or potential roadblock. This activity

enhances the collaboration and effectiveness of the team. Communication happens throughout the workday. Formal meetings for long durations are planned for the sprint demo and review discussion. Conflicts are recommended to be discussed in focused meetings with examples of working models and discussion on the same, instead of endless discussions. Working together in a co-location environment is another recommended approach for project success. It may not be possible to co-locate for all the workdays of the week, but even some level of co-location helps in enhancing the project success.

▸ **Business and customer involvement**
Success of the SAP IBP project in agile and agile add-on to ASAP is based on the involvement of business and system customers (planners, business teams, etc.) in providing the user stories, helping with the aimed value, and reviewing the planning models as delivered in different stages of the project. Involvement of customers (planners, business users, etc.) guarantees that the solution under creation is aligned to customer expectations and requirements.

▸ **Product backlog management**
User stories and product backlog are the guides to the solution scope. The right participants from the business must get involved for user story development. Ruthless ranking of the product backlog is recommended by the product owner based on the value of the requirement. This helps in segmenting the requirement into must-have and not relevant, so that the solution model meets the business requirements and value areas. The product backlog must be used as an active live document with detailed review for the priorities after every sprint based on additional feedback received from the customers on previously delivered or completed planning models.

▸ **Documentation**
Documentation should be considered a value area, and the team should devote efforts only on creating and maintaining the documents that add value to the customer. Any documentation that doesn't add value to the customer should be avoided. This approach requires a review by the product owner based on the industry background and any organizational and regulatory requirements.

▸ **Sprint cycle**
Sprint cycles for the SAP IBP project should be considered between two weeks and four weeks. This duration of the sprint provides enough time to develop or adjust a model with a group of requirements. At the end of every sprint, a sprint demo should be performed for the customer. This needs to be followed by the sprint review, which involves the customer actually working with the

model. Sprint review and actual working opens new horizons that help the customers decide on further enhanced models (or sometimes a simplified model) that can add value to the business. This review feedback must get captured in updating and reviewing the product backlog.

▸ **Training**
The agile approach may be new to the organization and the team members implementing the SAP IBP solution. Trainings should be planned to share the knowledge, processes, and working principles of the agile project management approach with the team members. This helps in understanding the expectations and delivering on the same.

In addition to agile approach training, which can be led by the trainer outside of the delivery team, there should be short training sessions planned to share the knowledge among the team members. These knowledge-sharing sessions can be focused on SAP IBP knowledge, supply chain principles, business processes, IT processes, data management, system architecture, and so on. Sharing the knowledge enhances the overall effectiveness of the team and results in a much more robust planning solution delivery.

17.5 Summary

The release of cloud-based, new-breed solutions such as SAP IBP are more suited for implementation through the agile project management approach than the traditional waterfall or ASAP methodology. The ASAP methodology from SAP has been updated with an agile add-on to enhance the efficiency of SAP implementation by achieving the advantages of the agile methodology. Against the linear solution development methodology of traditional approaches, the agile approach works on the iterative principle by delivering a working model of the system very early in the project. This helps the business users and customers refine and prioritize the requirements. The agile approach for SAP IBP is followed through Scrum methodology in a cross-skilled team comprising the product owner, Scrum master, and team members. Close collaboration in the team and constant communication with the stakeholders and customers are essential for the successful delivery of the SAP IBP solution implementation project.

The next chapter brings together everything we have covered in the previous ones by presenting stories about actual SAP IBP customers and how they achieved value from their implementations.

This chapter examines a broad variety of customer use cases for SAP Integrated Business Planning. Each customer represents a different industry, and they range from mid-size to very large global enterprises. The intent is to demonstrate the flexibility of the solution and its ability to create value across a diverse set of business conditions.

18 Customer Use Cases

The use cases in this chapter are based on information collected from actual customer implementations of SAP Integrated Business Planning (SAP IBP). For each use case, we'll describe the company's state of affairs prior to the SAP IBP implementation, their objectives, how SAP IBP helped them meet those objectives, and the benefits that were gained. While you may find similar conditions within your own organizations, any implementation recommendations should be based primarily on a detailed business requirements analysis.

18.1 Sales Planning

This use case describes how a company was able to improve its sales planning and sales and operations planning (S&OP) processes and results with SAP IBP.

18.1.1 Situation and Objectives

A global manufacturer that serves consumer, industrial, and commercial markets was facing growing complexity due to the number of products, channels, and markets it managed. The company's biggest issues were inconsistent sales planning and immature S&OP processes. In 2012, the company partnered with SAP to address these issues through new technology.

SAP Advanced Planning and Optimization (SAP APO) Demand Planning was the tool used for the existing sales planning process. This wasn't very effective, as SAP APO required too much detail for the supply chain planners and didn't provide sufficient detail for the sales planners. In addition, there was a high degree of manual effort in gathering sales data, leaving little time for analysis, and limited ability to do dynamic aggregation and disaggregation. Finally, the company needed to implement a continuous planning cycle for budgeting and forecasting.

18.1.2 Solution and Benefits

In 2013, the company began a SAP IBP project with a six-week proof of concept to test the foundational capabilities of the solution, which was very successful in securing buy-in from the sales and financial planning organizations. This was followed by a six-month sales planning implementation in one region. In this process, the sales teams developed a two-month sales plan at the product level using the SAP IBP Excel planning views. This plan was transferred to SAP APO, where the supply chain team developed the six-month consensus forecast and two-year statistical forecast. These forecasts are then passed back to SAP IBP for margin analysis, and a rolling financial forecast is created that is transferred to SAP Business Warehouse (SAP BW) for the budgeting process. All of these data transfers are managed using SAP Cloud Platform Integration.

The company realized the following benefits as a result of this project:

- User-driven dynamic aggregation/disaggregation
- Ability to create complete revenue plans, including non-products (services)
- Significantly improved new product introduction through like-modeling
- Significantly improved collaboration with sales managers on the final forecast
- Improved overall quality of the forecast
- Improved efficiency of the sales planning process
- Rapid scenario planning for revenue and margin analysis
- Support of rolling financial plans

18.1.3 Conclusions

Through this project, the company was able to establish a standard process for sales planning and budgeting that it plans to roll out globally. This will be done in conjunction with the implementation of a complete S&OP process that will be enabled by SAP IBP. In addition, the company has been able to improve its use of SAP APO by allowing the supply chain teams to focus on the mid- and long-term forecasting processes.

18.2 Collaborative Demand Management

This use case describes how a company was able to improve its demand planning process and results with SAP IBP.

18.2.1 Situation and Objectives

A vertically integrated natural resources company with expanding operations across several continents was facing major challenges due to the geographic diversity of the markets it serves. The company's IT was lacking standardization from both a systems and process perspective. In 2015, the company embarked on an initiative to improve its demand planning process and technology. After evaluating several alternatives, the company decided to go forward with SAP IBP based on what it identified as promising functionality and integration to its existing SAP ERP backend.

The existing process was mostly manual with a heavy reliance on Excel to manage the forecast, which was done at the product level for each country. Two days were required for each demand planner to gather input with little time left to review or analyze the numbers. The process of collecting the total demand for all markets took approximately two weeks, and the numbers were often inconsistent and difficult to reconcile. This led to a lack of trust in the results and low planner productivity.

18.2.2 Solution and Benefits

SAP IBP was implemented as a collaborative demand management tool. The initial project duration was eight months and focused on a single market and product line. The benefits achieved included the following:

▶ The ability to create multiple planning scenarios to simulate the impact of different sales volumes on cost and margin using the SAP IBP Excel planning views

▶ A highly automated demand planning process that produced valid results which were readily accepted by the business

▶ A 50% reduction in overall demand planning cycle time

▶ A 50% improvement in planner productivity

▶ Significant improvement in sales margins

18.2.3 Conclusions

The business was reported to be very satisfied with the results of this project. The plan is to expand the use of SAP IBP into additional markets as well as other processes such as production planning.

18.3 Forecasting and Replenishment Planning

This use case describes how a company was able to improve its forecasting and replenishment planning results with SAP IBP and SAP Enterprise Inventory and Service-Level Optimization.

18.3.1 Situation and Objectives

This Fortune 100 company distributes products globally via retail and wholesale channels. In 2012, the company embarked on an initiative to improve its forecasting process and supply chain visibility. SAP IBP was ultimately selected as the tool to address its business requirements.

The company employs a hub and spoke distribution model that includes both internal and customer distribution centers, as well as contract manufacturers and suppliers. The company's data volumes are extremely large due to the number of products and orders that are generated. The existing forecasting process was highly manual, spreadsheet-based, and disconnected from the supply side of the business. Thus, the company was unable to effectively anticipate and respond to an increasing level of demand and supply variability.

18.3.2 Solution and Benefits

The initial project was for a single business unit with the focus on statistical forecasting. The process begins with a weekly delta load of sales history from SAP ERP for all forecasted items at a ship-to level. All data integration is done using SAP Cloud Platform Integration. Due to the variability of demand, a new forecast is generated over the weekend to drive replenishment for the upcoming week. The results of the forecast are made available in an Excel planning view that supports dynamic aggregation and disaggregation, making it much easier for the planners to manage these large data sets. They also make extensive use of alerts to manage exceptions using the SAP IBP dashboards. These capabilities allow the planners to effectively handle large numbers of products using only a few screens. They are also able to make on-the-fly changes to the forecast based on new information and understand the impact of these changes before committing them to the live plan.

In addition to using SAP IBP for forecasting, the company also uses SAP Enterprise Inventory and Service-Level Optimization to calculate replenishment levels for the distribution centers. The SAP IBP weekly forecast is loaded into SAP Enterprise Inventory and Service-Level Optimization, and on-hand inventory and incoming supply orders are brought in nightly from SAP ERP. As discussed in an earlier chapter, the SAP Enterprise Inventory and Service-Level Optimization multistage planning engine understands demand and supply variability. Thus, it's able to use this data to determine the optimal replenishment levels for every product/distribution center combination. These replenishment signals are then transferred to SAP ERP where purchase orders and stock transfer orders are created to procure or position product appropriately. As a final step, the replenishment quantities are sent back to SAP IBP so that the planner can compare them to the original forecast to identify potential supply constraints. It should also be noted that the planners interact primarily with SAP IBP while SAP Enterprise Inventory and Service-Level Optimization operates purely as a planning engine.

This closed-loop process has enabled the company to achieve the following benefits:

▶ Respond rapidly to demand changes and optimize inventory targets across the entire distribution network.

▶ Improve forecast accuracy and plan performance due to the ability to generate key performance indicators (KPIs), and apply learning's from past performance into future plans.

▶ Assess the impact of constrained supply on customer demand, and determine the optimal supply plan.

▶ Develop an optimal business plan to meet financial targets.

▶ Collaborate and communication interactively in real time across organizations and with external partners.

18.3.3 Conclusions

The business is reported to be very satisfied with these results. The Excel planning views and web-based dashboards enabled a very fast learning curve, and didn't require highly experienced planners to use these tools productively. The company has begun to roll out SAP Jam for collaboration, and it plans to replace SAP Enterprise Inventory and Service-Level Optimization with SAP IBP for inventory to take advantage of the seamless integration this would provide.

18.4 Multilevel Supply Planning

This use case describes how a company was able to leverage SAP IBP to improve its inventory and supply planning results

18.4.1 Situation and Objectives

This mid-sized company manufactures and distributes several leading brands globally through the service provider and retail channels. Rapid growth both organically and inorganically led the company to select SAP IBP to help manage its supply chain more effectively.

In 2014, the company started an initiative to improve its demand and supply planning processes. The goal was to operate on a harmonized data model that was able to manage the thousands of finished goods and raw materials, plus multiple planning levels that comprised its supply chain. The company also wanted to improve its capability to plan safety stock levels to buffer against uncertainty, as well as provide real-time analytics to the end users at both aggregate and detailed levels of granularity. Finally, the company also needed to improve collaboration and orchestration of the end-to-end S&OP process.

18.4.2 Solution and Benefits

The first phase of the project focused on the consensus demand planning and statistical forecasting processes for several brands across a small segment of customers. Historical sales data from the SAP ERP environment was loaded into SAP IBP on a nightly basis using SAP Cloud Platform Integration. In week one of the monthly S&OP process, the demand plan is created, which includes the statistical forecast as well as input from sales and marketing. Week two begins the consensus review process where the various stakeholders come to a final agreement on the monthly demand plan. The forecasting and demand planning processes are enabled by SAP IBP Excel planning views, which are used to generate the forecast and collect sales and marketing data. The consensus process is enabled by SAP IBP process modeling and management and by SAP Jam for collaboration.

In phase two, the focus moved to supply planning. Master data, inventory positions, and supply plans are loaded into SAP IBP nightly from the SAP ERP environment using SAP Cloud Platform Integration. The SAP IBP multilevel heuristic is used to determine capacity and production requirements from both internal and external sources based on the consensus demand plan. In the supply review, the supply planning team evaluates resource constraints, supply projections, and shortages. This is followed by a series of pre-S&OP meetings where production is leveled and customer expectations are reset where necessary. As a final step, there is an executive review that analyzes the new plan from both an operational and financial perspective. The approved production plan is then published back to SAP ERP as planned independent requirements via SAP Cloud Platform Integration. All of these processes are enabled by the SAP IBP planning views and analytical dashboards.

Both phases of the project utilized an agile implementation methodology, which helped achieve the following benefits:

▶ **Acceleration of the company's S&OP process maturity**
Collaboration and process cadence are defined with measurable tasks.

▶ **Visibility to demand and supply in a single solution**
Sales, marketing, operations, and finance work from a single plan.

▶ **Real-time scenarios anywhere in the supply network**
Real time what-if scenarios in supply planning give quick insight to adjustments required to meet demand.

▶ **Real-time analytics to support key decisions**
Access is provided to key decision-making data with defined and ad hoc analytics and planning views.

18.4.3 Conclusions

The customer provided several lessons learned as an early adopter of SAP IBP:

▶ Use an agile approach to implementation that will provide flexibility when changes are required and deliver rapid time to value.

▶ Take time to understand the right level of detail required for planning; too much or too little detail can produce erroneous results.

▶ Make sure to enlist the help of skilled SAP IBP resources to properly configure the system, which needs to be done correctly from the beginning.

18.5   Cost-Optimized Supply Planning

This use case describes how a company was able to leverage the SAP IBP supply optimizer to better manage its supply chain costs.

18.5.1   Situation and Objectives

This division of a diversified corporation serves industrial and consumer markets. The division is very mature in its supply chain planning processes and an advanced user of SAP ERP and SAP APO. However, as the business grew and market conditions changed, it began to feel the need to investigate new technologies to enhance current planning capabilities.

Due to the commodity-driven nature of the business, the company's supply chain is very cost sensitive. The existing solution was lacking two critical capabilities to help optimize the supply chain costs: enablement of a complete S&OP process and what-if scenario planning. In late 2014, the division ran a successful SAP IBP proof of concept to address these shortcomings.

18.5.2   Solution and Benefits

In early 2015, the company began a pilot project for a large business unit, which was focused on S&OP and supply optimization. The detailed design was eight weeks in duration, followed by an agile deployment, which was completed in six months. Historical sales, pricing, and cost data was sourced on a monthly basis from SAP Business Warehouse (SAP BW), as well as some existing flat files using SAP Cloud Platform Integration. Master data was sourced from SAP ERP, SAP APO, and SAP Cloud Platform Integration. This provided the company with a complete supply chain model in SAP IBP that enabled several key processes.

The sales history and pricing data was used to create volume and revenue projections. These projections were used by the SAP IBP optimizer to generate monthly supply requirements using the cost and capacity data. To convince the business of the validity of this process, it did a comparison of the baseline optimized supply plans in SAP IBP and SAP APO, which were found to be very close at the beginning of the cycle. The company then used the SAP IBP supply optimizer to run multiple what-if scenarios to evaluate the impact of different volume, capacity, and cost assumptions on margin. In addition to these core planning functions, extensive use was made of SAP IBP dashboards for scenario analysis and support of the overall S&OP process. The ultimate result of this process is a constrained, cost-optimized supply plan that is passed back to SAP ERP and SAP APO for execution via SAP Cloud Platform Integration.

In mid-2016, a second SAP IBP project was initiated for another large business unit in several selected markets in conjunction with a broader SAP rollout. This business unit was less mature with respect to supply chain planning and the goal was to start simple and get some quick wins by leveraging the learnings from the previous project. The project was focused on the demand planning process. Historical sales data was loaded from flat files, and the system was configured to enable the sales and marketing teams to participate in a consensus demand planning process. Basic statistical forecasting was used to project volume, and pricing data was included to generate revenue projections. The total duration of this second project was approximately five months.

Following is a summary of the benefits achieved:

▶ Single data model tying together supply chain, commercial, and financial information to enable a true integrated business planning process

▶ Ability to generate revenue, cost, and margin projections supporting the S&OP process and what-if analysis

▶ User friendliness that reduces the learning curve and improves user adoption

▶ Real time analytics that improve effectiveness in decision-making

▶ Scalable and flexible to meet diverse business and process maturity levels

18.5.3 Conclusions

The business is reported to be very optimistic about SAP IBP. Future plans include expansion of supply planning and other SAP IBP solutions to additional business units and cost-to-serve analytics.

18.6 Sales and Operations Planning

This use case describes how a company was able to successfully transition from a spreadsheet-based process to an integrated S&OP process with SAP IBP.

18.6.1 Situation and Objectives

A vertically integrated global company was experiencing rapid growth through acquisition and expansion into new markets and product lines. It had a well-established manual monthly S&OP process that helped deal with the resulting complexity and challenges. In 2015, the company embarked on an initiative to streamline this process by implementing SAP IBP.

The legacy S&OP process was limited by the technology in place—a series of Excel spreadsheets manually updated with sales and inventory data from SAP ERP. These are ultimately consolidated into a single massive spreadsheet for S&OP. This sequential process, which consumed many hours each week, is summarized as follows:

1. Multiple sales update spreadsheets are consolidated into a single forecast.
2. Spreadsheets are updated manually with sales and inventory data from SAP ERP.
3. Supply planners wait for demand planners to complete the forecast prior to starting supply planning for packaging lines.
4. Excel is used to generate forecasts and supply plans.
5. Multiple supply plans are aggregated into one overall plan.

While the process itself was quite mature and stable, the limitations of the technology made it impossible to keep up with the rapid growth the company was experiencing.

18.6.2 Solution and Benefits

One of the main reasons SAP IBP was selected as the tool to manage the S&OP process was its configurability and the opportunity for rapid implementation. Working with a certified SAP partner, a blueprinting and modeling exercise was completed in 12 weeks. The new process included monthly meetings between demand planners and sales teams, as well as the generation of a weekly bucketed supply plan. The live data feed between SAP ERP and SAP IBP allowed the resulting production requirements to be quickly communicated to the schedulers and contract manufacturers. Another benefit was the ability to have up-to-date inventory data, which had become increasingly important with the accelerated introduction of new products. Having full visibility to demand, supply, and inventory enabled the company to create a balanced, profitable S&OP plan that was accepted by the sales and manufacturing teams. Several additional benefits are as follows:

- Compliance could be measured to plan between the SAP IBP plan and the production schedule.

- The appropriate level of target stock could be built up using custom calculations in SAP IBP as opposed to rules of thumb.

- The forecast developed in SAP IBP could also be used by finance for the annual budgeting process.

18.6.3 Conclusions

After the initial implementation of SAP IBP, the users became very proactive about learning how the model behaved and how the tool worked. The knowledge they gained led to a continuous improvement process to fine-tune the model and make the use of SAP IBP even more effective. The company also began expanding its use into other regions using the pilot model as a template.

18.7 End-to-End Planning and Visibility

This use case describes how a company leveraged SAP IBP to improve its S&OP, demand, inventory, and supply planning processes, as well as enable end-to-end supply chain visibility

18.7.1 Situation and Objectives

This global company is a mature SAP supply chain customer, including extensive use of SAP APO. In 2013, the company began an initiative to speed up its supply chain through the use of SAP IBP.

The company had successfully implemented SAP APO for demand and supply planning across all regions and product lines. However, it was still lacking system support for its S&OP process, which was spreadsheet-based and required significant manual effort to gather and consolidate information from sales, marketing, and the supply chain. In addition, the company had challenges with inventory visibility across the regions due to multiple instances of SAP APO. Finally, it needed to become more responsive to increasing demand and supply variability through improved operational planning.

18.7.2 Solution and Benefits

In late 2012, a pilot project began to implement SAP IBP for a complete product line in a single region to replace the existing spreadsheet-based process. The project spanned approximately five months and delivered the following benefits:

▸ Provided the ability to meet commitments on sales, profit, and share targets

▸ Improved the quality of the decision-making process and reduced cutting planning cycle time

▸ Empowered business users to perform what-if analyses in real time, helping drive consensus in business planning meetings

▸ Created a unified picture of sales, marketing, and financial data for real-time planning at any level of granularity

▸ Provided intuitive interfaces and an embedded collaboration platform, helping boost productivity at the individual and team levels

With SAP IBP for sales and operations in place to cover its tactical planning requirements, the company now turned its attention to resolving the operational planning and visibility issues. In 2014, several new regionally focused SAP IBP pilot projects began, which included advanced capabilities for demand sensing, inventory optimization, constraint-based supply planning, and real-time analytics. Most of the data required for these applications was sourced from existing SAP APO and SAP BW environments using SAP Cloud Platform Integration. This included forecasts, sales orders, shipments, inventory positions, and supply plans. The results generated in SAP IBP included a short-term demand plan and optimized inventory targets, which were pushed to SAP APO for execution, as well as a constrained supply plan that was used in the S&OP process to transition from a consensus to a constrained demand plan. Following are some of the key benefits realized:

▸ Enablement of daily responsiveness to demand variability

▸ Significant inventory reduction

▸ Fewer out-of-stock occurrences

▸ End-to-end visibility with real-time analytics

18.7.3 Conclusions

One of the key lessons learned from this project is that SAP IBP is a journey that requires the right balance of people, process, and technology to deliver the desired results. The ultimate goal is fully integrated end-to-end planning that enhances operations across all time horizons.

18.8 Integrated Business Planning

This use case describes how a customer was able to use SAP IBP to improve forecast accuracy and reduce working capital requirements through an integrated financial and operational planning process.

18.8.1 Situation and Objectives

A mid-sized manufacturing company had grown significantly through acquisition and had initiated a supply chain process transformation. One of the main goals of this transformation was to dramatically reduce working capital requirements through improved S&OP. SAP IBP was selected as the technology to enable this improvement.

As a result of its growth strategy, the company consisted of multiple business units with decentralized, spreadsheet-based S&OP processes. This made it very difficult to measure forecast accuracy. In addition, each division was responsible for its own inventory, which caused large imbalances in both shortages and excesses across the company. To resolve this, the company needed to establish a consistent global S&OP process with a monthly cadence that allowed the company to plan the business in an integrated fashion. They also needed a consistent set of KPIs that provided a complete view of the health of the company across the divisions.

18.8.2 Solution and Benefits

The monthly process the company adopted was as follows:

- ▸ Week 1: Sales and demand collection
- ▸ Week 2: Consensus demand planning
- ▸ Week 3: Rough-cut capacity and material planning
- ▸ Week 4: Demand/supply balancing, executive S&OP
- ▸ Planning horizon: 18 months, 3 frozen
- ▸ Planning level: Product/customer/location

SAP IBP was initially implemented to support this process in one division. The new S&OP process steps and activities were modeled in the system and orchestrated using SAP Jam. Excel planning views were designed specifically for the sales, demand, and supply planners. From these views, demand planners were able to build the baseline plan using statistical forecasting techniques, and run what-if scenarios to support the consensus demand planning step. The supply planners used the multilevel heuristic, also from within their planning views, to propagate the consensus demand plan to the distribution centers and plants. Finally, there were both planning and analytical views designed to support the demand/supply balancing and executive S&OP steps. The analytical views incorporated both standard and customized KPIs, while the planning views provided dynamic aggregation and disaggregation and what-if scenario analysis.

SAP Cloud Platform Integration was used for both inbound and outbound integration. Master and transactional data was sourced from SAP ERP, and historical data was sourced from SAP BW. The final agreed-upon S&OP plan was published to material requirements planning (MRP) in SAP ERP for operational planning and to SAP BusinessObjects Planning and Consolidation (SAP BPC) for financial planning.

18.8.3 Conclusions

A second division was subsequently added to the project. The implementation was done in conjunction with a certified SAP IBP partner and took approximately six months for the two divisions. The result is a closed-loop process that integrates sales, supply chain, and finance and will enable the company to reduce working capital requirements and improve forecast accuracy.

18.9 Summary

This chapter marks the conclusion of this book whose primary objective is to help current and prospective users of SAP IBP understand how this solution can apply to their organization. It begins with a discussion of the current business and technology environment that is driving the evolution of the digital supply chain, along with the role that planning plays in helping companies better anticipate and respond to the resulting changes. This is followed by an overview of SAP supply chain planning solutions, including SAP APO, SAP Enterprise Inventory and Service-Level Optimization, and SAP IBP. The goal is to understand what capabilities these solutions deliver and how they fit into the overall SAP supply chain strategy.

This final chapter is dedicated to the most important aspect of any solution, the customers that are using it. These are taken from actual interviews with individuals from these companies and written in narrative form to convey their personal as well as business perspectives. The goal is to provide you with a compelling set of stories that will help you envision how SAP IBP can benefit your own company.

A   Supply Chain Management Acronyms

Acronyms are widely used in supply chain management. Many of these terms have become the norm in everyday communication for business professionals. We have provided a list of commonly used acronyms in supply chain planning to help you understand the business language of supply chain planning professionals. Though we have covered all of the most common acronyms, this is not an exhaustive list. Many of the terms mentioned here are used in different sections of this book.

3PL	Third-party logistics provider
4PL	Fourth-party logistics provider
ATO	Assemble-to-order
ATP	Available-to-promise
BI	Business intelligence
BOM	Bill of material
BTO	Build-to-order
BW	Business warehouse
COGS	Cost of goods sold
CPFR	Collaborative planning forecasting and replenishment
CRP	Capacity requirement planning
CT	Control tower
CTO	Configure-to-order
DC	Distribution center
DP	Demand planning
ECC	Enterprise central component
EDI	Electronic data interface
EOQ	Economic order quantity
ERP	Enterprise resource planning
ETA	Estimated time of arrival
ETO	Engineered-to-order
FC	Forecast
FIFO	First-in, first-out

GATP	Global available-to-promise
IBP	Integrated business planning
IO	Inventory optimization
JIT	Just-in-time
KPI	Key performance indicators
LIFO	Last-in, first-out
LOC	Location
MAD	Mean absolute deviation
MASE	Mean absolute scaled error
MM	Materials management
MPE	Mean percentage error
MRP	Materials requirement planning
MSE	Mean square error
MTO	Make-to-order
MTS	Make-to-stock
NPI	New product introduction
POS	Point of sale
PP	Production planning
PPDS	Production planning and detailed scheduling
PPR	Product planning and review
PRD	Product
RCCP	Rough cut capacity planning
RES	Resource
RFID	Radio frequency identification
RMSE	Root mean square error
S&OP	Sales & operations planning
SC	Supply chain
SCCT	Supply chain control tower
SCM	Supply chain management
SCN	Supply chain network
SCOR	Supply chain operations reference model
SCP	Supply chain planning

SIOP	Sales, inventory, and operations planning
SKU	Stock keeping unit
SL	Service level
SMI	Supplier-managed inventory
SNP	Supply network planning
SNP	Supply network planning
SOP	Sales & operations planning (alternative)
SP	Supply planning
TM	Transportation management
VMI	Vendor-managed inventory
WAPE	Weighted absolute percentage error
WIP	Work in progress
WM	Warehouse management
WMAPE	Weighted mean absolute percentage error

B   The Authors

Sandy Markin has four decades of experience in manufacturing and supply chain management. He began his career in operations management in the consumer products industry and subsequently worked for a several software providers. He joined SAP in 1994 where he is currently the senior director for the digital supply chain. During his tenure at SAP he has been instrumental in bringing to market several industry-leading supply chain solutions including SAP APO and SAP IBP. Sandy is a lifelong Chicago-area resident and received his B.S. from the University of Illinois and his MBA from Loyola University of Chicago.

Amit Sinha is a leader in SAP supply chain practices at Deloitte Consulting, LLP. He has more than 14 years of experience in supply chain planning and business transformation projects. He has worked extensively with different industry sectors across the globe in the areas of S&OP (sales and operations planning), demand planning, supply planning, inventory optimization, and supply chain analytics. He is an expert in SAP IBP and other SAP supply chain applications. Amit has also authored a text book on supply chain management, published numerous articles in international journals, and has been a speaker at supply chain conferences.

Index

- ▶ Learn how SAP S/4HANA enables digital transformation
- ▶ Explore innovative financials and logistics functionality
- ▶ Understand the technical foundation underlying SAP S/4HANA advances

Baumgartl, Chaadaev, Choi, Dudgeon, Lahiri, Meijerink, Worsley-Tonks

SAP S/4HANA

An Introduction

Looking to make the jump to SAP S/4HANA? Learn what SAP S/4HANA offers, from the Universal Journal in SAP S/4HANA Finance to supply chain management in SAP S/4HANA Materials Management and Operations. Understand your deployment options—on-premise, cloud, and hybrid—and explore SAP Activate's implementation approach. Get an overview of how SAP HANA architecture supports digital transformation, and see what tools can help extend your SAP S/4HANA functionality!

449 pages, pub. 11/2016
E-Book: $59.99 | **Print:** $69.95 | **Bundle:** $79.99

www.sap-press.com/4153

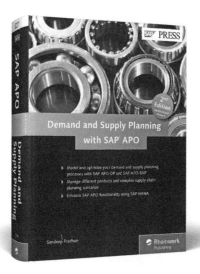

- ▶ Model and optimize your demand and supply planning processes with SAP APO-DP and SAP APO-SNP
- ▶ Manage different products and supply chain planning scenarios
- ▶ Enhance SAP APO functionality using SAP HANA

Sandeep Pradhan

Demand and Supply Planning with SAP APO

Keep up with consumer demand using this guide to SAP APO! Learn how to use DP and SNP to forecast demand and capture demand patterns to perform tactical supply planning. Blending big-picture descriptions with step-by-step instructions, this book offers information on everything from implementing SAP APO to using it for interactive, characteristic-based, and collaborative planning.

831 pages, 2nd edition, pub. 04/2016
E-Book: $69.99 | **Print:** $79.95 | **Bundle:** $89.99

www.sap-press.com/4011

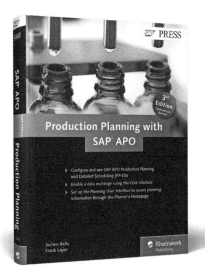

- ▶ Configure and use Production Planning and Detailed Scheduling (PP-DS)

- ▶ Enable a data exchange using the Core Interface

- ▶ Set up the Planning User Interface, a tool for end users to access planning information through the Planner's Homepage

Jochen Balla, Frank Layer

Production Planning with SAP APO

Immerse yourself in the complex world of Production Planning/Detailed Scheduling with this comprehensive guide. Discover how to set up the CIF, transfer master data between SAP APO and SAP ERP, and customize PP/DS to best meet the needs of your unique business. This one-stop resource is sure to help you learn everything you need to know about SAP APO-PP/DS!

431 pages, 3rd edition, pub. 10/2015
E-Book: $69.99 | **Print:** $79.95 | **Bundle:** $89.99

www.sap-press.com/3927

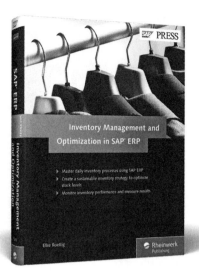

- ▶ Master daily inventory processes using SAP ERP
- ▶ Create a sustainable inventory strategy to optimize stock levels
- ▶ Monitor inventory performance and measure results

Elke Roettig

Inventory Management and Optimizaiton in SAP ERP

Avoid having too little or too much stock on hand with this guide to inventory management and optimization with SAP ERP! Start by managing the stock you have through replenishment, goods issue, goods receipt, and internal transfers. Then plan for and optimize your future by avoiding bottlenecks, setting lead times, using simulations, and more. Finally, evaluate your operations using standard reports, the MRP Monitor, and KPIs. Keep your stock levels just right!

523 pages, pub. 02/2016

E-Book: $69.99 | **Print:** $79.95 | **Bundle:** $89.99

www.sap-press.com/3977

- ▶ Implement, customize, and use SAP ERP for materials planning
- ▶ Evaluate and monitor your materials planning process
- ▶ Model your materials planning calculation using simulations

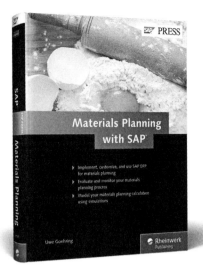

Uwe Goehring

Materials Planning with SAP

Balance the art and science of materials planning! Learn how to use SAP ERP to calculate what, when, and how many items are required for production with this comprehensive guide. From portfolio management and policy setting to exception monitoring and inventory optimization, you'll see the complete materials planning picture. Move your materials planning from routine to strategic!

519 pages, pub. 10/2015
E-Book: $69.99 | **Print:** $79.95 | **Bundle:** $89.99

www.sap-press.com/3745

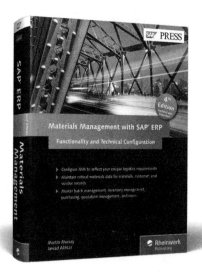

▶ Configure MM to reflect your unique logistics requirements

▶ Maintain critical materials data: materials, customer, and vendor records

▶ Master functionalities like batch management, inventory management, purchasing, and quotation management

Martin Murray, Jawad Akhtar

Materials Management with SAP ERP: Functionality and Technical Configuration

Get the most out of your Materials Management implementation with this updated, comprehensive guide to configuration and functionality. You'll learn the ins and outs of Materials Management in SAP, from goods receipt and invoice verification to early warning systems and special procurement types. Dive into master data and other configuration tasks to ensure your MM system is optimized for your logistics needs!

739 pages, 4th edition, pub. 02/2016
E-Book: $69.99 | Print: $79.95 | Bundle: $89.99

www.sap-press.com/4062

Interested in reading more?

Please visit our website for all new
book and e-book releases from SAP PRESS.

www.sap-press.com